SSSP

Springer
Series in
Social
Psychology

Springer Series in Social Psychology

SSSP

Basic
Group Processes

Edited by
Paul B. Paulus

Springer-Verlag
New York Berlin Heidelberg Tokyo

Paul B. Paulus
Department of Psychology
University of Texas–Arlington
Room 313 Life Science Building
Arlington, Texas 76019
U.S.A.

With 11 Figures

Library of Congress Cataloging in Publication Data
Main entry under title:
Basic group processes.
    (Springer series in social psychology)
    Bibliography: p.
    Includes index.
    1. Social groups—Addresses, essays, lectures.
2. Influence (Psychology)—Addresses, essays,
lectures. 3. Exchange theory (Sociology)—Addresses,
essays, lectures. 4. Social interaction—Addresses,
essays, lectures. I. Paulus, Paul B. II. Series.
HM131.B355   1983   302.3   83-10363

Typeset by Publishers Service, Bozeman, Montana.
Printed and bound by R.R. Donnelley and Sons, Harrisonburg, Virginia.
Printed in the United States of America.

9 8 7 6 5 4 3 2 1

ISBN 0-387-90862-5 Springer-Verlag New York Berlin Heidelberg Tokyo

ISBN 3-540-90862-5 Springer-Verlag Berlin Heidelberg New York Tokyo

Preface

Research on groups has been a major focus of concern among psychologists and sociologists for many years. The study of groups certainly deserves a central role in these disciplines since much of our behavior occurs in groups and many important social phenomena involve groups. Issues such as leadership, conformity, group decision-making, group task performance, and coalition formation have had a long history of research. However, recently a number of other areas of research have blossomed that provide interesting new perspectives on group processes (e.g., social impact). In addition, topics of research have developed outside the commonly accepted domain of group dynamics (e.g., self-disclosure) which seem to be concerned with rather basic group processes.

Basic Group Processes was designed to bring together in one volume a representative sample of the broad range of work currently being done in the area of groups. Some of the chapters provide a review of the literature while others focus more specifically on current programs of research. All, however, provide new insights into basic group processes and a number provide broad integrative schemes. All of the authors were asked to emphasize theoretical issues rather than a detailed presentation of research. *Basic Group Processes* suggests that research on groups is a lively enterprise and forging interesting new theoretical and empirical directions.

Basic Group Processes can serve as a text for both graduate and higher level undergraduate courses in groups. It not only provides a broad overview of the area but also should help stimulate further theoretical and empirical development.

I am most appreciative of all those who encouraged and supported me in this project. A special thanks is due the staff of Springer-Verlag for their role in bringing this volume to fruition.

Arlington, Texas   Paul B. Paulus

Contents

Contributors

Richard L. Archer, Department of Psychology, Southwest Texas State University, San Marcos, Texas 78666, U.S.A.

Duane Buhrmester, Department of Psychology, University of California–Los Angeles, Los Angeles, California 90024, U.S.A.

Martin M. Chemers, Chairman, Department of Psychology, University of Utah, Salt Lake City, Utah 84112, U.S.A.

Walter B. Earle, Department of Psychology, University of Texas at Austin, Austin, Texas 78712, U.S.A.

Robert G. Folger, Department of Psychology, Southern Methodist University, Dallas, Texas 75275, U.S.A.

Jerald Greenberg, Faculty of Management, Ohio State University, Columbus, Ohio 43210, U.S.A.

Stephen G. Harkins, Department of Psychology, Northeastern University, Boston, Massachusetts 02115, U.S.A.

William Ickes, Department of Psychology, University of Texas at Arlington, Arlington, Texas 76019, U.S.A.

Martin F. Kaplan, Department of Psychology, Northern Illinois University, De Kalb, Illinois 60115, U.S.A.

Linda J. Keil, Department of Psychology, University of North Carolina at Chapel Hill, Chapel Hill, North Carolina 27514, U.S.A.

Samuel S. Komorita, Department of Psychology, University of Illinois, Champaign, Illinois 61820, U.S.A.

David A. Kravitz, Department of Psychology, University of Kentucky, Lexington, Kentucky 40506, U.S.A.

Charles G. McClintock, Department of Psychology, University of California–Santa Barbara, Santa Barbara, California 93106, U.S.A.

Charles E. Miller, Department of Psychology, Northern Illinois Univeristy, De Kalb, Illinois 60115, U.S.A.

Serge Moscovici, Ecole des Hautes Etudes en Sciences Sociale, Groupe de Psychologie Sociale, 75006 Paris, France

Gabriel Mugny, Faculte de Psychologie et des Sciences de l'Education, University of Geneva, Geneva, Switzerland

Paul B. Paulus, Department of Psychology, University of Texas at Arlington, Arlington, Texas 76019, U.S.A.

Richard E. Petty, Department of Psychology, University of Missouri–Columbia, Columbia, Missouri 65201, U.S.A.

Catherine E. Seta, Department of Psychology, University of North Carolina at Greensboro, Greensboro, North Carolina 27412, U.S.A.

John J. Seta, Department of Psychology, University of North Carolina at Greensboro, Greensboro, North Carolina 27412, U.S.A.

Phillip Shaver, Department of Psychology, University of Denver, Denver, Colorado 80210, U.S.A.

Frank J. Stech, MITRE Corporation, McLean, Virginia 22102, U.S.A.

Chapter 1
Introduction

Paul B. Paulus

A predominant concern in the field of social psychology for the last 25 years has been the intrapsychic processes such as cognitive consistency, attitudes, attribution, social cognition, and self-awareness. Although an understanding of these processes is potentially important for understanding social behavior, the research and theory in these areas often demonstrate a limited concern with social behavior. Thus research in these areas tends to have a nonsocial flavor (cf. Taylor & Brown, 1979) and often represents extensions of work in other areas of psychology (e.g., social cognition). In contrast, research on groups has an explicitly social flavor. Furthermore, such research represents a domain unique to social psychology and not reducible to the concerns of other areas of psychology. Yet in spite of these positive features, research on groups tends to be the primary concern of only a small percentage of social psychologists. The reason for this limited activity may lie in part with the relatively greater time, subject, and space demands of groups research. However, it is also possible that the low rate of activity is related to a perceived lack of exciting theories or theoretical controversies in contrast to the state of affairs in such areas as cognitive social psychology.

The purpose of this volume is to highlight research in groups which deals with basic theoretical issues and processes. Although each chapter is unique in its approach, all focus on theoretical issues either in the context of a broad overview of areas of research or in relation to a program of research on a certain aspect of group behavior. As a result, the various chapters necessarily differ in their scope, but all of the chapters together provide a relatively complete overview of the basic issues in groups. All of the authors were encouraged to write in a style that would make lively and interesting reading. Obviously, this task was easier with some topics than with others. However, all of the authors have taken pains to provide a clear and readable presentation.

This volume is divided into four parts which focus on different types of group processes. The first part deals with the various elements of groups which influence the behaviors and ideas of group members. Group members are often subject to such sources of influence, and much research in groups has focused on the nature of the social and informational processes involved. For example, one of the major concerns in the study of groups has been the influence of leadership on group functioning. Early efforts focused on discovering the qualities of good leaders with little success. Current research has taken a much broader perspective by considering the joint influence of leader, group, and situational factors on leadership effectiveness. In Chapter 2, Chemers reviews the history of research on leadership and presents a comprehensive summary of the current status of research on leadership. He examines four different approaches to analyzing the leadership process: leader-oriented, transactional, cognitive, and cross-cultural. The review includes an extensive evaluation of Fiedler's contingency model, path-goal theory, and Vroom and Yetton's normative decision model. One important feature of the chapter is the presentation of an integrative model of leadership which incorporates and highlights the variables that are important in leadership and their interrelationship.

Moscovici and Mugny provide a detailed and provocative analysis of the nature of minority influence in groups in Chapter 3. A primary focus in social psychology has been the tendency for individuals to conform to groups because of their dependency on groups for approval and other resources. Social influence is seen as a means of controlling group members and keeping deviants in line. Deviants are generally viewed in negative terms as hindering group progress or goal achievement. Moscovici and Mugny emphasize that deviants in fact can be an important source of influence in groups and a source of innovation. Deviants or active minorities have their impact because of their behavioral style. (Behavioral style is the way in which the minority organizes and presents its position.) By consistently, repeatedly, and forcefully promoting its position, the minority can turn the initial negative reactions of the majority into some degree of acceptance of the minority position. Moscovici and Mugny provide significant insights into this minority influence process and demonstrate its unique features.

The study of the influence of group discussion on judgments and group decisions has been a major concern in the area of groups since the 1920s. Most recently it has been examined in the context of group polarization research and studies of jury decision-making. In Chapter 4, Kaplan and Miller analyze this research in light of informational and normative processes. Much evidence is presented in support of an informational analysis based on information integration theory. Kaplan and Miller also focus on the group decision processes involved in combining individual preferences into a group decision. Their chapter thus provides a broad and insightful analysis of the processes involved in group decision-making. They also relate this analysis to other areas of study such as the group's influence on the quality of judgments.

The second part of this volume also deals with influence processes in groups but focuses primarily on how the group can influence an individual's motivation and ability to perform tasks or process information. In Chapter 5, Paulus reviews and analyzes research on individual task performance in groups. This issue has long been of interest to social psychologists and has been studied under various labels such as social facilitation, crowding, and more recently, social loafing. Each of these areas of study has examined the influence of group presence or absence or group size variations on task performance. Research and theory in these different areas is reviewed and an integrative model is proposed to deal with the wide variety of results obtained.

One of the most basic issues in social psychology is the impact of simple social presence on the behavior and task performance of individuals. Much of this research has been done under the rubric of social facilitation. Seta and Seta provide a careful analysis of this phenomenon and related issues in Chapter 6. They note that existing models do not adequately account for the variety of findings in this area and they propose an alternative model based on a theory of personal equity. This model holds that task interest or effort depends on the value of the task and the costs that will be endured in its performance. Seta and Seta propose that group settings influence the willingness and ability to allocate intellectual or physical resources and in turn the degree to which individuals perform successfully on various tasks. They present a number of studies in support of their model and relate the model to competing theoretical perspectives.

In Chapter 7, Harkins and Petty analyze the social context of the persuasion process. Attempts at persuasion may involve single individual sources (e.g., a preacher) or multiple individual sources (e.g., witnesses at a trial). Similarly the recipient of the persuasive attempt may be one individual or many individuals. What happens when one increases the number of sources and targets of persuasion is the concern of this chapter. Using Latané's theory of social impact and cognitive response theory of persuasion as guiding frameworks, Harkins and Petty have generated the first comprehensive treatment of social context factors in persuasion. They present the fruits of an impressive research program designed to test their ideas.

Part III deals with the important issue of how group members deal with the problem of the combining, dividing, or allocating resources available to the group or individual group members. For example, people are frequently involved in coalitions in their relations with others. Coalitions involve an agreement among a number of individuals to cooperate or pool resources in order to attain a particular goal. Such coalitions are found among workers (unions), in politics, among teenagers (clubs), and many other groups. Yet, what determines how people form coalitions? A number of theories have been proposed to account for this process. Komorita and Kravitz, in Chapter 8, evaluate these theories in light of the current research for a variety of coalition formation situations. The research and theorizing on coalition formation is relatively unique in its mathematically based precision. Yet, it has provided important insights into normative and strategic behavior in small groups.

In many situations people are dependent upon one another for satisfactory level of attainment of goals. In reaching such goals as profitability in business, nuclear disarmament, and a satisfactory marriage, individuals have to come to agreements with others about the exchange of behaviors, commodities, or concessions. The processes involved in dealing with such dilemmas are the focus of research on bargaining. In Chapter 9, McClintock, Stech, and Keil provide an overview of the research and theory on this bargaining process. They review the major characteristics of the process and the different types of bargaining paradigms, such as the

Prisoner's Dilemma and the Commons Dilemma games, employed by researchers. The main focus of Chapter 9 is on the role of communication. This communication can take both verbal and nonverbal forms, but most research has been directed at the study of verbal or informational communication. The authors conclude the chapter by considering some of the processes that may underlie the influence of communication on the bargaining process.

It seems to be common sense that providing employees with some degree of control over their own working conditions will increase satisfaction and productivity. It has been proposed that the outcomes of a process in which individuals have participated will be perceived as far more acceptable than nonparticipative outcomes. This fair process effect is the focus of Chapter 10, by Greenberg and Folger. They briefly review the research on various participative programs in organizations—participative management programs, nonauthoritarian leadership styles, flexible work schedules, and cafeteria-style pay plans. Although there is some evidence for beneficial effects of these types of programs, results are somewhat mixed. Greenberg and Folger analyze the reasons for these apparent inconsistencies and present research in support of their analyses. In countering commonly accepted ideas about participatory programs, this chapter should stimulate a reexamination of this important issue.

Part IV deals with the nature of the interaction process among individuals that characterizes most group situations. This aspect of group dynamics has been ignored in most treatments of groups, yet some of the most dynamic new work is occurring in this domain. Part IV presents three different perspectives on the interactive process. In Chapter 11, Shaver and Buhrmester provide the first extensive attempt to relate perspectives and research on loneliness to groups. Loneliness may take both emotional and social forms as reflected in needs for psychological intimacy or for integrated involvement. Satisfactions with relations or groups depends on the degree to which individuals can satisfy these needs. They also cite parallels between the intimacy dimension and feminine social styles and the integrated involvement dimension and masculine social styles. The importance of intimacy and integrative involvement processes in various other group phenomena—cohesiveness, conformity, leadership styles, and group entry behavior—is discussed.

Archer and Earle deal with the process of revealing personal information to others in Chapter 12. In particular, they emphasize interpersonal aspects of the disclosure process. Although self-disclosure is a basic feature of many group processes, it has been largely ignored by most investigations in group behavior. Archer and Earle develop a perspective that should serve as a basis for bringing self-disclosure into the mainstream of groups research. They review the roots of the self-disclosure tradition and the role of communication in groups. They critique some initial attempts to analyze the interpersonal aspects of disclosure and propose a broader perspective of the disclosure process. The chapter by Archer and Earle does much to clarify the broad variety of self-disclosure relationships that may exist and highlight the important social aspects of this process. They suggest a need for investigations to focus on these social forms of disclosure and for researchers on related group processes to be aware of the importance of these processes in group relationships.

It has been painfully obvious to most of us that people are differentially skilled in human relations or are successful in some relations but not others. The idea that our past relationships play an important role in the nature and success of future relations is the focus of Chapter 13 by Ickes. The center point of the chapter is Toman's family constellation theory which proposes that people will be most comfortable and successful in relationships that duplicate relationships experienced in the family. Ickes reviews research which directly or indirectly bears on Toman's theory. Although the research is not directly supportive of Toman, it does provide strong evidence that order of birth influences one's behavior in social relationships. The processes that may underlie this phenomenon are examined and a new approach which may lead to even more fruitful study of the influence of past relationships on future ones is presented.

Reference

Taylor, D. M., & Brown, R. J. Towards a more social social psychology? *British Journal of Social and Clinical Psychology*, 1979, *18*, 173-180.

Part 1
Social Influence Processes in Groups

Chapter 2
Leadership Theory and Research: A Systems-Process Integration

Martin M. Chemers

Leadership is a concept of importance and centrality to the study of group processes and effectiveness. Leadership research has been extensive, however, until quite recently the field of leadership has been characterized by contradiction, controversy, and disorder. This chapter aims to compare and contrast contemporary research and theory, to identify important areas of consensus and divergence, and to suggest a potentially useful integrating framework for future study.

We will begin with a brief review of the historical trends in leadership research. Then, recent research and theory will be discussed under four general categories: (a) leader-oriented approaches, (b) transactional approaches, (c) cognitive approaches, and (d) cross-cultural approaches. Finally an integrative model of leadership stressing a multivariate systems approach will be offered.

Brief History

Leadership research may be seen as having passed through three major eras, that is, the trait, behavior, and current contingency eras, each characterized by a dominant strategy, and is now poised for movement into a new fourth era.

Trait Era

The period stretching roughly from the turn of this century to World War II was characterized by the search for personality traits that were associated with leadership. In the nineteenth century, Thomas Carlyle (1841/1907) propounded the "great man" theory of leadership. Its main premise was that leaders emerge and are successful because of certain unique characteristics. Alexander the Great, Napoleon, and Joan of Arc are examples of such specially endowed persons.

Later trait researchers attempted to identify exactly which personal characteristics were associated with leadership. The research strategy was to locate a group or organization with leaders and followers and administer a personality measure thought to reflect some aspect of leadership. Measures were made of a broad range of variables, including intelligence, dominance, social sensitivity, height, weight, speech fluency, and so on. In 1948, Stogdill reviewed the results of 124 studies relating personal characteristics to leadership status, behavior, or effectiveness. He concluded that, while certain traits such as intelligence, knowledge, and dependability are likely to characterize many leaders, the pattern and strength of the relationships revealed that the trait approach was too simplistic to be useful ultimately. Anticipating the direction of the field by some 15 to 20 years, Stogdill concluded:

> A person does not become a leader by virtue of the possession of some combination of traits, but the pattern of personal characteristics of the leader must bear some relevant relationship to the characteristics, activities, and goals of the followers. . . . The evidence suggests that leadership is a relation that exists between persons in a social situation, and that persons who are leaders in one situation may not necessarily be leaders in other situations. (1948, p. 64)

Other reviewers (Bird, 1940; Jenkins, 1947; Mann, 1959) reached similar conclusions.

Behavior Era

The period following World War II up to the early sixties was distinguished by an emphasis on the identification and measurement of leader behavior. The distressingly poor yield of the trait studies, combined with a growing emphasis on behavior in all fields of psychology, turned leadership research to the study of what it is that leaders actually do. Several groups of researchers, using somewhat different methods, attacked this issue.

A classic study which set the tone for much of the later research on leadership styles was done by Lewin, Lippitt, and White (1939). Graduate students acting as leaders in clubs for adolescent-age boys were trained in three styles of leadership. *Autocratic* leaders emphasized directive control of the group by the leader, while the *democratic* leaders employed a participative style, and *laissez-faire* leaders exercised very little of any kind of leadership activity. Results indicated that the democratically led groups had the highest level of member involvement and satisfaction. However, later research (e.g., Haythorn, Couch, Haefner, Langham, & Carter, 1956) indicated that the relationship between leadership style and group process was more complicated, being affected by the followers' attitudes and expectations as well as the leader's behavior. Leadership styles research did not yield the hoped for answer to the leadership question, and research became even more concretely focused on the description of observed leader behavior.

The most influential and long lasting of the behavioral research programs was conducted at Ohio State University (Shartle, 1956). The thrust of this research was the development of a rating scale for measuring leader behavior (Hemphill, 1950; Hemphill & Coons, 1957). The Leader Behavior Description Questionnaire (LBDQ) was a 150-item scale to rate the degree to which the leader engaged in specific behaviors. Factor analysis of the LBDQ (Halpin & Winer, 1957) indicated that most of the variation in leader behavior could be described by two factors or behavioral clusters. One of these, *consideration*, described behavior indicating open communication between leader and followers, mutual trust, respect, and interpersonal warmth. The second factor, *initiation of structure*, referred to behaviors designed to organize group activities, define relationships, and direct followers toward task accomplishment.

At the same time, researchers at the University of Michigan (Kahn, 1951; Katz & Kahn, 1953) were studying the behavior of industrial supervisors. Using interviews with the supervisors' subordinates, these researchers identified two general styles of supervision, which they labelled *production-oriented* and *employee-oriented*. The production-oriented supervisor emphasized planning, direction, and goal achievement. The employee-oriented supervisor was typified by rapport with subordinates, an open and accepting style, and a concern for the feelings and problems of subordinates.

At Harvard University, Bales and Slater (1945) observed the behavior of college students in leaderless discussion groups. They found that two types of leaders were likely to emerge in these groups. One type, the *task specialist*, engaged in many organizing, summarizing, and directing behaviors in order to carry out the task. The *socioemotional* specialist, on the other hand, acted to reduce tension, raise morale, and instigate group participation.

These three lines of research, as well as others (e.g., Couch & Carter, 1959), seemed to reach a consensus. Although measured with different techniques and given somewhat different labels, leader behavior could reasonably be described by two reliable sets of behaviors, the task directed and the socioemotional or relationship directed. This consensus represented a major step forward in our understanding of leadership. Unfortunately, later research, conducted primarily with the LBDQ (Fleishman, 1957; Fleishman & Harris, 1962), failed to find consistent relationships indicating which of these styles led to more effective leadership (Korman, 1966). The benefit of current research allows us to recognize that a research strategy which attempted to find the "one best" style of leadership or leadership trait, without a consideration of the situation, was likely to be unsuccessful.

During this period some researchers were also addressing aspects of the leadership situation. Leavitt (1951) showed that communication structures have a powerful impact on leadership emergence. The role of task characteristics was studied (Carter & Nixon, 1949; Hemphill, 1950; Stogdill, Shartle, Scott, Coons, & Jaynes, 1956) as was the influence of follower characteristics (Barnlund, 1962; Haythorn et al., 1956). The realization was slowly dawning on researchers that a comprehensive theory of leadership would have to integrate both personal and situational characteristics. The stage was set for the development of contingency theories which ushered in the modern era of the leadership theory.

Current Research and Theory

We will examine the current work from several vantage points. The *leader-oriented approaches* are those in which the leadership process is seen to revolve primarily around the personality or behavior of the leader. While followers are considered, their role is not focused upon. The *transactional approaches* treat leadership as a phenomenon arising from the relationship between the leader and follower. Recently, several theories which stress a *cognitive approach* have been developed. These theories focus primarily on the evaluations and judgments made by leaders and followers. Finally, the long neglected area of *cross-cultural* leadership research has begun to emerge in a systematic way. Each of these approaches has important contributions to make to a general theory of leadership.

Leader-Oriented Approaches

At present, three major theories seem to dominate the leadership field. All three are primarily leader-oriented approaches.

Contingency model. Beginning in the early 1950s, Fred Fiedler began research with a measure of leadership orientation called the "esteem for the least preferred co-worker" (LPC) scale. The scale, containing from 16 to 24 bipolar adjective scales, asks a leader to rate a person in his or her experience with whom the leader had great difficulty getting a job done. Scale items include pleasant-unpleasant, intelligent-stupid, open-closed, friendly-unfriendly, cooperative-uncooperative, and so on. The emotional response to this least preferred co-worker is thought to reflect important aspects of the leader's orientation towards work itself.

The most enduring and widely used interpretation of LPC is as a measure of relative task versus interpersonal orientation (Chemers & Rice, 1974; Fiedler, 1978; Fiedler & Chemers, 1974). A low LPC score indicates that the leader has evaluated a poor co-worker in generally negative terms which is assumed to indicate that the low LPC leader strongly values task success. A high LPC score, reflecting a relatively positive evaluation of a poor co-worker, is thought to reflect the high LPCs greater concern for relationship rather than task success. Because the LPC scale is not a direct measure of leader behavior, considerable controversy has ensued about its exact meaning. Critics such as Ashour (1973) and Korman (1974) have suggested that it is too "mysterious" a measure to be of very much value. Indeed, for many years, attempts to tie LPC to behavioral measures led to considerable confusion (Chemers & Rice, 1974; Chemers & Skrzypek, 1972; Fiedler, 1973).

A recent comprehensive review by Rice (1978) has done much to establish the construct validity of the scale. Rice categorized a large body of LPC research and concluded that the LPC score reflects a "value-attitude" orientation. As had long been thought, the low-LPC leader places a high value on task success. This value, in turn, gives rise to a set of attitudes, interests, motivation, and behaviors. The low-LPC leader is more influenced by task factors, derives more satisfaction from task success, and is more attentive to task-related cues. The high-LPC leader shows a similar pattern with respect to the interpersonal aspects of the leadership situation. Behaviorally, across a wide range of situations, the high-LPC leader is likely to engage in relatively high levels of considerate and participative behavior. The low-LPC leader tends to be more inclined toward directive and structuring behavior, although the low-LPC leader tends to be somewhat more considerate in very low stress situations and somewhat punitive under high stress conditions.

Early work with the scale indicated that leader LPC was often strongly associated with group performance in a variety of military, business, and laboratory settings. However, the pattern of relationships between LPC and performance was inconsistent, at times favoring the low-LPC leader and at times, the high. Fiedler (1964, 1967) reasoned that the leadership situation should determine which leader orientation would be more successful. The critical feature of the leadership situation was thought to be the extent to which the situation gave the leader predictability, certainty, and control with respect to group activities. This situational dimension was labelled *situational favorability* (Fiedler, 1967) and later *situational control* (Fiedler, Chemers, & Mahar, 1976).

Fiedler (1967) hypothesized that situational control was determined by three variables, which, in order of importance, are: (a) leader-member relations, that is, the amount of loyalty and support given to the leader by followers; (b) task structure, that is, the clarity and specificity of the group's task; and (c) position power, that is, the leader's formal authority to reward and punish followers. To test these notions, Fiedler reanalyzed data on many studies done prior to 1964. Each set of groups was dichotomized on each of the three variables resulting in a classification along the dimension of situational control. Then within each level of situational control, the leader's LPC score was correlated with a measure of group performance. The derived pattern of results is shown in Figure 2-1. The figure indicates that low-LPC leaders are most effective in situations of very high or very low control. High-

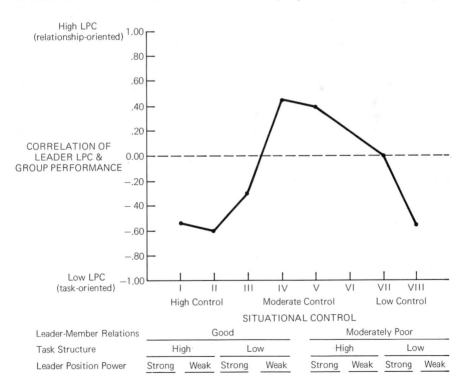

Fig. 2-1. **Contingency model.**

LPC persons are most effective in situations of moderate control. The rationale for these results is as follows.

Under high control conditions, when the group is responsive and the task is clear, effective leadership is embodied by the considerate, but firm and directive style of the low-LPC leader. However, under conditions of some uncertainty created by an unclear task or an unresponsive group, the more considerate, interpersonally sensitive, and participative style of the high-LPC results in greater follower involvement, motivation, and decision quality. Under the extremely difficult conditions of very low situational control, the no-nonsense, directive style of the low-LPC leader is thought to catalyze the group toward, at least some goal-directed activity.

The immediate impact of the *contingency model* in 1967 was profound. It helped explain the failure of the earlier trait approaches and provided a model of person-situation interaction. However, the honeymoon was a short one, and the model soon became a center of controversy. Criticism and reevaluation of theory came from both inside and outside Fiedler's laboratory (Ashour, 1973; Graen, Alvares, Orris, & Martella, 1970; McMahon, 1972; Mitchell, Biglan, Oncken, & Fiedler, 1970; Schriesheim & Kerr, 1977; Shiflett, 1973). The most serious of these criticisms was made by Graen et al. (1970). They argued that the contingency model was developed on the basis of data already collected. Such a post hoc analysis must be validated by data collected after the theory had been collected. Graen et al. cited data, including an extensive experimental test of their own, which failed to confirm predictions. They also pointed out that many of the findings in support of the contingency model were based on marginally significant results. They concluded that the theory was not valid. Fiedler (1971) answered the critique by pointing out that the research done by Graen et al. (1970) suffered from serious methodological inadequacies. Fiedler presented results from a number of laboratory and field studies in support of his model. Again, however, many of these findings were only marginally significant. He argued that the sample sizes in many studies were too small to achieve statistical significance, but that the great preponderance of results were in the direction predicted by the theory.

The validity controversy continued. Strong experimental support in some studies (e.g., Chemers & Skryzpek, 1972) was contrasted by disconfirmations in others (e.g., Vecchio, 1977). The methodology, statistical analyses, and explanatory approaches were often quite different from one study to another. It became clear that no single study would answer the validity question. However, a recent comprehensive review by Strube and Garcia (1981) may well have broken the deadlock on this previously fruitless controversy. Strube and Garcia employed "meta-analysis," in which the results of each individual study are converted into standard scores, which can be combined to test the probability of obtaining the effects observed across all studies. Combining the results of 145 tests of the contingency model, they reported extremely strong support for the model. The probability of getting these results by chance was equal to 2.99×10^{-28}, an infinitesimally small likelihood.

Recent research with LPC has broadened and extended the model in several interesting directions, including (a) the relationship of situational control to other organizational variables, (b) follower satisfaction, (c) the effects of leader intelligence and experience, and (d) the process characteristics of the model. Each of these areas will be dealt with briefly.

Some critics have argued that the situational control dimension, specified by its three components, is too narrow a description of the leadership situation. However, research has shown that when naive subjects are asked to rate the ease of leadership or potential for control in leadership situations, their ratings agree closely with predictions made by the model (Beach, Mitchell, & Beach, 1978; Mai-Dalton, 1975; Nebeker, 1975). However, two studies have taken this issue a bit further. Csoka (1975) demonstrated experimentally that the situational control dimension is very close to Burns and Stalker's (1961) more general notion of mechanistic and organic organizational climates. Also, Nebeker (1975) found the dimension to be analogous on an individual level to Lawrence and Lorsch's (1967) construct of environmental certainty in organizations. The integration of the situational control dimension with other theoretical approaches to leadership situations is a useful direction for further development. Broadening the methods of measuring situational control and relating the measures to other organizational constructs helps to enhance the cross-situational validity of contingency model research.

The contingency model has focused primarily on group productivity as the criterion of leadership effectiveness. However, recent research indicates that it has excellent potential for predicting leader and follower satisfaction. Rice (1981) reviewed the available literature and found that the interaction of LPC and situational control yields effects on subordinate satisfaction which are quite similar to the effects for productivity. Low-LPC leaders have more satisfied subordinates in high control situations and high-LPC leaders generate more follower satisfaction in moderate to low control situations. These results may reflect the fact that people are often more satisfied when their performance is high. Rice (1981) and Chemers, Goza, and Plumer (1979) also report that satisfaction in dyads is higher when members of the dyad have complementary rather than similar LPC scores. Rice, Marwick, Chemers, and Bentley (1982) found that low-LPC persons express more satisfaction with a group experience if they believe that the group performed well. High-LPC persons report higher satisfaction if they perceive that interpersonal relations were good. This last finding adds more support to the task versus relationship meaning of LPC.

Some extremely promising research by Fiedler and his associates (Fiedler & Leister, 1977; Fiedler, Potter, Zais, & Knowlton, 1979; Potter & Fiedler, 1981) is attempting to assess the effects of situational variables on the impact of the leader's intelligence and experience. The findings indicate that stress plays a key role in this equation. Under conditions of low stress with superiors, leader intelligence is positively correlated with group performance, but not so under highly stressful conditions. Under the high stress conditions, the leader's experience, rather than intelligence, predicts performance. In other words, when the situation becomes too stressful for thought, the effective leader falls back on the tried and true lessons of experience. Thus, dominant, well-learned responses are easier to perform under conditions of anxiety or stress. Fiedler and Leister (1977) have proposed a "multiple-screen" model of intelligence effects. A leader's intelligence will result in a good group performance provided that it is not blocked by lack of motivation or poor relations with the boss or with subordinates. This research appears to be moving the contingency model toward a more multivariable system orientation with an increasing emphasis on group process.

Another study shows movement in a similar direction. Konar-Goldband, Rice, and Monkarsh (1979) studied the relationship among LPC, leader-member relations, and performance over time. They measured each variable at two times during a 9-week intramural basketball season. The findings indicate that low-LPC leaders perform better if they have good leader-member relations, *and* the good performance serves to further enhance the leader's perceptions of those relations. Thus, a positive feedback loop is set up in which good relations lead to good performance, which leads to further good relations, and so on.

In another process-oriented experiment, Chemers, Goza, and Plumer (1979) examined the reactions of high- and low-LPC leaders and followers to conflict in the group. The conflict was generated by giving each member in a three-person group different and sometimes contradictory information about the best solution in a problem-solving task. Using a technique labelled the "psychological isotope" the experiment traced the utilization of information given to each group member. The results indicate, as predicted, that relationship-motivated (high-LPC) leaders were much more likely to use participative decision-making techniques to resolve the conflict than were low-LPC leaders. An interesting, unexpected finding was that the best performing groups had leaders and followers with complementary rather than the same leadership style.

The contingency model seems at this point to retain its viability as an instigator of research. Recent research has helped to elucidate the meaning of LPC and the underlying process of leadership effectiveness. New variables such as intelligence and stress are being integrated into the existing framework. However, considerably more work remains. Further clarification is necessary in all of these areas. The relationships of LPC to leader behavior and of leader behavior to subordinate satisfaction and group effectiveness have not been sufficiently systematically described.

Path-goal theory. This theory, which was strongly influenced by the Ohio State leadership studies, attempts to integrate the *consideration* and *structuring* factors of leader behavior with current conceptions of work motivation (House, 1971; House & Dessler, 1974). House has argued that "one of the strategic functions of the leader is to enhance the psychological states of subordinates that result in the motivation to perform or in satisfaction with the job" (House & Dessler, 1974, p. 30). The leader can accomplish these strategic functions by recognizing the needs of subordinates, enhancing the relationship between the subordinate's needs and organizational goals, and by clarifying and facilitating movement on the *path* to the *goals*. Because the motivational functions of the leader are stated in terms of paths, needs, and goals, the theory is referred to as the *path-goal theory* of leadership.

The second major tenet of the theory is that the specific leader behavior that will help to clarify and enhance path-goal relationships is determined by the situation in which the leader operates. In other words, the effect of consideration and structuring behavior by the leader are *contingent* upon situational characteristics.

The particular situational influences which the theory addresses are (a) characteristics of subordinates and (b) environmental demands and pressures on the subordinate. House and Dessler (1974) discuss two subordinate characteristics that might determine the acceptability or utility of specific leader behaviors. One characteristic is the particular values or needs of the subordinate (e.g., needs for affiliation, social approval, and extrinsic or intrinsic rewards). The second personal characteristic of subordinates is their degree of perceived ability to accomplish their tasks. For example, a subordinate who perceived himself or herself to have insufficient ability to perform the task, might value and welcome direction, coaching, and structuring from a boss, whereas a more confident subordinate might resent such "interference."

The features of the environment which enter into the path-goal equation are those factors over which the subordinate has no control, but which affect his or her ability to satisfy needs or perform effectively. Three general groups of these variables relate to (a) the subordinate's task, (b) the formal authority system of the organization, and (c) the primary work group. To the extent that these factors help to clarify the task or satisfy needs directly, they diminish the importance or utility of the leader's behavior. On the other hand, to the extent to which these factors fail to enhance, or even reduce, path-goal relationships, leader behavior becomes more important.

In its most actively researched form, path-goal theory makes two sets of hypotheses with respect to the effects of structuring and consideration behavior on the part of the leader. Specifically, the theory predicts that structuring behavior (i.e., direction, coaching, specifying goals, assigning duties, clarifying expectations, etc.) will result in positive effects on motivation and satisfaction when the subordinate's job or role is unclear and lacking in structure. If the job is already clearly specified, leader structuring will be seen as overly close and redundant supervision and will have negative effects. Consideration behavior by the leader is likely to have beneficial effects when the subordinate's job is aversive or boring, that is, when it fails to supply intrinsic satisfaction. If the job is already satisfying, supportive leader behavior is seen to be superfluous and will have few or no effects.

The early articles on which the theory is based (House, 1971; House & Dessler, 1974) reviewed a number of studies which were done prior to the development of the theory and a few studies specifically designed to test the path-goal hypotheses. Results reported, while not totally consistent, provide good support for the theory. A number of studies have been conducted since the House and Dessler (1974) paper. In general, the results of these investigations are supportive of the theory. The research suggests, however, that some refinements could increase the validity of the theory.

Most of the research has focused on environmental variables, especially those related to the degree of ambiguity in the subordinate's job. The measurement or operationalization of this variable has varied widely. Several studies have used the degree of task structure, in the subordinate's job usually, as rated by the subordinate (Downey, Sheridan, & Slocum, 1975, 1976; Stenson & Johnson, 1975). Other studies have taken a more general measure of role ambiguity (Dessler & Valenzi, 1977; Valenzi & Dessler, 1978), task variety (Schriesheim & DeNisi, 1981), or job factors affecting intrinsic motivation (Johns, 1978). Still others have inferred the degree of role ambiguity from formal structure variables such as administrative level (Sims & Szilagyi, 1975), group size (Schriesheim & Murphy, 1976), and organizational size (Miles & Petty, 1977). Most of this research provides support for the model. In studies which fail to clearly support the hypotheses, the most typical findings are that consideration behavior is positively related to satisfaction regardless of condition (Downey et al., 1975) or the pattern of results is confusing and difficult to interpret (Dessler & Valenzi, 1977; Stenson & Johnson, 1975; Valenzi & Dessler, 1978).

A number of methodological and conceptual issues have been suggested as reasons for some weak or inconsistent results across different studies. One important issue relates to the measurement of leader behavior and the choice of the measuring instrument. Different measures of leader behavior operationalize structuring and consideration in different ways. In the newer version of LBDQ, Form XII (Stogdill, 1963) items relating to autocratic and punitive behavior have been removed from the structuring scale, leaving items primarily concerned with the leader's attempts to clarify the task. Likewise, the consideration factor of Form XII dropped items related to subordinate participation in decision-making. Several path-goal researchers (Schriesheim, House, & Kerr, 1976; Schriesheim & Von Glinow, 1977) advise that the new scales more appropriately measure the leader behaviors in which House and Dessler (1974) are interested.

Recent research and theorizing suggests some valuable new developments in path-goal theory. A broadening and systematization of the organizational variables affecting leadership has been suggested by Kerr (1977) and Kerr and Jermier (1978). These authors propose that a number of organizational and job variables such as training, formal rules, feedback from the job or from co-workers, and routine technologies may channel and direct a worker's activities so that the behavior of his or her supervisor becomes irrelevant. The presence of these "substitutes for leadership" will affect many of the hypothesized relationships among leader behavior and subordinate motivation, satisfaction, and performance. Similar notions have been developed by Osborn and Hunt (1975) who argue that much of the leader's behavior may also be constrained by organizational factors. J. F. Schriesheim (1980) provides support for this view in a study which showed that group cohesiveness was a strong moderator of the effects of leader behavior. This recent work indicates a movement among leadership theorists to recognize the complex system of situational and individual characteristics that interact to produce leadership effects.

Some exciting research on individual difference effects in the path-goal relationships also reflects a movement towards integration of more variables. As early as 1976, Downey, Sheridan, and Slocum reported that task structure alone was insufficient to explain the relationship of leader behavior to subordinate satisfaction and performance. They reported that individual variables such as perceived needs and values also moderated these relationships. Schuler (1976) also found that subordinate authoritarianism affected the subordinate's acceptance of leader behavior under various conditions.

In a very useful synthesis of two research approaches, Griffin (1980) integrated the variable of *growth need strength* (Hackman & Oldham, 1976) into path-goal theory. Growth need strength (GNS) refers to an individual's expressed desire to work in a job which allows for personal learning, growth, and autonomy. Griffin looked at the effects of GNS on the relationship between directive, participative, and supportive leader behavior and subordinate satisfaction and performance. While no results were obtained with respect to subordinate performance, very clear and consistent effects were seen on satisfaction. Path-goal theory suggests that subordinates desire structuring and directive behavior from leaders when task structure is low. Griffin found that this was true only for subordinates who were low in growth need. Subordinates high in growth need, who are excited by challenging jobs, valued participative leader behavior under these conditions. Under conditions of high task structure, supportive, considerate leader behavior had positive effects for high-GNS subordinates, who were bored by the job. The positive effects of consideration were not found for low-GNS subjects who we might assume did not find the highly structured, routine job as aversive.

At present, path-goal theory represents a promising research approach, but one which has not realized its full potential. The research evidence, while generally supportive, lacks coherence. The situational and individual variables studied do not seem to follow any comprehensive plan. The operationalization of variables such as task structure needs a more clearly articulated rationale. The integration of more individual and situational variables into path-goal theory should increase its viability and potential. It may also make it possible to integrate the theory with other leadership and motivational approaches.

Vroom and Yetton's normative decision model. Vroom and Yetton's (1973) *normative model of decision-making* represents the third of the dominant contingency perspectives on leadership. These authors drew together a number of well-documented findings relating to (a) the effect of participation on subordinate commitment and motivation and (b) informational needs for making quality decisions. By integrating these two streams of thought on decision-making, Vroom and Yetton were able to develop a model which predicts which of several possible leadership decision styles will be most effective given various situational conditions.

Building on some earlier work by Maier (1963), Vroom and Yetton describe five styles of decision-making prevalent among contemporary managers. The styles range from a relatively individualistic, directive, and unresponsive style to a very group-oriented, responsive, and participative style. As such they again reflect a compatibility with the general leadership styles or orientations we have been discussing thus far. The relative effectiveness of the decision styles is determined by a set of rules. The rules fall into two general classes: those concerned with the quality of the decision and those concerned with acceptance of the decision by subordinates. A very rough distillation of the rules is that when the leader needs help in solving the problem or making a decision he or she must use a more participative approach. When the task is structured and he or she has the full support of subordinates the leader can use the less time-consuming autocratic methods. This model is based on a set of widely accepted data-based assumptions: (a) participative decision-making results in higher subordinate motivation and commitment, (b) complex or unstructured tasks benefit from high levels of input and diverse viewpoints, and (c) group decisions take more time than individual decisions. To facilitate the applicability of the model, Vroom and Yetton (1973) have constructed a flow chart or decision tree, by providing Yes or No answers to seven questions, related to the decision styles which can effectively be used in that particular situation.

A direct validation test of the normative decision model would require an objective assessment of the effects of a specific decision style on group performance in various situations. No such research has been done. Vroom and Jago (1978) do report the results of a procedure which asked 96 managers to recall the circumstances surrounding two decisions they had made in the past. The managers were asked to describe the situational context in terms of the characteristics of the Vroom and Yetton model, the decision style chosen, and outcome in terms of subordinate acceptance and effectiveness. The authors analyzed each description to see if the decision style employed adhered to the set of solutions which the model regards as feasible or correct. The results of this analysis strongly support the model. The probability of a successful decision was higher when the decision mode employed was in the feasible set than when it was not. In another analysis of the same descriptions, Jago and Vroom (1980) compared the Vroom and Yetton Model to two simpler alternatives proposed by Field (1979). Jago and Vroom report that the normative decision model was superior to the other models in differentiating successful from unsuccessful decisions. It should be recognized, however, that data recalled from memory, as was the case in the two reports, may be subject to a number of biases and distortions. These analyses provide only weak support for the model.

In a slightly different approach, Margerison and Glube (1979) asked a group of managers to respond to the set of problem decisions developed by Vroom and Yetton (1973). They found that managers whose responses were in high agreement with the model elicited higher satisfaction ratings from subordinates. While this was not a test of actual behavior, it does indicate, at least, that managers who can identify the correct behaviors are evaluated more highly. Studies by Hill and Schmitt (1977) and by Jago (1978a) and Jago and Vroom (1977) indicate that subjects who are asked to respond to the problem set scenarios are, in fact, influenced by the situational characteristics included. The tendency is for subjects to choose decision styles within the feasible set. However, there are also individual differences in a person's likelihood of choosing either more participative or more autocratic styles. Jago and Vroom (1977) and Jago (1978b) report that there is a marked tendency toward the greater use of participative decision procedures at higher levels of organizations.

Hill and Schmitt's (1977) finding of individual differences suggests that theories such as the contingency model which focus on personality or individual differences, might be usefully integrated with the models which focus on behavior or decision style. For example, a value attitude like LPC might predispose a leader toward relatively greater reliance on autocratic or participative decision styles. The findings on the influence of hierarchical level may be important to path-goal theory researchers who sometimes employ organizational level as an operationalization of task structure or role ambiguity (Sims & Szilagyi, 1975). In such designs, it may be difficult to differentiate the effects of individual differences from those of situational factors.

Some other research suggests that decision style may prove to be a useful variable, especially when tied to personal characteristics. Bernard Bass and his associates

(Bass & Valenzi, 1974; Bass, Valenzi, Farrow, & Solomon, 1975; Shapira, 1976) have analyzed a large set of data relating decision styles to intrapersonal, interpersonal, and organizational variables. The five styles identified include directive, manipulative, consultative, participative, and delegative. The styles of consultative, participative, and delegative seem to be highly correlated and may reflect a high loading on the Vroom and Yetton dimension of subordinate participation. The findings indicate that leaders do tend to rely on one set of related style suggesting that individual differences are important determinants of leadership style.

The normative decision model must be regarded as an extremely promising and attractive, but yet untested theory. Further empirical validation research will be welcomed.

Integration. These three leader-oriented theories are the central core of contemporary research in leadership. It seems warranted, then, to compare and contrast their respective systems and to attempt some integration if possible. Difficulties arise in this endeavor because, although the theories share some similarities, they also diverge quite drastically. All three attempt to integrate personal and situational factors into a prediction of group outcomes. Similarities exist in these situational and personal parameters.

The person variable in each theory reflects the influence of the task/relationship dichotomy which pervades the field. A reasonable interpretation of the LPC variable would indicate considerable similarity to Vroom's decision styles. Likewise, the structuring and considerate leader behavior of path-goal theory seem compatible with the task and relationship motivations of the contingency model. One very critical point of divergence, however, is that current research in path-goal theory does not address the participative versus autocratic behavior distinction which is so central to both Fiedler's and Vroom's formulations.

The situational variable in all three theories addresses the degree of certainty and structure in the leadership situation. Fiedler and Vroom seem quite close in their specifications while House ignores the variable of subordinate support for the leader.

Finally in terms of outcomes, the theories diverge even more. Path-goal theory focuses primarily on subordinate satisfaction and motivation. There is little emphasis on group performance, and empirical findings generally fail to yield performance effects. Normative decision theory is concerned with effectiveness but only of specific decisions. The contingency model has primarily been concerned with overall group or organizational effectiveness. This more general criterion in the contingency model may subsume subordinate motivation and decision quality. Research designs which include a broader range of dependent variables should help to integrate findings from different theoretical approaches.

In terms of the predictions generated in each theory, the contingency model and the normative decision model seem closest. Both approaches predict that structuring directive behavior will be most effective when the leader has high certainty, and considerate participative behavior would be most effective when certainty or control is lacking.

Superficially, path-goal theory appears to predict the opposite. That is, structuring behavior is best when low certainty exists, and considerate behavior is best when high structure or certainty exists. This apparent contradiction becomes more understandable when we review, again, the differences. Decision-making and problemsolving are not part of the path-goal theory, which really focuses more on supervision. Thus the use of the participation to gather information for decision-making is not as relevant as it is in Fiedler's and Vroom's formulations. Further, in Vroom's and Fiedler's models, uncertainty or ambiguity exists for the *leader as well as the followers*. In path-goal theory the uncertainty is the *subordinate's*. It is assumed that the leader, in fact, knows the appropriate structure and can provide it for the subordinate.

In summary, where similar antecedents and consequences are considered, the theories agree reasonably well. The points of their contradiction are the results of differences in assumptions or objectives. Research designed to bridge the gaps between these theories could be quite useful. Specifically, leader behaviors and styles need to be related to the personality and attitudinal variables which generate the observed behavior. The relative explanatory utility and possible congruence between the situational variables in each theory should be studied. And all three theories need a greater emphasis on the role of follower characteristics.

Transactional and Exchange Theories

The transactional approaches begin with the assumption that leadership is a relationship between persons. The relationship is created, bonded, and validated by the mutual exchange of valued resources. Hollander and Julian (1970) state:

> The leader who fulfills expectations and helps to achieve group goals provides a rewarding resource for others which is exchanged for status, esteem, and greater influence. Thus, he gives something and gets something. And what he gets contributes to his legitimacy insofar as he is "validated" in his role by followers. It is the leader's sense of this legitimacy which then seems as the base on which he may operate to exert influence. (p. 117)

Note that the leader-oriented theories acknowledge that leadership is an influence relationship. Fiedler and Vroom specifically integrate a factor representing the acceptance and support of the leader by followers. However, the leader-oriented theories do not specifically attend to the processes by which such relationships are developed and maintained.

Hollander's (1958) work has provided us with exceptional insight into that process. As Festinger (1950) pointed out, in order for a group to make progress toward a goal there must be some unanimity of opinion on what the goal is and conformity to the procedures for moving toward that goal. Leadership, however, implies the influencing and developing of group goals rather than simply conforming to them. But, if groups place great value conformity to normative positions, how does the leader gain the freedom to innovate, that is, Hollander and Julian's (1970) "legitimacy"? Hollander noted that we are talking about the group's acceptance of some unique (idiosyncratic) behavior by high status group members. Hollander (1958) has shown that "idiosyncrasy credits" are earned through two kinds of contributions to the group. The first contribution is conformity to core group values which demonstrates that the individual shares and validates the group's concerns. The second area of contribution is through competency, for example, acts that help the group to achieve its goals.

The contributions combine to identify those individuals who should lead. Competence without shared values may be dangerous to the group's integrity. Conformity without competence contributes little. These notions suggest that our understanding of leadership can be enhanced by attention to those exchange processes with influence the leader's role since the leader's legitimacy is regarded as a given in most theories. Furthermore, the emphasis in Hollander's work on the objectives and outcomes of leader behavior rather than on the simple counting or rating of behavioral categories helps us to recognize leadership as a process of social, goal-oriented, activity.

A leadership theory which also focuses on the exchange between leader and subordinates is the *vertical dyad linkage model* (Dansereau, Graen, & Haga, 1975; Graen, 1976; Graen & Cashman, 1975). Rather than focusing on why a good or poor exchange develops, these authors have investigated the outcomes of good and poor exchanges. They argue that leadership approaches which treat leadership as a group phenomenon rather than a dyadic phenomenon miss a valuable part of the leadership process. Dansereau et al. (1975) maintain that the quality of the exchange between a boss and subordinate is reflected in the negotiating latitude or the relative degree of freedom that a boss gives to a subordinate in development of their respective roles. Graen and Schiemann (1978) found that the nature of this interdependent role could vary in quality from a true "partnership" in which boss and subordinate have reciprocal influence, trust, respect, and liking, to a relationship more like an "overseer" and hired hand, in which these positive and mutual exchanges are absent.

By focusing on the group as the level of analysis we miss the fact that most leaders treat individual subordinates differently (Graen, Cashman, Ginsburgh, & Schiemann, 1977; Graen & Ginsburgh, 1977; Liden & Graen, 1980). Management dyads with good exchange relationships are characterized by a relationship which improves over time, results in higher agreement about important work activities (Graen & Shiemann, 1978), more delegation of authority (Dansereau, Graen & Haga, 1975), higher satisfaction, and less turnover (Graen & Ginsburgh, 1977). Wexley, Alexander, Greenawalt, and Couch (1980) also found that greater common understanding or perceptual congruence in managerial dyads was associated with higher subordinate satisfaction.

Methodological criticisms of the vertical dyad linkage model have been made, but vary in their import. A serious criticism arises out of the findings of Ilgen and Fujii (1976). They found that individual ratings of leader behavior and group outcomes were more likely to be in error than aggregated ratings. Furthermore, when several aspects of leadership functioning are rated by the same individual, biases are likely to distort the ratings. In an apparent misunderstanding of the model, Schriesheim (1979) completed a study to show that ratings of leader style made by individuals were very highly correlated with aggregate group ratings. He concluded that the model's assertion that leaders treat individual members differently was in error. Schriesheim failed to recognize that the model is concerned with the quality not the style of interaction. A manager can show relatively high levels of structuring or directive behavior with all subordinates and still have very different exchanges with them. For example, a manager may be seen by all of his or her subordinates as being relatively directive and task-oriented. Nonetheless, the manager's dyadic relationship with each subordinate could be quite different, perhaps ranging from very good to very poor exchanges.

The vertical dyad linkage model, like much of the recent work in leadership, is useful in pointing out the longitudinal process relationships which underlie leadership. A useful next step would be to identify the antecedents and the behavioral characteristics which characterize good and poor exchanges. This might allow for the integration of a dyadic perspective into the more comprehensive leadership theories.

Follower characteristics. Although not organized into a comprehensive theory, a number of studies have looked at the effects of follower characteristics on leadership and leader behavior. For example, Beckhouse, Tanur, Weiler, & Weinstein (1975) found that leader behavior is highly influenced by follower acceptance. When followers react positively to the leader's initiatives, the leader will increase his or her activity. Similar results have been reported by Bavelas, Hastorf, Gross, & Kite (1965) and Gruenfeld, Rance, and Weissenberg (1969).

The impact of individual differences in follower traits on the leadership process has long been an area of interest. Studies by Haythorn et al. (1956) and Sanford (1952) showed that difference in the authoritarian versus egalitarian values of followers affected their reactions to the leader's style. Recently, Weed, Mitchell, and Moffitt (1976) similarly found that followers who are high in dogmatism respond better to leaders who engage in a lot of structuring behavior. Low dogmatism followers perform better with leaders who engage in high levels of considerate behavior. Individual follower characteristics, like need for achievement (Steers, 1975), work values (Aldage & Brief, 1975; Blood, 1969), and locus of control (Durand & Nord, 1976; Ruble, 1976) have all been shown to have an impact on the leadership process.

At present, the research on follower characteristics is scattered and not well integrated. This parallels the early research on situational variables in the leadership process, prior to the integration of situational features into the contingency theories. Future leadership theorizing will benefit from greater attention to follower characteristics and dyadic processes.

Cognitive Approaches

Recently, social psychology has been heavily influenced by attribution theory (Heider, 1958; Jones & Davis, 1965; Kelley, 1973), which is concerned with the cognitive processes which underlie interpersonal judgments. One of the key features of such judgments is the strong tendency for people to develop causal explanations of another person's behavior. Attempts to explain why an individual has engaged in a particular behavior revolve around the question of whether the behavior was determined by factors internal to the actor, such as motivation or ability, or factors external to the actor, such as situational forces, conformity pressures, or luck.

Most central to the present discussion is the reliable finding that observers tend to attribute the causes of an actor's behavior to internal factors (Jones, 1979). Internal attributions may be appealing because they give the observer a sense of certainty and predictability with respect to the actor's future behavior. This effect is enhanced when the attribution process is related to the observer's judgments of self. For example, a teacher may be inclined to attribute a student's poor academic progress to internal factors (e.g., the student's ability) when a situational attribution might imply that the teacher was responsible for the student's failure. In other words, the enhancement or protection of self-esteem affects judgments.

Green and Mitchell (1979) have adapted attribution theory to the process by which leaders make causal judgment about subordinate performance. The theory hypothesizes that the types of attributions made by supervisor about subordinate performance will affect the actions taken toward subordinates. Furthermore, the attribution process will be affected by factors which are not directly related to subordinates' behavior. Knowlton and Mitchell (1980) found that when a supervisor is led to believe that a subordinate's poor performance was the result of a lack of effort, the supervisor made a more negative evaluation than when the performance was the result of a lack of ability. Two studies (Mitchell & Kalb, 1981; Mitchell & Wood, 1980) indicate that supervisors make much more negative evaluations of a subordinate's poor performance when the outcomes of that performance are severe than when they are not. The work of Mitchell and his associates appears very promising. Any longitudinal model of leadership which considers the process of role relationships between leader and follower such as the vertical dyad linkage model, can greatly benefit from an understanding of the dynamics of the attribution process.

Calder's (1977) attribution theory of leadership examines the leadership process from a different perspective. Calder argues that leadership processes and effects exist as perceptual processes in the minds of followers and observers. Since perceptual processes are often biased and distorted, our views of leadership may also reflect such distortion and bias. Every individual has an implicit causal theory of leadership which influences the perception of the leadership process. Individuals organize their perception of leadership around this implicit theory. For example, if a follower believes that structuring leadership behavior is likely to result in good performance, the follower, upon seeing good performance, may falsely infer that the leader behaved in a structuring manner. Salancik and Pfeffer (1978), in a discussion of job attitudes, echo Calder's warning. They argue that attitudes toward one's job are heavily influenced by the "social reality" created by group consensus. A person's attitudes are further affected by the need to justify or rationalize his or her own behavior. Thus, implicitly held theories, social reality, and self-esteem interact to bias an individual's perception of the organizational environment.

These theories raise a serious problem for leadership research. Thomas and Kilman (1975) point out that this problem becomes more dangerous when social desirability is considered. Individuals who have a strong desire to make a socially desirable self-presentation will receive higher scores on socially desirable measures. Thus, these measures will be correlated. In an experimental examination of this effect Schriesheim, Kinicki, and Schriesheim (1979) developed a "leniency" measure to test the likelihood that individuals will give socially desirable positive ratings to an attitude object, such as their supervisor. Their findings indicate the correlation of ratings of consideration behavior with other positive outcomes (e.g., satisfaction) were strongly affected by leniency. Berkowitz (1980) reports that because of such biases, subjects may show very strong and consistent relationships among organizational variables, even when none of these ratings are related to objective measures of performance. Rather than simple response sets of social desirability factors, ratings may reflect a subject's implicit theory of leadership. In other words, subordinate's ratings of leader behavior may reflect what the subordinate thinks good or bad leaders do, rather than any objective measure of what their leader really does. A number of recent studies (Downey, Chacko, & McElroy, 1979; Eden & Leviatan, 1975; Lord, Binning, Rush, & Thomas, 1978; Phillips & Lord, 1981) strongly indicate that implicit theories of leadership held by individuals affect their ratings of leader behavior. For example, raters who are led to believe that a group has performed well will give higher ratings of both structuring and consideration behavior to an observed leader than will raters who have observed the same behavior but were told that the group performed poorly.

Certain leadership researchers, such as those related to path-goal theory (House & Dessler, 1974), the normative decision model (Vroom & Yetton, 1973), and the vertical dyad linkage model (Graen, 1975) are especially vulnerable to problems associated with implicit leadership theories. In many tests of these theories, a single subordinate is asked to rate job characteristics such as structure or role ambiguity, negotiating latitude, leader behavior or decision style and also their own satisfaction, motivation, or performance. There is a very strong possibility that the resultant pattern of relationships is at least partially influenced by cognitive biases and implicit assumptions. Leadership researchers must be especially sensitive to the problems associated with broad data collection from a single source.

The cognitive research makes us aware of the complex processes which affect interpersonal perception. Our own implicit theories, biased perceptions, and ego-defensive judgments became part of the bases for our intentions and actions. Since expectations, intentions, and eventually behavior are affected by our perceptions of reality, a comprehensive theory of the leadership process must include a cognitive component.

Cross-Cultural Approaches

Berry (1969) has argued that American psychology is "culture-bound" and "culture-blind." The generalizability of our findings is bounded by the fact that most of our research is done with Euro-American samples. Furthermore, because we rarely compare cultures, we are blind to the potential effects of cultural differences. Chemers (Note 1) points out that this problem becomes more salient when we attempt to export our theories and training programs to cultures which are different from those in which the theories were developed.

Cross-cultural research can benefit leadership theory in two ways. Comparative studies can show us the generalizability of Euro-American theories, helping us to recognize the inherent limitations in their transfer to other cultures. More importantly, comparative research give us a much broader range of variables which may highlight relationships previously ignored. For example, since most studies done in the developed countries are done on subjects who are relatively well educated and technologically sophisticated, educational levels become a background variable to which we pay little attention. However, in a broader context, the socialization or educational background of workers may be an important determinant of work-related attitudes and responses.

Organizational psychologists have not totally ignored culture, but the results of the comparative research leaves much to be desired. Reviews by Roberts (1970), Nath (1969), and Barrett and Bass (1970) all concluded that the cross-cultural research on leadership was characterized by weak methodologies and by a gross absence of theory, both of which make the interpretation of the scattered findings very difficult. Since the time of those reviews, the situation has improved somewhat. Negandhi (1975) presented a model of cultural effects on organizational structure in which cultural or national differences act indirectly on management practices by affecting the organizational structure, and managerial policy is more important than cultural factors in determining behavior. This view contrasts with earlier views (e.g., Farmer & Richman, 1965) which saw culture as directly determining managerial values, attitudes, and behavior.

The actual role of culture probably lies somewhere between these two views. Neither culture nor organizational structure are static forces. Rather, they interact with dynamic process influencing one another, and both contribute to managerial attitudes and behavior. For example, studies which have compared the attitudes or behaviors of managers have found national differences somewhat moderated by organizational policy (Tannenbaum, 1980). Unfortunately, after we have dealt with the broad question of whether culture is important, we are still left with few theories making any specific predictions about the role of culture in shaping leadership process.

More recent reviews by Tannenbaum (1980) and Barrett and Bass (1975) indicate that comparative research in management attitudes and practices is growing, but the research is rarely guided or explained by clearly articulated theory. The most popular area of comparative research focuses on surveys or values of managers of different nationalities (Barrett & Bass, 1970; Haire, Ghiselli, & Porter, 1966). A common problem of studies of this kind is that the nationalities chosen for study are usually based on convenience (i.e., the availability of subjects) rather than on the basis of some theoretical relationship. Kraut (1975), in a review of cross-national management research, was able to discern that similarity in values can partially be explained by linguistic commonality, geographical proximity, and level of technological development. However, it is not clear how particular sets of values are related to particular aspects of the leadership process.

A potentially useful theoretical framework relating values to managerial and organizational process has been offered by Hofstede (1976, 1980, 1981). Comparing responses to a value survey from managers from 40 countries, Hofstede found that the pattern of results could be described by four factors. These were (a) power distances, that is, the relative importance of status, (b) tolerance for uncertainty, (c) individualism versus collectivism, and (d) masculinity. Hofstede (1981) presents a theory on how a culture's standing on these four value dimensions determines the kind of organizational structure and managerial policies that will be most likely to develop. For example, he argues that cultures which have a low tolerance for uncertainty, combined with a low emphasis on status, are likely to develop highly bureaucratic organizational structures to reduce ambiguity. Cultures which are also low in tolerance for uncertainty but high in power distance, will develop autocratic organizational structures, in which the high status persons resolve ambiguity by fiat.

The validity of much of the cross-cultural research has been questioned by Ayman and Chemers (Note 2). In a study of the leadership behavior of Iranian managers, these researchers found that traditional measures of leadership behavior and subordinate satisfaction resulted in very different factor structures in their Iranian sample than did those measures when used with European or American samples. Ayman and Chemers (Note 2) and Chemers (Note 1) argue that the imposition of Euro-American theories, measures, and research designs on other cultures may lead to very inaccurate conclusions.

Thus, more than a decade after Roberts' (1970) highly critical review of cross-cultural organizational research, we must conclude that there has been some, but not a great deal, of improvement. Cross-cultural research is complex, time-consuming, and very expensive. The quick gathering of some questionnaire data from a group of managers attending an international conference is much easier than careful, on-site, field studies of ongoing leadership processes. It is also true, however, that the latter strategy offers the greatest potential for a valid understanding of the role of culture in leadership.

Integrative Systems/Process Model

A theme which has permeated this chapter is that there are a number of promising theoretical approaches in leadership, but that they tend to be disconnected from one another. Each approach explains some aspect of the leadership process but fails to provide a comprehensive explanation. In this section a model will be presented which attempts to tie together the various approaches to leadership and suggest fruitful avenues for future research.

It must be stressed that the model which follows is not a theory. It is a heuristic which highlights the sets of variables which are thought to be important to leadership process, but it does not predict the specifics of the relationships among those variables. The model does assume that leadership process is a multivariable system in which each set of variables is influenced by, and in turn, influences numerous other sets of variables. It emphasizes multiple and bidirectional causality in which any specific variable can be both a cause and effect of other variables in the system.

Figure 2-2 is a graphic representation of the model. The boxes in the model represent major sets of variables. The lines indicate relationships among variables. It is not intended that the relationships indicated are the only ones possible. Rather, these relationships are the ones which have been identified by past research and

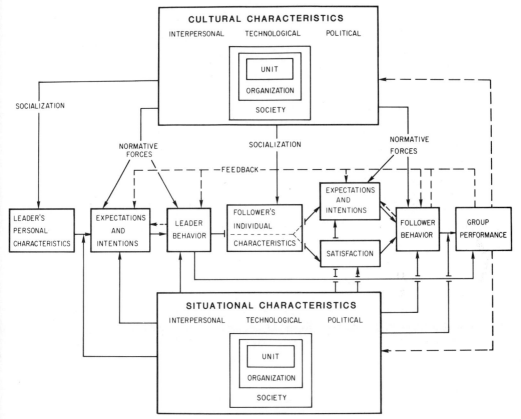

Fig. 2-2. Systems/process model of leadership.

seem to be promising points of departure for future research. The arrows which indicate direction of causal influence are, likewise, not meant to be exhaustive or exclusive, only suggestive.

Beginning on the left side of the graph, the model suggests that personal characteristics of the leader, such as leadership orientation (e.g., task vs. relationship orientation, locus of control, gender, etc.), help to determine the leader's perception of what actions are likely to result in various outcomes. These expectations and intentions in turn give rise to leader behavior, such as consideration, structuring, decision styles, and so on. The leader's perceptions, intentions, and actual behavior are influenced both directly and indirectly by situational characteristics, such as relationships with followers, peers, and superiors, task characteristics, authority, and organizational policy.

The effects of the leader's actions on the psychological states of followers, such as expectations and satisfaction, are influenced by the specific characteristics of those followers, such as LPC, locus of control, and growth need strength. The psychological states of followers along with situational characteristics influence the behavior of followers. Such behavior in interaction with situational characteristics results in group outcomes such as productivity, turnover, and grievances.

An example of one hypothetical set of relationships might be that leader LPC results in different leader expectations for the utilization of autocratic or participative leadership in a specific situation. Followers respond to that leader behavior on the basis of their own needs and personalities as well as their perception of the situation. The ongoing interaction of the leader and follower over time can be conceptualized as a dyadic role-making process. The behavior of the leader and followers, moderated by the situation, results in a variety of group outcomes.

However, the process is not unidirectional, linear, or static. The observed group outcomes act as feedback in the system, changing the situation, as well as the cognitions of both leaders and followers. For example, the expectations and future intentions of leaders and followers are modified by the attribution process. The unit, organization, society, and eventually culture are affected by the actions and outcomes of goal-directed groups.

Finally, in both the short and long term, both directly and indirectly, culture influences all aspects of the process. For example, the socialization and parenting practices of the society help to determine the personalities, values, and needs of leaders and followers. Expectations and intentions are influenced by the social reality or group consensus. Behavior of leaders and followers is affected by norms and conformity pressures. These effects of culture can take place at the level of the family, work group, organization, or society.

The contemporary research and theory discussed in this chapter might lead us to some tentative conclusions about where the field is heading and what productive avenues exist. This author believes that two dominant dimensions of personal need underlie much of the variation in observed leader attitudes, expectations, and behavior. These are the need for control and the need for social acceptance. High control needs lead to the perception of control in the environment and the use of orderly, directive, and relatively autocratic behavior patterns. High needs for social acceptance result in a leadership pattern which is open and participative and necessarily more fluid and responsive. The relative success of these behavioral practices and decision-making styles in terms of group performance and satisfaction depends both on the personal characteristics and expectations of followers and on the control potential of the leadership situation, that is, the degree to which problems can be clearly analyzed and decisions effectively executed.

The conflict between social acceptance and personal control can be elucidated by cross-cultural analyses. In many cultures outside of Europe and America, no such conflict exists. It is expected that the leader will be nurturant and considerate, but also directive and controlling. Thus the leader can ensure acceptance and control at the same time. The strong emphasis on individualism and freedom in the Western democracies results in the dichotomy of leadership styles which we observe.

The potentially fruitful areas of research which rise out of the foregoing analysis involve the integration of the relationships outlined in Figure 2-2. The following five recommendations for research represent a by-no-means-exhaustive list of starting points.

1. Traits and values of leaders and followers should be tied to the various aspects of leader behavior and decision style, as moderated by cognitive states.

2. The various partial and overlapping measures of leader behavior should be integrated into a common set of measures which could be in widespread use. Better observational techniques for the assessment of those behaviors should be developed to reduce our reliance on the use of self-reports.

3. Dyadic leader-follower processes, including a consideration of follower personality, should be integrated into the heavily leader-oriented approaches.

4. The psychological states of followers, such as motivation and satisfaction, need to be tied to actual follower behavior and group outcomes.

5. Cultural and national characteristics, such as level of development, political system, and values, need to be organized and dimensionalized. The resultant categories or culture types could be studied for their effects on personality and behavior of leaders and followers in a way that would allow for theory-based prediction and explanation.

If leadership theory is to move beyond its current stage of development, researchers must go beyond narrow squabbling between limited theories, toward an integration among theories. The research of recent years which emphasizes longitudinal process explanations of broad multivariable systems holds the promise for a more valid and more useful leadership field.

Reference Notes

1. Chemers, M. M. *Leadership and social organization in cross-cultural psychology*. Paper presented to the Meetings of the American Psychological Association, Los Angeles, 1981.
2. Ayman, R., & Chemers, M. M. *A cross-cultural study on the effect of leadership style on worker productivity and job satisfaction*. Paper presented at the International Association for Cross-Cultural Psychology, Munich, 1978.

References

Aldage, R. J., & Brief, A. P. Some correlates of work values. *Journal of Applied Psychology,* 1975, *60,* 757-760.
Ashour, A. S. Further discussion of Fiedler's contingency model of leadership effectiveness: An evaluation. *Organizational Behavior and Human Performance,* 1973, *9,* 339-355.
Bales, R. F., & Slater, P. E. Role differentiation in small decision making groups. In T. Parsons & R. F. Bales (Eds.), *Family, localization, and interaction processes.* New York: Free Press, 1945.
Barnlund, D. C. Consistency of emergent leadership in groups with changing tasks and members. *Speech Monographs,* 1962, *29,* 45-52.
Barrett, G. V., & Bass, B. M. Comparative surveys of managerial attitudes and behavior. In J. Brandburn (Ed.), *Comparative management: Teaching, training, and research.* New York: Graduate School of Business Administration, New York University, 1970.

Barrett, G. V., & Bass, B. M. Cross-cultural issues in industrial and organizational psychology. In M. D. Dunnette (Ed.), *Handbook of industrial and organizational psychology*. Chicago: Rand McNally, 1975.

Bass, B. M., & Valenzi, E. R. Contingent aspects of effective management styles. In J. G. Hunt & L. L. Larsen (Eds.), *Contingency approaches to leadership*. Carbondale, Ill.: Southern Illinois University Press, 1974.

Bass, B. M., Valenzi, E. R., Farrow, D. L., & Solomon, R. J. Management styles associated with organizational, task, personal, and interpersonal contingencies. *Journal of Applied Psychology*, 1975, *60*, 720-729.

Bavelas, A., Hastorf, A. H., Gross, A. E., & Kite, W. R. Experiments on the alteration of group structure. *Journal of Experimental Social Psychology*, 1965, *1*, 55-70.

Beach, B. H., Mitchell, T. R., & Beach, L. R. A note on judgements of situational favorableness and probability of success. *Organizational Behavior and Human Performance*, 1978, *22*, 69-74.

Beckhouse, L., Tanur, J., Weiler, J., & Weinstein, E. And some men have leadership thrust upon them. *Journal of Personality and Social Psychology*, 1975, *31*, 557-566.

Berkowitz, E. N. Role theory, attitudinal constructs, and actual performance: A measurement issue. *Journal of Applied Psychology*, 1980, *65*, 240-245.

Berry, J. W. On cross-cultural comparability. *International Journal of Psychology*, 1969, *4*, 119-128.

Bird, C. *Social psychology*. New York: Appleton-Century, 1940.

Blood, M. R. Work values and job satisfaction. *Journal of Applied Psychology*, 1969, *53*, 456-459.

Burns, T., & Stalker, G. *The management of innovation*. London: Tavistock Publications, 1961.

Calder, B. J. An attribution theory of leadership. In B. M. Staw & G. R. Salancik (Eds.), *New directions in organizational behavior*. Chicago: St. Clair, 1977.

Carlyle, T. *Heroes and hero worship*. Boston: Adams, 1907. (Originally published, 1841.)

Carter, L., & Nixon, M. Ability, perceptual, personality, and interest factors associated with different criteria of leadership. *Journal of Psychology*, 1949, *27*, 377-388.

Chemers, M. M., Goza, B. K., & Plumer, S. I. Leadership style and communication process: An experiment using the psychological isotope technique. *Resources in Education*, September, 1979. Accession Number, ED169 421.

Chemers, M. M., & Rice, R. W. A theoretical and empirical examination of the contingency model of leadership effectiveness. In J. G. Hunt & L. L. Larsen (Eds.), *Contingency approaches to leadership*. Carbondale, Ill.: Southern Illinois University Press, 1974.

Chemers, M. M., & Skrzypek, G. J. An experimental test of the contingency model of leadership effectiveness. *Journal of Personality and Social Psychology*, 1972, *24*, 172-177.

Couch, A., & Carter, L. F. A factorial study of the related behavior of group members. *American Psychologist*, 1959, *8*, 333.

Csoka, L. S. Relationship between organizational climate and the situational favorableness dimension of Fiedler's contingency model. *Journal of Applied Psychology*, 1975, *60*, 273-277.

Dansereau, F. Jr., Graen, G., & Haga, J. Vertical dyad linkage approach to leadership within formal organizations: A longitudinal investigation of the role making process. *Organizational Behavior and Human Performance*, 1975, *13*, 46-78.

Dessler, G., & Valenzi, E. R. Initiation of structure and subordinate satisfaction: A path analysis test of path-goal theory. *Academy of Management Journal*, 1977, *20*, 251-259.

Downey, H. K., Chacko, T. I., & McElroy, J. D. Attribution of the "causes" of performance: A constructive, quasi-longitudinal replication of the Staw (1975) study. *Organizational Behavior and Human Performance*, 1979, *24*, 287-289.

Downey, H. K., Sheridan, J. E., & Slocum, J. W., Jr. Analysis of relationships among leader behavior, subordinate job performance, and satisfaction: A path-goal approach. *Academy of Management Journal*, 1975, *18*, 253-262.

Downey, J. K., Sheridan, J. E., & Slocum, J. W., Jr. The path-goal theory of leadership: A longitudinal analysis. *Organization Behavior and Human Performance*, 1976, *16*, 156-176.

Durand, D. E., & Nord, W. R. Perceived leader behavior as a function of personality characteristics of supervisors and subordinates. *Academy of Management Journal*, 1976, *19*, 427-431.

Eden, D., & Leviatan, U. Implicit leadership theory as a determinant of the factor structure underlying supervisory behavior scales. *Journal of Applied Psychology*, 1975, *60*, 736-741.

Farmer, R. N., & Richman, B. M. *Comparative management and economic progress*. Homewood, Ill.: Irwin, 1965.

Festinger, L. Informal social communication. *Psychological Review*, 1950, *57*, 271-282.

Fiedler, F. E. A contingency model of leadership effectiveness. In L. Berkowitz (Ed.), *Advances in experimental social psychology* (Vol. 1). New York: Academic Press, 1964.

Fiedler, F. E. *A theory of leadership effectiveness*. New York: McGraw-Hill, 1967.

Fiedler, F. E. Notes on the methodology of the Graen, Orris, and Alvares studies testing the contingency model. *Journal of Applied Psychology*, 1971, *55*, 202-204.

Fiedler, F. E. Personality and situational determinants of leader behavior. In E. M. Fleishman & J. G. Hunt (Eds.), *Current developments in the study of leadership*. Carbondale, Ill.: Southern Illinois University Press, 1973.

Fiedler, F. E. The contingency model and the dynamics of the leadership process. In L. Berkowitz (Eds.), *Advances of experimental social psychology*. New York: Academic Press, 1978.

Fiedler, F. E., & Chemers, M. M. *Leadership and effective management*. New York: Scott-Foresman, 1974.

Fiedler, F. E., Chemers, M. M., & Mahar, L. *Improving leadership effectiveness: The leader match concept*. New York: Wiley, 1976.

Fiedler, F. E., & Leister, E. F. Leader intelligence and task performance: A test of a multiscreen model. *Organizational Behavior and Human Performance*, 1977, *20*, 1-14.

Fiedler, F. E., Potter, E. H., III, Zais, N. M., & Knowlton, W. A. Organizational stress in the use and misuse of managerial intelligence and experience. *Journal of Applied Psychology*, 1979, *64*, 635-647.

Field, R. H. G. A critique of the Vroom-Yetton contingency model of leader behavior. *Academy of Management Review*, 1979, *4*, 249-257.

Fleishman, E. A. A leader behavior description for industry. In R. M. Stogdill & A. E. Coons (Eds.), *Leader behavior: Its description and measurement*. Columbus: Ohio State University, Bureau of Business Research, 1957.

Fleishman, E. A., & Harris, E. F. Patterns of leadership related to employee grievances and turnover. *Personnel Psychology*, 1962, *15*, 43-56.

Graen, G. Role-making processes within complex organizations. In M. D. Dunnette (Ed.), *Handbook of industrial and organizational psychology*. Chicago: Rand McNally, 1975.

Graen, G., Alvares, K. M., Orris, J. B., & Martella, J. A. Contingency model of leadership effectiveness: Antecedent and evidential results. *Psychological Bulletin*, 1970, *74*, 285-296.

Graen, G., & Cashman, J. F. A role-making model of leadership in formal organizations: A developmental approach. In J. G. Hunt & L. L. Larsen (Eds.), *Leadership frontiers*. Kent, Ohio: Kent State University Press, 1975.

Graen, G., Cashman, J. F., Ginsburgh, S., & Schiemann, W. Effects of linking-pin quality on the quality of work life of lower participants. *Administrative Science Quarterly*, 1977, *22*, 491-504.

Graen, G., & Ginsburgh, S. Job resignation as a function of role orientation and leader acceptance: A longitudinal investigation of organizational assimilation. *Organizational Behavior and Human Performance*, 1977, *19*, 1-17.

Graen, G., & Schiemann, W. Leader-member agreement: A vertical dyad linkage approach. *Journal of Applied Psychology*, 1978, *63*, 206-212.

Green, S. G., & Mitchell, T. R. Attributional processes of leaders in leader-member interactions. *Organizational Behavior and Human Performance*, 1979, *23*, 429-458.

Griffin, R. N. Relationships among individual, task design, and leader behavior variables. *Academy of Management Journal*, 1980, *23*, 665-683.

Gruenfeld, L. W., Rance, D. E., & Weissenberg, P. The behavior of task oriented (low LPC) and socially oriented (high LPC) leaders under several conditions of social support. *Journal of Social Psychology*, 1969, *79*, 99-107.

Hackman, J. R., & Oldham, G. R. Motivation through the design of work: Test of a theory. *Organizational Behavior and Human Performance*, 1976, *16*, 250-279.

Haire, M., Ghiselli, E. E., & Porter, L. W. *Managerial thinking: An international study*. New York: Wiley, 1966.

Halpin, A. W., & Winer, B. J. A factorial study of the leader behavior descriptions. In R. M. Stogdill & A. E. Coons (Eds.), *Leader behavior: Its description and measurement*. Columbus, Ohio: Ohio State University, Bureau of Business Research, 1957.

Haythorn, W., Couch, A., Haefner, D., Langham, P., & Carter, L. F. The effects of varying combinations of authoritarian and egalitarian leader and follower. *Journal of Abnormal and Social Psychology,* 1956, *53,* 210-219.

Heider, F. *The psychology of interpersonal relations.* New York: Wiley, 1958.

Hemphill, J. K. Relations between the size of the group and the behavior of "superior" leaders. *Journal of Social Psychology,* 1950, *32,* 11-22.

Hemphill, J. K., & Coons, A. E. Development of the leader behavior description questionnaire. In R. M. Stogdill & A. E. Coons (Eds.), *Leader behavior: Its description and measurement.* Columbus: Ohio State University, Bureau of Business Research, 1957.

Hill, P. E., & Schmitt, N. Individual differences in leadership decision-making. *Organizational Behavior and Human Performance,* 1977, *19,* 353-367.

Hofstede, G. Nationality and espoused values of managers. *Journal of Applied Psychology,* 1976, *61,* 148-155.

Hofstede, G. Motivation, leadership, and organization: Do American theories apply abroad? *Organizational Dynamics,* Summer, 1980.

Hofstede, G. *Culture's consequences: International differences in work-related values.* London: Sage, 1981.

Hollander, E. P. Conformity, status, and idiosyncrasy credit. *Psychological Review,* 1958, *65,* 117-127.

Hollander, E. P., & Julian, J. W. Studies in leader legitimacy, influence, and innovation. In L. Berkowitz (Ed.), *Advances in experimental social psychology,* Vol. 5. New York: Academic Press, 1970.

House, R. J. A path-goal theory of leadership. *Administrative Science Quarterly,* 1971, *16,* 321-338.

House, R. J., & Dessler, G. The path-goal theory of leadership: Some post hoc and a priori tests. In J. G. Hunt & L. L. Larsen (Eds.), *Contingency approaches to leadership.* Carbondale, Ill.: Southern Illinois University Press, 1974.

Ilgen, D. R., & Fujii, D. S. An investigation of the validity of leader behavior descriptions obtained from subordinates. *Journal of Applied Psychology,* 1976, *61,* 642-651.

Jago, A. G. A test of spuriousness in descriptive models of participative leader behavior. *Journal of Applied Psychology,* 1978, *63,* 383-387. (a)

Jago, A. G. Configural utilization of implicit models of leader behavior. *Organizational Behavior and Human Performance,* 1978, *22,* 474-496. (b)

Jago, A. G., & Vroom, V. H. Hierarchical level in leadership style. *Organizational Behavior and Human Performance,* 1977, *18,* 131-145.

Jago, A. G., & Vroom, V. H. An evaluation of two alternatives to the Vroom/Yetton normative model. *Academy of Management Journal,* 1980, *23,* 347-355.

Jenkins, W. O. A review of leadership studies with particular reference to military problems. *Psychological Bulletin.* 1947, *44,* 54-79.

Johns, G. Task moderators of the relationship between leadership style and subordinate responses. *Academy of Management Journal,* 1978, *21,* 319-325.

Jones, E. E. The rocky road from acts to dispositions. *American Psychologist,* 1979, *34,* 107-117.

Jones, E. E., & Davis, K. E. From acts to dispositions. In L. Berkowitz (Ed.), *Ad-

vances in experimental social psychology (Vol. 2). New York: Academic Press, 1965.

Kahn, R. L. An analysis of supervisory practices and components of morale. In H. Guetzkow (Ed.), *Groups, leadership, and men*. Pittsburgh: Carnegie Press, 1951.

Kahn, R. L., & Katz, D. Leadership practices in relation to productivity and morale. In D. Cartwright & A. Zander (Eds.), *Group dynamics*. New York: Harper & Row, 1953.

Kelley, H. H. The processes of causal attribution. *American Psychologist*, 1973, *28*, 107-128.

Kerr, S. Substitutes for leadership: Some implications for organizational design. *Organization and Administrative Sciences*, 1977, *8*, 135-146.

Kerr, S., & Jermier, J. M. Substitutes for leadership: Their meaning and measurement. *Organizational Behavior and Human Performance*, 1978, *22*, 375-403.

Knowlton, W. A., Jr., & Mitchell, T. R. The effects of causal attributions on supervisors' evaluations of subordinate performance. *Journal of Applied Psychology*, 1980, *65*, 459-466.

Konar-Goldband, E., Rice, R. W., & Monkarsh, W. Time-phased interrelationships of group atmosphere, group performance, and leader style. *Journal of Applied Psychology*, 1979, *64*, 401-409.

Korman, A. "Consideration," "initiating structure," and organizational criteria— A review. *Personnel Psychology*, 1966, *19*, 349-362.

Korman, A. K. Contingency approaches to leadership: An overview. In J. G. Hunt & L. L. Larsen (Eds.), *Contingency approaches to leadership*. Carbondale, Ill.: Southern Illinois University Press , 1974.

Kraut, A. I. Some recent advances in cross-national management research. *Academy of Management Journal*, 1975, *18*, 538-549.

Lawrence, P. R., & Lorsch, J. W. *Organization and environment*. Boston: Harvard Graduate School of Business Administration, 1967.

Leavitt, H. J. Some effects of certain communication patterns on group performance. *Journal of Abnormal and Social Psychology*, 1951, *46*, 38-50.

Lewin, K., Lippitt, R., & White, R. K. Patterns of aggressive behavior in experimentally created "social climates." *Journal of Social Psychology*, 1939, *10*, 27-299.

Liden, R. C., & Graen, G. Generalizability of the vertical dyad linkage model of leadership. *Academy of Management Journal*, 1980, *23*, 451-465.

Lord, R. G., Binning, J. F., Rush, M. C., & Thomas, J. C. The effect of performance cues and leader behavior in questionnaire rating of leadership behavior. *Organizational Behavior and Human Performance*, 1978, *21*, 27-39.

Mai-Dalton, R. *The influence of training and position power on leader behavior* (Tech. Rep. 75-72). Seattle: University of Washington, Organizational Research, 1975.

Maier, N. R. F. *Problem solving discussion and conferences: Leadership methods and skills*. New York: McGraw-Hill, 1963.

Mann, R. D. A review of the relationship between personality and performance in small groups. *Psychological Bulletin*, 1959, *56*, 241-270.

Margerison, C., & Glube, R. Leadership decision-making: An empirical test of the Vroom and Yetton model. *Journal of Management Studies*, 1979, *16*, 45-55.

McMahon, J. T. The contingency model: Logic and method revisited: *Personnel Psychology*, 1972, *25*, 697-710.

Miles, R. R., & Petty, M. M. Leader effectiveness in small bureaucracies. *Academy of Management Journal*, 1977, *20*, 238-250.

Mitchell, T. R., Biglan, A., Oncken, G. R., & Fiedler, F. E. The contingency model: Criticisms and suggestions. *Academy of Management Journal*, 1970, *13*, 253-267.

Mitchell, T. R., & Kalb, L. S. Effects of outcome knowledge and outcome valence in supervisors' evaluations. *Journal of Applied Psychology*, 1981, *66*, 604-612.

Mitchell, T. R., & Wood, R. E. Supervisors' responses to subordinate poor performance: A test of an attributional model. *Organizational Behavior and Human Performance*, 1980, *25*, 123-138.

Nath, R. A. A methodological review of cross-cultural management research. In J. Boddewyn (Ed.), *Comparative management and marketing*. Glenview, Ill.: Scott, Foresman, 1969.

Nebeker, D. M. Situational favorability and perceived environmental uncertainty: An integrative approach. *Administrative Science Quarterly*, 1975, *20*, 281-294.

Negandhi, A. R. Comparative management and organization theory: A marriage needed. *Academy of Management Journal*, 1975, *18*, 334-344.

Negandhi, A. R., & Prasad, S. B. *Comparative management*. New York: Appleton-Century-Crofts, 1971.

Osborn, R. N., & Hunt, J. G. An adaptive-reactive theory of leadership. *Organization and Administrative Sciences*, 1975, *6*, 27-44.

Phillips, J. S., & Lord, R. G. Causal attributions and perceptions of leadership. *Organizational Behavior and Human Performance*, 1981, *28*, 143-163.

Potter, E. H., III, & Fiedler, F. E. The utilization of staff member intelligence and experience under high and low stress. *Academy of Management Journal*, 1981, *24*, 361-376.

Rice, R. W. Construct validity of the least preferred co-worker score. *Psychological Bulletin*, 1978, *85*, 1199-1237.

Rice, R. W. Leader LPC and follower satisfaction: A review. *Organizational Behavior and Human Performance*, 1981, *28*, 1-25.

Rice, R. W., Marwick, N. J., Chemers, M. M., & Bentley, J. C. Least Preferred Co-worker (LPC) score as a moderator of the relationship between task performance and satisfaction. *Personality and Social Psychology Bulletin*, 1982, *8*, 534-541.

Roberts, K. H. On looking at an elephant: An evaluation of cross-cultural research related to organizations. *Psychological Bulletin*, 1970, *74*, 327-350.

Ruble, T. L. Effects of one's locus of control and the opportunity to participate in planning. *Organizational Behavior and Human Performance*, 1976, *16*, 63-73.

Salancik, G. R., & Pfeffer, J. A social information processing approach to job attitudes in task design. *Administrative Science Quarterly*, 1978, *23*, 224-253.

Sanford, F. Research on military leadership. In J. Flanagan (Ed.), *Psychology in the world emergency*. Pittsburgh: University of Pittsburgh Press, 1952.

Schriesheim, C. A. The similarity of individual directed and group directed leader behavior descriptions. *Academy of Management Journal*, 1979, *22*, 345-355.

Schriesheim, C. A., & DeNisi, A. S. Task dimensions as moderators of the effects of instrumental leadership: A two sample replicated test of path-goal leadership theory. *Journal of Applied Psychology*, 1981, *66*, 589-597.

Schriesheim, C. A., House, R. J., & Kerr, S. Leader initiating structure: A reconciliation of discrepant research results and some empirical tests. *Organizational Behavior and Human Performance*, 1976, *15*, 297-321.

Schriesheim, C. A., & Kerr, S. Theories and measures of leadership: A critical appraisal of current and future directions. In. J. G. Hunt and L. L. Larsen (Eds.), *Leadership: The cutting edge*. Carbondale, Ill.: Southern Illinois University Press, 1977.

Schriesheim, C. A., Kinicki, H. A., & Schriesheim, J. F. The effect of leniency on leadership behavior descriptions. *Organizational Behavior and Human Performance*, 1979, *23*, 1-29.

Schriesheim, C. A., & Murphy, C. J. Relationship between leader behavior and subordinate satisfaction and performance: A test of some situational moderators. *Journal of Applied Psychology*, 1976, *61*, 634-641.

Schriesheim, C. A., & Von Gilnow, M. A. The path-goal theory of leadership: A theoretical and empirical analysis. *Academy of Management Journal*, 1977, *20*, 398-405.

Schreisheim, J. F. The social context of leader-subordinate relations: An investigation of the effects of cohesiveness. *Journal of Applied Psychology*, 1980, *65*, 183-195.

Schuler, R. A. Participation with supervisor and subordinate authoritarianism: A path-goal theory reconcilation. *Administrative Science Quarterly*, 1976, *21*, 320-325.

Shapira, Z. A facet analysis of leadership styles. *Journal of Applied Psychology*, 1976, *61*, 136-139.

Shartle, C. L. *Executive performance and leadership*. Englewood Cliffs, N.J.: Prentice-Hall, 1956.

Shiflett, S. The contingency model: Some implications of the statistical and methodological properties. *Behavioral Science*, 1973, *18*, 429-440.

Sims, H. P., & Szilagyi, A. D. Leader structure and subordinate satisfaction for two hospital administrative levels: A path analysis approach. *Journal of Applied Psychology*, 1975, *60*, 194-197.

Steers, R. M. Task-goal attributes, n achievement, and supervisory performance. *Organizational Behavior and Human Performance*, 1975, *13*, 392-403.

Stenson, J. E., & Johnson, T. W. The path-goal theory of leadership: A partial test and suggested refinement. *Academy of Management Journal*, 1975, *18*, 242-252.

Stogdill, R. M. Personal factors associated with leadership: A survey of the literature. *Journal of Psychology*, 1948, *25*, 35-71.

Stogdill, R. M. *Manual for the Leader Behavior Description Questionnaire—Form XII*. Columbus: Ohio State University, Bureau of Business Research, 1963.

Stogdill, R. M., Shartle, C. L., Scott, E. L., Coons, A. E., & Jaynes, W. E. *A predictive study of administrative work patterns*. Columbus: Ohio State University, Bureau of Business Research, 1956.

Strube, M. J., & Garcia, J. E. A meta-analytical investigation of Fiedler's contingency model of leadership effectiveness. *Psychological Bulletin,* 1981, *90*, 307-321.

Tannenbaum, A. S. Organizational Psychology. In H. C. Triandis & R. W. Brislin (Eds.), *Handbook of cross-cultural psychology: Social psychology*, Vol. 5. Boston: Allyn and Bacon, 1980.

Thomas, K. W., & Kilman, R. H. The social desirability variable in organizational research: An alternative explanation of reported findings. *Academy of Management Journal,* 1975, *18*, 741-751.

Valenzi, E., & Dessler, G. Relationships of leader behavior, subordinate role ambiguity, and subordinate satisfaction. *Academy of Management Journal,* 1978, *21*, 671-678.

Vecchio, R. P. Empirical examination of the validity of Fiedler's model of leadership effectiveness. *Organizational Behavior and Human Performance,* 1977, *19*, 180-206.

Vroom, V. H., & Jago, A. G. On the validity of the Vroom-Yetton model. *Journal of Applied Psychology,* 1978, *63*, 151-162.

Vroom, V. H., & Yetton, P. W. *Leadership and decision-making.* Pittsburgh: University of Pittsburgh Press, 1973.

Weed, S. E., Mitchell, T. R., & Moffitt, W. Leadership style, subordinate personality, and task type as predictors of performance and satisfaction with supervision. *Journal of Applied Psychology,* 1976, *61*, 58-66.

Wexley, K. N., Alexander, R. A., Greenawalt, J. P., & Couch, M. A. Attitudinal congruence and similarity as related to interpersonal evaluations in manager-subordinate dyads. *Academy of Management Journal,* 1980, *23*, 320-330.

Chapter 3
Minority Influence

Serge Moscovici and Gabriel Mugny

Two Social Influence Models

Dependency and Conformity Bias

Research on minority influence, that is, the impact of an individual on the group or of a group on a collectivity, is of recent origin. Why did it take so long to recognize this influence? There are several reasons. One is the conception and model on which studies about group phenomena generally, and social influence in particular, were based. From the early days of social psychology until quite recently, interest was focused on conformity, on the way a group affects individuals and brings about social uniformities (Festinger, 1950). Another reason is the perspective from which relations between individuals and groups were mainly envisaged, that is, dependency. Hence the well-known formulation: The fundamental influence mechanism, in its various guises, is social dependency (power, competence, etc.). A final reason is the emphasis on the social control process, which is presumed to facilitate cohesion and to enable a group of individuals to reach its goals. The only function attributed to social influence is therefore the group's social control over its members. Within this context deviants are presented as obstacles to group progress. They are viewed as "weak" individuals trying to reinsert themselves into the social system. These points are too familiar to delve into them at length. We only wish to point out that they underlie the classical view of groups and group dynamics (see Levine, 1980). Their joint effect has been to instill a conformity bias in social thought and research, as will become more evident when we examine each of these aspects in turn and look at them more closely.

Let us examine for instance the main question: Why does a source exert an influence on a target? The classic reply is quite simple: because the former has an advantage over the latter; because the two social entities under consideration, the majority and the minority, do not have the same resources at their disposal. The sources of influence will be individuals enjoying the highest social status, the greatest prestige, a greater expertise, more authority, or individuals with a bigger numerical backing, and so on. Publications are filled with experimental examples along these lines, showing that social influence seen in this light is regulated by a form of dependency. Dependency obviously implies a quantitative difference between the source and the target with respect to a physical or psychological resource at the disposal of each of them. Whoever is better endowed with this resource will affect the opinions and judgments of the one who has less, in an almost mechanical way. The way individuals or groups interact would appear to have little intrinsic importance since it would be limited to bringing to the surface the prior social givens, as old-time photographers merely revealed a picture captured by the negative. In a way, the die is already cast ahead of time, a natural conclusion from a social rationale that assigns each one a role, a capacity for being right or wrong, for being normal or "deviant." The picture we are sketching is of course oversimplified, but it is not far removed from reality.

From the above rationale there emerges a view of groups based on majorities, whose purpose it is to socialize individuals and make them adapt to group norms and values. Confronting the group are deviant individuals. Stereotypically, they are maladjusted, lacking information, or have a distorted view of reality. They serve as obstacles to group progress, and the purpose of influence is to remove these obstacles by integrating the deviants and making them conform to the group. In case of failure, the deviants will be excluded, stigmatized. In an extreme version, deviants (defined merely by their being different) were presented as trying to hide (Freedman & Doob, 1968) or to make themselves invisible (Personnaz, 1979). These passive deviants fail to assert themselves and sometimes seem, quite plausibly, to deserve their fate (Lerner, 1971). Unquestionably this type of deviant really exists and represents a kind of "withdrawal" or anomie. However, one must also, perhaps primarily, concern oneself with another kind of poorly integrated individuals or groups—active minorities. These individuals and groups, though they may be at times set apart, dominated, or isolated, do display a certain autonomy. They try to modify their position and propagate their views. To this type of minorities we might assign social movements (ecologists, student movements, etc.), artistic schools in their early days, scientific movements propounding new theories, some political parties, heterodox religious sects (Protestantism), and also all individuals with a special or original message. What these minorities all share is the tendency to seek visibility, to forge an identity, to convert the majority to their ideas and beliefs, in short, to change the groups or societies to which they belong. In other words, they are factors of innovation.

Innovation and Active Minorities

Recent studies concerned with influence processes, at least in Europe (Moscovici, 1976), have abandoned the classical perspective. They envisage groups and social systems in terms of their capacity to change, to grow in an environment that is being constantly modified by human activity. This is by no means an intrinsically novel idea. Biologists and historians have long since realized that societies progress by making a break with the past, just as mutations give rise to new species. However, this idea applied to social psychology generates a reversal in outlook. It is usually assumed in the social sciences that order, normalcy, and hence conformity, represent regularity, the basic state of social operation. For this reason, any deviation, any "novelty" seems to emerge as a deviance, and innovation as a perturbation or dysfunction (Merton, 1957).

As history, biology, and, of course, reality teach, the basic condition is actually a composite of many small or large modifications and breaks, of mutations and innovations. Some of these recur, are weeded out and normalized, gradually turning into a normal and uniform state of affairs. Stability, cohesion, and so on are thus merely temporary and apparent. This leads to the conclusion that innovation is not a secondary process, a case of failed conformity, but a process that is at least as basic if not more basic than conformity. Once this point of view has been accepted, it is natural to conclude that the function of social influence is also to guarantee social change, the evolution and diversity of ideas and behaviors, not just to assure their uniformity, stability, and conformity. The problem ceases to be, in this case, to determine how the group operates to carry out its goals most effectively. It is to determine how a group takes shape, is modified, and chooses these very goals, or more accurately, how it changes and grows.

Once social interaction and groups came to be viewed in the context of innovation, it was natural for the studies with which we are dealing here to focus on active minorities, which are in a way the most typical, if not the only, factors in innovation. History, and even biology, generally teach us that changes take place in societies or species in conjunction with the appearance of a new line of thought, of a pioneering, heterodox subgroup or group. The latter may succeed, after many attempts and even by dint of sacrifices, in bringing forth a novelty, in modifying the course of events. Rather than presenting an obstacle to the group's progress, it serves as a driving force. Indeed, what counts is not how many individuals there are but the fact that these minorities have a special position, transgress certain beliefs or reject certain behaviors, have their own identity and conception. In addition, they seek to convert other people. This is what makes them active minorities. These few points summarize intuitively what we have presented more abstractly and theoretically elsewhere (Moscovici, 1976; Mugny, 1982).

To go one step further, if we assume that minority influence is geared to bringing about change and innovation, dependency can no longer be conceived as the main factor in minority and majority relations and interaction. There are two reasons for this. On the one hand, the majority's dependence on the minority is too weak and the latter is at a disadvantage with respect to resources (power, competence, etc.), so that it could not exert influence on the strength of these resources (Moscovici & Nemeth, 1974). On the other hand, dependency, as well as influence, is viewed as unilateral in classical theories of social psychology. Only the active source (authority, majority, group, etc.) is considered capable of modifying the responses of the passive target (minority, deviant, individual, etc.). Of course, if we deal with a minority or an individual influencing the group or majority, it must be a matter of reciprocal action. In other words, both the source and the target can be and are, theoretically, equally active. This reciprocity is an essential principle in all social relations. No one involved in any social interaction is wholly unconcerned about the others with whom he is dealing. Every partner in the relation also changes the other, even if in varying degrees. Let us just recall Schachter's (1951) famous experiment about the reactions to different types of deviants. The stablest and firmest deviant concentrated group communication on himself, he focused the other members of the group on the causes of his deviance. Even though it was not considered desirable at the time to look into this reciprocal influence, and even though the experiment demonstrated the final rejection of the deviant, the fact remains that the deviant did modify something in the interaction.

It is this something that will be examined in this chapter. The question will be raised how active minorities, despite this rejection, modify the opinions and judgments of the majority and change the social field. To anticipate, let us state that they derive their influence from their behavioral style, in other words, from their way of expressing their point of view, of organizing their responses. To be fair, it must be admitted that dependency or status on the one hand and behavioral style on the other may go hand in hand or may clash, serve to reinforce or impede each other. Determining which of the two is more decisive in a group cannot be done theoretically. It must be verified experimentally. It would be valuable for sociology and social psychology to pay more attention to the relation between the two. This would already be a change with respect to the prevailing view which tries to reduce everything to social status, to a form of dependency. Behavioral style, as such, a concept that we have introduced elsewhere, is greatly neglected. It is our central proposition that in the case of social influence most phenomena can be explained and predicted by taking behavioral style as a starting point, dependency serving as a parameter facilitating or counteracting its effects.

We can summarize what we have just stated in the following way. Innovation is a fundamental process in group life, and minority influence is a typical expression of this process. Influence has a twofold function: to bring about change as well as social control. Consequently it can have a minority (deviants, individuals, etc.) as its source as well as a majority. The decisive element in the outcome is the behavioral style of the group members. Several of these ideas give a new slant to certain neglected aspects of group theory, while other of these ideas are clearly in conflict with group theory. After the publication of the first studies on minority influence and innovation, for instance, Hollander's (1960) traditional point of view was refurbished as an antidote. Taking leadership phenomena as his starting point, Hollander postulated the notion of idiosyncratic credit to explain how innovation succeeds through conformity. By a show of initial overconformity, an individual can gain group leadership. This status then allows him or her to present innovative solutions as long as his or her idiosyncratic "credits" are not overdrawn. The individual thus accumulates status by his or her conformity as though he or she were accumulating capital, and his or her surplus capital allows him or her to innovate until he or she has exhausted this surplus. Both innovation and conformity are associated with high social status. It is an elegant solution, which remains true to the classical model in that dependency plays a decisive role.

Supposing that this hypothesis had been verified by experiments, which is not exactly the case (Moscovici & Nemeth, 1974), what would it imply? There are innovations both from the top and from the bottom that are introduced in a group. Hollander's solution obviously illustrates a change from above, introduced by those who have resources and already enjoy a high status. But most changes, among them those of some historical significance and of the greatest theoretical interest as well, were introduced from the bottom. We have examined them in the context of active minorities, which generally have neither the means nor the urge to accumulate these idiosyncratic credits by the circuitous route of a conformism that they have long since rejected. And besides, to paraphrase a French sociologist (Crozier, 1979), society cannot be changed by decree. The strategies of these minorities for convincing others can be manyfold. One of them, the most sensible, would be along the following lines. Taking into account the possibilities at hand, the minority would first attempt to gain acceptance and respect of group members by making a series of concessions within the framework of existing norms. Thanks to this conformity, it would acquire both status and expertise, so as to be acknowledged by everyone in the group. Then and only then the minority could deviate from the group norms and convince others into following it. Its influence would be increased owing to its previously acquired status and expertise. This strategy assumes that the innovation process is one form of conformity and also that the majority is ready to include the minority in its system. We have shown elsewhere that even if the strategy is possible, it is not necessarily more efficient with regard to experimental findings (Moscovici, 1976).

When the changes are more important and social or ethical discrimination stronger, when it is not so much a question of deviating from group norms as of proposing another norm, then minorities have to resort to another strategy. It does not consist in making compromises, smoothing away conflicts in order to place themselves under the protection of an established power. On the contrary, they do their best to create conflicts, to smash the uniformity upheld by those in power, in order to make people share their views and aspirations. Let us quote Lewin (1973, p. 163) because what he writes about the Jewish minority has a broader psychological interest.

> More than words of self-defense are necessary to change social reality. Certainly Jews have to try everything to ally themselves with any other force seriously fighting Fascism. Being but few in number, it is incumbent upon us to try to win the help of other groups. However, the Jew will have to realize that for him as well as for any underprivileged group the following statement holds: only the efforts of the group itself will achieve the emancipation of the group.

This is a point that deserves to be stressed. Groups have been conceived for too long as conformity-producing machines and deviants as troublemakers, anomic, nonassertive individuals. One of the very few questions asked regarding them was: how to increase the resistance to majority influence? A broader perspective of reality has long been overdue, in which these nonconformist individuals are considered as more self-assertive, having their own goals and relying upon themselves. This entails a theory of the influence exerted by active minorities which answers another question: how to change or convince the majority? Our effort in group psychology is directed toward an evolution which leads from the idea of *resistance to* majority to the idea of *changing* the majority.

Impact of Behavioral Style

Social Context of Innovation

Any theory of the mechanics of minority influence must take the following two facts into account. First of all, as we have seen, minority influence cannot be explained by invoking one kind of power (or dependency) or another, for the sound reason that minorities do not have these at their disposal. They have no means of control or coercion available, and they have no social resource allowing them to impose their views, beyond making them known (and they usually have only limited or no access to the information media). The explanations accounting for majority influence are therefore not applicable.

A second fact should be noted. We are used to thinking that the influence source owes its influence precisely to the fact that it is respected, liked, and competent, and so on. Yet, initially the minority does not have a positive social image. At the start the minority is viewed as deviant, incompetent, unreasonable, unappealing, and unattractive. Minorities take root in a social context of tensions and conflicts, and the whole complexity of this normative context must be taken into account to explain their influence (Mugny & Papastamou, 1983). It is only in the wake of a social process leading to the raising of the barriers against it and the imposing (to some extent or other) of its innovations that the minority will reach a point where it may even be seen as attractive.

It should also be noted that the content of minority propositions cannot be invoked as an explanation. This is not due to the fact that the content is immaterial, or because its novelty and originality are without any appeal. Obviously this factor of novelty and originality is necessary. It is rarely sufficient, however, even in science where most theories have had to fight and use the means of persuasion in order to assert themselves. The scientists who put them forward have been in the situation of every minority, as testified by Heisenberg (1975, p. 157), one of the creators of quantum mechanics:

> On the whole, then, it is possible to conclude in retrospect that in this century there have been two great revolutions in our science, which have displaced foundations of physics and thereby altered the whole edifice of the subject. We must now ask how such radical alterations have come about, or—to put it in more sociological terms, though also quite misleadingly—how was a seemingly small group of physicists able to constrain the others to these changes in the structure of science and thought? It goes without saying that the others at the first resisted the change, and were bound to do so.

If things happen this way in physics, we may well think that in the other fields, where the ideological and material interests are more direct, the process has an even more stressed character. It stands to reason that the contents of minority propositions are rejected insofar as they diverge from the existing ideas or norms. At first they can be ignored, judged ludicrous, as in the case of Heider's ideas when they were first proposed (see Harvey, Ickes, & Kidd, 1976), or even considered erroneous or dangerous, as was the case with psychoanalysis or evolution theory. If after a time these contents are accepted and admired for their originality, this comes mostly as a result of a minority influence process. Thanks to it a basic innovation and a new social perspective will have won out.

What then is the source of minority influence, if it is neither one or another kind of power or dependency, nor a mark of social distinction, nor the appeal of the content of the minority propositions as such? The minority influence process relies on the minority's only resource, an inner resource—its own actions. The explanation for minority influence must therefore be sought in its behaviors (in the broadest sense, including its actions, the expression of attitudes and opinions, speeches, non-verbal clues, etc.) and more specifically in its behavioral styles, which constitute a sort of formal structure whereby the different behaviors a minority displays in various occasions and situations are organized. Behavioral styles are its rhetoric in that they define the temporal organization of behaviors and opinions as well as the intensity of their expression.

The most important among the behavioral styles that serve as underpinnings for minority influence is consistency. There are two complementary levels actually defining consistency, one involving the organization of the contents of the minority alternative and its stability over time (designated as diachronic consistency) and the other involving interindividual organization (referred to as synchronic consistency).

The Repetition Effect

Diachronic consistency refers to the systematicness with which the active minority keeps drawing attention to its positions and makes them socially visible. Diachronic consistency thus implies a certain repetition over time, as was illustrated in one of the first experiments concerned directly with minority influence (Moscovici, Lage, & Naffrechoux, 1969). In a color perception task, subjects were asked to attribute a simple color label to slides that were obviously blue (as proven by the almost complete absence of mistakes when the subjects responded spontaneously and alone). They expressed their judgments orally, in groups of six, consisting of four real subjects and two confederates of the researcher, the latter giving the incorrect response "green." In one experimental condition, the two confederates gave the wrong response together for two-thirds of the items and responded (correctly) like the real subjects for one-third of the trials. In this condition, their influence was almost nil. In another experimental condition, the two confederates also gave their "green" response to what they saw, but this time they did so consistently for the whole set of trials, without ever giving the impression that they were uncertain or undecided as to the obviousness of their response. In this condition, consistency induced minority influence and yielded more than 8% "green" responses on the part of the experimental subjects. This effect of systematically repeating one and the same response does indeed constitute an influence condition within the reach of a minority, as confirmed by other experiments (cf. Moscovici & Faucheux, 1972).

It should be noted, however, that this repetitiveness requirement does not imply that the minority must give one and the same more-or-less fixed response in order to draw attention to its consistency. Some variations are possible, as long as they are systematically structured, as can be seen in an experiment by Nemeth, Swed-lund, & Kanki (1974), using the "blue-green" paradigm. In the conditions that are of interest to us here, a distinctive feature of the stimuli was exploited. Although they were all blue, some were brighter, others duller. This pecularity made it feasi-ble to introduce consistent variations in the minority responses. In two so-called "correlated" conditions, the two confederates responded "green" to half of the 28 items and "blue-green" to the other half. In one case the "green" response was given to the brightest stimuli (correlated condition I), while in the other condition the "green" response was given for the dullest stimuli (correlated condition II) and the converse in each condition for the "blue-green" response. In a third condition, vari-ations in response were random rather than dependent on the brightness of the slides. The results obtained are shown in Table 3-1.

In the control condition (without minority confederates) no "green" response is ever given by the subjects. The experimental paradigm is therefore quite unambigu-ous. In the condition where minority responses vary randomly, their influence is nil. On the average fewer than 1 out of 28 items includes a "green" response. On the other hand, when these variations are related to variations in the physical character-istics of the stimuli, there is a clear minority influence, on the order of 20%. What is even more interesting is the fact that the influence is not significantly affected by the content of the variations (correlated I vs. correlated II). What matters, thus, is not so much the content of the responses but the systematicness within the "differ-entiated" repetition.

To summarize, consistency does not require a rigid repetition of the same response. It is perfectly compatible with certain variations as long as these variations are structured systematically and consistently match actual variations of the situation.

Consistency Effect

It is a fact that the setting within which and on which the minority exerts an influ-ence is not one-dimensional. The only reason it sometimes is one-dimensional in experiments is to prove a point. In such a one-dimensional setting, consistency must be characterized by a certain type of repetition. Here the minority must reassert its system of alternative responses over time, this being the only way it can display the consistency of its responses. In a multicriteria universe, consistency will refer to the

Table 3-1. Mean Number of Trials Subjects Said Green (max = 28)[a]

Condition	
Control	0.00
Random	0.06
Correlated I	6.37
Correlated II	5.31

[a](Based on Nemeth et al., 1974, p. 58.)

systematicness of its behaviors in various realms. Thus, when a minority upholds a given stand on a problem, it must also uphold an equally consistent stand with respect to other problems. A study by Allen and Wilder (1978) makes this point clear. In the two conditions relevant to our discussion, the subjects were given information about opinions on five topics (which were actually not spelled out) submitted by a person six times during a year (once every two months). On the first topic, the stimulus person remained consistent the whole year (responding either −3 or +3 on a 6-point scale) for two experimental conditions. In one condition, the source remained equally consistent on four other topics (responding always in the same way, either −3 or +3 for three of them, and always 0 for the last topic). In the other condition, on the contrary, the source was not consistent over time. Every two months it changed by a point on each of the four other topics, gradually moving in a positive or negative direction on each of these topics. The subjects were asked, among other things, to evaluate how persuasive they thought the stimulus person would be in arguing in favor of its position with respect to the first topic (on which all persons maintained a consistently extreme position). The subjects responded on a 9-point scale (1 = not at all persuasive; 9 = very persuasive). When the source was consistent for all the other topics, it was perceived on the whole as persuasive ($\bar{X}$ = 6.22). Conversely, when the source was not equally consistent on the other topics, it was perceived as having a weak power of persuasion ($\bar{X}$ = 3.31). Consistency must therefore extend beyond the particular topic on which the source is exerting its influence. The minority is expected to be consistent in several different dimensions. This is the only way the minority can present an authentic alternative.

Consistency between various responses is an aspect of consistency which emphasizes the firmness of the minority's stand in the overall social field. The study of judgments relating to social matters (rather than perceptive judgments) should therefore be particularly appropriate in evaluating the impact of consistency. In this instance, consistency is characterized not only by the systematic maintenance of a given stand over time, but also by the internal consistency of the minority's discourse, as demonstrated by the following experiment (Mugny, 1975). In this experiment, the subjects did not interact directly with confederates. They were asked to read a minority appeal drawn up in the form of a leaflet. After having first responded to an opinion questionnaire on attitudes toward foreigners, half the subjects were given an appeal disseminated by an anti-foreign-minority group, while the other half received an appeal disseminated by a pro-foreign-minority group. In both cases, half the subjects were given a consistent appeal and half of them an inconsistent appeal. Consistency was defined by the "repetition" of a compatible stand (either extremely pro- or anti-foreign) with respect to various dimensions of the problem. Thus the minority group demanded (or spoke against, according to the conditions) political rights for foreigners, economic equality, housing rights, or respect for cultural identity. The group, furthermore, defended its positions firmly, its consistency underscored by the certainty and intensity of expression reflected stylistically in the language used. Conversely, inconsistency was defined by an explicit reluctance to take a stand (this in spite of the position upheld in the body of the appeal, which was identical in both conditions), by contradictions between assertions and certain conclusions, as well as by the ambiguity of the solutions advanced. Scores of opinion changes demonstrate clearly that only minorities with a firm and consistent presentation (i.e., consistent minorities) had a positive influence. The same result was obtained for the anti-foreign and the pro-foreign minorities (though the latter had the greater influence), proving that, except for slight qualifications (cf. Mugny, 1982), the essential requisite for minority influence is not the content as such but the organization and the stylistic modalities of the minority's behavior with respect to this content.

Need for Minority Consensus (Asch Reinterpreted)

Let us now broach the second aspect of consistency (synchronic). Minorities generally consist of more than a single individual (though occasionally such relatively isolated instances of dissidence do occur (cf. Moscovici, 1979, on the Solzhenitsin case). In the case of several individuals, the consistency requirement is translated into the need to present a united unanimous front. To make itself heard, the minority cannot allow itself to seem lacking in consistency and must demonstrate at any given time and in the course of time a consensus that guarantees a single-minded stand on the part of the members of the minority. To be sure, the fact that the minority must create an impression of consensus does not imply that disagreements and conflicts might not arise within the minority group. These disagreements must remain internal to the group and even concealed, inasmuch as one of conditions of its influence is the impression of unanimity it conveys.

We shall refer to Asch's (1951, 1956) famous experiment in order to illustrate the impact of synchronic consistency. In the Asch paradigm the subject is asked to judge which of three bars of different sizes in sets of different sizes is equal to a standard bar. The right response is obvious, but the subject is confronted with a unanimous "majority" of confederates giving a wrong answer. Our interest in this experiment is twofold. First, this paradigm has always been considered the prototype for studying majority influence, but such an interpretation is actually too limited. It reduces the social implications of the experiment to the narrow framework of the experiment setup. By defining the more numerous entity as the majority and the one including fewer individuals as the minority, the most original aspect of this paradigm is obscured. Asch, in effect, shows in these experiments under what conditions a new, incorrect, as well as unpopular response can assert itself. Far from merely studying "majority" influence, *Asch was actually studying processes for disseminating an innovation*! Are the subjects confronted with the experimental setup not in fact equipped with the necessary sociocognitive instruments for evaluating the differences with certainty? And are the confederates not innovating by suggesting wrong answers which challenge the usual principles for evaluating perceived differences? Secondly, if one is willing to envision Asch's paradigm as approximating innovation phenomena, his different variables and their results actually give us direct insight into minority influence! Surely in the various results we can see the effects of consistency in their different guises!

From this point of view, the effect of diachronic consistency is demonstrated by Asch's manipulation of the relative rate of critical items (where the source is innovating) and neutral items (where the source gives the correct response). Influence increases as the number of incorrect responses increases and the number of correct responses declines. Hence it does in fact increase with minority consistency.

Similarly, Asch's experiment illustrates the effect of synchronic consistency. Asch certainly disrupted source consensus by introducing an additional experimental subject or a confederate. Thus, while the influence rate in his initial experiment was higher than 30% it fell to 10% when he introduced another subject who did not always respond in the same way as the numerical "majority" and thereby supported the minority response. The influence rate even fell to 5.5% when a confederate who happened to respond correctly was introduced. It is striking that influence diminished even when one of the confederates disrupted the consensus by giving an even more incorrect response than the other confederates, without giving direct social support (see Allen, 1975; Allen & Levine, 1968; Doms & Van Avermaet, 1980) to the subject. All this further confirms the fact that the precondition for successfully disseminating a minority innovation is its being supported "to the last man" by all the members of the group.

It must also be noted that the actual number of minority individuals does make a difference. Asch observed that influence increased with the number of influence sources, stabilizing at around three or four. The same point was investigated in connection with the "blue-green" paradigm conceived to study minority influence. One experiment was designed to determine the influence of a given consistent style displayed either by a single or by two minority individuals (Moscovici, 1976). While the two synchronically and diachronically consistent confederates obtained about 10% influence, the single confederate obtained no more than 1%. It is likely that subjects confronted with a single deviant individual were able to make an internal attribution by imputing his deviance to some sort of visual or personal anomaly. Such an internal attribution would be less plausible and therefore less likely to be invoked in the case of two or several individuals maintaining the same position than it would be for an isolated minority individual (see Mugny & Papastamou, 1980; Papastamou, Mugny, & Kaiser, 1980; Papastamou, 1983). The existence of a consensus would thus have the effect of counteracting such attributions which, when they can be invoked, may well cancel out a source's influence, at least if it is a minority source.

Why Is Minority Consistency Effective?

Let us at this point take as settled the fact that a minority wishing to exert influence urgently needs to show itself diachronically and synchronically consistent. Obviously the evidence is limited to individual cases which will be found in other studies as well (Moscovici, 1976; Mugny, 1982). We shall now raise the central question: For what reason is consistency the source of minority influence?

Social Visibility

One explanation lies in the content of the positions to be structured into a consistent pattern. Even where the content is not viewed by the majority as erroneous and distasteful, it has the disadvantage of unfamiliarity. One of the functions of consistency is therefore to spell out this content, to gain conspicuousness and visibility for it in the social field. Through the systematic repetition of the same (or similar) positions the minority provides potential targets with a convenient opportunity to get a feeling for the minority alternative as a whole. Having already acquired conspicuousness as a result of the law of relative visibility, the minority further reinforces the visibility of its positions in a social field that bears the imprint of its eagerness to express itself forcefully by word and deed.

This cognitive function is certainly an important factor. The minority can exert an influence only if its alternative norm is clearly recognized and defined. There is more to it than that, however. We must remember that minority positions are by definition initially rejected. One might even argue that the risk of rejection might be increased by consistency, inasmuch as it makes the content of the minority counternorms conspicuous. Hence we must look for the source of minority influence elsewhere than in its simply clarifying its position.

Conflict Creation

The true minority "power" lies in its ability to create a field of social tensions by its consistency, producing a break where there used to be uniformity and creating social effervescence in an otherwise "pacified" social system. The conflict induced or made explicit by the active deviance of the minority presents two facets. By defining a specific antinormative position, the minority replaces the homogeneity of the dominant social model with a heterogeneity of models, since it opposes its own norm to the established norm. By so doing, the minority undermines the dominant model, underlines its flaws, and introduces uncertainty by giving complexity to the social field, by inserting the possibility of choice, and even threatening to replace the old norm with its own norm. Beyond undermining previously dominant norms, the minority exerts an even more important effect. It disrupts a social agreement that guarantees the power of the majority. By its consistency, the minority spells out its refusal to submit to this logic, which it deliberately defies. Thus the minority is not only assaulting specific social norms (although all activism must necessarily be somewhat specific) but often questions the power structure itself, which it disorganizes and sometimes even paralyzes. The minorities' power to disorganize and conflictualize a system stems from the fact that consistency actually expresses a sort of intransigence, of refusal to compromise, a way of blocking negotiations with the other social entities (cf. Schachter, 1951; Mugny, 1982). This destabilizing effect is illustrated in a study by Paicheler (1976), in which women students were asked to discuss briefly, in groups of four, various attitudes toward women. They were instructed to reach an agreement, a single response for the group as a whole. In one of the experimental conditions relevant to our point, one of the subjects (in fact a confederate) upheld an extremely antifeminist position against experimental subjects with a rather profeminist outlook. The result was rather striking. In 94% of the cases, the subjects were unable to follow the experimental instructions, namely to reach a consensus. This incapacity to reach a consensus, moreover, had its repercussions on the opinions later expressed individually by the subjects, in that it led to a bipolarization of the group. By blocking negotiation, the minority confederate actually split the group in two: some reacted negatively, others positively. In any case, something had broken down in the group because of minority consistency.

Innovative Impact of Minority Influence

The social instability induced by minority consistency has another important aspect. By its consistency the minority breaks the social contract, the rules of the social game according to which individuals must conform to the majority. The minority therefore becomes a *model of dissidence*, and may induce subjects to give more independent and even innovative—neither majority nor minority—responses. Let us first take the example of an experiment by Kimball and Hollander (1974). The authors led their subjects to believe that they were participating in groups of five. They were really each on their own and tied in with a Crutchfield apparatus that provided them with programmed responses. The setup was presented to them as one allowing them to explore the procedures which radar teams or air traffic controllers use to collate and communicate perceptual information. The task consisted of judging for a whole series of trials which of three blue lights was turned off first. The lights were first turned off at random, then with such a short lag that it became impossible to discriminate which light was turned off first. Influence was studied in this last phase, when there could be no correct responses. At this stage they were given the responses presumably uttered by the other members of the group. Three "subjects" always chose one identical response among the three possible responses, a fourth (minority) subject always chose a different response. In other words, the subject was faced each time with three possibilities: to respond like the majority, like the deviant confederate, or independently, by choosing the third responses.

In certain conditions the subjects thought that the "bogus minority subject" had already some experience in this kind of task, in other conditions that he had none. Results show that agreement expressed with the minority is the same in both cases. A significant difference distinguishes the two conditions, however. For the minority confederate with experience, the subjects were induced to show a greater independence toward the majority, as indicated by the increase in "original" responses, that is, either majority or minority responses. To put it differently, minority influence manifests itself not merely as acceptance of the minority's stands, but as the product of creative activity set in motion by the minority's break with uniformity. This conclusion is confirmed by another experiment on social influence involving a problem-solving task in groups, where the minority also had a creative influence. In this experiment (Nemeth & Wachtler, 1983) majority influence was created by combining four confederates with two subjects and minority influence was created by a combination of four subjects and two confederates. The task involved hidden figures. Subjects were shown a standard figure, as well as several figures among which they were to pick out the ones containing the standard figure. Some of the standard figures were very easy to pick out, others could be picked out only with the greatest difficulty (and furthermore, half of them were correct and half incorrect). In every instance, the majority of minority confederates showed agreement on each item, choosing the easiest as well as one of the difficult figures. It was found that the confederates had more influence when they were in the majority than when they were in the minority. In the latter case, however, it appears that the subjects found many more difficult and correct responses than an uninfluenced control group. On the contrary the novel and correct responses did not increase in the presence of the majority.

It is obvious from these two experiments that the conditions under which majority and minority influence is exerted differ, as do the processes whereby responses change. The influence exerted by a majority (or authority) is direct and socially manifest. Such is not the case with minority influence, which is more latent and indirect in nature (Moscovici, 1980). While it does have some direct influence, this influence is weaker than the majority's. However, the minority succeeds in rupturing the singleness of the norm by its consistency. By putting forward its own system of responses (which some persons, thought not many, will actually adopt), the consistent minority allows the subjects to look for new and original normative systems themselves. The minority in a way liberates the individual from the stranglehold of conformity and uniformity, without necessarily integrating him or her into its own orthodoxy. As a model of dissidence, it encourages other dissidence, all of them challenging the previously dominant norm.

Minority Image

Active and creative minorities generate conflict. Minority behaviors, in this conflict, provide information on two levels: with respect to the contents of the minority's positions and regarding the minority itself. A minority induces the subjects to envision itself in a certain way. The image it thus elicits will be a critical feature of its social impact.

Disliked But Confident

This image, which makes behavioral consistency meaningful, implies that minority influence is contingent upon the minority's actually being perceived as consistent. Hence, consistency must be occasionally made explicit by psychosocial processes suitable for highlighting it. For this purpose certain dramatic actions, a special intonation or certain rhetorical devices are indispensable. A study of Nemeth and Wachtler (1974) reveals this requirement and also give us some insight into the content of the minority image. In their experimental setup the authors simulated a jury and studied how much it affected the influence of a minority confederate, who was consistently maintaining a very unpopular judgment, whether he explicitly and of his own accord chose a seat at the head of a rectangular table (this position tends to guarantee a greater influence to its occupant; cf. Strodtbeck & Hook, 1961). The consistent minority gained greater influence when it deliberately chose the seat at the head of the table than if this same seat was assigned to it by the experimenter or if it chose a seat along one of the sides. To have its consistency recognized, the minority may thus occasionally strive to attract attention to itself, to make its consistent behavioral style visible and conspicuous (irrespective of the contents of the stand that its consistency structures).

What are the contents of this image? The subjects in this same experiment were asked to describe all the participants on a whole set of scales. Let us see what distinguishes the perception of the minority confederate from that of the other participants. First of all, it appears that on several scales the confederate is evaluated less positively than the other participants. He is viewed as *less* reasonable, fair, perceptive, warm, cooperative, liked, admired, and wanted. As we already mentioned, a minority's influence is not due to its attractiveness. That is hardly surprising, since it is the instigator of a social conflict involving psychological tensions for the other members of the group. It would be a mistake, however, to believe that the minority is perceived in exclusively negative terms. In fact, the minority confederate is generally perceived as *more* consistent, independent, active, central, confident, and strong-willed. He is also credited with stimulating more thought in the subjects and with making them reconsider their stands.

Behavioral consistency is therefore successful in making the subjects aware of the minority's characteristics, notably the strength of its convictions, its autonomy, its intransigence, and its aims. The minority makes clear that it will not give in but will maintain the positions of which it is convinced with all necessary independence, no matter what the circumstances, against all odds.

The Cognitive and the Social Dimensions

While the minority, therefore, is not liked and fails to exert any social attraction, it does stand out in two dimensions, the cognitive and the social. Although a minority does not convey an image of competence, it is recognized (if it is consistent) as self-assured, confident, convinced, even original. Further, its firmness and consistency may be viewed as guarantees of its integrity, independence, and autonomy. All these characteristics attract the attention of the subjects provoking and challenging them. These positive "cognitive" qualities—for they are indeed positive—confer on the minority a bit of credibility, which will serve to unsettle the norm or even the social system itself.

The difficulty of having these cognitive qualities of the minority properly recognized constitute a major stumbling block to its influence. For instance, the minority is forced to keep recalling its consistency by means of actions highlighting it. But its main problem lies in the intensity of the social conflict instigated by the minority and in the way it is perceived. Sometimes the cognitive dimension of consistency may be salient: in this case, the more salient the cognitive characteristics, the more effective the minority's influence. Most often however, a more "social" dimension will be salient, that concerned with the minority intransigence in blocking the negotiation. In that case, conversely, the more conspicuous the social characteristics of intransigence, the less effective the minority's influence.

Here an experiment by Ricateau (1970-1971) is particularly relevant. Using a simulated jury paradigm, a confederate takes a stand at odds with that of the subjects by consistently maintaining an unpopular judgment. The main manipulation consists of making the subjects use a larger or smaller number of judgmental categories (after a pre- and before a postmeasure of subjects' opinion relative to the jury case). For this purpose the subjects are asked several times during the negotiations to describe the confederate and the other participants by means of two (condition I), five (condition II), or eight (condition III) judgmental scales (such as activeness/passiveness or realism/romanticism). In this way the subject could be induced to take a few or many judgmental dimensions into account. Supposedly the fewer dimensions they took into account, the more they would focus on the most conspicuous dimensions notably intransigence, in blocking the negotiation. As far as influence is concerned (see Table 3-2), the results demonstrate that increasing the number of scales does in fact increase minority influence. The main difference arises between the condition involving the use of no more than two scales (here only 4 out of 16 subjects change their minds) and the two other conditions where 18 (9 in each condition), of the 27 subjects change their opinion toward the one advocated by the minority.

What accounts for this effect? The answer is supplied by a measurement of the source image carried out at the end of the experiment. The subjects were asked to select from among about 100 descriptive terms those that characterized the minority confederate most accurately. The traits related to various minority characteristics such as personality, appearance, emotional and cognitive attitude, and blocking negotiations. Of course the latter two dimensions (cognitive attitude and blocking negotiations) are those of interest to us. Table 3-2 presents the number of traits chosen from these two categories in each condition, as well as the average number chosen from all the other categories. The results emphasize the importance of these two dimensions of the minority image, one of them focusing on the more cognitive aspects of consistency, the other on those social aspects associated with minority intolerance in blocking negotiations. The more conspicuous the cognitive aspects of consistency, the greater minority influence. Influence, on the other hand, is reduced if minority intransigence is particularly conspicuous, as a result of which the cognitive aspects become obscured. In this case, intransigence outweighed all

Table 3-2. Number of Traits Chosen Relating to Cognitive and Negotiation-Blocking Dimensions, Average of Traits Relating to Other Dimensions, and Number of Subjects Changing Their Opinions Toward the Minority's[a]

	Conditions		
Dimensions	I (two scales) (n = 16)	II (five scales) (n = 14)	III (eight scales) (n = 13)
Cognitive	52	71	86
Blocking	75	59	53
Others	38	27	39
Number of influenced subjects	4	9	9

[a] Based on Ricateau (1970-71, p. 916).

other aspects and the minority may effectively be categorized as dogmatic (Mugny, 1982). Viewing a source as dogmatic is tantamount to considering it overexclusive. Its intransigence automatically removes any chance of conciliation. The minority is therefore rejected because it is perceived as itself rejecting the subject (Mugny & Papastamou, 1982).

Consistency and Uniformity Pressures

Retaliatory Threat and "Going Underground"

Let us now examine a final point. In the last analysis, consistency also emphasizes commitment and involvement on the part of its adherents. It is indicative of their courage in assuming the potential social costs (Larsen, 1974) of active deviance. Bringing conflicts into the open, the minority is surely always at risk from the thunderbolts of the majority.

We have so far stressed the fact that consistency structures minority behaviors. However, the way consistency is perceived is of prime importance. As we have seen, there are several procedures for calling attention to the consistency of minority behavior. Paradoxically, consistency can sometimes be inferred, even in the absence of behavioral correlates, or even appearances to the contrary, as attested by Galileo. For it must be recognized that sometimes social pressures exerted on minorities are so great that unbearable social costs would be imposed on the minority whose very existence might be jeopardized. This is likely when repression is part of the social arsenal deployed by the social system to restore uniformity, "pacify" social relations, and reduce conflict. In these limiting situations, the minority may admittedly be compelled to go underground (so that its behaviors become in effect invisible), or even to recant, without losing any of its consistency or influence.

Personnaz (1979) investigated this question experimentally, in a situation where a subject and a confederate (the source) were instructed to agree on the (green or blue) color of a light source briefly presented several times in a row. For the sake of conforming to this need for social consensus, the source, having consistently maintained an opinion contrary to the subject's, suddenly "gives up" its response. It stressed, however, that it acted solely to make a consensus possible, making it clear that its private response, its own perception, remained unchanged. Notwithstanding this "recantation," influence effects appear to the same extent that they do when the source maintains its own response during the experiment in a situation where the need for consensus was not introduced. This result clearly demonstrates the obvious point that consistency is not identifiable with any particular behavioral equivalents. Situational factors, such as the uniformity pressures operating in the above case, are taken into consideration in recognizing consistency.

Consistency and Chance of Rejection

An experiment by Wolf (1979) shows that consistency is perceived differently depending on whether there does or does not exist a chance to reject the minority

individual. Female students participated in groups of four in simulated juries deciding on compensation and interest claims in which the plaintiff asked for $45,000.
The report was worded so as to encourage the subjects to propose a judgment
between $20,000 and $30,000. The subjects were retained for the experiment only
if they had proposed at least $10,000 at the beginning of the experiment. They
received a bogus distribution in which two group members suggested a compensation comparable to the amount suggested by the subject (one $2,000 below that
amount, the other $3,000 above that amount). A minority suggestion was presented
by the fourth subject, who asked for $3,000 in damages, a highly unpopular
response. The experimenter then distributed the stands that the various participants
had supposedly written down during the ensuring exchange of positions (actually
manipulated by the experimenter).

Three variables were introduced in this paradigm. The minority was either consistent or inconsistent. The consistent minority adhered to its initial position
($3,000) even in the final exchange of notes. The inconsistent minority handed in a
final message couched in these words: "I thought $3,000 was the fairest judgment,
but now I'm not so sure." It thus expressed a state of doubt about the legitimacy of
its suggestion. In half of the cases, the subjects could take some countermeasures
against the minority. The experimenter announced that subsequently she wanted to
study what happened with groups consisting of an uneven number of participants,
that is, groups of three. The decision of whom to eliminate was to be left up to the
subjects themselves, a vote being taken which person to eliminate. In this case the
minority "subject" would be the perfect target for this rejection. In the other condition it was announced that this choice would be based on a random procedure, so
that the minority could in no way be subjected to intentional discrimation. Finally,
two types of groups were formed, cohesive and noncohesive. For this purpose, the
subjects were asked, after having become acquainted, to describe each other and to
express how much liking they felt for one another. The experimenter then handed
a bogus distribution of these responses to each subject. Half the subjects were made
to think that they were viewed very positively by the other members of this jury
(high cohesion condition) and the other half that they were held in very low esteem
by all the others (low cohesion condition). We will not go into the results for the
subjects in the noncohesive groups. Suffice it to say that they modified their initial
responses only slightly, regardless of the other conditions, either because they did
not care for the group or because under these conditions they were not interested
in reaching a consensus. Table 3-3 shows the changes which occurred in the judgments between the initial measurement and the final measurement for the cohesive
groups.

Where the possibility of rejecting one of the members is not mentioned, consistency has its fullest impact, significantly more than inconsistency. Conversely, where
the possibility of rejection is made explicit, the opposite is true. How can we
account for this inversion? Apparently, where minority rejection is excluded, the
subjects had to come to terms with the conflict maintained by the minority's consistency—and one which the minority explicitly intended to maintain throughout
by its obvious blocking of negotiation. When the minority displayed some incon-

Table 3-3. Average Reduction in Suggested Compensation and Interest (High Cohesion Condition Only)[a,b]

	Minority	
	Consistent	Inconsistent
No chance of rejection	− $6,530	− $3,500
Chance of rejection	− $2,870	− $6,000

[a] Subjects initially suggested between $10,000 and 45,000, while minority suggested only $3,000.
[b] Based on Wolf (1979, p. 389).

sistency, it was in some way telling the subjects that it would revise its position, that it might try to narrow the gap. That was in fact the essence of its inconsistency and the cause of its lesser influence. By breaching its certainty, by tampering with its initial position, the minority proclaimed its intention to compromise. Paradoxically—but is not all fair in love and war?—the subjects then reinforced their own position in the negotiation that was about to begin, or at least they were careful not to give in too much.

Where there was a chance for rejection, things took an entirely different course. It was now possible for the subjects to resolve the conflict produced by the minority's intransigence by excluding the minority. By its very intransigence, the minority somehow legitimized its possible rejection: "Since it shows no desire to negotiate, I will reject it." The subjects no longer look at the minority position as a challenge to their own views. They concern themselves instead with the social relation that they may be able to modify by excluding the deviant (an ad hoc measurement indicated, in fact, that in the subjects' opinion the minority individual would be the most likely choice for exclusion from the group). But why does inconsistency in this case exert such great influence? Perhaps the subjects are caught between the two horns of a dilemma: the possibility of rejection on the one hand and on the other hand the fact that the minority individual was making honorable amends and envisaging a revision of her judgment, thus attenuating the conflict. In so doing, she was surely diminishing the likelihood of her exclusion by raising the question of a compromise that would be indispenable at a later stage, presuming she were kept in the group for the next stage.

It then appears that the effects of minority styles of behavior are not independent of the social context (i.e., the ability of the majority to reject the minority). In reality it is this context that gives meaning to the behavioral styles. In the case of impossibility of rejection, the "cognitive" dimension of consistency would be more conspicuous: Firmness means consistency, and doubt means inconsistency. The converse is true in the case of a possibility of rejection. The possibility of such a social regulation of the conflict would make salient a more "social" dimension. Consistency now takes the meaning of a rigidity that by itself justifies the rejection, and inconsistency now means the willingness of the minority to consider a compromise solution which prevents the subjects from considering rejection as the only way of resolving the social conflict.

The Snowball Effect

But how can we account for the subjects' intransigence toward a consistent confederate when the chance for rejecting him or her is available? The answer is obvious. The subjects realize that the minority may be persuasive. When we recall that the minority instigates social conflict, that it converts certain individuals to its stand, and that it can even arouse original responses counter to the dominant norm, it becomes clear that the disturbing element in minority consistency is not so much the actual content of the antinormative positions but primarily its potential influence.

Further, minority consistency is actually more effective if the minority succeeds not only in asserting its own stand but also in convincing others, leading a member of the majority to identify with it, as Kiesler and Pallak (1975) demonstrate. The subjects believed that they were participating in a decision group consisting of eight persons. The case under discussion was similar to the one of Johnny Rocco, a boy whom the report presented in a very negative light. The majority propositions were sure to be very severe. The subjects, who had been placed in isolation booths, were given a first feedback about the opinions of the eight participants. Table 3-4 reproduces this first distribution (the subject being represented by the letter S) for a subject who had responded 9. The distribution was along the same lines and with the same spread for subjects giving a response other than 9. The subjects then discover that their responses match those of the majority and that two minority members have an opinion that goes clearly counter to their own. By an appropriate manipulation, the experimenters have a second opinion survey and once more produce a bogus distribution of opinions. At this stage several manipulations are introduced. We shall only discuss those regarding the behaviors of the members of the majority. In the control condition, the second distribution is identical to the first.

In the second (reactionary) condition, the subjects discover that subject B has modified his response and has become even more extremist (changing from position 9 to the extremist position 11 for example in Table 3-4). In the third (majority compromise) condition, the same subject B is shown as deviating by two points from his initial response, but in the direction of a compromise with the minority (changing from 9 to 7). In the final condition (majority defection) subject B is shown as converting to position 4, the one maintained by the minority individuals. The average changes on the various questions measuring influence on a scale of 11 points are shown in Table 3-5.

Table 3-4. Bogus Opinion Distribution Given to Subjects (S)[a]

							E		
							D		
	G						S		
	C				F	B	A		

Lenient _____ Severe

| 1 | 2 | 3 | 4 | 5 | 6 | 7 | 8 | 9 | 10 | 11 |

[a] Based on Kiesler and Pallak (1975, p. 244).

These results show that minority influence increases when it has proved effective in producing change in other individuals, particularly when the exmajority subject is completely converted to the minority. It should be added that this result is not just a reflection of pressures operating in connecting booths. At the end of the experiment, the subjects were given a chance to write notes to one of the participants. The most frequently chosen target was a minority member. However, the content of these notes varied. Whereas 30% of the communications expressed disagreement with the minority in the first two (control and reactionary) conditions, this percentage rose to nearly 65% in the last two conditions—those involving the strongest minority influence. Minority influence unquestionably has a dynamic of its own, one that is original and very different from the dynamics of majority influence. When the minority is able to prove that its consistency is effective and that it can induce some people to identify with it, its influence increases accordingly. For after all, this is surely one of the conditions for the strengthening and growth of minorities and for their finally succeeding some day, possibly, in imposing their own orthodoxies.

Conclusion

There can be no doubt that the study of minority influence offers a fresh point of view for the study of relations within social groups and the actions of these groups. Its contribution is twofold. In the first place, it allows us to undertake the analysis of a category of groups that had until now been systematically neglected by social psychology, namely all kinds of minorities: social minorities and dissident minorities, critical minorities and rebellious minorities. No matter what their label, they all share a specific position. They all offer a new idea or a new life-style which they wish to propagate by taking a stand against the majority. In other words, they are all active minorities. In the second place, the study of minority influence shows that innovation is as fundamental in influence mode as conformity and that relations within a group can be envisaged as a dialectic between the majority and the minority. This dialectic in a way replaces the previously accepted dialectic between the "deviant" and the "normal" part of the group, which is not so much wrong as simply incomplete. In the process, stress shifts from the problem of group control to the problem of group change. The reason for this shift is clear. While the former

Table 3-5. Average Changes on an 11-Point Scale of Severity [a,b]

Condition	Change
Control	+0.385
Reactionary	+0.307
Majority compromise	+0.611
Majority defection	+0.953

[a] + denotes a positive influence.
[b] Based on Kiesler and Pallak (1975, p. 246).

point of view focused on how to reduce deviance to normalize the group, the new point of view is concerned with the way majority and minority reciprocally modify their judgments or opinions. These modifications always lead to new relations and new points of view in the group in question.

Interest in minority influence, to be sure, is largely contingent upon social psychology's concern with groups as such, a concern which, to put it mildly, is presently at a very low ebb. But even with this handicap in mind, the concept we are advocating here is open to serious criticisms. There are those who reject the role we attribute to behavioral styles in general and consistency in particular, for the sake of maintaining the role of dependency, which is seen as the mainspring of influence. We do not claim, of course, that dependency serves no functions, inasmuch as, wherever social relations exist, there is also dependency. However, when we view the influence phenomenon within the context of such a relation, the decisive difference must be attributed to behavioral styles. There are enough experiments to confirm this hypothesis. Others insist that conformity and innovation, majority and minority influence, involve the same psychological and social processes, the only difference between them being merely a question of numbers. Minorities would then represent small numbers and majorities large numbers. From this the conclusion is drawn at once that since the process involved is the same, nothing special can be expected from the study of minority influence. There is therefore no need to study it separately, all we need to do is to apply it to what has been learned about majority influence. This implies, as Hollander suggested, that innovation should be viewed as a sort of conformity. Of course the different forms of influence do share certain features (Moscovici, 1976). Nonetheless, as experience has shown, there are differences. Minority influence tends to be hidden, majority influence tends to be more explicit. To put it in a nutshell, people are converted by minorities. They submit to majorities. But it is out of the question to state here the detailed arguments in favor of our position, nor the arguments against it, as would be only fair. Let us therefore merely restate that the study of minority influence can make an invaluable contribution to the study of groups by providing useful concepts and by identifying neglected phenomena. However tentative the findings, research in social psychology has in any case been greatly enriched through these efforts.

References

Allen, V. L. Social support for nonconformity. In L. Berkowitz (Ed.), *Advances in experimental social psychology* (Vol. 8). New York: Academic Press, 1975.

Allen, V. L., & Levine, J. M. Social support, dissent and conformity. *Sociometry,* 1968, *31*, 138-149.

Allen, V. L., & Wilder, D. A. Perceived persuasiveness as a function of response style: Multi-issue consistency over time. *European Journal of Social Psychology,* 1978, *8*, 289-296.

Asch, S. E. Effects of group pressure upon the modification and distortion of judgment. In H. Guetzkow (Ed.), *Groups, leadership and men.* Pittsburgh: Carnegie Press, 1951.

Asch, S. E. Studies on independence and conformity: a minority of one against an unanimous majority. *Psychological Monographs*, 1956, *70*, 416.

Crozier, M. *On ne change pas la societe par decret*. Paris: Grasset et Fasquelle, 1979.

Doms, M. The minority influence effect: an alternative approach. In W. Doise & S. Moscovici (Eds.), *Current issues in European social psychology*. Cambridge: Cambridge University Press, 1983.

Doms, M., & Van Avermaet, E. Social support and minority influence: the innovation effect reconsidered. In S. Moscovici, G. Mugny, & E. Von Avermaet, *Perspectives on minority influence*. Cambridge: Cambridge University Press-L.E.P.S., 1983.

Festinger, L. Informal social communication. *Psychological Review*, 1950, *57*, 271-282.

Freedman, J. L., & Doob, A. N. *Deviancy: The psychology of being different*. New York: Academic Press, 1968.

Harvey, J. H., Ickes, W. N., & Kidd, R. F. (Eds.), *New directions in attribution research* (Vol. 1). Hillsdale, N.J.: Lawrence Erlbaum, 1976.

Heisenberg, W. *Across the frontiers*. New York: Harper Torchbooks, 1975.

Hollander, E. P. Competence and conformity in the acceptance of influence. *Journal of Abnormal and Social Psychology*, 1960, *61*, 360-365.

Kiesler, C. A., & Pallak, M. S. Minority influence: The effect of majority reactionaries and defectors, and minority and majority compromisers, upon majority opinion and attraction. *European Journal of Social Psychology*, 1975, *5*, 237-256.

Kimball, R. K., & Hollander, E. P. Independence in the presence of an experienced but deviate group member. *Journal of Social Psychology*, 1974, *93*, 281-292.

Larsen, K. S. Social cost, belief incongruence, and race: Experiments in choice behavior. *Journal of Social Psychology*, 1974, *94*, 253-267.

Lerner, M. J. Justice, guilt, and veridical perception. *Journal of Personality and Social Psychology*, 1971, *20*, 127-135.

Levine, J. M. Reaction to opinion deviance in small groups. In P. B. Paulus (Ed.), *Psychology of group influence*. Hillsdale, N.J.: Lawrence Erlbaum, 1980.

Lewin, K. *Resolving social conflicts*. London: Souvenir Press, 1973.

Merton, R. K. *Social theory and social structure*. New York: Free Press, 1957.

Moscovici, S. *Social influence and social change*. London: Academic Press, 1976.

Moscovici, S. La dissidence d'un seul. Appendix in S. Moscovici, *Psychologie des minorites actives*. Paris: Presses Universitaires de France, 1979.

Moscovici, S. Toward a theory of conversion behavior. In L. Berkowitz (Ed.), *Advances in experimental social psychology* (Vol. 13). New York: Academic Press, 1980.

Moscovici, S., & Faucheux, C. Social influence, conformity bias, and the study of active minorities. In L. Berkowitz (Ed.), *Advances in experimental social psychology* (Vol. 6). New York: Academic Press, 1972.

Moscovici, S., Lage, E., & Naffrechoux, M. Influence of a consistent minority on the responses of a majority in a color perception task. *Sociometry*, 1969, *32*, 365-379.

Moscovici, S., & Nemeth, C. Social influence II: Minority influence. In C. Nemeth (Ed.), *Social psychology: Classic and contemporary integrations.* Chicago: Rand McNally College Publishing Co., 1974.

Mugny, G. Negotiations, image of the other and the process of minority influence. *European Journal of Social Psychology,* 1975, *5*, 209-228.

Mugny, G. *The power of minorities.* London: Academic Press, 1982.

Mugny, G., & Papastamou, S. When rigidity does not fail: Individualization and psychologization as resistances to the diffusion of minority innovations. *European Journal of Social Psychology,* 1980, *10*, 43-61.

Mugny, G., & Papastamou, S. Minority influence and psychosocial identity. *European Journal of Social Psychology,* 1982, *12*, 379-394.

Mugny, G., & Papastamou, S. L'influence du social dan l'influence sociale. In S. Moscovici, G. Mugny, & E. Van Avermaet, *Perspectives on minority influence.* Cambridge: Cambridge University Press-L.E.P.S., 1983.

Nemeth, C., Swedlund, M., & Kanki, B. Patterning of the minority's responses and their influence on the majority. *European Journal of Social Psychology,* 1974, *4*, 53-64.

Nemeth, C., & Wachtler, J. Creating the perceptions of consistency and confidence: A necessary condition for minority influence. *Sociometry,* 1974, *37*, 529-540.

Nemeth, C., & Wachtler, J. Creative problem solving as a result of majority vs. minority influence settings. *European Journal of Social Psychology,* 1983, *13*, 45-55.

Paicheler, G. Norms and attitude change I: Polarization and styles of behavior. *European Journal of Social Psychology,* 1976, *6*, 405-427.

Papastamou, S. Strategies of minority and majority influence. In S. Moscovici & W. Doise (Eds.), *Current issues in European social psychology* (Vol. 1). Cambridge: Cambridge University Press, 1983.

Papastamou, S., Mugny, G., & Kaiser, C. Echec a l'influence minoritaire: La psychologisation. *Recherches de Psychologie Sociale,* 1980, *2*, 41-56.

Personnaz, B. Niveau de resistance a l'influence de responses nomiques et anomiques: Etudes des phenomenes de referents clandestins et de conversions. *Recherches en Psychologie Sociale,* 1979, *1*, 5-27.

Ricateau, P. Processus de categorisation d'autrui et les mecanismes d'influence sociale. *Bulletin de Psychologie,* 1970-1971, *24*, 909-919.

Schachter, S. Deviation, rejection, and communication. *Journal of Abnormal and Social Psychology,* 1951, *46*, 190-207.

Strodtbeck, F. L., & Hook, L. H. The social dimensions of a twelve-man jury table. *Sociometry,* 1961, *24*, 397-415.

Wolf, S. Behavioral style and group cohesiveness as sources of minority influence. *European Journal of Social Psychology,* 1979, *9*, 381-395.

Chapter 4
Group Discussion and Judgment

Martin F. Kaplan and Charles E. Miller

Introduction

The influence of group discussion on individual judgments and group decisions is one of the oldest problems in the experimental study of small groups (Bechterev & DeLange, 1924; Burtt, 1920; Marston, 1924). Early interest was focused primarily on the *quality* of group versus individual products, that is, on the question are groups *better* than individuals? Attention has turned more recently to examining judgmental shifts per se, without regard to improvement or decline in quality. We will be concerned primarily with changes induced by discussion, and will not deal at length with the perplexing question of whether the changes are for the better. The judgments and decisions with which we will deal are those where alternatives are along a bipolar, unidimensional scale of some sort, for example, "How large should the damage award be in a civil trial?"

After a period of dormancy, interest in the influence of group discussion was renewed, spurred largely by Stoner's (1961) startling finding that group discussion enhanced risk-taking—the famous "risky shift" phenomenon. Stoner's finding, reported in an unpublished master's thesis, started a flurry of studies of risk-taking, from which evolved a more general phenomenon: A group judgment, or the average of group members' individual responses following discussion is usually more extreme in the same direction than the average of members' prediscussion judgments. The more general phenomenon is known as *group polarization* (see Cartwright, 1973; and Pruitt, 1971a, 1971b, for historical reviews of the evolution of the concept).

The "discovery" of a phenomenon often attracts a host of explanatory theories in the early stages of its explication, and group polarization did not disappoint on this count. After a period of theoretical exploration (see, e.g., the collection of papers in *Journal of Personality and Social Psychology,* 1971, volume 20, number 3), three major theoretical approaches have emerged as most viable (see reviews by Myers & Lamm, 1976, and Lamm & Myers, 1978), and these will be treated in this chapter. Though the approaches have often been compared in a spirit of confrontation (e.g., Kaplan, 1977) it is not our contention that they are mutually exclusive. Indeed, it is likely that each comes into play at different points in the group influence process, and under different conditions (see also Laughlin & Earley, 1982).

The first two approaches deal primarily with the individual as the unit of analysis, that is, they concern the mechanism by which discussion influences the individual member. *Normative influence* suggests that judgment shifts result from exposure to others' preferences, and subsequent conformity to judgmental norms. *Informational influence* attributes shifts to incorporation of relevant arguments, or information about the judged object, which are shared between discussants.

The third approach, *group decision rules,* has typically been applied to the aggregation of individual preferences into a group product. The group decision rules approach seeks the decision rule implicit in the combination of individual preferences into a group decision (with or without the formal requirement of consensus) in functioning groups. This theory is explicitly more quantitative in description than the first two, but has not been as explicit in specifying the psychological mechanism by which decision rules are applied in shifting group responses. This omission does not preclude incorporation of the other two theories—or of other qualitative theories for that matter—as mechanisms for described decision rules.

In our discussion, we will first expand on normative and informational modes of influence. We will propose a mechanism for informational influence based on integration of shared information. This mechanism treats the thorny question of why responses polarize when discussed information is no more extreme than information previously incorporated into judgment. It also accounts for instances where judgment shifts toward more moderate preferences. Research pitting normative and informational influences will be reviewed, and it will be shown that the two influence modes are not mutually exclusive, but that their usage may depend on task characteristics, preference distribution of members, and decision rule. Next, it will be suggested that issues endemic to the *process* of group influence are applicable to *outcome* as well, that is, to the question of *quality* of group judgment. Finally, it will be suggested that the group decision rules approach need not be restricted to group products, but can apply to influences on individual judgments. Task characteristics and prediscussion distributions of member preferences elicit different implicit decision rules, which are associated with different modes of influence on the individual.

Group Discussion and Individual Judgment

It is of little surprise that individual members will change their judgments after group discussion of some issue. More surprising is the fact that changes will occur even when all members are in substantial agreement prior to discussion. This fact has generated a considerable amount of work over the past 15 years, and will be the focus of our attention. In treating this phenomenon, it will be emphasized that any theoretical interpretation must be able to account for shifts in *either* direction on the judgmental scale, that is, toward a more-or-less extreme judgment than that initially reached. In other words, we are interested in *general* models of the effects of discussion on individual judgment rather than models of polarization alone.

In his now classic study, Stoner (1961) faced subjects with choices between risky and cautious solutions to fictitious situations (*Choice Dilemma Questionnaire*). In each dilemma, subjects chose the lowest probability of the risky action proving successful for which they would be willing to recommend that action (e.g., 1 choice in 10, 2 in 10, . . ., 9 in 10), or indicated no risky action at all. Stoner found that groups were more risky after discussion of choice-dilemmas than their average individual member before discussion. This finding, subsequently replicated many times, was labelled the "risky shift" phenomenon, and it gave rise to a host of theoretical explanations (see Cartwright, 1971, Pruitt, 1971a, 1971b, and Lamm & Myers, 1978). Before long, it was noted that more cautious shifts could also follow discussion of choice dilemmas, and in fact, shifts were noted as well with quite different judgmental materials, such as social and political attitudes, interpersonal impressions, and jury cases. The shift was observed to fall in the direction of the prediscussion judgments of individual members, but towards greater extremity on the response continuum. For example, items which elicited initial assessments of defendant guilt evoked shifts farther along the guilt continuum after discussion, and items eliciting initial impressions of innocence evoked shift toward greater certainty of innocence after discussion (Myers & Kaplan, 1976). Accordingly, the risky shift was given the broader label of *group polarization* (Cartwright, 1973; Moscovici & Zavalloni, 1969), describing an increase in extremity of the average response of individuals in the group, in the same direction as initial responses. Thus, discussion enhances the dominant prediscussion tendencies of individual group members in a variety of tasks (see Myers & Lamm, 1976). It should not be concluded that polarization is a necessary consequence of discussion; Lamm and Myers (1978, pp. 148-149) cite several instances where polarization was not robust, or where the direction of shift is toward more moderate positions. They suggest that something other than the relevant merits of the problem enter into postdiscussion judgments (e.g., generalized values) in such instances. This implies that the direction of the shift depends on the substance of discussion. Consequently, a theory of discussion effects needs to consider *both* polarization *and* moderation, and should take the nature of discussion into account.

While many theories have been proposed for polarization (see Cartwright, 1973, Lamm & Myers, 1978, and Pruitt, 1971a, 1971b, for an itemization), most have fallen by the wayside, either because they are bound only to riskiness and cannot deal with other shifts, or because they predict only polarization. Others (e.g., those invoking the introduction of participants' values) are vague with respect to the *mechanism* by which factors external to the issue are woven into discussion and, subsequently, the response. Two theories have emerged, however, as prime, though not necessarily competing, candidates for describing the mechanism of polarization. *Normative influence* attributes individual shifts to exposure to the preferences of others. These preferences convey a judgmental norm, so that if other discussants show preferences more extreme than the individual's, the individual will conform to the norm. Others' preferences may exert normative pressure to conform, or may "release" the individual to express his or her position more strongly. In either event, the individual shifts toward the norm in order to minimize conflict and/or present a favorable appearance.

Informational influence attributes shifts to the informational content of arguments presented during discussion. In addition to revealing their responses to the issue during discussion, participants also share the arguments which produced those responses. Change is induced when the information is incorporated into the individual's response. When the information is provided forcefully, the label *persuasive argumentation* is applied (e.g., Burnstein, Vinokur, & Trope, 1973), implying some form of persuasive message effect. Informational influences need not be limited, however, to active argumentation; passive sharing of information is also sufficient to produce shifts (Anderson & Graesser, 1976; Ebbesen & Bowers, 1974; Kaplan, 1977).

At the heart of the normative/informational distinction is the question of whether group influence on judgment is a source or a message effect (Myers & Lamm, 1976). Broadly speaking, do judgments change to conform to those of others so that behavior will be more acceptable, or does discussion provide information to be incorporated into prior judgment? This distinction is central to general treatments of group processes and social motivation. On the one hand, people are viewed as social *reward-seekers,* aiming to maximize acceptance and reward in interaction with others. On the other, people are characterized as *information-seekers,* using information from others to augment personal experiences in knowing their environment. These models of human nature have been contrasted in treatments of conformity (Deutsch & Gerard, 1955), interpersonal attraction (Kaplan & Anderson, 1973), social modeling (Bandura, 1965), persuasion (Greenwald, Brock, & Ostrom, 1968; Petty, Ostrom, & Brock, 1981), and learning (Tolman, 1948), so it is little wonder that they emerge as prime explanatory schemes for group polarization effects. The next two sections deal with tests of the two influence models, and with the cognitive mechanism for informational influence.

Normative and Informational Influence

The two major models of group influence on judgment, normative and informational, have been pursued in a spirit of confrontation. Brown (1965), for example, contends that the content of discussion is of no importance; polarization is effected only by exposure to others' judgmental preferences. Similarly, though in a superficially more conciliatory vein, Sanders & Baron (1977) suggest that persuasive arguments facilitate polarization, which is primarily due to comparison with the preferences of others. These strong normative views contrast with the assertion of Burnstein and co-workers (Burnstein & Santis, 1981; Burnstein & Vinokur, 1973, 1975, 1977) that the preponderance and distribution of arguments *entirely* predicts shifts. It is not surprising, then, that tests of the models over the years have aimed at critical comparisons of their implications.

The most straightforward test might involve varying one form of influence in the absence of the other form. Some studies have provided individuals with the judgments or positions of other group members, without giving arguments or reasons for the positions. Damaging to the normative model, polarization shifts following exposure to positions alone are either weak (Clark & Willems, 1969; Teger & Pruitt, 1967) or fail to materialize (Wallach & Kogan, 1965). Moreover, even when no arguments are explicitly given, Burnstein & Vinokur (1975) suggest that knowledge of anothers' position may enable inference of supportive arguments. They demonstrated that knowledge of position alone will lead to polarization only when the subject thinks of arguments on which the others' positions are based.

On the other side of the coin, when arguments are shared by participants, without giving their positions, strong polarization is found (Clark, Crockett & Archer, 1971; St. Jean, 1970). It can be argued, though, that normative influence is not ruled out since arguments can also inform about the participants' position. This criticism is circumvented, however, in Burnstein & Vinokur (1973), where individuals were unaware whether other participants were giving their own arguments, or role-playing contrary positions. Consequently, while polarization can be induced by sharing informational arguments without giving other participants' positions, it is unclear whether knowledge of positions alone, that is, normative influence, is sufficient to produce shifts.

Another test consists of manipulating the content of arguments so that they fall on one or the other side of the issue. Here, individuals will shift in the direction of the argument content (Roberts & Castore, 1972; Silverthorne, 1971). But, this test is open to the criticism, once again, that the arguments imply the arguers' positions.

A stronger test involves the covariation of positions and informational content. When others' judgments are opposed to the information they share, polarization is in the direction of the latter (Burnstein & Vinokur, 1973; see also discussion of Kaplan, 1977, below). That is, suppose others say they are in favor of some outcome, but then give arguments against the outcome. The individual will shift towards the information value of the arguments.

Finally, one can compare the two influences by covarying the number of arguments (i.e., amount of information) and the number of participants (normative base). Presumably, the more arguments that are presented, the greater the informational influence, and the more people giving their positions, the stronger the normative pressure. Using different designs, both Vinokur & Burnstein (1974) and Kaplan (1977) found extent of polarization to be related to number of distinct arguments in favor of a position, but not to number of participants in favor of a position.

A series of studies by Kaplan and his co-workers can illustrate the distinction between the two influence models. These studies utilized courtroom materials; in all, subjects were exposed to synopses of contrived trials, and asked individually to rate the guilt appearance and recommend sentence for the defendant. They then discussed the trial, and again rated guilt and punishment.

In a preliminary study, a polarization effect was demonstrated (Myers & Kaplan, 1976). After discussing cases contrived to give a predominantly low initial appearance of guilt, subjects were, on the average, more extreme in their judgments of innocence and more lenient in recommended punishment, and after discussing high guilt cases they shifted towards harsher judgments of guilt and punishment. No shifts were observed for control sets of cases which were judged twice, but without intervening discussion.

In three additional experiments (Kaplan, 1977), the content of discussion was manipulated by having participants pass notes to one another rather than engaging in face-to-face interaction. Notes were intercepted and replaced by bogus notes which were varied according to the experimental design. In the first experiment, subjects were exposed to a contrived trial which was designed to give either a high or low appearance of defendant guilt. After individually rating guilt and recommended punishment, subjects were formed into six-person juries, each person in a separate room. Each person prepared a set of five written arguments, one to an index card, giving the five most salient reasons for their judgment. These were to be exchanged with other participants. In their place, the experimenter substituted five bogus cards, each containing a trial fact not given by a particular individual in his or her notes. The facts given to each individual were selected to be in either the same or opposite guilt/innocence proportion as he or she had given. That is, if a person had given four guilt-appearing facts and one innocent-appearing fact, he or she received either a 4:1 or 1:4 ratio of guilt/innocence items. Where shared information was in the *same* proportion cited by subjects, judgments polarized, that is, became more extreme in the same direction as initial judgments. Where the proportion of shared information was *opposite* to that given by subjects, responses shifted *away* from extremity (see Figure 4-1). In short, post discussion judgments shifted toward the value of shared information.

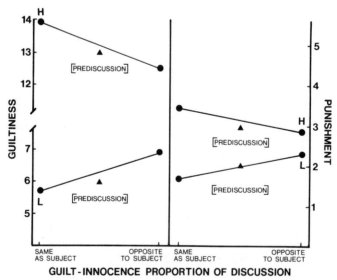

Fig. 4-1. Postdiscussion judgments (filled circles) as a function of shared information. H: Guilt-appearing cases; L; innocent-appearing cases. From Kaplan (1977, Experiment 1).

It is possible, of course, that subjects inferred the positions of others from their arguments, and so the second experiment made these positions explicit. This experiment was an exact replication of the preceding one, except that participants' judgments were also provided, in the following manner. Each argument was attributed to a different participant, who was also ascribed a guilt rating. All five ratings (one to each remaining participant) were devised to be within two scale units of the subjects' initial rating, with the mean value being the same as that of the subject. Results were statistically identical to the pattern of shifts in the first experiment; addition of participants' *positions* did not have any effects beyond those produced by shared information alone (see Figure 4-2). Particularly noteworthy is the fact that in those conditions where shared information was in opposite proportion to the subject's emitted evidence (and therefore at odds with other participants' positions), shift was towards the information, and not towards the incongruent positions. It should be noted that providing information which argues for the opposite position taken by the source allows a strong test of the relative influence of information and norms. That the magnitude of shift was no less than in the first experiment (Figure 4-1) suggests that the judgmental norm, even though it agreed with the subject's initial position, exerted no influence.

The same trials (high or low guilt appearance) were used in the third experiment. The five shared items were selected to be either mutually redundant or nonredundant. *Redundant* statements repeated the same piece of evidence, varying only in phrasing. In addition, this evidence was one of the items cited by the subject. *Non-*

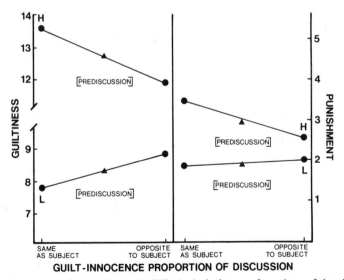

Fig. 4-2. Postdiscussion judgments (filled circles) as a function of incrimination value of shared information, and where participants also gave preferences consistent with case appearance. H: Guilt-appearing cases; L: innocent-appearing cases. From Kaplan (1977, Experiment 2).

redundant statements gave five different facts, none of which duplicated facts given by the subject. Unlike the first two experiments, the facts were uniformly of the same valence (i.e., guilty or innocent in appearance) as the predominant value of the trial. According to an informational view (e.g., Vinokur & Burnstein, 1974), influence should be greater when arguments are nonredundant, presenting effectively *new information.* However, if an argument is persuasive because it conveys the *normative* position of the participant, and not for its informational content, (non)redundancy should not matter, since the same norm is conveyed in either case. To provide another test of normative influence, the five shared items were ascribed to either one participant, or to five participants (one item to each group member). If shifts occur because of normative pressure, the norm provided by five people should be greater than knowledge of one person's judgment (see, e.g., Harkins & Petty, Chapter 7, this volume). But, if informational content is paramount, the number of sources should not have a bearing. Results were in line with the informational influence predictions. No statistical effects were found for number of sources, but polarization following discussion was greater for nonredundant than for redundant shared information (see Figure 4-3).

In sum, jurors shifted judgments in the direction of shared information, and were uninfluenced by normative positions of others, even when the norms were opposed to the information content, or were augmented by increased numbers of people holding the *same* position as the individual. These studies, along with those previously cited (see also Burnstein & Santis, 1981), seem to speak powerfully against normative influences in group polarization. Yet, we should not be too hasty

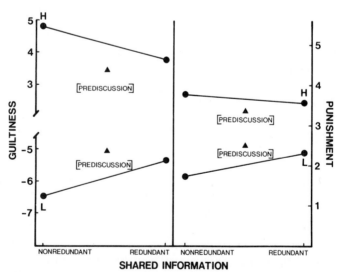

Fig. 4-3. Postdiscussion judgments (filled circles) as a function of redundancy of shared information. Extent of polarization for H (guilt-appearing) and L (innocent-appearing) cases is reflected in deviation from prediscussion judgments. From Kaplan (1977, Experiment 3).

in dismissing influence based on the positions of others. For one reason, the study of normative conformity in simple judgmental situations (i.e., those involving minimal information) has a long and successful history. For another, most attitude polarization studies do not engage strong pressure to agree for agreement's sake, that is, do not require unanimity or even consensus for reaching a judgment. Acquiescence to norms may be a real phenomenon in decision contexts requiring group action. Given certain decision rules, for example, unanimity, it is conceivable that a clear majority would abandon information sharing and resort to normative pressure to win over the recalcitrant few. In a similar vein, whether the task is one which elicits concerns with achieving and maintaining group membership (*group set*) or which leads one to view others as mediators of facts (*task set*) may determine the form of influence (Thibaut & Strickland, 1956). For example, longterm groups may elicit social concerns which predominate over reality testing needs. Engaging the need to be liked may facilitate normative influence, while arousal of the need to be correct may maximize informational influence. To more fully gauge the role of normative pressure, the next generation of studies should vary decision requirements and analyze the sorts of communications (i.e., information sharing, forceful argumentation or normative pressure) that ensue. It is likely that the decision rule, by holding the balance between the two forms of influence, affects the very information being communicated during discussion.

It is also useful, in gauging the proper roles of normative and informational influence, to revive the distinction made between public and private conformity (e.g., Allen, 1965). Studies testing normative and informational influence typically ask for an individual, private response following discussion. As we have shown, these typically find for informational influence. Accordingly, it might be suggested that informational influence is most impactful on private, subjective response, for example, on one's subjective judgment of guiltiness. But ultimately, in functioning group decisions, the private response must be transformed to a public judgment, for example, a guilty/innocent vote. One determinant of this transformation is the criterion adopted for the decision. One can, for example, privately entertain a high subjective certainty of guilt, and yet vote "innocent" if the criterion is set higher (see Kaplan, 1982, pp. 214-217). On a related note, Stasser (1977, cited in Stasser, Kerr, & Davis, 1980) found that revisions of *certainty* of preference followed the form expected on the basis of information exchange during discussion, while changes in *preferences* seemed more sensitive to normative pressures. Normative and informational influences were not directly assessed, but were inferred from the total number of opinion advocates of a particular position (for the former influence) and the ratio of advocates of one position to another (for the latter influence). Together with our discussion, this suggests that it is not a question of *whether* normative or informational influences account for discussion-induced shifts, but *when* one or the other is operative in the process (i.e., in certainty or in criterion-setting for preference), and for *what* response (public or private). It would be instructive to see whether normative influences operate largely on criterion-setting, and consequently on the public manifestation of private judgments (see also Kaplan & Schersching, 1981, for a related discussion).

Mechanism for Informational Influence

In many studies, including those cited here (Kaplan, 1977, Experiments 1 and 2), the polarization effect takes on an odd character. How can it be that, when people are given arguments during discussions which mirror the value and extremity of those which formed the initial judgment, they will shift to a more extreme position? In other words, the phenomenon is in need of a mechanism for shift which goes beyond the mere invocation of persuasive arguments which, after all, are no more extreme than those the individual initially took into account.

An information integration analysis provides such a mechanism (Anderson, 1981; Anderson & Graesser, 1976; Kaplan, 1977, 1982; Kaplan & Schersching, 1981). This analysis, which provides a general model for judgment, proposes that a unitary judgment flows from an integration of separate pieces of information about the judged object or issue. Each piece of information is represented by two quantitative parameters: scale value and weight. *Scale value* refers to the subjective position of a piece of information on the judgment dimension. For example, if a defendant had a grudge against the victim, this might represent a scale value of 8 on a 10-point scale of guilt appearance. *Weight* represents the functional importance of that information, that is, its contribution to the judgment. Information about the grudge might, for example, have less weight than information about the defendant's ability to carry out the crime. Reduction of information to component scale values and weights permits separation of *what* an item tells us about the issue and *how much* it contributes to the judgment—the latter being closely related to the familiar concepts of validity and reliability. The central role of these parameters also permits the integration of substantively disparate pieces of information, such as motives and opportunities, or risks to self and costs to society, into a single judgment.

To reach a judgment, the weighted scale values are combined by means of an *integration rule* of some algebraic function. Although a variety of algebraic functions have been demonstrated in certain tasks (see Anderson, 1981), a weighted averaging rule seems to fit most instances. That is, the scale values of information about the issue are averaged, each value weighted by its importance relative to the others. Central to our analysis, it should be noted that the integration equation also contains an allowance for an *initial impression*. This refers to the scale value of the judgment existing prior to apprehending information about the issue, and may be equated with a dispositional bias in the individual. In many judgments, such as in the judicial tasks cited in the present chapter, this disposition assumes a neutral or near-neutral value (Kaplan, 1975). Accordingly, any judgment will be an average of the values of information about the issue and of the initial impression. If the former is more extreme than the latter, that is, if the information has a predominant value direction, then the judgment will be moderated by the less-extreme initial impression. The more information of a univalent nature that is added, or the greater the weight of the information, the less the initial impression will affect the outcome, and therefore the more extreme will be the response. These implications of the averaging rule with initial impressions have been supported (Kaplan, 1975).

Prior to discussion, a preliminary judgment is made by individuals. This judgment is based on a limited subset of available or potential information. All information may not be represented in this preliminary integration since some may have been overlooked, disbelieved, misunderstood, forgotten, or not integrated due to limited processing capability. If the total information set has some predominant univalent value (e.g., promotes a risky decision), or in any event is more polar in value than the initial impression, the individual's judgment will be less extreme than warranted by the information alone. This is because (a) the integrated average is moderated by the less extreme initial impression, and (b) not all information is integrated into the judgment.

During discussion, participants share the information that was salient to their preliminary judgments. Since the subset of information used and therefore shared by each participant will not be identical, some shared information will be *effectively* new, that is, previously unintegrated. The subset of information now utilized in the postdiscussion judgment will be enlarged, shifting the response away from the initial impression and toward the more extreme information value. The net result of this information-enlarging process is the polarization effect. Note that polarization would not be predictable from merely incorporating more information *of the same value* as that originally taken into account if an allowance for a moderating, near-neutral initial impression were not present. Some readers will recognize that this treatment of the polarizing effect of added information underlies accounts of the set-size effect in impression formation (Anderson, 1967; Kaplan, 1981), which describes the polarization of person impressions with added information of uniform scale value.

Three implications of this analysis are apparent. First, if groups are constrained to share only one valence of information, even when it is opposite in value to the majority of information, individuals will shift toward the value of shared information (Kaplan, 1977, Experiments 1 and 2). The direction of shift is determined by the valence of discussed information; while this is usually in the same direction as the prediscussion choice (e.g., Ebbesen & Bowers, 1974; Kaplan, 1977), shift can also be toward a minority position, if such is overrepresented in shared comments (Nemeth, 1979; see also Moscovici & Mugny, Chapter 3, this volume). Second, the extent of shift depends on the extent to which shared information is different from that previously incorporated by a given individual (Vinokur & Burnstein, 1974; Kaplan, 1977, Experiment 3; Kaplan & Miller, 1977). Groups whose members share among them a wider pool of facts show a larger mean shift after discussion. Third, where group members have different initial impressions (e.g., some jurors are dispositionally lenient, others are harsh), the individual differences manifested in prediscussion judgments will be reduced after discussion (Kaplan & Miller, 1978, Experiment 3). This is because more information is integrated after discussion, lessening the impact of the divergent initial impressions.

This analysis is based on incorporation of previously ignored information into the cognitive equation. What about the instance where discussed facts overlap completely with information which has already been integrated into judgments? Here too, the model allows for polarization. If the facts are presented forcefully, the persuasiveness of the arguments may increase the *weight* of the already incorporated facts. Increasing the weight of nonneutral information relative to the initial impression will shift the average toward the information value, that is, toward greater polarity (see Kaplan, 1971, for an example in person impressions).

Further elaboration of the informational influence mechanism is found in Kaplan and Miller (1977). We reasoned that groups that have been exposed to the same information prior to discussion may nevertheless base their individual judgments on different subsets of information due to differences in information attended to and remembered. If the remembered information differs among individuals, the variety of facts shared during discussion will be larger, leading to greater polarization as facts related by other members which were not initially used by an individual are now incorporated. In the study, six-member groups listened to 30 pieces of evidence in an assault trial, given in one of six different orders. In half the groups, all members heard the same ordering (*homogeneous condition*), and in the remaining groups, each member heard the same facts in different orders (*heterogeneous conditions*). Within the two ordering conditions, half the groups heard facts contrived to give a predominant appearance of guilt, and half were given facts with an appearance of innocence. Pilot testing had shown recency effects in memory, so that within heterogenous groups, the members would tend to recall different facts from each other (though all would remember facts with similar guilt or innocence values), whereas within homogeneous groups, factual recall among members would overlap more. Analysis of discussion content showed a greater variety of facts was introduced in the heterogeneous-order groups. Likewise, these groups showed greater polarization of judgment following discussion, confirming expectations (see Figure 4-4).

We have presented an information-integration mechanism for informational influences in group discussion. This analysis can account for shifts produced by persua-

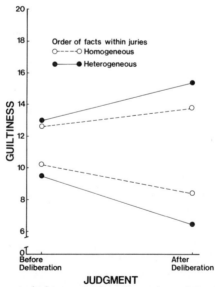

Fig. 4-4. Guilt judgments before and after discussion of facts presented in homogeneous or heterogeneous orders within groups. Extent of polarization is reflected in line slope; upper lines are for guilt-appearing facts, and lower lines are for innocent-appearing facts. From Kaplan and Miller (1977).

sive arguments as well as by more passively shared information. It can also account for shifts toward polarization or moderation. Finally, it can handle polarization shifts when other members have initial positions that are *more* extreme than the individual's, and the more bothersome instance when the other participants give the *same,* or even less polar initial responses. By considering the initial impression—the response in the absence of information—polarization is predicted even when others share information no more extreme than that originally considered by an individual.

A Word About Discussion and Quality of Judgment

While our intended focus has been on judgment-formation and not the quality or correctness of judgment, we would be remiss in not briefly pointing out some parallels. These observations are suggestions and do not wholly encapsulate the topic.

Dashiell (1935), in an early review of findings in group versus individual productivity, contrasted shared information and "arguments" (the latter referring to active influence on solutions, not information) as agents of changed judgments in groups. In a later review of models of group problem-solving, Kelley & Thibaut (1969) distinguished between *information-distribution* and *response-distribution* models. The former refers to the distribution within the group of *attributions* about the nature of the problem, and the latter focuses on the distribution of *solutions.* It is strikingly apparent that comparisons of the quality of group versus individual judgment and problem-solving resort to the same distinctions made for discussion polarization. The question in both generations of *Handbook of Social Psychology* chapters is whether groups differ from individuals in the quality of their problem-solving due to the influence of the *information* possessed by members, or to the press of members' *solutions* (see also Marvin Shaw, 1981, pp. 57-68, for a more recent statement).

In what is likely the first systematic comparison of group versus individual judgment quality, Bechterev (1920, cited in Dashiell, 1935) found groups superior to individuals, and attributed this to an improvement in quantity of details observed and recalled (see also Bechterev & deLange, 1924). Shaw (1932) also found groups superior to individuals, but at a cost of greater time to reach decisions. She observed that groups have the advantage of checking errors in information and rejecting incorrect information. Jenness (1932) also suggested that groups possess wider knowledge than individuals, and went further in concluding that member differences in knowledge are directly related to group judgment accuracy. This can be seen as an early statement of the notion that variety of pooled information affects postdiscussion judgments (Kaplan, 1977; Kaplan & Miller, 1977). On a similar note, Dashiell (1930) attributed improvement in groups to the greater *range* of available information; he found that the greater the initial diversity of information between members, the more the improvement in judgment. Shaw (1981), in summing up the available research, concluded that groups have more information available. Finally, Kelley & Thibaut (1969) suggested that influences based on response distribution are involved when all members of a group have the *same* information. Taken as a whole, these works show the importance of information about the issue, and its distribution among members, in affecting the *quality* of group judgment, parallel to the role of informational influence on judgment polarization documented earlier in this chapter.

It is not surprising that explications of quality shifts look toward informational influences. Elsewhere, Laughlin & Earley (1982; see also the following) distinguish between intellective and judgmental tasks. The former refers to tasks where correctness is the issue, and the latter to value-laden tasks. They suggest that decision rules generated by informational processes apply better to intellective tasks, while rules generated by normative processes fit judgmental decisions. They offer some indirect evidence in support of the influence/task interaction: Items producing strong shifts after discussion were best fit by decision rules which implied informational processes, and items producing weak shifts were best fit by decision rules implying both normative and informational influences. In turn, subjects viewed the former items as intellective, and the latter as judgmental. Since the tasks used in studies of *quality* of group decisions are, of necessity, intellective, it is reasonable to expect a predominance of informational influence.

In a comprehensive treatment of gains and losses in problem-solving groups compared to individuals, Kelley & Thibaut (1978) elaborate on informational influences. Group discussion can provide a gain or loss in quality depending largely on the informational offerings of members. *Gain* from sharing information requires coordination of presentation. This includes the proper timing and sequencing of individual offerings (*synchronization*), and *patterning* of information distribution. Optimum patterning exists where (a) information (expertise) does not conflict among individuals, (b) information is low in interindividual redundancy, but (c) contains enough overlap between individuals to facilitate communication. *Loss* can derive from three sources. With more people contributing, there is greater chance that information will be repeated, or brought up in the wrong sequence. Further, there is a better chance that "blind alleys" will be entered. Finally, there is a motivational loss due to diminished feelings of responsibility for the outcome, anonymity, and social loafing, or "freeloading" on the work of others (Latané, Williams, & Harkins, 1979). There is some evidence that motivational loss is likely for easy but not difficult tasks (Harkins & Petty, Chapter 7, this volume).

This elaboration may be usefully applied to the polarization phenomenon, leading to finer analyses of informational influence. For example, is the extent of polarization shift influenced by variations in synchronization and patterning? *Quality* of group problem-solving is enhanced by maximizing coordination of informational input; will *polarization* be enhanced as well? There is reason to believe this would be so; inducing greater variety (Kaplan, 1977; Vinokur & Burnstein, 1974) and spread among members (Kaplan & Miller, 1977) in the patterning of information does increase polarization. Optimizing the sequence in which information is shared should likewise enhance polarization. Informational treatments of quality and polarization may have much in common, and attempts at their convergence may be overdue.

Group Decision Rules

Whereas the normative and informational influence approaches have been concerned primarily with the influence of group discussion on individual judgments, the group decision rules approach has dealt primarily with the aggregation of individual judgments into a group decision. This approach focuses on the most fundamental elements involved in any group decision-making task: A group of *individuals* must somehow combine their *preferences* regarding a set of *alternatives* in order to arrive at a *group decision* (preference) regarding the alternatives. The preferences of the individuals are viewed as being combined by means of a group decision *rule*. We are all familiar with formal or explicit decision rules such as majority rule (commonly used in committee decision-making) or unanimity rule (under which juries often function). But this approach holds that whether or not a group operates according to an explicit, formal rule, it can be viewed as functioning according to some informal or implicit rule. The problem is to find what that implicit rule is.

The group decision rules approach has been something of a poor cousin to the normative and informational influence approaches, having been the focus of far fewer studies (most of these by Davis and his co-workers and students; Davis, 1973; Stasser, Kerr, & Davis, 1980) and having generally been regarded as a less adequate explication of the polarization or choice-shift phenomenon. This assessment of the inadequacy of the group decision rules framework is probably due in large part to the often-cited and influential review of group polarization research by Myers and Lamm (1976). We believe that this assessment of the group decision rules approach is not entirely merited, and that the approach has several advantages, or at least potential advantages, that have not been sufficiently recognized or exploited.

The decision rule most frequently suggested to account for choice shifts is some version of majority rule (e.g., Cartwright, 1971). As Myers and Lamm (1976) point out, majority rule predicts shift toward the dominant pole when the majority favors that direction and when there is skewness in the distribution of initial preferences. Myers and Lamm believe that while the decision rule approach is intuitively appealing, the available data "sharply contradict it, at least as far as majority rule is concerned" (p. 611). They consider several facts that they believe provide evidence against this approach, the most important of which is that "*skewness cannot account for group polarization*" (p. 612). With the majority rule scheme, positively skewed distributions on Choice Dilemmas Questionnaire (CDQ) items (i.e., with a risky majority) should produce risky shifts, and negatively skewed distributions should produce cautious shifts. Unfortunately, as Myers and Lamm note, there is little evidence of any relationship between skewness and shifts (e.g., Fraser, 1971; Moscovici & Zavalloni, 1969; Vinokur, 1969). Moreover, they cite the rather mixed results of attempts directly to apply a majority rule model to discussion-induced shifts (e.g., Cvetkovich & Baumgardner, 1973; Moscovici & Zavalloni, 1969; Zaleska, 1976).

Nevertheless, we believe that the group decision rules approach is often a useful tool in explicating the group polarization or choice-shift phenomenon. In what follows, we give several illustrative examples of this approach: We present, first, a reanalysis by Cartwright (1971 of some data from a study by Cecil (1967), then an example of Davis' well-known social decision scheme approach, along with some recent interesting variants, and finally a model proposed by Harnett (1967) that appears promising and does not require skewness to account for shifts.

Example of the Group Decision Rules Approach

In one of the first reviews to stress the importance of viewing the group-polarization phenomenon within the wider context of group decision-making literature, Cartwright (1971) presented a decision rule reanalysis of data from a study by Cecil (1967). In the Cecil study, 43 three-person groups made unanimous decisions for each of four CDQ items. The alternatives among which the groups could choose were 1 chance in 10, 3 in 10, 5 in 10, 7 in 10, 9 in 10, or "not at all" (10 in 10). Cartwright attempted to account for the group decisions through the application of three decision rules: majority rule, coalition rule, and mean rule.

In 90 of the 172 distributions, two or more of the group members preferred the same odds. For these groups, Cartwright suggested that the natural thing to do would be choose the alternative preferred by the *majority*. Actually, 79% of them did just that. Moreover, essentially the same results were obtained regardless of whether the majority was relatively risky or relatively cautious.

For 60 of the remaining 82 distributions, Cartwright suggested the application of a *coalition rule*. In 36 of the distributions, two of the preferences were adjacent on the odds scale, while the third was separated from them by at least one position (e.g., 9, 7, and 3). Here, Cartwright assumed that the pair of adjacent members would form a coalition based on their relative similarity of preferences. For the other 24 distributions, the three preferences were adjacent, but the distribution was not symmetric around 5 in 10 (e.g., 1, 3, and 5). Arguing that there is reason to believe that more extreme choices are made with more confidence or commitment, Cartwright assumed that the two more extreme members would form a coalition. He predicted that coalitions would choose one of the two preferences of their members, and he found that 80% of the group decisions were consistent with this principle.

In the remaining 22 distributions, either the preferences were all adjacent but symmetric around 5 in 10, or no two were adjacent. There is no obvious basis for forming coalitions in these instances, but Cartwright suggested that the simplest rule might be to choose the alternative closest to the *mean* of the distribution. This actually occurred in 50% of the groups.

Overall, the principles of majority or coalition rule were applicable for 87% of the group decisions, and correctly predicted 79% of these. The principle of mean rule applied to 13% of the decisions, and correctly predicted 50% of them. (Of course, the predictions of coalition rule were for either of two alternatives.)

Cartwright's analysis is illustrative in several respects. First, notice that in order to map every possible distribution of initial individual preferences into a predicted group decision, it was necessary to posit alternative rules (so-called *subschemes* or *subrules*). For example, although coalition rule might be considered sufficient to generate predictions for most distributions (majority rule might be considered a version of coalition rule), for 13% of the distributions it could not supply predictions. For these cases an alternative rule was required—in this case, mean rule. The group decision rules approach typically requires the use of alternative rules because terms such as "majority rule" and "coalition rule" are generally not well-defined, that is, do not specify a mapping of every conceivable distribution of individual preferences into a group decision.

Second, notice that the analysis relies primarily on the first preferences of the group members. This is true of most group decision rule models. Yet, for some of the distributions considered under coalition rule, it was useful to make an assumption having to do with the *strength* of preferences (commitment, confidence). Such an assumption is one way of potentially getting around the skewness problem mentioned previously (note that the assumption is made to deal with distributions that are not skewed). Similar assumptions are made in some of the other examples of group decision models at which we will look (Harnett, 1967; Stasser & Davis, 1981).

Third, notice that for the most part Cartwright's analysis leads to specific point predictions, that is, to the prediction of a specific alternative, given some distribution of initial individual preferences. The group decision rules approach often makes much stronger predictions than do the normative and informational influence approaches. These latter approaches usually predict only that a particular choice shift will or will not occur, or will be stronger or weaker under various circumstances. They do not ordinarily make predictions regarding the choice of a specific alternative; they make weaker, directional predictions.

A fourth, related point is that the more precise predictions of decision rule models typically require more extensive information (about the distribution of preferences) than do the social comparison and informational influence approaches. The latter approaches usually ignore specific information about individual preferences and consider only a summary characterization of the distribution, for example, they rely heavily on comparisons of pre-and postdiscussion mean responses on the attitudinal or risk dimension (see Stasser et al., 1980, for an excellent discussion of the important information that is potentially lost through relying solely on summary statistics).

Finally, the accuracy with which the majority/coalition rule accounts for the group decisions of Cecil's study is encouraging for the group decision rules approach. We turn now to what is probably the best-known of the work using this approach— that of Davis and his co-workers (Davis, 1973; Stasser et al., 1980).

Social Decision Schemes

In the *social decision schemes* (SDS) approach adopted by Davis, the goal is to predict the probability of the group choosing each of several possible decision alternatives. There are two considerations that are important in determining the likelihood that a group will choose a given alternative. The first is the initial distribution of preferences in the group, that is, the number of group members initially supporting each of the alternatives. Table 4-1 gives an example of all the possible ways a group of four persons can distribute themselves over three alternatives.

The second consideration is the SDS. For each one of the distinguishable distributions of preferences, the SDS specifies the probability that the group chooses each of the alternatives. The SDS is represented as a matrix, D. Table 4-1 gives an example of a plurality rule/averaging decision scheme (note the use of a subscheme).

Now, in order to calculate the probability of each decision, all we need is to know the SDS and know or be able to estimate the likelihood of occurrence of each of the distinguishable distributions of preferences. The predicted probabilities of the

Table 4-1. A Plurality/Averaging Social Decision Scheme Matrix for Four-Person Groups on a Three-Alternative Task in Which Alternatives Reflect an Underlying Continuum[a]

	A_1	A_2	A_3
(4, 0, 0)	1.00	0.00	0.00
(0, 4, 0)	0.00	1.00	0.00
(0, 0, 4)	0.00	0.00	1.00
(3, 1, 0)	1.00	0.00	0.00
(3, 0, 1)	1.00	0.00	0.00
(1, 3, 0)	0.00	1.00	0.00
(0, 3, 1)	0.00	1.00	0.00
(1, 0, 3)	0.00	0.00	1.00
(0, 1, 3)	0.00	0.00	1.00
(2, 2, 0)	0.50	0.50	0.00
(2, 0, 2)	0.00	1.00	0.00
(0, 2, 2)	0.00	0.50	0.50
(2, 1, 1)	1.00	0.00	0.00
(1, 2, 1)	0.00	1.00	0.00
(1, 1, 2)	0.00	0.00	1.00

[a]If a simple plurality exists, it determines the outcome. Otherwise the alternative nearest the average of the preferred alternatives is chosen. (Averages falling exactly between two adjacent alternatives are treated by assigning equal probabilities to the two alternatives.)

various decisions can be tested for goodness-of-fit to observed data. This procedure is characteristic of a *model-testing* approach, in which several possible decision schemes are postulated and then contrasted against one another in their ability to account for the observed data.

Another approach is the *model-fitting* strategy. Instead of postulating different SDS matrices, one estimates a matrix D' that best describes the transition from distinguishable distributions of preferences to final group decisions. The estimated SDS matrix is then examined in an attempt to understand the group decision-making process it seems to represent (see, for example, Kerr, Atkin, Stasser, Meek, Holt, & Davis, 1976).

An excellent example of the model-testing approach as applied to the group choice-shift phenomenon is provided by a recent study by Laughlin and Earley (1982). Laughlin (1980) has proposed that many of the tasks with which groups deal can be thought of as located along a continuum anchored by intellective and judgmental tasks. Intellective tasks involve a demonstrably correct solution, whereas judgmental tasks involve decisions regarding nondemonstrable behavioral, ethical, or aesthetic judgments. According to Laughlin and Earley, there is evidence that the SDS that best describes group decision-making differs for intellective and judgmental tasks. For intellective tasks, the typical group decision rule is truth-supported wins; if and only if two or more group members are correct, the group will be correct. For judgmental tasks, the typical group decision rule is that a majority (simple or two-thirds) of the member preferences determines the decision. In their study, Laughlin and Earley predicted different best-fitting SDS models based on informational influence—specifically, relevant arguments theory (Burnstein & Vinokur, 1975; Vinokur & Burnstein, 1974; Vinokur, Trope, & Burnstein, 1975), and normative influence—specifically, social comparison theory (Goethals & Zanna, 1979; Sanders & Baron, 1977).

Four choice dilemma items were used in the study: one that consistently results in a strong risky shift, one a weak risky shift, one a weak cautious shift, and one a strong cautious shift. Laughlin and Earley interpret relevant arguments theory as predicting that the best-fitting model on the item with a strong risky shift would be risk-supported wins and the best-fitting model on the strong cautious-shift item would be caution-supported wins. (Risk-supported means two or more members preferring risk, and caution-supported means two or more members preferring caution.) For the weak risky- and cautious-shift items, the best-fitting model would be majority rule. Basically, the notion is that during group interaction members share and evaluate on their merits, arguments for or against a given course of action, and that some of these arguments have not previously been considered by all of the members. A choice shift occurs to the extent that members who had not previously considered these arguments become convinced of their merits (see related discussion earlier in the chapter). The degree of shift is related to the strength and distribution of arguments. A strong risky shift, for example, occurs when a number of persons who had not previously considered certain arguments favoring risk consider the merits of these arguments and are convinced by them. A weak shift occurs if the arguments are not as convincing, or if only a few members had not previously considered them. Laughlin and Earley suggest that the placement of choice dilemma items on the intellective-judgmental task continuum corresponds to the balance of arguments. Items with a balance strongly favoring risk or caution are closer to the intellective end of the continuum (i.e., there is a demonstratively correct answer in the sense that consensus is attainable on an appropriate course of action). Items with a balance less strongly favoring risk or caution are more in the judgmental direction.

Laughlin and Earley interpret the social comparison approach as predicting that the best-fitting SDS on all items would be majority wins. The notion here is that some minority of members discover during group interaction that they fail to at least equal the modal group member on some positively valued dimension that is (either directly or indirectly) related to the decision task. A choice shift occurs to the extent that these members change in order to make themselves at least equal to the average group member on the valued dimension. Hence, it is the majority position that is important.

Individuals and five-person groups responded to the choice dilemmas three successive times, either always as individuals, or in the order individual-group-individual. The predictions of nine a priori social decision models, including risk-supported wins, caution-supported wins, and majority rule, were considered. For purposes of their analysis, Laughlin and Earley dichotomized the odds scale into risky (1-5 in 10) and cautious (6-10 in 10) preferences. For each of the four items, the vector of relative frequencies of occurrence of distinguishable distributions (i.e., proportions of 5-0, 4-1, 3-2, etc., risky-cautious splits in the groups) was multiplied by the appropriate matrix D for each of the social decision models. The predicted proportions of occurrence of risky and cautious decisions for each model were then tested against the obtained proportions for the four items. As predicted from persuasive arguments theory, risk-supported wins was the best-fitting model on the most risky item, and caution-supported wins was the best-fitting model on the most cautious item. And as predicted by both persuasive arguments theory and social comparison theory, the best-fitting model on the two less extreme items was majority rule.

Laughlin and Earley point out that these results correspond to the results of previous research using intellective and judgmental tasks. Choice dilemmas that result in strong shifts (risky or cautious) are apparently closer to the intellective end of the intellective-judgmental task continuum. Just as the truth-supported wins rule has provided the best fit for other intellective tasks, a risk- (or caution-) supported wins rule provides the best fit for choice dilemmas with strong shifts. Such items may be regarded as having demonstrably correct solutions, and persuasive arguments are most persuasive and important for such items. Two members of the group are necessary and sufficient to demonstrate to the others, by their arguments, the correctness of the solution.

Choice dilemmas that result in moderate shifts are apparently closer to the judgmental end of the continuum. Just as majority rule provides the best fit for other judgmental tasks, it provides the best fit for choice dilemmas with moderate shifts. Here, there are no arguments persuasive enough to establish a consensus on the correctness of a particular course of action, that is, there is no demonstrably correct solution. For such items, the opinions of others are relatively more important, and a majority tips the balance.

The Laughlin-Earley findings are, of course, open to alternative interpretation, especially inasmuch as Laughlin and Earley did not directly assess the number, nature, or persuasiveness of the various arguments that were advanced during group discussions. Moreover, although the truth-supported wins rule provided the best fit for the strong-shifting items, just as it has for intellective tasks, one may question the notion that such items have a "demonstrably correct" solution in the ordinary sense. Nevertheless, the findings are suggestive and represent an excellent example of the complemental nature of the informational influence, normative influence, and group decision rules approaches.

Beyond Social Decision Schemes

One of the difficulties of attempting to account for group polarization effects via the SDS approach is that individual preference changes can occur as a result of group discussion without a group decision having been made or a consensus reached. Although one can argue that postdiscussion individual preferences may reflect an implicit consensus, this is not always a compelling argument. Moreover, the application of an SDS analysis requires that there be some group (point) outcome. There are two extensions of the SDS approach that deserve mention here, since they suggest possible ways of dealing with this difficulty.

Social Transition Schemes (STS). This approach focuses not on the group's final decision, but rather on the successive changes in preferences of the group members during decision-making. Instead of predicting the final decision from distinguishable distributions of preference, the STS model predicts (or estimates) the likelihood of transition from one distinguishable distribution to another. For example, suppose that a six-person group must choose from among four decision alternatives. Then the STS approach would predict or estimate the likelihood of shifting from a given distinguishable distribution such as $(4, 0, 1, 1)$ to $(3, 1, 1, 1)$ or $(4, 0, 2, 0)$ or $(5, 0, 0, 1)$ or so on.

Whether the STS approach predicts or estimates the likelihood of shifting from one distinguishable distribution to another depends on whether a model-testing or a model-fitting strategy, respectively, is adopted. We give one relevant example of the former strategy, from a study by Godwin and Restle (1974). In this study, groups of 3-6 members attempted to attain consensus on which of four stimulus arrays another group had chosen as "most outstanding." Each member's preference was continuously monitored during group discussion. Godwin and Restle proposed several possible processes that might underlie transitions of preference. They found that the best-fitting model was one that assumed that the "drawing power" of a subgroup (ability of the subgroup to attract other members) was a function of the size of the subgroup and also the overall size of the group. Subgroups with all but one group member [i.e., a distinguishable distribution such as $(0, 5, 0, 1)$ in the six-person groups] were very attractive, and subgroups with at least a majority were much more attractive than subgroups without a majority. For example, denoting the attractiveness of a subgroup with i persons as G_i and setting $G_1 = 1.00$, Godwin and Restle obtained maximum likelihood estimates for $G_2 = 2.48$; $G_3 = 8.33$; $G_4 = 46.0$; $G_5 = 189.1$. Thus, the drawing power of a subgroup increased rapidly as the size of the subgroup reached and exceeded a majority.

Stasser et al. (1980) point out that the Godwin and Restle results may have implications for the question of the relative importance of informational versus normative influence in group decision processes. If the number of arguments advanced by a faction or subgroup is even roughly proportional to its relative size, the drawing power of the faction should also be roughly proportional to its size. In other words, G_i should be approximately equal to iG_1. But in the six-person groups of the Godwin-Restle study, G_i far exceeds iG_1. This seems to imply that some sort of normative influence process is prevalent. For example, Stasser et al. suggest that perhaps small minorities recognize the low likelihood of their winning, and thus they yield to the majority.

Social Interaction Sequence (SIS) model. This model is an extension of the SDS and STS approaches; it is concerned with group members' changes of preference and changes of subjective certainty. Its primary purpose is to relate the direction and rate of such changes to the existing distinguishable distribution or group state. The model recognizes that an individual's preferences and the subjective certainty of those preferences are affected by the preferences of other group members, and that changes in any one individual's preferences and (indirectly) certainty will subsequently affect the preferences and certainty of others. Thus, the model is interactive and sequential in nature.

So far the SIS model has been applied only to decision tasks involving two alternatives, and there have been few such applications (e.g., Stasser & Davis, 1981). In principle, however, the approach could be extended to situations involving several alternatives, including those in which the alternatives are ordered along a continuum. For this reason, and because the concept of certainty of (or commitment to) preference is of interest, we will discuss the model, albeit briefly and only in rudimentary detail.

For the case of two alternatives, denoted A_1 and A_2, the model assumes that group members can be classified into one of four *individual states,* as follows: S_1 — prefers A_1 and is certain of that opinion; S_2 —prefers A_1 but is uncertain of that opinion; S_3 —prefers A_2 but is uncertain; S_4 —prefers A_2 and is certain. Certainty is defined in the SIS model by two criteria: (a) an individual will not change his or her preference if currently certain; (b) an individual who has changed his or her preference will not immediately be certain of the new preference.

According to the SIS model, group interaction involves the movement of members into and out of the individual states over time. An individual can either become more or less certain of a given preference, or change the preference. Interaction can be described in terms of the relative frequency or probability that each type of change occurs. The probabilities of the various types of changes—opinion changes and certainty revisions—are thought to be a function of the distinguishable distribution. The *influence function,* which relates the probabilities of uncertain individuals changing their preferences, or certain individuals becoming uncertain, to the number of individuals holding each preference, may take a number of forms. An important question is what the form of the influence function actually is.

Stasser (1977) (reported in Stasser et al., 1980, and Stasser & Davis, 1981) examined the ability of two general forms of influence functions (linear and positively accelerating) to describe the rate of opinion changes and certainty revisions in four- and six-person mock juries. During deliberations, jurors periodically indicated their opinions regarding guilt, and the certainty with which they held those opinions. These responses determined the group state (distinguishable distribution) at each balloting and were also used to place individuals in one of the four individual states of the model. Thus, movement between individual states could be directly related to the group state.

For four- and six-person juries Stasser found that the estimated probability of a change from S_2 to S_3 (guilty to not guilty) was equal to .0852 (r_2/r_1), whereas the estimated probability of change from S_3 to S_2 (not guilty to guilty) was equal to .0271 (r_1/r_2). (Hence, changes of opinion from guilty to not guilty were much more likely than changes from not guilty to guilty.) In each instance, the estimated probability of an opinion change is a positive accelerating function of the number or proportion of advocates of that opinion change. The ratio r_2/r_1, for example, increases rapidly as r_2 exceeds r_1 (that is, as r_2 moves from a minority to a majority). Stasser et al. (1980) note that such a positive accelerating function probably reflects both informational and normative influences. As the number of advocates of a preference increases, both the amount of information favoring the preference in the discussion and the amount of normative pressure to adopt the preference increase.

Revisions of certainty were best described as a function of the proportion of persons favoring the alternative in the direction of the revision. For example, the estimated probability of moving from S_3 to S_4 (becoming certain of a not guilty opinion) was equal to .1487 (r_2/r), where r is the group size. Such linear functions are the form we might expect if revisions of certainty were due mostly to the exchange of information in the group.

Stasser et al. (1980) and Stasser and Davis (1981) note that revisions of certainty are, for the most part, private events within the context of group interaction, whereas changes of preference are largely public events. To the extent that behavior is public, it is subject to influence through normative pressures. Changes of preference are therefore likely to be the result of normative pressure as well as the information exchanged during group discussion. The addition of normative influence should cause the probability of preference change to increase more rapidly as the number of advocates for a preference approaches and exceeds a majority than the consideration of informational influence alone would suggest. Moreover, there is often pressure to obtain a consensus in decision-making groups (for example, juries typically operate under a formal requirement of unanimity), and this represents a kind of normative pressure. Such pressure should favor one alternative disproportionately as the number of advocates of that alternative increases to and exceeds a majority, because once a majority is attained, the easiest path to consensus is for the remaining minority members to acquiesce.

Harnett's (1967) Level of Aspiration Model

It seems possible that some of the lack of success of group decision rules in accounting for choice shifts arises from a too-narrow definition of preference. Group decision rule models have typically been applied to the distribution of *most*-preferred alternatives. That is, each individual's preference is defined as the alternative that he or she most favors. An individual's preferences encompass more than this, however. An individual will typically have alternatives that he or she prefers second-most, third-most, and so on. And an individual may greatly prefer one alternative as opposed to another, or may prefer it only slightly, or may be indifferent between the two. If an attempt were made to take into consideration not only each individual's most-preferred alternative, but the individuals's rank ordering of the alternative and/or some information about the strength of the individual's preferences, decision rule models might do a better job of accounting for choice-shifts. (The notions of commitment, confidence, and certainty seen in the Cartwright analysis and the SIS approach may be regarded as assumptions about, or assessments of, strengths of preference.)

The problem with group decision rules that fail to consider information beyond the first preferences of individuals can be illustrated by considering the application of majority rule to a three-person group in which one member so strongly prefers alternative x to alternative y that y is unacceptable, and the other two individuals slightly prefer y to x, but find either acceptable. Majority rule would predict that y would be the group decision, even though all three individuals might reasonably agree on alternative x as a better *group* outcome.

A very interesting group decision rule that attempts to take account of information beyond the first preferences of group members and that is applicable to preferences of the kind that have been the focus of polarization and choice-shift studies has been suggested by Harnett (1967). The Harnett model begins with information about preferences that involve not only a ranking of the preferences, but a ranking of the relative distances between adjacently ranked alternatives as well. (Such information is obtainable by means of a scaling technique that is fairly simple to apply, as long as the number of alternatives does not exceed 5 or 6—Siegel, 1957). This information is used to determine each individual's *level of aspiration*. An individual's level of aspiration is defined as the more preferred of the two adjacent alternatives between which the distance (in terms of preference or utility) is greatest, that is, it is the upper bound of the point at which there is the largest difference in how much the individual prefers adjacent alternatives.

With level of aspiration defined in this way, an individual is considered to be satisfied with any decision that meets or exceeds his aspiration level, and dissatisfied with any decision that does not. The group decision is then predicted to be the alternative that satisfies more individuals than any other alternative. In other words, the group decision depends only upon the number of individuals satisfied (i.e., attaining their aspiration level). In instances in which there is a "tie," that is, two or more alternatives satisfy the same number of group members, the group decision may be predicted by applying a version of majority rule. (The version to be applied may vary slightly, but we need not be concerned with that here.)

Harnett (1967) provided some support for this level of aspiration model. One interesting finding from his work is that the model did especially well in predicting decisions when there was no obvious majority solution (i.e., no alternative that was most preferred by a majority). The model also did better when unanimity was required than when majority rule was the formal decision procedure. This is of interest since a number of polarization and choice-shift studies have required consensus, either formally or informally.

Castore, Peterson, and Goodrich (1971) have tested the level of aspiration model in three- and four-person decision-making groups, using CDQ-like items. The model correctly predicted 80% of all group decisions. Moreover, this level of accuracy was not due to the groups simply failing to shift, since 59% of the predictions that were correct involved a risky shift, and 25% a cautious shift. All the errors of prediction were instances in which the model predicted a risky shift, but the group decisions were riskier than the predictions (cf. Zaleska, 1976). Therefore, the model could not fully account for the risky shift. However, the *directions* of the model's predictions (risky or cautious shift or no shift) were correct 100% of the time! In addition, the decisions not correctly predicted by the model were cheifly instances in which a relatively unconcerned (indifferent) majority confronted a minority member with consistent preferences (few cases of indifference among the alternatives) and few satisfactory alternatives. In these instances the group decision appeared to be a compromise between the position preferred by the committed minority member and the relatively unconcerned majority (cf. Moscovici & Faucheux, 1972).

Castore et al. (1971) note that the main reason the level of aspiration model predicted group decisions that were riskier than average was apparent from inspection of the preference data. In most cases, the second choices of individuals were riskier than their first choices. Thus, unless there was a clear majority rule solution evident in the members' first preferences, it would seem natural for the group to move in the direction of considering riskier alternatives. It seems possible that subjects were reluctant to advocate strongly a riskier but actually more admired alternative (cf. Levinger & Schneider, 1969; Pruitt, 1971b). When it became apparent that the group could not reach a decision from consideration of first preferences, the members could then consider the riskier (and more admired) alternatives. That is, the necessity to consider alternatives to achieve a consensus would lead to support of greater risk by the group.

Summary

This chapter has addressed theoretical accounts of how group discussion influences individual and group decisions. In dealing with these accounts, we have focused largely on judgmental shifts toward greater polarity of response. Treatments of this shift most frequently invoke either normative (social comparison) or informational influences, the latter including both persuasive argumentation of facts, and more passive information sharing. In addition, quantitative treatments look toward the implicit decision rules adopted by a group, which can be based on either normative or informational pressure, some combination of both, or other factors.

Comparative tests of normative and informational influence, while often flawed, favor the informational interpretations somewhat. A mechanism for informational influence is suggested herein, and studies providing evidence for this mechanism are described. The mechanism extends an information integration model of social judgment to group influence. In this model, judgments are an integration of the values of information about the issue and of a preinformational response (initial impression), with each piece of information and the initial impression weighted by effective importance. Given an averaging integration rule for information and initial impression, and given a more extreme value for the former (which would be true where the information has some predominant value, as in choice dilemmas tending toward risky solutions), the individual judgment would not be as extreme as warranted by the facts, due to the integration of the more neutral initial impression. Facts shared during discussion are subsequently integrated into the cognitive equation, moving the average toward the value of the information set, and away from the more neutral initial impression. This polarization effect would be particularly strong where the shared and newly integrated facts were not previously considered by the individual, though polarization could also follow from an increase in the *weight* of previously integrated facts as a consequence of persuasive argumentation.

Informational and normative influences are not mutually exclusive. The form of influence operative at any point may depend on the process stage, response requirements, the nature of the task, and the decision rule adopted by the group. It is suggested that informational influences are more relevant to subjective certainty responses (e.g., "how guilty does the defendant appear?") while normative influences may apply more to criterion setting (e.g., "how much certainty is needed for a

guilty verdict?"). Similarly, private judgments may be more influenced by information, and public judgments more susceptible to normative influences. Tasks which
are primarily intellective (correctness is at issue) evoke informational pressures,
while judgmental tasks (values are at issue) evoke both types of influence. In addition, different task requirements and prediscussion distributions of preferences
among members call forth different implicit decision rules which, in turn, are associated with different forms of influence. In fact, any of a number of social psychological explanations of group decision-making are translatable into decision rules.
One advantage of the group decision rules approach is that it often makes relatively
precise predictions (predicts the choice of a specific alternative, given an initial distribution of preferences). These predictions frequently prove to be accurate,
especially if the strength of individual preferences is taken into account. Moreover,
variations of the group decision rules approach (STS, SIS) are not restricted to
making predictions of group outcomes, but instead make predictions regarding
individual preferences.

References

Allen, V. L. Situational factors in conformity. In L. Berkowitz (Ed.), *Advances in
    experimental social psychology* (Vol. 2). New York: Academic Press, 1965.
Anderson, N. H. Averaging model analysis of set-size effect in impression formation.
    Journal of Experimental Psychology, 1967, *75*, 158-165.
Anderson, N. H. *Foundations of information integration theory*. New York: Aca-
    demic Press, 1981.
Anderson, N. H., & Graesser, C. C. An information integration analysis of attitude
    change in group discussion. *Journal of Personality and Social Psychology*, 1976,
    34, 210-222.
Bandura, A. Vicarious processes: A case of no-trial learning. In L. Berkowitz (Ed.),
    Advances in experimental social psychology (Vol. 2). New York: Academic Press,
    1965.
Bechterev, V. M., & de Lange, M. Die ergebnisse des experiments auf den gebiete
    der kollectiven reflexologie. *Zeitschrift für Angewandte Psychologie*, 1924, *24*,
    305-344.
Brown, R. *Social Psychology*. New York: Free Press, 1965.
Burnstein, E., & Santis, K. Attitude polarization in groups. In R. E. Petty, T. M.
    Ostrom, & T. C. Brock (Eds.), *Cognitive responses in persuasion*. Hillsdale, N. J.:
    Lawrence Erlbaum, 1981.
Burnstein, E., & Vinokur, A. Testing two classes of theories about group-induced
    shifts in individual choice. *Journal of Experimental Social Psychology*, 1973,
    9, 123-137.
Burnstein, E., & Vinokur, A. What a person thinks upon learning he has chosen dif-
    ferently from others: Nice evidence for the persuasive-arguments explanation of
    choice shifts. *Journal of Experimental Social Psychology*, 1975, *11*, 412-426.
Burnstein, E., & Vinokur, A. Persuasive argumentation and social comparison as
    determinants of attitude polarization. *Journal of Experimental Social Psychol-
    ogy*, 1977, *13*, 315-332.

Burnstein, E., Vinokur, A., & Trope, Y. Interpersonal comparison versus persuasive argumentation: A more direct test of alternative explanations for group-induced shifts in individual choice. *Journal of Experimental Social Psychology*, 1973, *9*, 236-245.

Burtt, H. E. Sex differences in the effect of discussion. *Journal of Experimental Psychology*, 1920, *3*, 390-395.

Cartwright, D. Risk taking by individuals and groups: An assessment of research employing choice dilemmas. *Journal of Personality and Social Psychology*, 1971, *20*, 361-378.

Cartwright, D. Determinants of scientific progress: The case of the risky shift. *American Psychologist*, 1973, *28*, 222-231.

Castore, C. H., Peterson, K., & Goodrich, T. A. Risky shift: Social value or social choice? An alternative model. *Journal of Personality and Social Psychology*, 1971, *20*, 487-494.

Cecil, E. A. *The effect of group composition on the level of risk in group decisions.* Unpublished doctoral dissertation, Indiana University, 1967.

Clark, R. D., Crockett, W. H., & Archer, R. L. Risk-as-value hypothesis: The relation between perception of self, others, and the risky shift. *Journal of Personality and Social Psychology*, 1971, *20*, 425-429.

Clark, R. D., & Willems, E. P. Where is the risky shift? *Journal of Personality and Social Psychology*, 1969, *13*, 215-221.

Cvetkovich, G., & Baumgardner, S. R. Attitude polarization: The relative influence of discussion group structure and reference group norms. *Journal of Personality and Social Psychology*, 1973, *26*, 159-165.

Dashiell, J. F. An experimental analysis of some group effects. *Journal of Abnormal and Social Psychology*, 1930, *25*, 190-199.

Dashiell, J. F. Experimental studies of the influence of social situations on the behavior of individual human adults. In C. Murchison (Ed.), *Handbook of social psychology*. Worcester: Clark University Press, 1935.

Davis, J. H. Group decision and social interaction: A theory of social decision schemes. *Psychological Review*, 1973, *80*, 97-125.

Deutsch, M., & Gerard, H. G. A study of normative and informational social influences upon individual judgment. *Journal of Abnormal and Social Psychology*, 1955, *51*, 629-636.

Ebbesen, E. B., & Bowers, R. J. Proportion of risky to conservative arguments in group discussion and choice shift. *Journal of Personality and Social Psychology*, 1974, *29*, 316-327.

Fraser, C. Group risk-taking and group polarization. *European Journal of Social Psychology*, 1971, *1*, 493-510.

Godwin, W. F., & Restle, F. The road to agreement: Subgroup pressures in small group consensus processes. *Journal of Personality and Social Psychology*, 1974, *30*, 500-509.

Goethals, G. R., & Zanna, M. P. The role of social comparison in choice-shifts. *Journal of Personality and Social Psychology*, 1979. *37*, 1469-1476.

Greenwald, A. G., Brock, T. C., & Ostrom, T. M. (Eds.) *Psychological foundations of attitudes*. New York: Academic Press, 1968.

Harnett, D. L. A level of aspiration model for group decision making. *Journal of Personality and Social Psychology*, 1967, *5*, 58-66.

Jenness, A. The role of discussion in changing opinion regarding a matter of fact. *Journal of Abnormal and Social Psychology*, 1932, *27*, 279-296.

Kaplan, M. F. Dispositional effects and weight of information in impression formation. *Journal of Personality and Social Psychology*, 1971, *18*, 279-284.

Kaplan, M. F. Information integration in social judgment: Interaction of judge and informational components. In M. F. Kaplan & S. Schwartz (Eds.), *Human judgment and decision processes*. New York: Academic Press, 1975.

Kaplan, M. F. Discussion polarization effects in a modified jury decision paradigm: Informational influences. *Sociometry*, 1977, *40*, 262-271.

Kaplan, M. F. Amount of information and polarity of attraction. *Bulletin of the Psychonomic Society*, 1981, *18*, 23-26.

Kaplan, M. F. Cognitive processes in the individual juror. In R. M. Bray & N. L. Kerr (Eds.), *The psychology of the courtroom*. New York: Academic Press, 1982.

Kaplan, M. F., & Anderson, N. H. Information integration theory and reinforcement theory as approaches to interpersonal attraction. *Journal of Personality and Social Psychology*, 1973, *28*, 301-312.

Kaplan, M. F., & Miller, C. E. Judgments and group discussion: Effect of presentation and memory factors on polarization. *Sociometry*, 1977, *40*, 337-343.

Kaplan, M. F., & Miller, L. E. Reducing the effects of juror bias. *Journal of Personality and Social Psychology*, 1978, *36*, 1443-1455.

Kaplan, M. F., & Schersching, C. Juror deliberation: An information integration analysis. In B. D. Sales (Ed.), *The trial process: Perspectives in law and psychology* (Vol. 2). New York: Plenum, 1981.

Kelley, H. H., & Thibaut, J. W. Group problem solving. In G. Lindzey & E. Aronson (Eds.), *The handbook of social psychology* (Vol. 4, 2nd ed.) Reading, Mass.: Addison-Wesley, 1969.

Kelley, H. H., & Thibaut, J. W. *Interpersonal relations: A theory of interdependence*. New York: Wiley, 1978.

Kerr, N. L., Atkin, R. S., Stasser, G., Meek, D., Holt, R. W., & Davis, J. H. Guilt beyond a reasonable doubt: Effects of concept definition and assigned decision rule on the judgments of mock jurors. *Journal of Personality and Social Psychology*, 1976, *34*, 282-294.

Lamm, H., & Myers, D. G. Group-induced polarization of attitudes and behavior. In L. Berkowitz (Ed.), *Advances in experimental social psychology* (Vol. 11). New York: Academic Press, 1978.

Latané, B., Williams, K., & Harkins, S. Many hands make light the work: The causes and consequences of social loafing. *Journal of Personality and Social Psychology*, 1979, *37*, 822-832.

Laughlin, P. R. Social combination processes of cooperative problem-solving groups on verbal intellective tasks. In M. Fishbein (Ed.), *Progress in social psychology*. Hillsdale, N.J.: Lawrence Erlbaum, 1980.

Laughlin, P. R., & Earley, P. C. Social combination models, persuasive arguments theory, social comparison theory, and choice shift. *Journal of Personality and Social Psychology,* 1982, *42,* 273-280.

Levinger, G., & Schneider, D. J. Test of the "risk is a value" hypothesis. *Journal of Personality and Social Psychology,* 1969, *11,* 165-169.

Marston, W. M. Studies in testimony. *Journal of Criminal Law and Criminology,* 1924, *15,* 5-31.

Moscovici, S., & Faucheux, C. Social influence, conformity bias, and the study of active minorities. In L. Berkowitz (Ed.), *Advances in experimental social psychology* (Vol. 6). New York: Academic Press. 1972.

Moscovici, S., & Zavalloni, M. The group as a polarizer on attitudes. *Journal of Personality and Social Psychology,* 1969, *12,* 125-135.

Myers, D. G., & Kaplan, M. F. Group-induced polarization in simulated juries . *Personality and Social Psychology Bulletin,* 1976, *2,* 63-66.

Myers, D. G., & Lamm, H. The group polarization phenomenon. *Psychological Bulletin,* 1976, *83,* 602-627.

Nemeth, C. The role of an active minority in intergroup relations. In Austin, W. G., & Worchel, S. (Eds.), *The social psychology of intergroup relations.* Monterey, Calif.: Brooks Cole, 1979.

Petty, R. E., Ostrom, T. M., & Brock, T. C. (Eds.). *Cognitive responses in persuasion.* Hillsdale, N. J.: Lawrence Erlbaum, 1981.

Pruitt, D. G. Choice shifts in group discussion: An introductory review. *Journal of Personality and Social Psychology,* 1971, *20,* 339-360. (a)

Pruitt, D. G. Conclusions: Toward an understanding of choice shifts in group discussion. *Journal of Personality and Social Psychology,* 1971, *20,* 495-510. (b)

Roberts, J. C., & Castore, C. H. The effects of conformity, information, and confidence upon subjects' willingness to take risks following a group discussion. *Organizational Behavior and Human Performance,* 1972, *8,* 384-394.

Sanders, G. S., & Baron, R. S. Is social comparison irrelevant for producing choice shifts? *Journal of Experimental Social Psychology,* 1977, *13,* 303-314.

Shaw, Marjorie E. A comparison of individuals and small groups in the rational solution of complex problems. *American Journal of Psychology,* 1932, *44,* 491-504.

Shaw, Marvin E. *Group dynamics: The psychology of small group behavior.* New York: McGraw-Hill, 1981.

Siegel, S. Level of aspiration and decision making. *Psychological Review,* 1957, *64,* 253-263.

Silverthorne, C. F. Information input and the group shift phenomenon in risk taking. *Journal of Personality and Social Psychology,* 1971, *20,* 456-461.

Stasser, G. *A model of social influence during group discussion: An application with four- and six-person mock juries.* Unpublished doctoral dissertation, University of Illinois, 1977.

Stasser, G., & Davis, J. H. Group decision making and social influence: A social interaction sequence model. *Psychological Review,* 1981, *88,* 523-551.

Stasser, G., Kerr, N. L., & Davis, J. H. Influence processes in decision-making groups: A modeling approach. In P. Paulus (Ed.), *Psychology of group influence.* Hillsdale, N.J.: Lawrence Erlbaum, 1980.

St. Jean, R. Reformulation of the value hypothesis in group risk taking. *Proceedings of the 78th Annual Convention of the American Psychological Association,* 1970, *5,* 339-340.

Stoner, J. A. F. *A comparison of individual and group decisions involving risk.* Unpublished Master's thesis, School of Industrial Management, Massachusetts Institute of Technology, 1961.

Teger, A. I., & Pruitt, D. G. Components of group risk taking. *Journal of Experimental Social Psychology,* 1967, *3,* 189-205.

Thibaut, J. W., & Strickland, L. Psychological set and conformity. *Journal of Personality,* 1956, *25,* 115-129.

Tolman, E. C. Cognitive maps in rats and man. *Psychological Review,* 1948, *55,* 189-208.

Vinokur, A. Distribution of initial risk levels and group decisions involving risk. *Journal of Personality and Social Psychology,* 1969, *13,* 207-214.

Vinokur, A., & Burnstein, E. Effects of partially shared persuasive arguments in group-induced shifts. *Journal of Personality and Social Psychology,* 1974, *29,* 306-315.

Vinokur, A., Trope, Y., & Burnstein, E. A decision-making analysis of persuasive argumentation and the choice-shift effect. *Journal of Experimental Social Psychology,* 1975, *11,* 127-148.

Wallach, M. A., & Kogan, N. The role of information and consequences in group risk taking. *Journal of Experimental Social Psychology,* 1965, *1,* 1-19.

Zaleska, M. Majority influence on group choices among bets. *Journal of Personality and Social Psychology,* 1976, *33,* 8-17.

Part 2

Group Influence on Task
Performance and Information Processing

Chapter 5

Group Influence on Individual
Task Performance

Paul B. Paulus

Psychologists have long had an interest in how being in a group affects task perfor-mance. Because many tasks are performed in social settings, a thorough understand-ing of the processes by which the group context influences task performance is important for both theoretical and practical reasons. Much research has focused on group problem-solving and group productivity and has been summarized by Davis (1969), Steiner (1972), Hackman and Morris (1975), and Hoffman (1965). The focus of this chapter, however, is on social settings in which individuals perform their own tasks "independent" of the others present. In this situation, individuals typically do not interact or share information as in the case of other group problem-solving and task performance paradigms (cf. Steiner, 1972). Many real-life settings such as athletic events, classrooms, and work environments have this feature. Research employing this coactive or additive paradigm has the advantage of permit-ting a relatively precise study of the influence of group variables on task perfor-mance unencumbered by the complexities of group interaction. Thus, such research provides basic information important for understanding effects in more complex group problem-solving and performance paradigms.

Research on the effects of the group on individual task performance has taken place along several different lines, each with a somewhat unique set of findings and concepts. Social facilitation studies have been concerned with the effects of an audience or of a coactor on task performance (cf. Geen & Gange, 1977). Classroom size studies have tried to determine the effect of number of students in a class on academic performance (e.g., Thomas & Fink, 1963). Studies of crowding have often assessed the effects of groups of varying sizes and density or "compactness" on individual task performance (cf. Paulus, 1980). Recent work on social loafing has dealt with the impact on individuals' motivation of their performing collectively, as a group, rather than as individually identifiable performers (Latané & Nida, 1980). Each of these areas of study and their relevant theories will be briefly summarized. I will then propose a broader model of task performance that can encompass each of these lines of research.

Social Facilitation

The study of social facilitation received a strong impetus from Zajonc's (1965) theoretical integration of the major findings. He suggested that the presence of others in audience and coaction situations serves as a source of drive arousal. According to Hull-Spence theory (Spence, 1956), this arousal should enhance dominant or strong responses relative to subordinate or weak responses. Dominant response enhancement should facilitate the performance of simple or well-learned tasks but produce decrements in the performance of complex or poorly learned tasks. This perspective has received fairly substantial support in the social facilitation area (Geen & Gange, 1977). There is much evidence that audiences or coactors have such effects and some direct evidence for increased arousal states. However, a number of competing theories have arisen in response to perceived inadequacies of the Zajonc formulation.

One position, known as the learned drive position (Cottrell, 1972; Henchy & Glass, 1968; Paulus & Murdoch, 1971), accepted the major elements of the Zajonc interpretation but held that the arousal state was a function of the learning history of the organism. Presumably, it is the anticipation of positive or negative outcomes in the presence of others that increases arousal levels in audience and coactive situations. Later research (Geen, 1980; Schkade, 1977; Weiss & Miller, 1971) has suggested that it is the concern for negative consequences that is the important factor. The learned drive position suggests that characteristics of the situation and the individual that affect the perceived consequences should influence the strength of social facilitation effects. Specifically, it has been found that increasing the degree and explicitness of evaluation, audience expertise, competition, and degree of test anxiety increases the effects of audiences or coactors (Geen, 1980). Zajonc (1980) has suggested, however, that while the learned drive position may account for effects related to evaluative factors, it does not account for effects obtained in non-evaluative contexts.

Another position in the social facilitation area is that the distraction due to the presence of others in task situations increases drive arousal (Baron, Moore, & Sanders, 1978). Others may be distracting because they may increase uncertainty about the appropriate responses and possible outcomes, increase evaluation apprehension (Geen, 1980), or because they induce a tendency to engage in social comparison as a means to evaluate one's own performance (Sanders, Baron, & Moore, 1978). The distraction position has received good support in a number of studies (cf. Sanders, 1981). However, it is difficult to differentiate distraction theory from learned drive theory since they seem to make similar predictions (cf. Geen, 1980, 1981). To the extent that situations are highly evaluative, they are likely to be both highly distracting and a source of increased drive.

Social facilitation effects can also be analyzed in terms of objective self-awareness theory (Duval & Wicklund, 1972). According to this interpretation, audiences produce an enhanced state of self-awareness. In this state an individual tends to become more aware of discrepancies between the "ideal self" or the standards that define it and the "actual self." In task performance situations, awareness that one's performance does not measure up to optimal levels should motivate an individual to improve his or her task performance. This motivation should facilitate performance on simple tasks. Decrements in performance on complex tasks are explained as due to "trying beyond one's capabilities" (Duval & Wicklund, 1972). The explanation of performance decrements is not very convincing, and the self-awareness approach has additional difficulty in explaining social facilitation effects with animals or the occurrence of arousal states.

A recent theory that is related to self-awareness theory is the cybernetic model of Carver and Scheier (1981). This model uses control-systems terminology to explain the facilitation of performance in the presence of others without recourse to drive arousal. Carver and Scheier presume the existence of a feedback loop often called TOTE (Test-Operate-Test-Exit) (Miller, Galanter, & Pribram, 1960) which serves to increase behavioral intensity in settings where others are present. The initial *test* phase involves comparing the existing state with a goal state or standard. If these are discrepant, attempts are made in the *operate* phase to reduce this discrepancy. If a subsequent *test* indicates that a discrepancy still exists, this process is repeated until the discrepancy disappears and the person *exits* the feedback loop. To the extent that social settings increase attention to the self, the test phase of the feedback loop occurs more frequently and behavioral intensity is increased. In everyday language, in social performance settings individuals are relatively more sensitive to relevant behavioral standards (e.g., performing well) and try harder to meet these standards. This would be reflected in superior performance on simple tasks.

Carver and Scheier (1981) explain the impairment of task performances in social settings by positing that subjects assess the likelihood of attaining a desired outcome or goal during task performance. This assessment is most likely to occur when the situation is highly evaluative and the performance appears to be going more poorly than expected. If the result of this assessment is favorable, the subject will continue striving to attain the standard. If unfavorable, the person will stop trying. Supposedly, with simple tasks favorable expectancies would occur, either limiting the outcome assessment process or resulting in favorable assessments. Task facilitation should occur under such conditions. With complex or difficult tasks, unfavorable expectancies should be relatively likely and impairment of performance should result. Carver and Scheier (1981) thus explain the effects of others on simple and complex tasks as due to the motivational effects of self-evaluations relative to a standard or goal and one's assessment of the likelihood of attaining that goal. Some support for this rationale was provided by the results of a study by Bond (1982). He found that when subjects performed a task with mostly simple items and a few complex ones, audience presence had no significant effects on the performance of either simple or complex items. However, when the task consisted of mostly complex items, the performance on both simple and complex items was hindered with an audience present.

In sum, there are a number of interpretations of social facilitation effects that have some degree of support. Although there has been much concern with the relative superiority of these differing positions (cf. Borden, 1980; Geen, 1980), it seems possible that all of these interpretations contain elements of truth. In that spirit, the model to be proposed will incorporate important elements from each of these theories. It should be noted that the present review has not been comprehensive. Two additional models have recently been proposed (Berger, Hampton, Carli, Grandmaison, Sadow, Donath, & Herschlag, 1981; Blank, 1980), but because these seem somewhat limited in their scope, they are not reviewed in this chapter.

Group Size and Crowding

In their review of the group size literature, Thomas and Fink (1963) mention only a small number of studies that had assessed the impact of group size on individual task performance. They concluded that although group size may be related to individual problem-solving or task performance, the direction/nature of the relationship is highly dependent on group conditions other than size. For example, superior performance typically was found to occur in large classes versus small ones, but sometimes no differences were observed. Other studies have favored small classes (McKeachie, 1980). Waxenberg (1974) has noted that most of these studies are plagued with various methodological problems that limit their usefulness. In a study that controlled for some of these problems, he found no effect of number of students in a class on student performance but did find that decreased interpersonal distance had a negative effect.

A second area reviewed by Thomas and Fink is that of work productivity. They noted one study in which group size reduced individual productivity (Marriot, 1949) and another in which an opposite trend appeared (Gekoski, 1952). Steiner (1966) concluded from his review of the group size/task productivity literature that increases in group size beyond some minimal point generally lead to reduced productivity for individual members.

Recent work on the topic of crowding also has examined the effects of group size on independent task performance. In these studies, group size is often varied in conjunction with the size of the room and/or interpersonal distance. In several studies, my students and I found that the variables of interpersonal distance, group size, and room size all can affect task performance (Paulus, Annis, Seta, Schkade, & Matthews, 1976; Paulus & Matthews, 1980a; Seta, Paulus, & Risner, 1977; Seta, Paulus, & Schkade, 1976). In these studies, using a novel maze task, we found that groups of four performed more poorly than groups of two, groups of eight performed more poorly than groups of four, groups of four placed close together performed more poorly than those placed far apart, and males but not females performed more poorly in a small room than in a large one.

We have obtained similar results using aptitude tests situations (Paulus, Matthews, & Chernick, Note 1). In one study, subjects performed more poorly on an IQ test in groups of eight as compared to groups of four. In a second study, male students who took the Scholastic Aptitude Test in a large room with about 50 students performed more poorly than those who took the exam in a small room with about 13 students. In contrast, Hillery and Fugita (1975) found that simple motor coordination tests are performed better in large groups than in small ones.

Several other studies have also obtained effects of group size on task performance in laboratory settings. Martens and Landers (1972) found that individual subjects performed more poorly on a difficult motor task as group size increased from one to four under highly evaluative conditions. Kalb and Keating (Note 2) found poorer performance on a word task for five- or six-person groups as compared to two- or three-person groups.

The effects of group size on task performance in the crowding literature can be easily handled by an extension of the drive arousal model of social facilitation (cf. Paulus, 1980). Increased group size and density increase arousal and thus hinder the performance of complex tasks (Paulus et al., 1976) while facilitating the performance of simple ones (Hillery & Fugita, 1975). There are also a number of other models of crowding that can explain the negative effects of crowding or increased group size on task performance. However, these models do not predict facilitation of performance on simple tasks. These models will be discussed briefly.

It has been proposed that increasing the number or density of individuals in a group can lead to stimulus overload (Milgram, 1970; Saegert, 1978). This overload can hinder task performance by overtaxing the attentional capacity of individuals (Cohen, 1978). Feelings of personal control also seem to be important (Baron & Rodin, 1979; Baum & Valins, 1977; Schmidt & Keating, 1979). Interference and unwanted intrusions in crowded settings may lead to a feeling of helplessness (Seligman, 1975) and consequent passivity and impaired cognitive functioning. Simply giving individuals a sense of perceived control over their crowded environment (e.g., giving them the option of leaving) can eliminate these negative effects (Langer & Saegert, 1977; Rodin, Solomon, & Metcalf, 1978; Sherrod, 1974).

Another set of models propose that attribution of the arousal experienced in crowded settings to crowding-related factors (such as group size, density, room size, or interference) leads to a feeling of crowding (Schaeffer & Patterson, 1980; Schmidt & Keating, 1979; Worchel & Teddlie, 1976). Based on the seminal work of Schachter and Singer (1962), these models presume that under crowded conditions, individuals will attribute the arousal experienced to crowding if crowding is a salient factor. If the arousal is attributed to other strong stimuli such as noise, then effects of crowding may not be obtained (Kalb & Keating, Note 2; Worchel & Yohai, 1979). However, a study by Paulus and Matthews (1980) found that having one definitive explanation of crowding-induced arousal (either crowding or noise) reduced the negative impact of the crowding. Because the type of attribution explanation did not seem to matter, this result was interpreted as support for perceived control theory.

The attributional model also implies that it is possible to feel crowded under conditions where crowding per se is not the primary causal factor (Gochman & Keating, 1980; Kalb & Keating, 1980). Unfulfilled goals or disconfirmed expectations in a course registration area or bookstore (Gochman & Keating, 1980; Kalb & Keating, 1980) and a dissonance manipulation (Kalb & Keating, 1980) all have led to increased feelings of crowding in settings where density was a salient factor, but was not the primary causal one (e.g., during course registration).

In sum, the effects of crowding and/or group size variations have been explained in terms of arousal, attribution of arousal, perceived control, and stimulus overload. Although these may be seen as competing positions, one can also view them as reflecting the different processes engaged in crowded environments or in large groups (cf. Paulus, 1980). It seems likely that crowded conditions or large groups simultaneously affect arousal, stimulus overload, feelings of control, and attributions. Alternatively, these different processes may vary in importance in differing situations. The integrative model presented later in this chapter attempts to encompass these various processes.

Social Loafing

Although the research in the social facilitation and crowding/group size areas has found considerable evidence for energization (heightened motivation or arousal) effects, some studies have demonstrated that increases in group size in a task performance situation leads individuals to exert less effort (Ingham, Levinger, Graves, & Peckham, 1974; Latané, Williams, & Harkins, 1979). Ingham et al. (1974) were concerned with replicating a frequently cited study by Ringlemann. This study, as cited in Moede (1927), used a tug-of-war (rope-pulling) task and found that increases in group size led to an increased discrepancy between actual performance and potential performance (based on the sum of the individual capabilities). Ingham et al. (1974) used six-man groups who were instructed to pull on the rope either alone or in groups of two, three, four, five, or six. Average individual pulling performance decreased as the group size increased to three, and then levelled off. As possible explanations for this result, it was observed that the decrement could be due to either coordination loss or to reduced task motivation (Steiner, 1972). In order to rule out the first of these explanations, task coordination problems were eliminated as a factor in a second study by having five experimental accomplices take on the role of subjects along with one naive subject. Similar results were obtained using this paradigm, with the individual exerting less effort as "perceived" group size increased to three, and leveling off after that. This indicates that motivation loss is one important factor underlying the results.

This motivational factor has been the focus of subsequent research by Latané et al. (1979). They have termed the loss of motivation with increased group size "social loafing." Individuals in their studies were asked to clap or cheer as loudly as possible. As the size of the group clapping or cheering increased, the intensity of sound produced per individual was reduced. In one study, individuals were blindfolded and wore earphones so that they could be led to believe that they were performing with a certain number of others while they actually performed alone. This allowed for an assessment of the extent to which the effects obtained were due to reduced effort as opposed to coordination loss or interference. The results of this study indicated that the group-induced performance decrement was due about equally to reduced effort and to loss of coordination. Petty, Harkins, and Williams (1980) extended this line of research to cognitive tasks. They had students evaluate either films of a therapist or written editorials. They varied whether these films or editorials made a positive or negative impression. Their general finding was that students who thought they were alone while evaluating the stimulus discriminated more clearly the positive or negative features of the stimulus than did students who thought they were one of a group of individuals evaluating the stimulus.

One limitation of these studies is that the size of the group was held constant in all of the experiments. In the Ingham et al. (1974) studies and those by Latané et al. (1979), groups of six were used. In the Petty et al. (1980) study, one experiment used only individual subjects while a second experiment used groups of 7 to 15. Thus, there was no systematic variation of actual group size in these studies. However, a study by Keating and Latané (1976) did vary actual group size by having individuals listen to a communication either alone or in a group (size unspecified). Attitudes of group subjects were less affected by the communication than attitudes of individual subjects. Kerr and Bruun (1981) also varied actual group size (one, two, three) and found decreased performance (social loafing) with increased group size using a pumping task.

The social loafing literature has thus demonstrated that increased group size can lead to decreased effort and decrements in performance on simple tasks. This finding, of course, contrasts with demonstration in the social facilitation and group size literature of facilitative effects on simple task performance. This apparent contradiction will be addressed by the theoretical model to be proposed.

Integrative Model

As we have seen, the available research offers considerable evidence that being alone versus in a group is an important variable influencing task performance. However, as pointed out by Thomas and Fink (1963), the exact direction and nature of this influence depends on a number of situational and/or group variables. We have discussed a variety of models designed to account for data in different areas of research related to individual task performance in groups. Each of these models has certain features which allow it to account quite well for a range of data within each of these areas. Yet, no single model has been developed to integrate the findings across these areas. Such a model is proposed in the following—one that incorporates important elements of many of the models discussed thus far. It is hoped this model will be useful in integrating the research in these differing areas and providing a basis for predicting new phenomena in these areas.

One major concern in developing this model will be the attainment of predictive power. This predictive power is presently lacking at two levels. First, we do not have a broad understanding of what characteristics of the group situation influence an individual's task-related state and how various components of this task-related state influence task performance. The importance of further specifying such group influence factors is illustrated by the fact that groups can both increase motivation (e.g., social facilitation) or decrease motivation (e.g., social loafing). What characteristics of the group determine when and to what extent these divergent effects occur? Previously discussed models have suggested that alterations in group setting can affect an individual's arousal, effort, and cognitive functioning. Yet how do these three effects combine to influence performance? Are these three outcome variables influenced differentially by certain group characteristics? More specifically, when would one expect facilitation of performance and when decrements? The above issues have been addressed by various models, but no single model enables precise predictions across the broad range of phenomena previously discussed.

A recent theoretical development in the area of anxiety is pertinent to our aims. Much research has examined the influence of anxiety on learning and memory (Eysenck, 1979). It has often been suggested that anxiety leads to task-irrelevant responses which interfere with the task performance of highly anxious subjects (e.g., Sarason, 1975; Wine, 1971). Eysenck (1979) proposed that anxious individuals process task-irrelevant information (e.g., worrisome thoughts) which in turn reduces the capacity available in working memory. These individuals then attempt to compensate by increasing their effort on the task. This may result in no observed differences in quality of task performance (performance efficiency). Yet because of the greater effort expended by the highly anxious subjects, they can be considered less effective processors (e.g., effectiveness = performance efficiency/effort). Eysenck (1979) proposes that anxiety will always reduce effectiveness but efficiency may be maintained if sufficient effort is exerted. Hence, the use of simple quality-of-performance measures may obscure the negative impact of high anxiety. Generally, it appears that research on anxiety involves many of the same issues and concepts that appear in the group task performance literature.[1]

The present model, which will be referred to as the cognitive-motivational model, views effort, arousal, and task-irrelevant cognitive activities as the primary task-relevant states. Although defining these three task-relevant states in precise operational terms may be difficult, it is felt that they are potentially distinguishable. Effort is viewed as the extent to which an individual desires to perform well on a task and should be reflected in behavioral manifestations such as speed, attentiveness, and carefulness. Arousal is presumed to be a psychological or emotional state of energization similar to that hypothesized in Hull-Spence theory (Spence, 1956). This state may be accompanied by physiological variations in arousal (e.g., GSR, heartrate). Task-irrelevant processing involves the focusing of attention on factors other than the task at hand. For example, task-irrelevant processing could consist of "worrying" about whether one's performance will measure up to the group's

---

[1] Eysenck's (1979) integration of the anxiety literature relies in part on the very influential work by Kahneman (1973). Kahneman dealt extensively with the interrelationship of effort, arousal, and task performance, using the terms "effort," "attention," and "capacity" somewhat interchangeably. He proposed that effort increases with increased difficulty of the task. However, decrements in performance can occur in spite of increased effort because the increased effort may not match the increased demand. Increased arousal up to moderate levels is seen as facilitating task performance. Capacity is supposedly increased at moderate levels of arousal. Furthermore, increased arousal levels lead to increased focusing on a limited range of dominant or obvious cues (cf. Easterbook, 1959). This may facilitate performance at moderate levels of arousal but hinder performance if it becomes too extreme. More complex tasks should be more sensitive to such a decremental effect since they require attention to a broader range of cues.

expectation. This factor appears to be the one emphasized by the distraction model of social facilitation (Sanders, 1981).

Effort, arousal, and task-irrelevant processing are influenced by certain features of group settings. The major factor determining the magnitude of influence is the extent to which the group affects the potential social consequences of the individual (Figure 5-1). Preliminary versions of this model can be found in Seta et al. (1976, 1977). Groups can either decrease or increase social consequences, and these consequences can be either negative, positive, or both.[2] For the sake of simplicity, it will be assumed that positive consequences dominate in some situations and negative consequences in others. I will deal first with the effects of variations in negative consequences.

In competitive and evaluative situations, such as exams or athletic competitions, being in groups or increasing group size increases the potential negative consequences –both in perceived probability and in magnitude–to which an individual can be exposed (e.g., embarrassment, disapproval, negative evaluation, or losing). This is particularly true when increased group size increases the focus of attention on the individual and there exists a concern with the extent to which the individual meets certain standards (as suggested by self-awareness theory, Duval & Wicklund, 1972). On the other hand, in cooperative or nonevaluative situations in which the focus is on group products rather than individual attainment of standards, being in groups or increasing group size should reduce the potential negative social consequences to which an individual can be exposed. In such settings the potential for being the focus of attention decreases (one can become lost in the group). Collective work on problem-solving endeavors and in communes exemplifies this type of paradigm. Latané and Nida (1980) make a similar distinction when they discuss division and multiplication of impact. When the individual is the focus of social influence, the greater number of sources of this influence (number of people), the greater the impact. When the individual is part of a group that is exposed to external social forces or influences, the impact of those forces will be reduced (i.e., "diffused") with increasing group size.

When being in a group increases the potential negative social consequences to an individual, increased effort, arousal, and task-irrelevant processing should occur. Evidence cited by Eysenck (1979) supports the notion that "anxiety-provoking" situations increase effort and task-irrelevant processing. The social facilitation and crowding literature provides evidence for the arousal component. With simple tasks, increased effort and arousal should have facilitatory effects while task-irrelevant processing should have negative effects. Whether overall facilitation will occur depends of course on the relative importance of these three factors. Research find-

---

[2] The degree of certainty of the consequences may also be an important factor. Complete certainty about positive or negative consequences may not be terribly arousing (McGrath, 1976). It is presumed that in most group situations some degree of uncertainty exists about the potential consequences. The focus of the cognitive-motivational model is on how group size affects the magnitude of these potential but uncertain consequences.

FOR SIMPLE TASKS

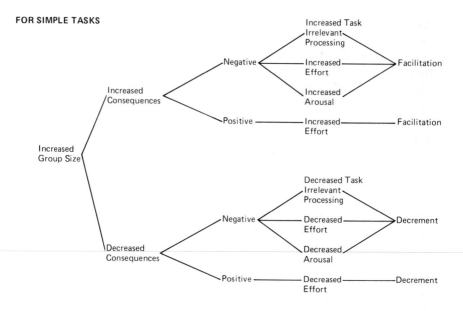

FOR COMPLEX TASKS

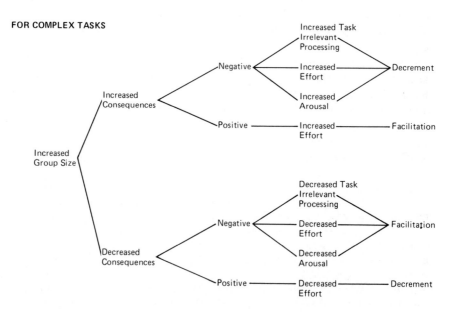

Note: Facilitation/Decrement is relative to smaller group size.

Fig. 5-1. The cognitive-motivational model of group task performance.

ings with simple tasks generally indicate facilitatory effects (Geen, 1980), suggesting that either effort and arousal outweigh task-irrelevant processing in their influence or that simple tasks are not very susceptible to task-irrelevant processing (cf. Child, 1954). Such tasks may not require much cognitive capacity. With complex tasks, effort should be facilitatory but arousal and task-irrelevant processing inhibitory. The general inhibitory effects of group presence and group size on complex task performance (Geen, 1980) indicates that the effects of the two inhibitory factors often outweigh those of the facilitatory one.

Under conditions where group presence or increased group size reduce negative social consequences, decreased effort, arousal, and task-irrelevant processing should occur. With simple tasks, we would expect relatively poorer performance in group settings, again presuming that a decrease in task-irrelevant processing is not important enough to offset the debilitating effects of decreased effort and arousal. With complex tasks, the lowered arousal and task-irrelevant processing should have facilitatory effects, while the effect of reduced effort should be inhibitory. This makes predictions somewhat difficult, but the study by Seta et al. (1976) suggests that facilitation of complex task performance can be demonstrated under such conditions, implying that the arousal and task-irrelevant processing effects can outweigh the effect of effort.

It was assumed in the previous discussion that the major social consequences of concern to the individual in competitive and evaluative settings are the potentially negative ones. However, positive consequences can also have motivational effects on behavior. This can be seen most clearly in settings that are neither evaluative nor competitive (in terms of potential negative consequences), but in which there are still positive incentives for doing well (e.g., social approval). These incentives would be greater (or magnified) in a group setting or with increasing group size. A prototype of this kind of situation is the case where an individual is highly skilled in a particular behavior (e.g., singing) and could receive a favorable response from observers. In such cases, group settings should serve mainly to increase effort, while having less impact on arousal and task-irrelevant processing. Both simple and complex tasks should be facilitated. If, however, the group setting (e.g., a commune) decreases the likelihood of recognition or reward, effort should be reduced. Both simple and complex task performance should be impaired in such situations.[3]

---

[3] In contrast to the implication of the model that an individual voluntarily controls the amount of effort in a task, Kahneman (1973) has proposed that voluntary control over effort is limited. He presented evidence that effort increases voluntarily with increased difficulty of the task. The problem with Kahneman's approach is that it was developed on the basis of research which focused primarily on the influence of task characteristics. The influence of external factors such as incentives and social influence was not systematically evaluated. The main external manipulation of arousal was noise. Presumably, in most of these settings a rather moderate level of evaluative concern existed in the subjects. Moreover, the practice of paying subjects or using sophisticated and motivated graduate students in many of the studies may have further restricted the range of motivation observed.

The cognitive-motivational model suggests that manipulation of the social consequences of task performance in groups can have a considerable influence on effort. Further, this influence is seen as reflecting a voluntary control over effort in response to the anticipated social consequences. In contrast, arousal is seen as an involuntary reaction to variations in social consequences and hence can be differentiated from effort.

In many situations group size variations may involve both positive and negative consequences. As can be seen from Figure 5-1, with simple tasks predictions remain rather straightforward. Increased potential for positive or negative consequences should facilitate performance, while decreased consequences should lead to decrements in performance. In the case of complex tasks predictions become difficult since changes in anticipation of positive and negative consequences have opposite effects on task performance. The potential counteractive effects of anticipation of positive and negative consequences may be a factor in the reported failures to obtain effects of group size variations on complex task performance (cf. Paulus, 1980).

In considering the effects of effort, arousal, and task-irrelevant processes, tasks have been dichotomized into simple or complex ones. In actual practice it is of course difficult to assign precise levels of difficulty to a task because of the lack of standard criteria. In most studies, investigators tend to pick tasks which are obviously at one extreme or the other. There is a need to establish guidelines for classifying tasks along a difficulty dimension so that predictions can be made for non-obvious cases and with "real tasks" in field settings.

It is quite likely that effort, arousal, and task-irrelevant processing differentially affect tasks varying in difficulty. In the case of simple tasks, if tasks are too simple, one may have to contend with ceiling effects and it will be difficult to demonstrate the impact of group settings. If such a ceiling is not a problem, there should be a rather straightforward relationship between effort and performance. Arousal is expected to have a smaller effect since it plays the role of a more subtle energizer. Task-irrelevant processing should have practically no effect because of the limited mental capacity required by such tasks. One might be able to assess the differential influence of effort, arousal, and task-irrelevant processing by assessing the effects of manipulations which should differentially affect them. For example, threat of shock noncontingent upon performance should primarily affect arousal (e.g., Morris & Liebert, 1973). Threat of failure contingent upon performance of a task should affect all three factors. If the failure threat is not contingent upon the performance of the criterion task, then the primary result may be task-irrelevant processing or worry (Morris & Liebert, 1973).

With relatively complex tasks, it is expected that task-irrelevant processing will be the major factor because of its negative effects on the working memory capacity which is so crucial in such tasks (Eysenck, 1979). While effort may be able to compensate for this, there are probably limits to this capability, especially with very difficult tasks (Kahneman, 1973). This is exemplified by the statement "trying too hard" frequently encountered in sports and other domains. In fact, while increased effort may increase processing resources (Kahneman, 1973), the autonomic, emotional, and physical cues associated with extremely high levels of effort may reduce processing resources. The effects of arousal on complex task performance independent of task-irrelevant processes are difficult to isolate since both should have negative effects. It is hard to think of manipulations that would affect only arousal and not task-irrelevant processing, except for physiological interventions. However, work on test anxiety has been able to demonstrate that both the emotionality (arousal?) and worry (task-irrelevant processing?) components of anxiety negatively affect task performance (Doctor & Altman, 1969). Yet, this research has also demonstrated that the worry component has a stronger negative effect on task performance than the emotionality component (Doctor & Altman, 1969; Morris & Liebert, 1970). This supports the contention that task-irrelevant processing may be a more important negative factor than arousal in task performance situations. In some cases, increased effort may be able to counteract and thus cancel out the negative effects of arousal and task-irrelevant processing on complex tasks, resulting in no observed effect of one's manipulation on task performance (Eysenck, 1979). This fact, as well as the counteractive effects of positive and negative consequences, may help account for frequently reported finding of null effects of crowding on task performance (cf. Paulus, 1980), failures to demonstrate effects in social facilitation paradigms (e.g., Manstead & Semin, 1980), and inconsistency in classroom size studies (Thomas & Fink, 1963).

I have proposed that the effects of group settings and variations in group size on task performance can be understood in terms of effort, arousal, and task-irrelevant processing. These factors have been part of a number of relevant theoretical models, but I know of no single model that has tied all three together. The model is proposed to explain a broad range of findings in the areas of social facilitation, crowding, social loafing, and anxiety. The major problem facing research and application in these areas is being able to specify the extent to which facilitation or impairment will occur. To that end, I have suggested relatively specific patterns of outcomes with simple and complex tasks.

Evaluation of the Cognitive-Motivational Model

Some Potential Problems

One problem with the model is that the three components of effort, arousal, and task-irrelevant processes can influence one another. For example, there may be a tendency for individuals to expend more effort when task-irrelevant processing becomes more debilitating (as with complex tasks) (Kahneman, 1973). Yet, as we have pointed out, high levels of effort may not be as beneficial with complex tasks as with simple ones. Consequently, subjects may not show the full benefit of this effort. It is likely that increased effort itself will be associated with increased physiological arousal (Kahneman, 1973) and become indistinguishable from it. For this reason, the model focuses on external sources of arousal. Yet, even then there is a confounding of effort and arousal since the model portrays them increasing and decreasing in concert with one another. In fact, one could eliminate arousal from the model and still come out with the same predictions.

Is arousal then superfluous? I think not. There are situations in which effort and arousal should be at different levels. For example, one could be in a setting where one anticipates potential negative consequences but there is no hope of avoiding them (e.g., an impossible task). Here one may observe high levels of arousal but low levels of effort. One could also demonstrate that arousal levels are higher when one anticipates increased negative consequences than when one anticipates positive ones. A major problem in resolving this arousal/effort issue is the lack of straightforward measures that could differentiate the two states. Physiological measures of arousal in social settings have had a mixed success, with palmar sweating being perhaps the most promising (Carver & Scheier, 1981; Geen & Gange, 1977). Kahneman (1973) has employed a pupil dilation measure of effort while others have employed a verbal measure (Petty et al., 1980). Until more definitive data is available, it is felt that a model that incorporates both effort and arousal will be a more useful integrative tool.

A second potential problem for the cognitive-motivational model is suggested by the Carver and Scheier (1981) cybernetic model. They propose that once individuals begin task performance, they assess the extent to which their performance matches pertinent standards or goals and the probability of matching them by continued performance. With simple tasks, the assessment should be positive and performance should be energized by continued effort. With complex tasks, the assessment is likely to be negative and task motivation or effort will be reduced. This model implies generally high levels of effort on simple tasks and low ones on complex tasks. While this may be fine under some conditions, it is an oversimplification of the dynamics likely to be operating.

First of all, one would expect an assessment of likelihood of success on a task to be related to past success on similar tasks. Since success is a relative matter and is related to norms of population success, subjective assessment of success should be affected by feedback provided about such norms or by the individual's personal estimation of such norms. On familiar tasks or tasks that involve skills for which the individual has a good sense of his or her standing relative to the population norms, subjective estimation of success may occur with some degree of confidence. On unfamiliar tasks, task feedback about relative success may be necessary and more influential for subjective estimation of success. The point is that performance assessments on both simple and complex tasks may lead to estimations of success or lack of success, depending on the particular performance norms or standards employed (cf. Seta, 1982; Seta & Hassan, 1980). So increased effort could come after assessments on both simple and complex tasks if such assessment suggest success, and there is no a priori reason to believe that such assessments are more likely with simple than with complex tasks. In fact, contrary to the Carver and Scheier suggestions, one might expect more effort to be exerted on complex tasks because more effort may be necessary to obtain a respectable level of performance and because such tasks may be more informative about the limits of one's capabilities (especially moderately difficult ones) (Trope & Brickman, 1975). Since high levels of performance are usually attained quite readily on simple tasks, low levels of effort quickly ensue because one has essentially obtained one's "goal."[4]

---

[4] The motivational effects of task difficulty has been the concern of several other scholars. For example, McGrath (1976) cites evidence that highly demanding tasks are associated with relatively more stress. Thus a "decrement" in task performance at high stress or arousal levels is a mere coincidence of these levels being associated with difficult tasks. This is similar to Kahneman's (1973) effort and task difficulty

Relation to Other Models

The proposed cognitive-motivational model explicitly incorporates the major elements of learned drive theory (Cottrell, 1972; Paulus, 1980) and Eysenck's (1979) theory about anxiety and task performance. It can handle data gathered within the rubric of social loafing, social facilitation, crowding, and group size. It can also accommodate the major elements of a number of prominent theories in the areas of social facilitation, crowding, and social loafing. One such example is the distraction theory of social facilitation (Sanders & Baron, 1975). Sanders and Baron proposed that distraction in audience situations can be a source of arousal and hence lead to the facilitation of simple tasks and decrements on complex ones. While they have provided strong evidence for this (e.g., Sanders, 1981), it also seems likely that social distraction in an evaluative task setting will lead to attempts to overcome the distraction. Such attempts can be seen as increased effort and should contribute to the overall quality of task performance. This increased effort should contribute to facilitation with simple tasks and help compensate for the detrimental effects of arousal with complex tasks. Distractions can be seen as contributing to task-irrelevant processing since they by definition take attention away from the task and reduce the available capacity. In other words, it is proposed that distraction has the same effects as increased negative consequences in our model. This may reflect the fact that increased consequences in social settings are the major source of distraction. So the distraction position can be subsumed by the cognitive-motivational model. Of course, a simple distraction model as proposed by Sanders et al. (1978) cannot account for the full range of data and situations covered by the present model.

The cognitive-motivational model can also readily accommodate the major elements of currently popular theories of crowding. Stimulus overload theories (Cohen, 1978; Saegert, 1978) seem to be emphasizing the task-irrelevant processes part of the model. Crowding stimuli take attentional capacity away from task stimuli and thus interfere with task performance. Perceived control theories (Baron & Rodin, 1978; Schmidt & Keating, 1979) emphasize the lack of perceived control in crowded settings. Presumably, the lack of perceived control or learned helplessness may lead to a deterioration of problem-solving capability and motivation (cf. Seligman, 1975). Others have argued that having perceived control over a stressful stimulus

_____

perspective. McGrath presents evidence from one study with Little League baseball teams that increased arousal or stress leads to enhanced task performance when one controls for task difficulty. However, the generality of these findings needs to be assessed. Certainly, considerable evidence exists for decrements in performance of complex tasks that cannot be easily explained away by the task difficulty factor (cf. Cohen, 1978).

The work by Harkins and Petty (Chapter 7, this volume) similarly suggests that task characteristics can affect an individual's task motivation. They found that on difficult or unique tasks, social loafing effects did not obtain. However, the cognitive-motivational model would predict that if the social consequences of identifiability or group size variations were great enough, effects of these variations would be obtained with unique and difficult tasks.

may ameliorate its stressful impact (cf. Cohen, Glass, & Phillips, 1979; Thompson, 1981).

Research on the effects of having a sense of perceived control during task performance is somewhat mixed. Some studies suggest that the effects of perceived control on task performance can be observed only after cessation of the aversive uncontrolled stimuli (Glass & Singer, 1972; Sherrod, 1974). Other studies suggest that simultaneous effects can be observed (Paulus & Matthews, 1980b). Beneficial effects (on complex tasks) observed from perceived control manipulations (as with Paulus & Matthews, 1980b) during exposure to the aversive stimuli could be due to decreased arousal and decreased task-irrelevant processing (worry) occasioned by perceived control. Detrimental aftereffects on task performance could be explained by the cognitive-motivational model in terms of residual effects of efforts, arousal, and task-irrelevant processes. For example, if during task performance a group stimulus is terminated, arousal may carry over into the new phase but effort may be reduced. This would lead to an overall decrement in task performance. While the cognitive-motivational model may be able to handle the perceived control data, future research will have to determine the precise role of this factor in the model.

The other major perspective in crowding is the attribution model as proposed by Worchel and Teddlie (1976), Schmidt and Keating (1979), and Schaeffer and Patterson (1980). This model holds that the extent to which the individual attributes his arousal state in a dense setting to crowding determines whether or not the experience of crowding and related negative effects occur. If such an attributional process exists, it could be incorporated into the present model. Attributing one's arousal state to the close proximity or large number of others may serve to enhance the worry process. This increase in task-irrelevant processing should have negative effects on task performance. The attributional theories presume the prior existence of an arousal state, and the attributional process is not seen as affecting this state. The attributional models appear to have only limited utility in predicting task performance effects in group settings. However, a detailed analysis of the importance of attributional processes in affecting arousal, effort, and task-irrelevant processes in group settings will be required for a definitive determination of this issue.

Research on social loafing (e.g., Latané et al., 1979) also can be incorporated easily into the cognitive-motivational model. This research found that in situations in which there is group responsibility for the quality of task performance, individuals seem to exert less effort and exhibit a lower level of task performance. This pattern of findings and accompanying perspective are representative of the decreased consequences part of the cognitive-motivational model. When increased group size decreases the potential consequences (positive or negative), reduced effort should ensue. However, as indicated by our model, only when the decreased consequences are primarily positive will decreased effort and resulting poorer task performance consistently be found (for both simple and complex tasks). When the primary consequences are negative, the situation is more complex, with decreased arousal and task-irrelevant processes also being contributing factors. While decrements in performance are still expected with simple tasks, increments can occur with complex tasks because of decreased arousal and task-irrelevant processing (cf. Seta et al.,

1976). In sum, social loafing can be seen as a demonstration of one type of outcome with group task performance, but this theory ignores the potential energizing effects addressed by this and other models.

Studies on social loafing have utilized both within-subject and between-subject paradigms. That is, in some studies subjects experienced only one group condition (e.g., Petty et al., 1980), while in others they experienced all conditions (Latané et al., 1980). Social loafing effects are obtained under both conditions (Harkins, Latané, & Williams, 1980; Kerr & Bruun, 1981). Yet, it should be noted that the within-group variations manipulated the number of people perceived to be working on the task, while keeping the actual size of the group present constant. I know of no studies that have involved actual manipulation of group size in a within-subjects paradigm. This is probably due to the cumbersomeness of this procedure. There would also be a number of inferential problems since one would not know whether the effects obtained were a result of the actual group size or the contrast between a particular group size and the other group sizes experienced.

Reduced Social Consequences and Complex Tasks

The cognitive-motivational model deals with the impact of both increased and decreased social consequences on task performance. Considerable evidence exists for the impact of increased social consequences on both complex and simple tasks under the rubric of social facilitation (Geen, 1980) and crowding (Paulus, 1980). Evidence for the impact of reduced social consequences on simple tasks has been provided by the social loafing research (Latané et al., 1979). However, the effect of reduced social consequences on complex tasks has received very little study relative to the other consequence and task combinations. Amoroso and Walters (1969) found that performance on a complex paired-associate task was facilitated when individuals who were under threat of shock were allowed to be in the presence of others for a period of time prior to task performance. This study's findings were consistent with others on affiliation (Schachter, 1959; Wrightsman, 1960) which indicate that being with others who are expecting the same aversive experience can reduce one's anxiety or fear level. Amoroso and Walters (1969) obtained physiological and affect data consistent with these notions. One problem with the Amoroso and Walters study is that it used calm confederates as co-others. This allows for anxiety to be reduced by modeling instead of perceived social consequences.

Seta et al. (1976) examined the above question using groups of naive subjects. In one study groups of two or four subjects performed a memory task under either cooperative or competitive conditions. In the competitive condition, individuals were told their performance would be compared with one another, so others should be a source of increased consequences. In the cooperative condition subjects were told they were competing as a group with other groups and that their scores would be combined into a common score. In this case, an increased number of others should be a source of decreased consequences. The results supported our line of reasoning. Within the cooperative condition increased group size facilitated word recall, while in the competitive condition increased group size decreased recall.

Similar findings were obtained using social distance as a variable instead of group size and a maze learning task (Table 5-1).

A third study that has dealt with reduced social consequences on complex tasks is that by Petty et al. (1980) on cognitive effort. They found that conditions of group responsibility reduced the impact of being exposed to an informational stimulus such as a film of a therapist or a persuasive communication. Those students who thought they were solely responsible for evaluating the stimulus discriminated more clearly the positive or negative features of the stimulus than did students who thought they were one of a group of individuals responsible for this task. This finding was interpreted as being due to diffusion of cognitive effort or loafing in the group responsibility condition.

This study has some interesting implications for a study of the effects of group size on task performance. To the extent that large groups reduce a feeling of accountability or responsibility, large groups may lead to a reduction in cognitive effort. Consequently, when one is exposed to information in groups (as in classrooms, conventions, meetings, etc.) one may be less attentive to it, process it less diligently, and consequently remember it more poorly, be less influenced by it, and evaluate it less accurately. This possibility has not been examined systematically, however. The Petty et al. (1980) study focused only on evaluative responses and did not obtain direct measures of task performance or information processing. If cognitive effort varies in response to group responsibility manipulations, measures of task performance or information processing should be affected. Also, they did not vary actual group size. Group size was the same in both the individual and group responsibility conditions. While the cognitive-motivational model can accommodate the effects of group responsibility manipulations as discussed earlier, actual group size variations are more likely to engage all of the various processes (arousal, effort, and task-irrelevant processes) discussed in our model.

Paulus, Noll, and Teng (Note 3) recently completed a study designed to address some of these issues. Employing the same paradigm as Petty et al. (1980), individuals in groups of 7 or 15 were asked to read an essay on instituting senior comprehensives. We also varied whether they were given a cooperative, competitive, or individualistic set. The cooperative set was similar to the group responsibility con-

Table 5-1. Task Performance as a Function of Group Set, Size and Proximity[a]

		Group Set	
		Cooperative	Competitive
Group Size[b]	2	8.06	10.56
	4	10.00	9.13
Proximity[c]	Close	34.67	38.03
	Far	39.85	34.67

[a] Adapted from Seta et al. (1976).
[b] Dependent measure is words recalled.
[c] Dependent measure is errors on maze task.

dition of the Petty et al. study while the individualistic set was the same as their individual responsibility conditions. The competitive set emphasized that the individual evaluations of the essay would be evaluated and discussed by the group afterwards. We employed the strong version of essay used by Petty et al. (1980). The main dependent measure of this study was free recall of the basic points of the essay. The recall measure simply involved the subject listing all of the arguments they could recall in favor of senior comprehensives.

The cognitive-motivational model's predictions are as follows. In the competitive condition, increased group size should lead to increased concern for negative social consequences and a resultant decrement in performance due to increased arousal and task-irrelevant processes. In the cooperative condition, increased group size should lead to facilitation of recall due to reduced concern for negative social consequences. Group size should not be a factor in the individualistic condition since it is not explicitly related to social consequences. The results obtained provided only partial support for these predictions (Table 5-2). The most important finding was that increased group size did facilitate task performance in the cooperative condition. This represents only the second demonstration of such a phenomenon in the literature. However, increased group size also facilitated performance in the individualistic condition. Possibly we did not effectively eliminate concern for potential negative social consequences in this condition and being in a nonevaluative group setting helped reduce the concern for such consequences (affiliation-related fear reduction). The failure to find an effect in group size in the competitive condition may lie in the offsetting effects of increased effort versus arousal and task-irrelevant processes.

Since this was the first study to assess the influence of task performance in this type of paradigm, any conclusions should be treated lightly. The results and the theoretical model do suggest that research in this area will need to delineate more precisely how various task characteristics are influenced by the arousal, effort, and task-irrelevant process components. Some types of tasks may be more sensitive to one component than the others. Certain procedural details such as the method of task presentation may also be important. For example, in this study subjects were given 10 minutes to write down as many arguments as they could remember from the essay. Use of different presentation and testing procedures might well influence the nature of the results. For example, time pressure is an important determinant of effort, with increased effort occurring under higher levels of pressure (Kahneman, 1973).

Table 5-2. Recall of Arguments About Senior Comprehensives as a Function of Group Set and Group Size

Group Size	Group Set		
	Cooperative	Individual	Competitive
Small	4.00	4.36	4.52
Large	5.26	5.20	4.63

Conclusions

In this chapter I have reviewed research and theories in a variety of areas concerned with the task performance of individuals in groups. Although each of these areas has somewhat unique concerns, they all offer important insights into the nature of task performance in groups. It is felt that progress in this area will be best served by developing a broader perspective that encompasses these various traditions. The cognitive-motivational model was proposed as one way to accomplish this goal. Much more precise and systematic research is required to evaluate its various components and to increase its predictive power. Such research will greatly enhance both our understanding of task performance in groups and our ability to make precise predictions about task performance in various real-life group settings.

Acknowledgments. The preparation of this chapter was facilitated by a Visiting Fellowship Award from the National Institute of Justice. The comments of Bill Ickes, Steve Harkins, Norbert Kerr, and John Seta on an earlier version of the chapter are greatly appreciated.

Reference Notes

1. Paulus, P. B., Matthews, R. B., & Chernick, L. *The effects of group size and anxiety on IQ scores*. Paper presented at the Midwestern Psychological Association Convention, St. Louis, 1980.
2. Kalb, L. S., & Keating, J. P. *The misattribution of nondensity induced arousal to perceived crowding*. Unpublished manuscript, University of Washington, 1981.
3. Paulus, P. B., Noll, V. L., & Teng, G. *The influence of group size and group set on an information-processing task*. Unpublished manuscript, University of Texas at Arlington, 1982.

References

Amoroso, D. M., & Walters, R. H. Effects of anxiety and socially mediated anxiety reduction on paired-associate learning. *Journal of Personality and Social Psychology*, 1969, *11*, 388-396.
Baron, R. S., Moore, D., & Sanders, G. S. Distraction as a source of drive in social facilitation research. *Journal of Personality and Social Psychology,* 1978, *36*, 816-824.
Baron, R. M., & Rodin, J. Personal control and crowding stress: Processes mediating the impact of spatial and social density. In A. Baum, J. Singer, & S. Valins (Eds.), *Advances in environmental psychology* (Vol. 1). Hillsdale, N.J.: Lawrence Erlbaum, 1978.
Baum, A., & Valins, S. *Architecture and social behavior: Psychological studies in social density*. Hillsdale, N.J.: Lawrence Erlbaum, 1977.
Berger, S. M., Hampton, K. L., Carli, L. L., Grandmaison, P. S., Sadow, J. S., Donath, C. H., & Herschlag, L. R. Audience-induced inhibition of overt practice

during learning. *Journal of Personality and Social Psychology*, 1981, *40*, 479-491.

Blank, T. O. Observer and incentive effects on word association responding. *Personality and Social Psychology Bulletin*, 1980, *6*, 267-272.

Bond, C. F. Social facilitation: A self-presentational view. *Journal of Personality and Social Psychology*, 1982, *42*, 1042-1050.

Borden, R. J. Audience influence. In P. B. Paulus (Ed.), *Psychology of group influence*. Hillsdale, N.J.: Lawrence Erlbaum, 1980.

Carver, C. S., & Scheier, M. F. The self-attention-induced feedback loop and social facilitation. *Journal of Experimental Social Psychology*, 1981, *17*, 545-568.

Child, J. L. Personality. *Annual Review of Psychology*, 1954, *5*, 149-170.

Cohen, S. Environmental load and the allocation of attention. In A. Baum, J. Singer, & S. Valins (Eds.), *Advances in environmental psychology*. Hillsdale, N.J.: Lawrence Erlbaum, 1978.

Cohen, S., Glass, D. C., & Phillips. S. Environment and health. In H. G. Freeman, S. Levine, & L. G. Reeder (Eds.), *Handbook of medical sociology*. Englewood Cliffs, N.J.: Prentice-Hall, 1979.

Cottrell, N. B. Social facilitation. In C. G. McClintock (Ed.), *Experimental social psychology*. New York: Holt, 1972.

Davis, J. H. *Group performance*. Reading, Mass.: Addison-Wesley, 1969.

Doctor, R. M., & Altman, F. Worry and emotionality as components of test anxiety, with replication and further data. *Psychological Reports*, 1969, *24*, 563-568.

Duval, S., & Wicklund, R. A. *A theory of objective self-awareness*. New York: Academic Press, 1972.

Easterbrook, J. A. The effect of emotion on cue utilization and the organization of behavior. *Psychological Review*, 1959, *66*, 183-201.

Eysenck, M. W. Anxiety, learning, and memory: A reconceptualization. *Journal of Research in Personality*, 1979, *13*, 363-385.

Geen, R. G. The effects of being observed on performance. In P. B. Paulus (Ed.), *Psychology of group influence*. Hillsdale, N.J.: Lawrence Erlbaum, 1980.

Geen, R. G. Evaluation apprehension and social facilitation: A reply to Sanders. *Journal of Experimental Social Psychology*, 1981, *17*, 252-256.

Geen, R. G., & Gange, J. J. Drive theory of social facilitation: Twelve years of theory and research. *Psychological Bulletin*, 1977, *84*, 1267-1288.

Gekoski, N. *The relationship of group characteristics to productivity*. Unpublished doctoral dissertation, Ohio State University, 1952.

Glass, D. C., & Singer, J. G. *Urban stress*. New York: Academic Press, 1972.

Gochman, I. R., & Keating, J. P. Misattributions to crowding: Blaming crowding for nondensity-caused events. *Journal of Nonverbal Behavior*, 1980, *4*, 157-175.

Hackman, J. R., & Morris, G. Group tasks, group interaction process, and group performance effectiveness: A review and proposed integration. In L. Berkowitz (Ed.), *Advances in experimental social psychology* (Vol. 8). New York: Academic Press, 1975.

Harkins, S., Latané, B., & Williams, K. Social loafing: Allocating effort or taking it easy? *Journal of Experimental Social Psychology,* 1980, *16*, 457-465.

Henchy, T., & Glass, D. C. Evaluation apprehension and the social facilitation of dominant and subordinate responses. *Journal of Personality and Social Psychology,* 1968, *10*, 446-454.

Hillery, J. M., & Fugita, S. S. Group size effects in employment testing. *Educational and Psychological Measurement,* 1975, *35*, 745-750.

Hoffman, L. R. Group problem solving. In Berkowitz (Ed.), *Advances in experimental social psychology* (Vol. 2). New York: Academic Press, 1965.

Ingham, A. G., Levinger, G., Graves, J., & Peckham, V. The Ringelmann effect: Studies of group size and group performance. *Journal of Experimental Social Psychology,* 1974, *10*, 371-384.

Kahneman, D. *Attention and effort.* Englewood Cliffs, N.J.: Prentice-Hall, 1973.

Kalb, L. S., & Keating, J. P. Nonspatial factors affecting crowding attributions in a dense field setting. In I. G. Sarason & C. D. Spielberger (Eds.), *Stress and anxiety* (Vol. 7). New York: Halsted Press, 1980.

Keating, J. P., & Latané, B. Politicians on TV: The image is the message. *Journal of Social Issues,* 1976, *32*, 116-132.

Kerr, N. L., & Bruun, S. E. Ringelmann revisited: Alternative explanations for the social loafing effect. *Personality and Social Psychology Bulletin,* 1981, *7*, 224-231.

Langer, E. J., & Saegert, S. Crowding and cognitive control. *Journal of Personality and Social Psychology,* 1977, *35*, 175-182.

Latané, B., & Nida, S. Social impact theory and group influence: A social engineering perspective. In P. B. Paulus (Ed.), *Psychology of group influence.* Hillsdale, N.J.: Lawrence Erlbaum, 1980.

Latané, B., Williams, K., & Harkins, S. Many hands make light the work: The consequences of social loafing. *Journal of Personality and Social Psychology,* 1979, *37*, 822-832.

Manstead, A. S. R., & Semin, G. R. Social facilitation effects: Mere enhancement of dominant responses? *British Journal of Social and Clinical Psychology,* 1980, *19*, 119-136.

Marriot, R. Size of working group and output. *Occupational Psychology,* 1949, *26*, 47-57.

Martens, R., & Landers, D. M. Evaluation potential as a determinant of coaction effects. *Journal of Experimental Social Psychology,* 1972, *8*, 347-359.

McGrath, J. E. Stress and behavior in organizations. In M. D. Dunnette (Ed.), *Handbook of industrial and organizational psychology.* Chicago: Rand McNally, 1976.

McKeachie, W. J. Class size, large classes, and multiple sections. *Academe,* February, 1980, 24-27.

Milgram, S. The experience of living in cities. *Science,* 1970, *167*, 1461-1468.

Miller, G. A., Galanter, E., & Pribram, K. H. *Plans and the structure of behavior.* New York: Holt, Rinehart & Winston, 1960.

Moede, W. Die Richtlinien der Leistungs-Psychologie. *Industrielle Psychotechnik,* 1927, *4*, 193-207.

Morris, L. W., & Liebert, R. M. Relationships of cognitive and emotional components of test anxiety to physiological arousal and academic performance. *Journal
of Consulting and Clinical Psychology,* 1970, *35*, 332-337.

Morris, L. W., & Liebert, R. M. Effects of negative feedback, threat of shock, and
level of trait anxiety on the arousal of two components of anxiety. *Journal of
Consulting Psychology,* 1973, *20*, 321-326.

Paulus, P. B. Crowding. In P. B. Paulus (Ed.), *Psychology of group influence.* Hillsdale, N.J: Lawrence Erlbaum, 1980.

Paulus, P. B., Annis, A. B., Seta, J. J., Schkade, J. K., & Matthews, R. W. Density
does affect task performance. *Journal of Personality and Social Psychology,*
1976, *34*, 248-253.

Paulus, P. B., & Matthews, R. W. Crowding, attribution, and task performance.
Basic and Applied Social Psychology, 1980, *1*, 3-13. (a)

Paulus, P. B., & Matthews, R. W. When density affects performance. *Personality and
Social Psychology Bulletin,* 1980, *6*, 119-124. (b)

Paulus, P. B., & Murdoch, P. Anticipated evaluation and audience presence in the
enhancement of dominant responses. *Journal of Experimental and Social Psychology,* 1971, *7*, 280-291.

Petty, R. E., Harkins, S. G., & Williams, K. D. The effects of group diffusion of cognitive effort on attitudes: An information-processing view. *Journal of Personality and Social Psychology,* 1980, *38*, 81-92.

Rodin, J., Solomon, S., & Metcalf, J. Role of control in mediating perceptions of
density. *Journal of Personality and Social Psychology,* 1978, *36*, 988-999.

Saegert, S. High density environments: Their personal and social consequences. In
A. Baum & Y. Epstein (Eds.), *Human responses to crowding.* Hillsdale, N.J.:
Lawrence Erlbaum, 1978.

Sanders, G. S. Driven by distraction: An integrative review of social facilitation
theory and research. *Journal of Experimental Social Psychology,* 1981, *17*,
227-251.

Sanders, G. S., & Baron, R. S. The motivating effects of distraction on task performance. *Journal of Personality and Social Psychology,* 1975, *32*, 956-963.

Sanders, G. S., Baron, R. S., & Moore, D. L. Distraction and social comparison as
mediators of social facilitation effect. *Journal of Experimental Social Psychology,* 1978, *14*, 291-303.

Sarason, I. G. Anxiety and self-preoccupation. In I. G. Sarason & C. D. Spielberger
(Eds.), *Stress and anxiety* (Vol. 2). London: Wiley, 1975.

Schachter, S. *The psychology of affiliation.* Stanford: Stanford University Press,
1959.

Schachter, S., & Singer, J. E. Cognitive, social, and physiological determinants of
emotional state. *Psychological Review,* 1962, *69*, 379-399.

Schaeffer, G. H., & Patterson, M. L. Intimacy, arousal, and small group crowding.
Journal of Personality and Social Psychology, 1980, *38*, 383-390.

Schkade, J. K. *The effects of expectancy set and crowding on task performance.*
Unpublished doctoral dissertation, University of Texas at Arlington, 1977.

Schmidt, D. E., & Keating, J. P. Human crowding and personal control: An integration of the research. *Psychological Bulletin,* 1979, *86*, 680-700.

Seligman, M. E. P. *Helplessness*. San Francisco: Freeman, 1975.

Seta, J. J. The impact of comparison processes on coactor's task performance. *Journal of Personality and Social Psychology*, 1982, *42*, 281-291.

Seta, J. J., Hassan, R. K. Awareness of prior success or failure: A critical factor in task performance. *Journal of Personality and Social Psychology*, 1980, *39*, 70-76.

Seta, J. J., Paulus, P. B., & Risner, H. T. The effects of group composition and evaluation on task performance. *Bulletin of Psychonomic Society*, 1977, *9*, 115-117.

Seta, J. J., Paulus, P. B., & Schkade, J. K. The effects of group size and proximity under competitive and cooperative conditions. *Journal of Personality and Social Psychology*, 1976, *34*, 47-53.

Sherrod, D. R. Crowding, perceived control, and behavioral aftereffects. *Journal of Applied Social Psychology*, 1974, *4*, 171-186.

Spence, K. W. *Behavior theory and conditioning*. New Haven: Yale University Press, 1956.

Steiner, I. Models for inferring relationships between group size and potential group productivity. *Behavioral Science*, 1966, *11*, 273-283.

Steiner, I. D. *Group process and productivity*. New York: Academic Press, 1972.

Thomas, E. J., & Fink, C. F. Effects of group size. *Psychological Bulletin*, 1963, *60*, 371-384.

Thompson, S. C. Will it hurt less if I can control it? A complex answer to a simple question. *Psychological Bulletin*, 1981, *90*, 89-101.

Trope, Y., & Brickman, P. Difficulty and diagnositicity as determinants of choice among tasks. *Journal of Personality and Social Psychology*, 1975, *31*, 918-925.

Waxenberg, F. *Effects of class size and density level on retention of lecture content in secondary school children*. Unpublished doctoral dissertation, Hofstra University, 1974.

Weiss, R. F., & Miller, F. G. The drive theory of social facilitation. *Psychological Review*, 1971, *78*, 44-57.

Wine, J. Test anxiety and direction of attention. *Psychological Bulletin*, 1971, *76*, 92-104.

Worchel, S., & Teddlie, C. The experience of crowding: A two-factor theory. *Journal of Personality and Social Psychology*, 1976, *34*, 30-40.

Worchel, S., & Yohai, S. M. L. The role of attribution in the experience of crowding. *Journal of Experimental Social Psychology*, 1979, *15*, 91-104.

Wrightsman, L. S. Effects of waiting with others on changes in felft level of anxiety. *Journal of Abnormal and Social Psychology*, 1960, *61*, 216-222.

Zajonc, R. B. Social facilitation. *Science*, 1965, *149*, 269-274.

Zajonc, R. B. Compresence. In P. B. Paulus (Ed.), *Psychology of group influence*. Hillsdale, N.J.: Lawrence Erlbaum, 1980.

Chapter 6

The Impact of Personal Equity Processes on Performance in a Group Setting

John J. Seta and Catherine E. Seta

The aim of this chapter is to use the knowledge gained from research on value to further our understanding of performance in a group setting. In doing so, we hope to suggest processes that underlie both the assignment of value and performance in groups. Toward this goal, we will first describe a theory which was proposed to account for the assignment of value (i.e., personal equity theory, Seta & Seta, 1982), and then we will try to apply this knowledge to performance in a group situation. We will discuss how this process may affect individuals' willingness to engage in performance and will highlight factors which may influence individuals' inability to perform well even though they may be willing to do so.

Since the study of performance in groups has had a long history in psychology, we will only discuss a subset of this literature. We are interested in task performance in group settings and the variables which influence this performance. Although other theories have emphasized a variety of variables such as drive arousal, dominant responses, distraction, and social comparison, theories thus far have not stressed the influence of the value of the task to the performer, the costs of performing the task, and the individual's resources for performing the task. These factors are important for a number of reasons. There are situations in which individuals are willing to perform well but do not have the resources. Or the individual may have the resources but not the willingness. Furthermore, the social context may affect the resources the individual can invest in the task or the willingness to perform the task. Unless one has a clear theoretical grasp of the influence of these variables, an explanation of performance in groups in a wide variety of settings will remain incomplete.

A relatively simple and inexpensive way to alter a task's value is to vary the number of people present while an individual is performing. This procedure varies the magnitude of potential consequences (e.g., praise, criticism) that can be derived from task performance. In the audience paradigm, researchers compare the performance level of subjects working in front of varying numbers of passive spectators. Alternatively, a coaction paradigm in which subjects work concurrently but independently on the same task is often used. In this paradigm, researchers can compare the performance level of the coactors or compare each coactor's performance to subjects working alone. Both of these paradigms are a part of the social facilitation literature (i.e., the study of how performance changes in group settings). We will discuss primarily audience and coaction paradigms with the understanding that our analysis should be generalizable across a number of different task performance contexts.

Our analysis has a direct application to classroom settings in which students must perform tasks in the presence of other individuals. Paulus (1980) has discussed his own very interesting research on this topic, and has also pointed out the similarities among a number of performance paradigms. As we will discuss later, social facilitation paradigms may involve anxiety-producing variables (e.g., negative outcome anticipation). Therefore, our analysis of the effects of anxiety may also bear upon issues concerning the relationship between anxiety and task performance. Furthermore, since an audience is a source of potential positive or negative consequences, our analysis should apply to those paradigms that make performance contingent on various tangible and intangible rewards and punishers. The research discussed in this chapter has generally defined performance rather narrowly. For example, we will discuss primarily performance on academically oriented tasks (e.g., list learning). Performance could, of course, be defined very broadly. An individual attempting to cope with a stressful situation at his or her office is involved in various tasks. Whether the individual is successful may depend upon the type of strategy that is used. We will attempt to address the issue of how consequences affect individuals' use of strategies. We will see that the strategies individuals use to organize information change in predictable ways when they are confronted with potential consequences of various magnitudes.

In sum, we feel that an understanding of how the presence of others can affect our behavior will benefit from an understanding of an individual processing system; we will consider conspecific presence as one type of input information into an intrapersonal comparator system. First, we will discuss the theory which described the operation of this system in the assignment of value (i.e., personal equity theory). Then we will use this theory to make some inferences about performance in a group setting.

Personal Equity Theory

Personal equity (Seta & Seta, 1982) is a consistency theory utilizing an economic view of man. The primary assumption of this approach is that an intrapersonal comparator process is instrumental in determining the value of rewards or goal objects. One type of information inherent in this process is a reward criterion which is an individual's expectation of what *should* be received (versus what will be received) given his or her investment or cost.

Typically, when a moderate rather than a minimal level of cost has been expended, individuals believe that they should receive a higher-valued outcome. Probably this criterion is not a formal or explicit expectation, given an exact amount of cost expenditure, but is a general expectation of the value warranted by a *range* of cost incurrence. Therefore, greater amounts of cost would be required to violate the general range of cost associated with high-valued objects than would be necessary to violate the range associated with objects of lower values.

Once the range of cost associated with a reward is violated, reward value might be expected to increase. When an intrapersonal comparison of the input information indicates that cost has been incurred over the range normally required to obtain a certain object, then the expectation is that the individual should receive an outcome value greater than the initial value of the object. In order to maintain personal equity, the value of the reward object would be raised to meet the individual's expectation of value that he or she should receive.

Another type of input information central to this comparator system that explains reward value decrements is the ceiling value of a goal object. It is derived from the reasonable assumption that any given object has an upper limit to its attractiveness. There should not be an infinite number of incremental value possibilities for all objects. Thus, a ceiling value most probably exists that would limit these increments and allow the highest possible value of an object to be expressed in finite terms. Therefore, once increments in the value of an object have pushed that object's value to its ceiling level, equity cannot be maintained by further increases in the attractiveness of that object. At this point, a process akin to perceptual contrast as discussed by Helson, 1964 may occur. The excessive amount of cost expenditure would lead an individual to expect that he or she should obtain a higher-valued outcome than possible given the ceiling value of the reward. This criterion could become the contextual background within which the figure (i.e., reward) is perceived. This comparison may result in perceptual contrast, since the reward that is obtained cannot meet the individual's criterion for an equitable reward. Relative to what *should* be obtained, the actual reward may appear less attractive than its ceiling value. As the criterion of what should be received increases, the magnitude of inequity should increase, thereby producing a corresponding decrement in the attractiveness of the reward.

In sum, an intrapersonal comparator system in which an object's ceiling value is compared to one's criterion of value was hypothesized to be operative within costly environments. A nonlinear relationship between effort/cost and the value of a goal is expected, given this comparison system analysis. Thus, as long as the reward's ceiling value has not been reached, individuals can match their perceptions of reward value through discovery of positive object properties, with their reward criterion. But once an individual's criterion of reward value surpasses the ceiling value of the goal object, a decrement in the value of the goal object is expected since a perceptual contrast phenomenon should occur.

Several experiments (Seta & Seta, 1982) have found results which support this analysis. Moderate amounts of cost or effort expenditure enhanced reward value whereas extreme amounts produced reward devaluation; reward value was seen to be a nonlinear function of cost. That is, as the number of cost or effort trials performed in pursuit of a reward was increased, the value of the reward showed an initial increment followed by an eventual decrease.

The initial value of the reward and the context in which cost was incurred were seen to be critical variables for predicting the rate at which cost or effort manipulations influenced the perceived value of the reward (i.e., the shape of the nonlinear function). Reward enhancement occurred sooner in contexts in which cost was very salient than in contexts in which cost was not very salient. Reward devaluation also occurred sooner in this cost-salient context. In two additional studies it was also found that fewer failure and effort trials were necessary to enhance the value of an initially low-valued reward than were necessary to enhance the value of an initially high-valued reward. Reward devaluation also occurred in fewer effort and cost trials when the reward was initially low valued. These results conform to predictions derived from personal equity theory and support its basic assumptions. Namely, individuals are sensitive to ranges of cost and/or effort expenditure and violations in these ranges lead to reward or outcome enhancements and devaluations.

This analysis seems to offer a viable alternative to the more traditional approaches to attraction and attitude change (e.g., dissonance theory, reactance, and self-perception). We are now doing research which seems to be successful in applying this approach to issues within the intrinsic motivation literature (e.g., Deci, 1975; Lepper, Greene, & Nisbett, 1973). The flexibility of the model is due to its reliance upon processes which operate within a general comparator system. Input information of many types, including incentives, can feed into this system and affect the value of stimuli.

Task Performance: Willingness and Capability

Before we can apply the information we have gained from our research on value, we must first consider some of the differences between value and instrumental value. In paradigms testing value, individuals are usually given an incentive (e.g., Deci, 1975) or required to incur cost for a valued stimulus (e.g., Aronson & Mills, 1959). Subsequent to the treatment, value is inferred either verbally (asking subjects to rate the stimulus) or by observing subjects' preferences in a free-choice setting. In a free-choice setting, an individual can interact with any number of activities, and there are no apparent immediate consequences contingent upon any of the activities. The more an activity is engaged in, the more valuable it is assumed to be. Performing a task in front of other conspecifics is quite different. There are immediate external consequences contingent upon a subject's activities. An audience will usually express approval of a quality performance but will often express disapproval of a poor performance. A subject is faced with a situation in which he or she must perform an activity at some given level (i.e., a criterion) in order to gain audience approval or avoid audience disapproval. Therefore, even if an activity per se would not be of value in a free-choice setting, an individual might vigorously engage in the activity in an audience setting. The activity may acquire instrumental value via its utility in procuring positive outcomes (e.g., audience approval) and/or avoiding negative outcomes.

Differences of these types highlight the fact that the knowledge gained from the research on value measured verbally or in a free-choice setting cannot be *directly* applied to performance in a group setting. Some modifications must be made.

In our discussion of performance we will make a distinction between the instrumental value of a task (i.e., its utility in procuring positive outcomes and/or avoiding negative outcomes) and the value of a task in an environment in which no apparent immediate external consequences are contingent upon its performance. The need for this distinction becomes clear if one considers situations in which an individual devotes a great deal of effort in performing a rather dull task, such as memorizing paired associates, in the presence of an evaluative audience, but would not do so in the absence of contingent stimuli or in a free-play environment. In a situation in which individuals' performance is being evaluated by external agents, the value of the task cannot be considered to be independent or separate from these consequences. We are assuming that a task's instrumental value is determined by the magnitude of the consequences to be derived from its performance. As mentioned earlier, its value is in its utility in procuring positive outcomes and/or in its utility for the avoidance of negative outcomes. Increases in the magnitude of these positive and/or negative outcomes are assumed to increase the instrumental value of a task. As the instrumental value of the task increases, individuals should be increasingly willing to allocate their resources in its performance.

As discussed earlier, personal equity theory assumes that there is a range of cost or resources which is commensurate with value; this range should exist for any value term including instrumental task value. In this context, this range is essentially information about how much cost or effort expenditure should be devoted to the instrumental task. As the instrumental value of the task increases, the range should indicate that more effort or resources should be expended in the task's performance. Since the performance of most tasks is improved by devoting more resources to the task, changes in performance levels can result from changes in instrumental task value.

Therefore, this analysis seems to provide a framework for understanding why increases in the saliency, number, or status level of audience members often increases individuals' performance. These audience variables are assumed to increase the instrumental value of tasks. This increase in instrumental value provides input information to an intrapersonal comparator system which analyzes resource-value relationships. The input information that value has increased provides impetus for personal equity maintenance, that is, the increase in value indicates that equity can be maintained by increasing resource output.

The previous discussion concentrates upon situations in which audience size is changing and all other aspects of the context, including expectations and the demands of the task, are held constant. Now we will discuss situations in which audience size and expectations are held constant and the demands of a task are increased. That is, what happens in an audience setting when individuals are asked to perform tasks which demand different amounts of cognitive or physical effort? An analysis of the amount of cost involved in performing a task in front of an audience would be necessary to an understanding of this situation.

Researchers interested in performance typically utilize cognitively demanding tasks such as anagrams, list learning, and paired associates. Therefore, in order to understand how much cost is generated in a task setting, one must take into consideration both task demands and the amount of capacity available for task performance.

For a number of years the concept of man as a limited-capacity organism has been used as a heuristic concept within both social and cognitive psychology (Cohen, 1981; Miller, 1956; Norman, 1968). Capacity refers to the available processing resources an individual can allocate to any given task. The recognition that man possesses only a limited amount of cognitive capacity has led to increased interest in semantic organizational strategies (e.g., Tulving, 1962) and in cognitive resource allocation (e.g., Shiffrin, 1975; Triesman, 1969; Triesman & Davies, 1973). Scant research, however, has been done on this topic within the area of social facilitation (Carver & Scheier, 1981, are a notable exception to this generalization).

The proposed analysis will utilize two different capacity components: (a) the amount of capacity demanded by tasks (see Norman and Bobrow, 1975) and (b) the amount of capacity available for processing or performance at any given time. These components combine to produce a cost component. The ratio of task demanded resources to available resources expresses the relationship between the two that defines an inherent cost of task performance. As this ratio becomes larger, while remaining less than one, the amount of cost in a setting is increasing. This reflects either an increment in task-demanded resources or a decrement in available resources (or both). The cost of performing a task is relative to the amount of available resources the individual possesses. Two people, for example, may pay the same amount of money for any object but they may have expended different amounts of cost or resources for its attainment. One person might be a millionaire, the other a pauper. It is clear that the pauper has expended more of his or her resources (money) in obtaining the object than the millionaire has, since the pauper has fewer monetary resources available. Similarly, two individuals may not possess equal amounts of resources at any given time. Therefore, task performance may be more costly to one individual than another given that he or she has fewer resources or less processing capacity available in this setting and is therefore allocating a greater percentage of his or her resources in order to perform. If the ratio becomes greater than one, the individual would be unable to perform because he or she lacks the necessary resources. That is, the task would demand more resources than the individual has available. For example, a student may desire an A on an important exam but in this stressful setting may not be capable of recalling the necessary information to do well. This cost ratio relationship should then serve as input information to an intrapersonal comparator system. If the amount of cost which would be incurred by performing is commensurate with the value of the outcome (e.g., the importance of a successful performance), then individuals should be willing to perform. If the amount of cost is too great, then individuals should be unwilling to perform and should allocate little or no resources to the task. For example, an athlete may be willing to expend all of his or her energy while performing in the Olympic trials but may not be willing to do so in a minor regional meet.[1]

---

[1] It may be the case that if task demands are held constant the instrumental value of the task will increase with increments in audience size. That is, since instrumental

Another implication of this analysis is that people would generally be willing to adhere to a more stringent performance criterion in front of a large rather than a small audience. It also implies that in the absence of explicit criterion (e.g., clear social norms or instructions) people would generally be willing to allocate greater resources in front of large rather than small audiences, since the outcome value associated with a large audience is usually higher than that of a small audience. Since the performance of complex tasks may be assumed to require a greater amount of cognitive resources than the performance of simple tasks, higher-valued outcomes may be necessary to produce optimal performance for complex than for simple tasks.[2] As will be discussed later in the distraction-conflict section, individuals may be willing to allocate the resources necessary for optimal task performance, but may not have these resources available. This lack of resources may produce performance debilitation. It seems that anxiety is augmented when expectations of not meeting criteria increase (Geen, 1979) and as the negative consequences associated with failure increase (Seta & Hassan, 1980).[3] Since anxiety depletes capacity and since we are limited-capacity organisms, increases in anxiety will eventually reduce the overall capacity one has available to allocate to a given task. This reduction in capacity has been shown to result in performance decrements (e.g., Kahneman, 1973; Mueller, 1978). Therefore, if subjects expecting failure are generally more anxious than those expecting success, it should take a smaller or less-evaluative audience to violate the capacity limits of subjects expecting failure than for those expecting success. Individuals expecting failure may become incapable of performing sooner than individuals expecting success. Therefore, individuals may be willing but incapable of performing well in some evaluative settings.

In sum, we have proposed that people are willing to incur cost or allocate more resources in evaluative or group settings for a high- than for a low-valued outcome. We have also pointed out that this increased willingness may manifest itself in improved or optimal task performance. Individuals, however, are not always able to

---

value is not an entity independent of the consequences that produce it, it may have no ceiling. It is solely determined by the potential consequences associated with the presence of evaluative others. Instrumental value may, however, asymptote if one's perception of costs and rewards follow a negatively accelerating function (e.g., Stevens, 1957, 1975).

On the other hand, since task value is not entirely set by immediate consequences, it can have a ceiling. Therefore, if one concentrates on task value per se rather than instrumental value, increases in audience size can result in task decrements and a corresponding decrement in willingness. This may occur because the rewards and costs may indicate that the task should have a value that cannot be met.

[2] If an explicit criterion (the quality or quantity of performance that is necessary to obtain a goal) is made salient to individuals in the situation, then an individual should simply attempt to meet or surpass this level rather than that which is produced by the outcome value. In an audience setting the audience composition can alter the criterion (Seta & Hassan, 1980).

[3] When subjects have a very low expectation of success, the instrumental value of the task would also be low.

allocate the necessary resources or are not always willing to allocate the necessary resources for success. This can occur because the individual does not have the resources available for allocation or because the resources to be spent would not result in a personally equitable outcome.

Social Facilitation: Audience and Coaction Paradigms

We will first provide an overview of the social facilitation literature. Then, we will apply our analysis to this literature.

Pioneering research on this topic indicated that performance was facilitated by the presence of others (see Dashiell, 1935). This effect was called social facilitation. It soon became apparent, however, that performance could be debilitated by the presence of others. On some "simple" motor tasks, performance was improved but on other more complex tasks, performance was impaired by the presence of others.

In 1965, Zajonc integrated the vast majority of social facilitation results into a Hullian analysis (Hull, 1952).[4] Briefly, he proposed that the mere presence of a conspecific was sufficient to increase generalized drive and the increments in drive increase the tendency to emit dominant responses. If the dominant response is correct, increases in drive presumably increase task performance. If, however, the dominant response is incorrect, performance debilitation occurs. Zajonc later clarified the meaning of his mere presence concept (Zajonc, 1980). He argued that the physical presence of others was always a source of drive induction because a conspecific's presence was associated with uncertainty. As noted by Sanders, "the most salient aspect of this hypothesis is that the simple physical presence of others should always increase drive, given that one never knows, for sure, what to expect from them" (1981, p. 230).

Cottrell (1972), following Zajonc, also used a Hullian analysis to make predictions about how behavior would change as a function of changes in drive. But Cottrell modified Zajonc's position by arguing that mere presence was *not* sufficient to provide increases in drive. Rather, a conspecific was a source of drive induction if and only if the presence of that conspecific was associated with positive or negative outcomes. It was the anticipation of positive or negative outcomes that was responsible for drive induction—conspecifics were a learned source of drive induction.

A number of controversies have arisen over the work of Zajonc and Cottrell. First, investigators have attempted to distinguish Zajonc's mere presence position from Cottrell's learned drive position (e.g., Henchy & Glass, 1968; Paulus & Murdoch, 1971; Rajecki, Ickes, Corcoran, & Lenerz, 1977). Researchers investigating this issue have generally argued that according to a learned drive position, the per-

---

[4] Zajonc and the learned drive theorists have stressed the notion of generalized drive at the expense of directive cues. Hull (1952), however, seemed to accept the notion that directive cues were part of the drive stimulus. Drive theory itself has undergone a number of changes since its inception. It is important to note that we are using the version of Hull's analysis adopted by Zajonc and other learned drive theorists within social psychology.

formance of a subject working alone should be equivalent to that of a subject working in front of a nonevaluative conspecific. This is because a nonevaluative conspecific is one who is not associated with anticipations of positive or negative outcomes. A number of studies have found results that presumably support a learned drive position (e.g., Henchy & Glass, 1968; Paulus & Murdoch, 1971; Sasfy & Okun, 1974).

Other studies have not supported a learned drive approach (e.g., Markus, 1978; Rajecki et al., 1977; Rittle & Bernard, 1977). These studies have found that even though a spectator could not evaluate a subject's performance, the performance level of these subjects differed from that of those working alone. Results such as these have been interpreted as support for a "mere presence" explanation. The spectators' presence was itself sufficient to alter a subject's drive level.

Unfortunately, these results do not offer clear support for a mere presence position. The fact that a nonevaluative spectator is observing a subject's performance in a given experimental context does *not* necessarily imply that the spectator's "mere presence" is responsible for alterations in the subject's drive level. The spectator may resemble a conspecific who has evaluated the subject in the past. One could easily argue from a learned drive position that it is this prior association that is responsible for the proposed mere presence effect. More importantly, it is not sufficient to argue that mere presence occurs when other effects (e.g., learned drive) are presumably not occurring. It is difficult, if not impossible, for a researcher to eliminate all "other" effects. And even if this elimination procedure is successful, what is left may or may not be mere presence defined as uncertainty. To be a viable concept, mere presence advocates need to identify variables that alter its occurrence. They need to tell us what aspects of a conspecific must be present for their predicted results to occur.

Even though Zajonc (1980) uses the concept of uncertainty to define mere presence, others like Rescorla and Wagner (1972) have used uncertainty to discuss the effects biologically important events have on performance. One interpretation of this work is that if a conditioned stimulus (CS) has been randomly associated with an unconditioned stimulus (US) the organism can learn to become uncertain about the consequences of the CS-US pairing. One could learn, in this fashion, to become uncertain in the presence of a conspecific. The conspecific may be the CS that has been randomly associated with a US. The conspecific can either be directly or indirectly associated with the US. Therefore, counter to Zajonc's conceptualization, one can envision uncertainty developing via the random pairings of conspecifics with motivationally laden events.

Alternatively, the presence of others can be considered an unconditioned stimulus. Sanders (1981) has suggested that the presence of a conspecific might be a US for an alertness reflex. To improve the testability of a mere presence concept, he has suggested that

> If such a reflex exists, in the Pavlovian sense, then it should be possible to discover an unconditioned stimulus, other than the presence of others capable of eliciting its occurrence: or it should be possible to elicit its occurrence via classical conditioning in which a neutral stimulus is repeatedly paired with the US of the presence of others. (1981, pp. 230-231)

The exploration of these possibilities would certainly help improve the testability of a mere presence concept. However, even if the above possibilities were confirmed, they would not rule out a learned drive position. Conditioning of the sort just described might easily be interpreted as an example of higher-order conditioning. That is, the presence of others may not be a US but rather a CS which has gained its evocative properties by association with other motivationally laden events.

At present, we can see that there is no definite resolution to the learned drive versus mere presence controversy. The experimental evidence supporting either learned drive or mere presence is subject to reinterpretation by the opposing approach. Even so, it is clear that the presence of others can have dramatic effects upon performance.

An additional controversy exists within the social facilitation literature. This controversy concerns the impact of positive and negative consequences on performance. The theorists engaged in this controversy have generally cast their analyses within a learned drive framework. Weiss and Miller (1971) have proposed an evaluation apprehension notion of social facilitation whereby conspecifics are a source of increased drive if they serve as stimuli for the anticipation of negatively evaluated outcomes. This evaluation apprehension viewpoint differs from that proposed by Cottrell (1968, 1972) and that of Good (1973). For Cottrell, conspecifics are a source of increased drive if they serve as stimuli for the anticipation of both positive and negative evaluations. For Good, variations in the degree of evaluation apprehension can alter drive and performance only when subjects anticipate a positive outcome.

Researchers testing these three evaluation apprehension notions have reached conflicting conclusions about the impact of positive and negative expectations. An increase in the number of spectators has been shown to be more likely to produce a decrement in performance (e.g., memory tasks) for subjects anticipating a negative outcome than for subjects anticipating a positive outcome (e.g., Geen, 1979, Experiment 1; Seta & Hassan, 1980). It has also been shown that on a simple motor task, performance increments can be obtained when subjects anticipate a negative outcome (e.g., Seta, 1982). All of the findings are consistent with Weiss and Miller's approach.

However, researchers have also found that performance increments can be obtained when subjects anticipate a positive outcome (Geen, 1979, Experiment 2; Good, 1973). Even though Weiss and Miller's approach has been shown to provide a theoretical explanation of Good's (1973) discrepant finding (see Seta & Hassan, 1980), it does not account for Geen's (1979, Experiment 2) results. Geen offered a two-factor analysis of his results. He suggested that the evaluation apprehension generated by a prior failure experience was responsible for the poor performance of subjects within the failure feedback condition. He also suggested that subjects given prior success needed to maintain a favorable impression for the experimenter and that this factor motivated their elevated performance level. Thus, Geen suggests that both evaluation apprehension and self-presentational processes are operative within the social facilitation paradigm. Even though Geen's analysis adequately accounts for the results of several experiments, it is not clear how it accounts for the results of several experiments which have not found differences in the performance of audience and "alone" subjects who have positive expectations of success (e.g., Geen, 1979, Experiment 1; Seta & Hassan, 1980).

To understand how the discrepant results of Geen and Seta and Hassan might be resolved we must first analyze the procedures of the two experiments. In Seta and Hassan's experiment, subjects performed either alone or in front of an audience of five, whereas in Geen's experiment, they performed alone or in the presence of one experimenter. It is possible that the audience of five (one older male and four unspecified individuals) used by Seta and Hassan was more evaluative than that used by Geen (one female experimenter). In addition, the alone condition used in Geen's experiment would seem to be less evaluative than that used in Seta and Hassan's experiment. In Geen's experiment subjects were told that any evaluation would be delayed whereas in Seta and Hassan's experiment subjects were not told that their evaluation would be delayed. Thus, it would seem that the procedures of Geen's and Seta and Hassan's experiments may have produced differing magnitudes of evaluation regardless of the type of feedback given to the subject.

In Geen's experiment, subjects may have experienced either a low (alone condition) or moderate (audience condition) level of evaluation apprehension. In Seta and Hassan's study, subjects may have experienced a moderate level of evaluation apprehension in the alone condition; subjects knew they would receive feedback from a male experimenter. A high level of evaluation apprehension may have been produced by Seta and Hassan's audience condition since subjects knew that they were observed by the evaluative male experimenter and four other individuals. If it is reasonable to draw inferences about the magnitude of evaluation apprehension from a comparison of these two studies, one might conclude that performance depends upon the interaction between subjects' expectation of success and the level of potential evaluation. For subjects expecting favorable outcomes, performance seemed to be facilitated by an increase from a low to a moderate level of evaluation (as suggested by Geen's results) whereas an increase from a moderate to a high level of evaluation did not seem to effect a change in performance (as suggested by Seta and Hassan's results). For subjects expecting an unfavorable outcome, increasing the level of potential evaluation seems to have a generally debilitating effect upon performance. The performance of moderate-evaluation subjects was inferior to that of low-evaluation subjects (Geen) and the performance of high-evaluation subjects was inferior to that of moderate-evaluation subjects (Seta & Hassan).

Thus, it would seem that performance in a social setting may be described by an interaction between expectations and level of potential evaluation. From the combined results of Geen (1979) and Seta and Hassan (1980) it appears as if initial increments in evaluation are more likely to produce increments in the performance level of subjects expecting success than those expecting failure. However, Seta (1982) found an increment in subjects' simple task performance in a negative expectation condition. Therefore, initial increments in evaluation have been shown to facilitate performance in both positive and negative expectation conditions. This is understandable since conspecifics' presence can increase the instrumental value of a task either because subjects are attempting to avoid negative outcomes and/or obtain positive outcomes. As Neal Miller (1944, 1959) has shown, however, approach/avoidance gradients are not mirror images of each other. The avoidance gradient is generally steeper than the approach gradient. Although this function has been shown to vary across contexts (Hearst, 1969), it is clear that approach and avoidance gradients are not always equivalent. Therefore, different performance levels may be expected depending upon whether instrumental value is determined by failure avoidance or success approach.

The second conclusion we may reach from the combined results of Geen (1979) and Seta and Hassan (1980) is that smaller increments in audience size are needed to produce performance decrements for subjects expecting failure than for subjects expecting success. These inferred results would be consistent with the analysis we have proposed. The anxiety generated by expecting failure in front of a large audience should be greater than that generated in front of a smaller audience. Therefore, the capacity available for task performance may be reduced more in the presence of a large audience than in the presence of a smaller audience.[5]

A number of studies have been conducted in our laboratory which lend credibility to this analysis (Seta, Seta, & Crisson, Note 1). In one experiment, a group of subjects was told that the task they would be working on was important (high outcome value) whereas a second group of subjects was told that the same task was relatively unimportant (low outcome value). Subjects worked alone or in front of an audience. In the alone condition, the performance of high-outcome-value subjects was significantly better than that of low-outcome-value subjects. This finding is consistent with our analysis. The amount of resources one is willing to allocate to a task should increase as the value of the outcome associated with that task increases, and this willingness may manifest itself in improved performance. Therefore, under low or moderate evaluative settings, the performance of subjects working on a high-value task is likely to be superior to that of those on a low-value task.

Opposite, though theoretically consistent results, were found within the audience condition. The performance of subjects working on a valuable task was inferior to that of those working on the low-outcome value task. The potential cost associated with failure should be greater for the important task than for the less-important task; and since this cost may eventually result in an anxiety-induced capacity overload, impaired performance should occur sooner for subjects working on an important than a relatively unimportant task.

In a second experiment, we varied three evaluation arrangements (low-alone, moderate-audience of one, and high-audience of five) and two expectation-of-success levels (high and low). The recall performance of subjects in the moderate evaluation condition was superior to that of those in the low evaluation condition (significant

---

[5] An inverted-U relationship between performance and arousal was first posited by Yerkes and Dodson (1908) and empirically suggested within an audience setting by Geen (1979). Yerkes and Dodson suggested that the inflection point of this function would occur sooner for simple than for the complex tasks. Results of this sort are consistent with our analysis and we are trying to provide an explanation for them.

for high expectation subjects only). This finding is also consistent with our analysis. Since the outcomes associated with doing well or with avoiding a poor performance are greater the larger the audience or the more evaluative the situation, performance facilitation is likely to be observed when comparing the performance of subjects in the moderate evaluation condition to that of subjects in the low evaluation condition.

The performance of high and moderate evaluation subjects did not differ when subjects expected success. For failure-oriented subjects, however, the performance in the high evaluation condition was inferior to that of both moderate and low evaluation conditions. These results are also consistent with our analysis. Failure-oriented subjects, due to their anxiety, should become overloaded more quickly than success-oriented subjects and this overload should demonstrate itself in impaired performance. These results indicate that evaluation affects the performance of subjects who primarily expect either success or failure. Evaluation, however, does not affect the performance of success- and failure-oriented subjects equivalently.

We have been assuming that the poor performance of failure-oriented subjects in the high evaluation condition was due to subjects' inability to perform well. One could argue, however, that their performance was due to decreased "trying." Subjects may have anticipated that a great deal of cost was associated with failure in the high evaluation condition and may not have been willing to allocate the necessary resources required for a good performance. Our third experiment was designed to determine if subjects' performance could decrease because of an inability to perform rather than because of an unwillingness to perform.

Experiment 3 was similar to Experiment 2. The major difference was the task used. In Experiment 2 we used a recall task whereas in Experiment 3 we used a speed-accuracy task and told subjects that speed and accuracy were both important evaluative criteria. If the accuracy, but not the speed, of failure-oriented subjects is inferior in front of a large audience relative to a small audience, then it would be reasonable to infer that failure-oriented subjects can be willing but incapable of performing well in front of large audiences. Further, if subjects are willing to perform well but incapable because of anxiety, we should notice less of a drop in the accuracy of success-oriented subjects than failure-oriented subjects. That is, it should take a larger or more evaluative audience to violate the capacity limits of success-oriented subjects than of failure-oriented subjects. Anxiety is augmented when expectations of not meeting criteria increase and as the negative consequences associated with failure increase. Since anxiety depletes capacity and since we are limited-capacity organisms, increases in anxiety will eventually reduce the overall capacity that one has available to allocate to a given task. Therefore, if subjects suspecting failure are generally more anxious than those suspecting success, a larger or more evaluative audience would be needed to violate the capacity limits of success- rather than failure-oriented subjects.

The results of the experiment indicated that subjects' speed was higher in an audience of five condition than in an alone condition. In addition, we found that when subjects expected success, their percent accuracy scores did not drop across audience conditions. When they expected failure, however, subjects' percent accuracy scores were lower in the audience than in the alone condition. These results are conceptually similar to those obtained in Experiment 2 and suggest that performance decrements can occur because subjects are incapable rather than unwilling to invest the resources necessary for optimal performance.

The results of these experiments indicate that performance is affected by evaluation in the form of the size or evaluative nature of the audience, and by subjects' expectations of success. In addition, the results indicate that (a) performance can improve as the instrumental or outcome value of the task increases, and (b) with further increases in outcome value performance decrements can occur, not because subjects are unwilling to perform well, but because they are incapable of performing well.

In sum, the results of the experiments discussed in this chapter and the results of Geen (1979) and Seta and Hassan (1980) suggest that performance increments are possible for individuals expecting either positive or negative outcomes. The non-equivalency of these effects was emphasized and discussed within a resource allocation analysis. In addition, it was observed that performance decrements were never observed for success-oriented subjects. These findings were taken as support for a model using the concept of anxiety-induced capacity overload as one potential explanation for performance decrements. In addition, these findings and those of Berger, Carli, Hammersla, Karshmer, and Sanchez (1979), and Bond (1982), as well as those of Manstead and Semin (1980), indicate the incomplete nature of Zajonc's drive analysis and the need to develop an approach that encompasses more than generalized drive and habit.

Processing Strategies

From drive theory (Hull, 1952), it has been argued that increments in drive increase the probability of a dominant response. In this section we will discuss how our analysis accounts for variations in the probability of a dominant response and how it accounts for changes in strategies used in task performance.

The proposed model rests upon the assumption that a limited amount of processing capacity is available for allocation to performance. Factors such as audience size and negative expectations can reduce the amount of processing capacity available for task performance by producing anxiety (e.g., Kahneman, 1973). If the anxiety produced by these factors is sufficient to reduce available capacity below an amount which is necessary in order to perform well, performance decrements on a resource-limited task are expected. The prediction of performance decrements is based upon Norman and Bobrow's (1975) distinction between data-limited and resource-limited tasks. Data-limited tasks are activities in which performance is limited by the quality of the sensory input (e.g., understanding the relationships portrayed in a double-exposure photograph); increments in processing resources do not affect the performance of these tasks. Resource-limited tasks are dependent upon the availability of adequate processing resources for their successful completion. For example, performance of a resource-limited task (e.g., anagram solving) can be improved by increasing the amount of processing devoted to the activity. Therefore, anxiety-induced limitations in available processing capacity can have damaging effects upon the performance of a resource-limited task.

However, it is important to note that performance decrements can be avoided if the available processing space can be used in an effective though less resource-demanding fashion. For example, organizational processing may require a great deal of processing space since the to-be-remembered items must be related to each other along some conceptual dimension in working memory. This type of elaborative rehearsal requires the transfer of categorical information from a semantic knowledge base into some sort of working space, as well as the maintenance of the to-be-related items within this space. The to-be-related items, as well as the semantic information necessary to form a conceptual relationship, must be present in the processing system simultaneously in order for one to be able to recognize the similarities along the items. Although organizational strategies are effective in producing good memory performance, other types of processing strategies can also produce good memory performance. For example, a processing strategy which entails the semantic elaboration of an individual item within a list may take up less processing space and still be an effective memory strategy. This type of strategy would require the elaboration of each individual item of information rather than necessitating the maintenance of other list items within working memory; thus, this type of processing strategy would make less of a demand upon available processing resources than an organizational processing strategy. Although research has shown that both organizational and individual item processing is necessary for optimal performance (e.g., Einstein & Hunt, 1980; Hunt & Einstein, 1981), either strategy may produce a sufficiently durable memory trace to adequately fulfill immediate recall task demands.

Mueller (1976) has shown that anxiety influences organizational strategies in a manner which would be expected given the above analysis. Subjects scoring high on a test-anxiety scale clustered less than those scoring low in test anxiety. However, there was no significant difference in the total recall scores of the two groups. Mueller (1976) interprets his results as indicating that anxious subjects initially utilize a small part of the available stimulus attributes during encoding. This analysis is consistent with that proposed in this paper. We would add the comment that subjects were unable to utilize these stimulus attributes because they were unable to maintain the items in working memory long enough to notice the similarities among the items along the relevant dimension.

We have recently completed an experiment which supports the hypothesis that increases in audience size can lead to increased anxiety levels which interfere with subjects' capacity to organize information. Subjects were asked to categorize a related word list into six relevant categories (i.e., an organizational orienting task) while performing either alone or in front of an audience of one or five. We found that although the total number of words recalled remain constant across conditions, subjects' ability to organize information differed when comparing the alone and the audience-of-five condition ($p < .06$, ARC scores, Roenker, Thompson, & Brown, 1971). That is, we found a similar pattern of data when we varied audience size as found by Mueller for high and low test-anxious subjects. This provides some evidence that increases in audience size may create anxiety which interferes with individuals' ability to organize information. A decrement in recall performance may not have been found because subjects engaged in less resource-demanding strategies that maintained a somewhat durable memory trace.

Of course, quality of memory performance is also greatly dependent upon the nature of the memory test (e.g., Morris, Bransford, & Franks, 1977; Stein, 1978; Tulving & Thompson, 1973). For example, the test used in the study just described was a free recall test in which subjects could output information in any order they chose with the restriction that they wrote the recall items in a column so that clustering measures could be taken. Our other recall studies required subjects to generate the category label presented at input and to list the recall items under their appropriate category headings. This type of test places greater demands upon organizational variables since subjects are required to duplicate the organizational structure of the input information. Thus, performance was seen to deteriorate in the presence of an audience under testing conditions which required information organization. Under conditions in which organization was relatively less important (e.g., the free recall test used in the study described earlier in this section), performance decrements as measured by overall recall were not observed.

Many times researchers have not obtained performance differences across audience conditions and have concluded that the task used was not "stress sensitive." The previous discussion suggests that a task might not appear to be stress sensitive, but if a more detailed analysis of the data is undertaken (e.g., clustering measures) one might conclude that the task was sensitive. Perhaps a more reasonable distinction to make between stress sensitive and stress insensitive would be that which could be derived from Norman and Bobrow (1975). Data-limited tasks are assumed to be insensitive to available resources whereas resource-limited tasks are assumed to be sensitive to changes in capacity. This would allow an a priori assessment of whether a task would or would not be sensitive to changes in stress level.

This analysis also offers some insight for why well-practiced responses seem to become highly probable with increases in evaluation or audience size. Responses can become "automatic" through repeated practice (e.g., Manstead & Semin, 1980; Norman & Bobrow, 1975). That is, the performance of the same task can take up less processing resources as the task is practiced. For example, when one is first learning to drive a car, this activity usually requires all of one's attention. Other activities such as talking, turning radio dials, or planning one's daily activities cannot be performed effectively in conjunction with driving. For most of us, driving eventually becomes relatively automatic and this frees us to perform other activities during our daily commuting route. In this example, driving comes to demand less of our cognitive resources through repeated practice and we now have resources available for allocation to other tasks. Since automatic tasks are assumed to take up minimal processing resources, reductions in capacity should not impede the performance of well-practiced responses as quickly as would be expected for a more resource-demanding task. If increases in audience size or evaluation produce decrements in the amount of capacity available for task performance, then one might expect individuals to use a performance strategy commensurate with their available processing resources. This could lead to an increased tendency for individuals to use a well-practiced strategy in some social settings. Thus, we see an increase in the probability of a dominant response. We would interpret this tendency as a product of limited processing capabilities or as a reflection of insufficient "incentive" (as defined as the potential attainment of an outcome value commensurate with the resources necessary for its procurement) rather than a multiplicative function of drive and habit strength.

A Comparison of Personal Equity Processes and Other Theoretical Perspectives

Carver and Scheier's Cybernetic Model

Carver and Scheier (1981) have recently proposed a provocative theory of human behavior. They have applied the cybernetic concepts of attention, standards, and expectancies to an understanding of a broad range of social psychological phenomena. Social facilitation is one topic, among many, which has been considered within their approach. Briefly, they propose that the presence of an audience serves to increase self-directed attention, either to public or private behavioral standards. The standard serves as the goal-state which a discrepancy-reducing feedback system strives to match. Social facilitation (higher performance levels in the presence of an audience than when alone) results whenever a single clear behavioral standard exists and when individuals expect to meet the standards. Impaired performance is expected whenever the task-appropriate response is unspecified (the behavioral standard is unclear) or whenever an individual attempts to meet two incompatible standards simultaneously. Self-attentive individuals are assumed to interrupt their behavior and determine the likelihood of attaining the desired outcome. Carver and Scheier suggest this expectancy development is likely to occur in highly evaluative settings in which the outcome is important or uncertain and when feedback from the individual's prior performance indicates that he or she has not been doing well on the task. If the individual develops a positive expectation, this momentary interruption is followed by a resumption of his or her matching-to-standard attempt. If a negative expectation is developed, "mental withdrawal," which would result in impaired performance, may occur.

The model suggested in this chapter has many features in common with Carver and Scheier's theory. Both invoke the concepts of attention, standards, and expectations. However, the particular usage of these concepts differs between the two models. Carver and Scheier use the concept of self-focused attention to connote an inner-directed sensitivity to self-schemata. Self-schemata may provide access to programs of action which serve to direct or guide attention and behavior. Our usage of "attention" differs from that of Carver and Scheier in its emphasis. Even though they emphasize the direction of attention toward program level activity during most behavioral regulation (1981, p. 137), we are emphasizing the amount of attentional resources which the individual may be willing or able to allocate to this activity. We are stressing conditions which may affect whether individuals are induced to allocate all, part, or none of the resources to this program level activity. If the program level activity is a resource-limited task then the amount of resources allocated to the activity may be critical in determining whether individuals will meet the standard successfully.

It should be noted that our usage of attention does not imply consciousness. It also does not imply a capacity which is allocated in an all-or-none fashion. Rather, we are using attention to refer to individual's central processing capacities and the process of allocating these resources to various inputs; individuals may or may not be aware of the operation of these processes (Posner & Klein, 1973; Posner & Snyder, 1974). Different tasks are assumed to require different amounts of processing capacity and the number of tasks which can be accomplished simultaneously is limited only by the amount of resources required for processing. The allocation of resources is assumed to be under the control of processes which are affected by outcome importance or value, and task demands, as well as the availability of processing resources. Individuals may allocate all, none, or part of their processing resources to the accomplishment of a task.

Again, this component of our analysis is not at all inconsistent with that of Carver and Scheier. In fact this component may be incorporated within their general approach. But without the addition of a process which derives input from task value and potential resource requirements, their analysis would suffer from an inability to predict various routes to identical goal attainments. Several different strategies may be used to accomplish similar goals and some strategies may require more processing resources than others (see prior discussion).

Carver and Scheier would also be unable to account for situations in which individuals have a positive expectation but do not pursue the activities necessary to obtain the outcome. Our analysis would account for this situation by weighting its potential outcome value to potential cost (Seta & Seta, 1982). If the cost necessary for goal attainment is not commensurate with outcome value, then the individual may not pursue the goal even if he or she has a favorable expectation of being able to obtain it.

Our suggested analysis also differs from Carver and Scheier's in its explanation of performance decrements. Carver and Scheier predict performance decrements whenever (a) the behavioral standard is unclear, (b) two incompatible standards exist simultaneously, or (c) negative expectations of meeting a standard create "mental withdrawal." However, our analysis predicts that performance decrements will occur whenever the amount of task-related anxiety is sufficient to infringe upon processing space necessary for successful task performance. Individuals having a negative expectation may not "mentally withdraw" from a task (although there are certainly situations in which one may quit). They may be allocating all their available resources for task performance but may lack the necessary resources for the successful performance of a resource-limited task (as seemed to be the case in Experiment 3).

Distraction-Conflict Theory

Sanders, Baron, and Moore (1978) have developed a distraction-conflict model to understand how the physical presence of a conspecific impacts performance. They argued

> That while any type of distraction presented during a task might give rise to drive effects, in most social facilitation/impairment research other people distract the subject in large part because the subject is interested in obtaining social comparison information regarding the adequacy of his or her performance. This could involve comparing one's own performance to that of coactors or it could involve comparing one's own opinion of one's performance to the opinion held by an audience. (Sanders et al., 1978, p. 292)

Sanders (1981) then elaborated upon the distraction-conflict model. Distraction has two effects. First, drive caused by distraction was proposed to facilitate simple task performance and impair complex task performance. These drive effects are consistent with the drive model proposed by Zajonc (1965). In addition, distraction was proposed to hinder both simple and complex task performance because distraction would reduce the likelihood of subjects engaging in task-related activities. It has a facilitating effect because it increases the probability of a correct dominant response, and it has a debilitating effect because it reduces task-related activities. Ultimate performance would presumably be determined by the relative strength of these opposing forces. On a complex task, however, distraction always has a debilitating effect on performance. First, it debilitates performance because it increases the probability of an incorrect dominant response and second it debilitates performance by reducing task-related activities.

A major strength of this theory is that it has been instrumental in highlighting the potential importance of distraction and social comparison processes within the social facilitation area. The focus on comparison processes has helped to broaden the scope of the social facilitation paradigm. This increase in scope can be attested to by the recent experiments involving the effects of feedback on coactors' task performance (Beck & Seta, 1980; Seta, 1982).

The propositions put forth in the distraction-conflict theory, however, do not seem sufficient to account for a number of findings within the social facilitation area. First, it has difficulty accounting for the combined results of coaction experiments (Carment, 1970; Moede, cited in Dashiell, 1935; Seta, 1982). In these experiments, the subjects' task performance was affected by the ability level of the other coactor. For example, Moede found decrements in the performance level of subjects (relative to an alone condition) upon the introduction of a coactor of inferior ability, and Seta (1982) found that (a) subjects' performance improved when paired with coactors who seemed to be performing at slightly superior levels, and (b) performance levels were not significantly affected by the presence of coactors who seemed to be performing at inferior, identical, or very superior performance levels. These studies tell us that once subjects compare, they gain information about their ability relative to that of the other coactor and that the discrepancy between the ability levels of the two coactors has a marked effect on task performance (Seta, 1982). Even though the distraction-conflict model tells us that subjects will compare, it does not delineate the effects of the information gained from the comparison process. That is, it does not tell us how the discrepancy between the ability levels of two coactors will affect task performance. This is not a criticism of the logic of the theory, but rather a limitation of the theory's present formulation.

Our resource allocation analysis can account for these results. The discrepancy in the ability level of a subject and coactor can indicate to the subject the level of performance (criterion) that must be obtained in order to obtain reward. Meeting or surpassing a coactor's performance, however, may not be the primary reward in every coaction setting. A subject may be concerned primarily about satisfying an evaluator (e.g., experimenter), and in a coaction setting, the evaluator's criteria may be implicit in the situation (see Seta, 1982). A subject's ultimate performance, then, will partially depend upon whether the criterion is set by a coactor, by an evaluator, or by both. In addition, performance will depend upon the resource cost involved in meeting a particular criterion. The person should be willing to meet a particular criterion if the necessary resource allocation does not far exceed the instrumental value associated with that criterion. Finally, it is necessary to understand a person's expectation of meeting a criterion. A negative expectation of meeting a criterion may produce anxiety which may limit an individual's available processing capacity. The individual may be willing to allocate the necessary resources to obtain an outcome but be unable to perform well because of the unavailability of sufficient capacity.

A more substantial problem for distraction-conflict theory is its inability to account for the expectation × audience interaction obtained by Bond (1982) and Geen (1979). According to this theory, if the task is complex the performance of a subject working in front of an audience should never be better than that of a solitary subject. First, since distraction increases the probability of an incorrect dominant response, an increase in distraction will reduce complex task performance. Second, distraction reduces related activities and this leads to impaired task performance. Geen used a version of the Spence, Farber, and McFann (1956) memory task, which has been assumed to be complex, within the Zajonc drive framework adopted by the distraction-conflict theorists. Geen found that relative to an alone condition, the presence of a spectator improved or had no effect on complex task performance if subjects expected success.

The results of Bond (1982) also question the utility of Zajonc's drive analysis which makes predictions about changes in the direction of performance based upon the nature of the task. Increments in drive are usually expected to produce performance decrements on complex tasks and performance increments on simple tasks. Bond found both performance increments and decrements on both simple and complex items within single lists. Whether performance was facilitated or debilitated depended upon whether the list was primarily composed of simple or complex items. These results are contrary to straightforward predictions from Zajonc's drive analysis since subjects presumably maintained the same drive level while working on the task.

Since the analysis we have proposed does not make the distinction between simple and complex tasks but defines task complexity in terms of the amount of capacity the task demands relative to the amount of capacity which is available, the results of Geen and of Bond are consistent with our approach. Increments in audience size can facilitate or debilitate performance on either "simple" or "complex" tasks depending upon the value of the task and whether the necessary processing resources are available. Their exact results, of course, will not always be obtained, because they used only two audience arrangements and the relationship between audience size and performance is not linear. Consequently, even with a set expectation level, an increase in audience size can lead to an increase or decrease in performance. The exact results then would depend upon which two audience arrangements are compared.

Bond used a self-presentational analysis which was similar to Geen's. As the analysis points out, it is important to note that individuals attempt to present themselves favorably. It is equally important, however, to understand when individuals will expend the necessary resources required to win or maintain the approval of others and when they will be able to do so. Our analysis speaks to this issue and offers some understanding of when self-presentational processes will appear to be operative and when they will not.

Social Impact Theory

Latané and his colleagues (e.g., Latané, 1980; Latané & Harkins, 1976; Latané & Nida, 1980) have developed a theory of social impact. Social impact may be defined as "any effect of the presence or actions of other people on the individual" (Latané & Harkins, 1976, p. 482). The intensity of social impact experienced by the individual will vary according to the composition and characteristics of these others. Specifically, it was proposed that impact is a function of the strength (S), immediacy (I), and number (N) of people comprising an evaluative group or audience. Strength, in this case, is defined as the salience, power, importance, or intensity of the group and may be operationalized by a manipulation of status as measured by age or educational level of the group members. Immediacy is defined as the proximity or closeness in time or space of the audience to the individual. Number is simply the numerical size of the group. Social impact theory further suggests that the amount of impact experienced by an individual should be described by a multiplicative function of the strength, immediacy, and number of the others present. Finally, social impact theory proposes that these three factors (i.e., strength, immediacy, and number) contribute to the overall impact experienced with marginally decreasing utility. That is, Latané and Nida (1980) propose a psychosocial relationship which corresponds to Stevens' (1957, 1975) psychophysical relationship. One implication of this analysis is that the difference in the impact produced by 0 and 1 individual is greater than that produced by 99 and 100 individuals.

We have been discussing situations in which there is one target and many sources of influence. In these situations the impact experienced is a multiplicative function of number, strength, and immediacy. There are situations, however, "where other people stand with the individual as the target of forces coming from outside the group. In such situations one would expect that increasing the strength, immediacy, or number of people should lead to a division or diminution of impact, with each person feeling less than he would if alone" (Latané & Nida, 1980, p. 11). This relationship can be described by the same mathematical equation as that used to describe the situation in which strength, immediacy, and number combine multiplicatively, except in this situation the exponent is negative ($I = SN^{-t}$). Using this formulation, Latané and his colleagues have argued that with large groups the impact would be divided among many individuals and with small groups it would be divided among few individuals. Given that the overall amount of impact is constant, it follows that each member of a large group would experience less impact than each member of a small group. This effect has been labeled social loafing.

Latané and his associates have generalized this psychophysical analysis to task performance. From their analysis the effort of each member of a large group would be less than that of each member of a small group if group members have responsibility for the task. This social loafing effect follows from their psychophysical analysis as long as there is a *direct relationship* between impact and effort. It was first thought (e.g., Williams, Harkins, & Latané, 1981) that the social loafing effect occurred when the performance of each group member was not identifiable, but did not occur when the performance of each group was identifiable. Harkins and Petty (Chapter 7, this volume), however, have shown that even if group members are not identifiable, a social loafing effect can be reduced and even eliminated if each group member works on a difficult task or works on a distinctive area. In these experiments, a loafing effect was obtained when subjects worked on easy or nondistinct tasks.

From our analysis there are situations in which an individual *may* be willing to allocate the necessary resources if part of a small group but *not* if part of a large group. In the large group, the instrumental value of success may not be great enough to encourage the subject to invest the necessary resources for optimal task performance, and a social loafing effect may be noticed. Harkins and Petty's data may also be incorporated into our analysis. In general, audiences are assumed to place more value on the successful performance of a difficult than an easy task, and most probably on a distinct versus a nondistinct task. Therefore, it is possible that the outcome value associated with task success was higher for Harkins and Petty's subjects working on a difficult as opposed to an easy task and on a distinct versus a nondistinct task. Consequently, loafing did not occur in this experiment when subjects worked on a difficult or distinct task. In these settings, the instrumental value associated with success may have been sufficiently high in both small and large groups to insure that subjects were willing to expend the necessary resources for optimal performance.

In addition, it is not clear how social impact would explain situations in which a subject does not expend effort even though he or she presumably experienced a great deal of impact. From our analysis, the cost/value relationship is critical to understanding when a person is or is not willing and/or is not capable of performing well. For example, a person may not respond simply because the amount of work that is required is too great for that which would be obtained. Consequently, even though the conceptual variables of strength, immediacy, and number predict that impact would be great, an individual might not engage in task-related activities.

Social impact also has difficulty accounting for situations in which a subject is incapable of performing well. That is, why should we obtain an inverted-U relationship between audience size and performance or between value and performance? From social impact one might expect that a negatively accelerating function describes the relationship between performance and audience size ($I = SN^t$, where $t > 0 < 1$), not an inverted-U relationship.

From these examples, it seems clear that knowing the reported impact of a subject does not allow us to predict performance accurately. If the proponents of social impact want to understand how task performance is affected by the social context, they must include additional concepts in their analysis.

Conclusion

In this chapter we used knowledge gained from research on value to further our understanding of performance in a group setting. We first described a theory which was developed to account for the assignment of value, and we then applied this knowledge to performance in a group setting. In doing this we considered some of the differences between task value and instrumental value. Theories to date have given little attention to the influence of the instrumental value of the task to the performer, the costs of performing the task, and the individual's resources for performing the task. By using this analysis to explain several empirical findings, we have, hopefully, shown how these factors can affect performance. We have pointed out situations in which individuals are willing to perform well but do not have the resources, or may have the resources but not the wiliingness.

Although we specifically addressed issues within social facilitation, our analysis is applicable to any setting that involves consequences and performance. We feel that we are describing a process that should be operative in a number of different contexts. For example, it should operate in a family setting and speaks to the issue of sibling rivalry; it should operate in an educational setting and speaks to the issue of how consequences alter a student's performance. A consideration of this analysis may provide a basis for a different perspective on attitudes as well as situations in which performance is contingent upon immediate external consequences. Although we have not specifically discussed complex schedule or sequential effects (e.g., discrete trial or free operant procedures) we feel that our analysis has potential for providing insights into these effects. In complex settings, such as these previously, processes in addition to personal equity are most likely operative. However, a consideration of value changes may provide useful information about behavior in these complex settings, as well.

Acknowledgments. Parts of this chapter were funded by grants from the University of North Carolina at Greensboro. We would like to thank Paul Paulus for his very helpful comments and suggestions on the chapter as well as for his support on this and other projects. James Crisson, Lenny Martin, and Aaron Brownstein's comments and support are also greatly appreciated. We would, in addition, like to thank Kendon Smith, Reed Hunt, and Hall Beck for their helpful suggestions.

Reference Note

1. Seta, J. J., Seta, C. E., & Crisson, J. E. *Value and task performance: A theoretical analysis.* Unpublished manuscript, University of North Carolina at Greensboro.

References

Aronson, E., & Mills, J. The effect of severity of initiation on liking for a group. *Journal of Abnormal and Social Psychology,* 1959, *55*, 177-181.

Beck, H. P., & Seta, J. J. The effects of frequency of feedback on a simple coaction task. *Journal of Personality and Social Psychology,* 1980, *38*, 75-80.

Berger, S. M., Carli, L. L., Hammersla, K. S., Karshmer, J. K., & Sanchez, M. E. Motoric and symbolic mediation in observational learning. *Journal of Personality and Social Psychology,* 1979, *37*, 735-746.

Bond, C. F. Social facilitation: A self-presentational view. *Journal of Personality and Social Psychology,* 1982, *42*, 1042-1050.

Carment, D. W. Rate of simple motor responding as a function of differential outcomes and the actual and implied presence of a coactor. *Psychonomic Science,* 1970, *20*, 115-116.

Carver, C. S., & Scheier. *Attention and self-regulation: A control-theory approach to human behavior.* New York: Springer-Verlag, 1981.

Cohen, C. E. Person categories and social perception: Testing some boundaries of the processing effects of prior knowledge. *Journal of Personality and Social Psychology,* 1981, *40*, 441-452.

Cottrell, N. B. Performance in the presence of other human beings: Mere presence, audience and affiliation effects. In E. C. Simmel, R. A. Hoppe, & G. A. Milton (Eds.), *Social facilitation and imitative behavior.* Boston: Allyn & Bacon, 1968.

Cottrell, N. B. Social facilitation. In C. G. McClintock (Ed.), *Experimental social psychology.* New York: Holt, 1972.

Dashiell, J. E. Experimental studies of the influence of social situations on the behavior of individual human adults. In C. Murchison (Ed.), *Handbook of social psychology.* Worcester, Mass.: Clark University Press, 1935.

Deci, E. L. *Intricsic motivation.* New York: Plenum Press, 1975.

Einstein, G. O., & Hunt, R. R. Levels of processing and organization, additive effects of individual item and relational processing. *Journal of Experimental Psychology: Human Learning and Memory,* 1980, *6*, 588-598.

Geen, R. G. Effects of being observed on learning following success and failure experiences. *Motivation and Emotion,* 1979, *3*, 355-371.

Good, K. J. Social facilitation: Effects of performance anticipation, evaluation, and response competition on free association. *Journal of Personality and Social Psychology,* 1973, *38*, 270-275.

Helson, H. *Adaption-level theory: An experimental and systematic approach to behavior.* New York: Harper & Row, 1964.

Hearst, E. Aversive conditioning and external stimulus control. In B. A. Campbell & R. M. Church (Eds.), *Punishment and aversive behavior.* New York: Appleton-Century-Crofts, 1969.

Henchy, T., & Glass, D. C. Evaluation apprehension and the social facilitation of dominant and subordinate responses. *Journal of Personality and Social Psychology,* 1968, *10,* 446-454.

Hull, C. L. *A behavior system.* New Haven, Conn.: Yale University Press, 1952.

Hunt, R. R., & Einstein, G. O. Relational and item-specific information in memory. *Journal of Verbal Learning and Verbal Behavior,* 1981, *20*, 497-514.

Kahneman, D. *Attention and effort*. Englewood Cliffs, N.J.: Prentice-Hall, 1973.

Latané, B. Psychology of social impact. *American Psychologist,* 1981, *36*, 343-356.

Latané, B., & Harkins, S. Cross-modality matches suggest anticipated stage fright is a multiple function of audience size and status. *Perception and Psychophysics,* 1976, *20*, 482-488.

Latané, B., & Nida, S. Social impact theory and group influence: A social engineering perspective. In P. B. Paulus (Ed.), *Psychology of group influence*. Hillsdale, N.J.: Lawrence Erlbaum, 1980.

Lepper, M. R., Greene, D., & Nisbett, R. E. Understanding children's intrincic interest with extrincic reward: A test of the "overjustification" hypothesis. *Journal of Personality and Social Psychology*, 1973, *28*, 129-137.

Manstead, A. S. R., & Semin, G. R. Social facilitation effects: Mere enhancement of dominant responses? *British Journal of Social and Clinical Psychology,* 1980, *19*, 119-136.

Markus, H. The effect of mere presence on social facilitation; an unobtrusive test. *Journal of Experimental Social Psychology,* 1978, *14*, 389-397.

Miller, G. A. The magical number seven, plus or minus two: Some limits on our capacity for processing information. *Psychological Review,* 1956, *63*, 81-97.

Miller, N. E. Experimental studies of conflict. In J. Mc. V. Hunt (Ed.), *Personality and the behavior disorders*. New York: The Ronald Press Co., 1944.

Miller, N. E. Liberalization of basic S-R concepts: Extensions to conflict behavior motivation and social learning. In S. Koch (Eds.), *Psychology: A study of a science* (Vol. 2). New York: McGraw-Hill, 1959.

Morris, C. D., Bransford, J. D., & Franks, J. J. Levels of processing versus transfer appropriate processing. *Journal of Verbal Learning and Verbal Behavior,* 1977, *16*, 519-533.

Mueller, J. H. Anxiety and cue utilization in human learning and memory. In M. Zuckerman and C. D. Spielberger (Eds.), *Emotion and anxiety: New concepts, methods and applications*. Hillsdale, N.J.: Lawrence Erlbaum, 1976.

Mueller, J. H. The effects of individual differences in test anxiety and type of orienting task on levels of organization in free recall. *Journal of Research in Personality,* 1978, *12*, 100-116.

Norman, D. A. Toward a theory of memory and attention. *Psychological Review,* 1968, *75*, 522-536.

Norman, D. A., & Bobrow, D. G. On data limited and resource limited processes. *Cognitive Psychology,* 1975, *7*, 44-64.

Paulus, P. B. Crowding. In P. B. Paulus (Ed.), *Psychology of group influence*. Hillsdale, N.J.: Lawrence Erlbaum, 1980.

Paulus, P. B., & Murdoch, P. Anticipated evaluation and audience presence in the enhancement of dominant responses. *Journal of Experimental Social Psychology,* 1971, *7*, 280-291.

Posner, M. I., & Klein, R. M. On the functions of consciousness. In S. Kornblum (Ed.), *Attention and performance IV*. New York: Academic Press, 1973.

Posner, M. I., & Snyder, C. R. R. Attention and cognitive control. In R. L. Solso (Ed.), *Information processing and cognition: The Loyola Symposium*. Hillsdale, N.J.: Lawrence Erlbaum, 1974.

Rajecki, D. W., Ickes, W., Corcoran, C., & Lenerz, K. Social facilitation of human performance: Mere presence effects. *Journal of Social Psychology,* 1977, *102,* 233-246.

Rescorla, R. A., & Wagner, A. R. A. A theory of Pavlovian conditioning: Variations in the effectiveness of reinforcement and non-reinforcement. In A. H. Black & W. F. Prokasy (Eds.), *Classical conditioning II.* New York: Appleton-Century-Crofts, 1972.

Rittle, R. H., & Bernard, N. Enhancement of response rate by the mere physical presence of the experimenter. *Personality and Social Psychology Bulletin,* 1977, *3,* 127-130.

Roenker, D. L., Thompson, C. P., & Brown, S. C. Comparison of measures for the estimation of clustering in free recall. *Psychological Bulletin,* 1971, *76,* 45-48.

Sanders, G. S. Driven by distraction: An integrative review of social facilitation theory and research. *Journal of Experimental Social Psychology,* 1981, *17,* 227-251.

Sanders, G. S., Baron, R. S., & Moore, D. L. Distraction and social comparison as mediators of social facilitation effects. *Journal of Experimental Social Psychology,* 1978, *14,* 291-303.

Sasfy, J., & Okun, M. Form of evaluation and audience expertness as joint determinants of audience effects. *Journal of Experimental Social Psychology,* 1974, *10,* 461-467.

Seta, J. J. The impact of comparison processes on coactors' task performance. *Journal of Personality and Social Psychology,* 1982, *42,* 281-291.

Seta, J. J., & Hassan, R. K. Awareness of prior success or failure: A critical factor in task performance. *Journal of Personality and Social Psychology,* 1980, *39,* 70-76.

Seta, J. J., & Seta, C. E. Personal equity: An intrapersonal comparator system analysis of reward value. *Journal of Personality and Social Psychology,* 1982, *43,* 222-235.

Shiffrin, R. M. The locus and role of attention in memory systems. In P. M. A. Rabbit & S. Dornic (Eds.), *Attention and performance V.* New York: Academic Press, 1975.

Spence, K. W., Farber, I. E., & McFann, H. H. The relation of anxiety (drive) level to performance in competitional and non-competitional paired-associates learning. *Journal of Experimental Psychology,* 1956, *52,* 296-305.

Stein, B. S. Depth of processing re-examined: The effects of precision of encoding and test appropriateness. *Journal of Verbal Learning and Verbal Behavior,* 1978, *77,* 165-174.

Stevens, S. S. On the psychophysical law. *Psychological Review,* 1957, *64,* 153-181.

Stevens, S. S. *Psychophysics: Introduction to its perceptual, neural, and social prospects.* New York: Wiley, 1975.

Triesman, A. M. Strategies and models of selective attention. *Psychological Review,* 1969, *76,* 282-292.

Triesman, A. M., & Davies, A. Divided attention to ear and eye. In S. Kornblum (Ed.), *Attention and performance IV.* New York: Academic Press, 1973.

Tulving, E. Subjective organization in free recall of "unrelated" words. *Psychological Review,* 1962, *69,* 344-354.

Tulving, E., & Thompson, D. M. Encoding specificity and retrieval processes in episodic memory. *Psychological Review,* 1973, *80,* 352-373.

Weiss, R. F., & Miller, F. G. The drive theory of social facilitation. *Psychological Review,* 1971, *78,* 44-57.

Williams, K., Harkins, S., & Latané, B. Identifiability as a deterrant to social loafing: Two cheering experiments. *Journal of Personality and Social Psychology,* 1981, *40,* 303-311.

Yerkes, R. M., & Dodson, J. D. The relation of strength of stimulus to rapidity of habit-formation. *Journal of Comparative and Neurological Psychology,* 1908, *18,* 459-482.

Zajonc, R. B. Social facilitation. *Science,* 1965, *149,* 269-274.

Zajonc, R. B. Compresence. In P. B. Paulus (Ed.), *Psychology of group influence.* Hillsdale, N.J.: Lawrence Erlbaum, 1980.

Chapter 7

Social Context Effects in Persuasion: The Effects of Multiple Sources and Multiple Targets

Stephen G. Harkins and Richard E. Petty

Attitudes are a central feature of our social lives. Daily, we are called upon or feel compelled to express our views on a variety of topics. Equally often, we are exposed to attempts to change these attitudes. Some classic research in social psychology clearly makes the point that the social context in which people find themselves is a crucial determinant of their attitudes. For example, Newcomb (1943) in his research on Bennington College coeds found that students who were initially highly conservative, gradually came to adopt the liberal views espoused by the college community over the course of their stay there. The fact that people and their attitudes are located in social matrices has been suggested as one reason that field studies of attitude change typically find weaker effects than laboratory studies (Hovland, 1959). In laboratory research people are typically exposed to a persuasive communication in social isolation, but in field research and in "real life" people often receive messages in the company of others. As a result, subjects in laboratory research may feel that the message is aimed at them in particular which enhances its impact, whereas in the natural environment the perception may be that the message is aimed at people in general. Also, when other people are present, a message recipient might hear various individual group members make statements in opposition to the position outlined by the message source. This would also reduce the impact of the message.

Despite the obvious importance of the social context of persuasion, an examination of the attitude-change literature reveals that with a few notable exceptions that will be addressed later in this chapter (e.g., the effects of group discussion on attitude change, Lamm & Myers, 1978), relatively little attention has been paid to the effects of the social context on persuasion. The incorporation of social context into the study of attitude change, while long overdue, introduces many complexities into the study of the persuasion process. In fact, it may well be the complexity of the endeavor that has led attitude researchers to employ the impoverished social settings that have characterized most investigations. While we readily acknowledge this complexity, and can only aspire to the goal of the development of a comprehensive model of the effects of social context on persuasion, in this chapter we will report a series of studies that represent a first step. In this initial work, we have limited the focus of our attention in several ways. (a) In social groupings people are often alternately the source and the target of persuasive communications. While we are interested equally in the effects of the production of and exposure to persuasive communications, in this chapter we will restrict our attention to the effects of the latter process. (b) People are exposed to persuasive communications that are generated both from within and from without the social groups in which they happen to be at a given time. We will limit our attention to communications originating from outside the social grouping. (c) People are sometimes exposed to persuasion in the company of friends and acquaintances, and sometimes in the presence of strangers. We will limit our attention to the effects of strangers.

By limiting the domain of our initial inquiry in this way, we have excluded from consideration many potentially interesting features of the social context. Nevertheless, even this restricted domain serves quite well as a first approximation, since it allows the control of many features of a very complex situation, and also provides an analog for many real-world persuasion settings that involve groups. For example, in the courtroom, opposing attorneys attempt to persuade a jury of the merits of their cases using a parade of witnesses to bolster their positions. The members of the jury are jointly exposed to the messages from multiple sources and are jointly responsible for evaluating these positions and reaching a verdict. At political rallies, a number of speakers may argue in favor of or against some position or candidate to groups of voters who are jointly responsible for the election outcome. Finally, we note that our consideration of these persuasion settings will be limited in another way. In the examples just given, people are often with others and at the same time are exposed to persuasive communications delivered by multiple sources. We have separated these features, so that, in our research, single or multiple targets were exposed to a persuasive communication delivered by a single source, or a single target was exposed to one or multiple sources. In addition to the advantage of reducing complexity, this conceptualization was suggested by Latané's (1981) theory of social impact, which proposes that the many ways in which people are affected by others can be described as operating in two basic types of social force fields: *multiplicative force fields,* in which a person stands alone as a target of social influence emanating from multiple sources, and *divisive force fields,* in which a person stands with others as a target of social influence. According to the theory, social impact increases with the number, status, and immediacy of sources attempting to influence us, but decreases with the number, status, and immediacy of the other targets of the influence attempt. Of course, the situation in which a person stands alone as the target of the persuasion attempts of multiple sources represents a multiplicative force field, whereas the situation in which a person stands with others as the target of an influence attempt represents a divisive force field. The theory would generally predict that increasing the number of message sources should increase the amount of persuasive impact, while increasing the number of message recipients (targets) should diminish it.[1]

Although Latané's theory of social impact makes predictions concerning the

---

[1] The theory also predicts the shape of these functions as the number of sources and/or targets increases, but these predictions are not tested in the present research since we did not parametrically manipulate number.

degree of attitude change in multiplicative and divisive force fields, the theory does not attempt to provide an account of the process that intervenes between exposure to these social contexts and attitude change. As Latané writes:

> It (social impact) does not purport to "explain" the operation of any of the number of particular social processes that are necessary to account for all of the effects I have labelled "social impact" or to substitute for theories that do. It does, however, provide general overall rules that seem to govern each and all of these individual processes. (1981, p. 343).

An account of the intervening process that we were interested in testing is provided by the cognitive response approach to persuasion (Petty, Ostrom, & Brock, 1981). Cognitive response theory contends that targets of persuasion attempts do not passively encode the content of persuasive messages; rather, as the message arguments are presented, people generate internal idiosyncratic reactions, termed cognitive responses. If these responses are preponderantly favorable, persuasion results; if they are primarily unfavorable (i.e., counterarguments), no persuasion results, and in fact, some boomerang might occur. The quality of the arguments making up the message plays a central role in determining the pattern of these cognitive responses. If the arguments are cogent, favorable thoughts are likely to predominate; if unconvincing, counterarguments are likely to be generated. Manipulations of both ability and motivation to think about the message arguments have been shown to interact with message quality in determining the pattern of cognitive responses and attitude change (see Petty & Cacioppo, 1981, for a review). Thus, manipulations of both greater ability (e.g., message repetition; Cacioppo & Petty, 1979) and greater motivation (e.g., issue involvement; Petty & Cacioppo, 1979) to think have been shown to enhance production of favorable thoughts and increase persuasion when the message was composed of convincing arguments, but increase counterargumentation and decrease persuasion when the message was composed of low-quality arguments. The importance of the cognitive response approach is that in contrast to social impact theory, which predicts a direct effect of number of sources and targets on persuasion, cognitive response theory predicts that the number of sources and targets will have an impact on persuasion primarily through their impact on a person's motivation and/or ability to think about the message arguments presented.

Division of Impact

We will consider first the situation in which a person stands with others as a target of social impact. In this type of social force field, social impact would predict that as the number of targets increases, persuasion should decrease. Consistent with this prediction, Latané (1981) reported a reliable *inverse* relationship between the proportion of Billy Graham crusade attenders persuaded sufficiently by the speaker to lead them to inquire for Christ, and crowd size. On the other hand, Newton and Mann (1980), who surveyed crusade attendance in Australia in 1979, found that for weekday meetings the *greater* the audience size, the greater the proportion of inquirers. Analysis of one crusade, in Melbourne, and the weekend crusades at all of the locations revealed no reliable relationship between crowd size and inquiry.

Latané (1981) did not break his data down on the basis of time of week or location, and so, these two sets of findings may not be as inconsistent as they seem, but even if there were a consistent relationship, since these are correlational studies, numerous alternative interpretations exist. As Newton and Mann (1980) point out, the positive relationship for weekday meetings "may be due to a tendency for larger crowds to include higher proportions of people whose independent predisposition is to go forward as inquirers" (p. 881). There are any number of other alternative interpretations. For example, weather and speaker enthusiasm are likely to covary with crowd size.

Fortunately, there are a few experimental studies of the effects of audience size on persuasion that do not fall prey to these types of alternative interpretations. For example, Knower (1935) found that a speaker presenting arguments concerning prohibition produced more attitude change among "alone" participants than was obtained by presenting the same speech to participants who were members of an audience. This was true for both alone "pro-wet" targets who became more "dry" in response to a pro-dry advocacy, and alone "pro-dry" targets who became more "wet" in response to a pro-wet advocacy than their respective "group" counterparts. This study was replicated using written messages, rather than speakers (Knower, 1936), and a similar pattern of results was obtained: Participants reading the arguments when alone in a room were more affected than participants who read the arguments in a classroom with others. More recently, Keating and Latané (1976) presented participants, who were either alone or in the company of others, messages concerning censorship and an all-volunteer army in one of four communication media (written, audio, TV, and live). For all but the written mode, the alone participants were much more convinced by the counterattitudinal message concerning the all-volunteer army than were the group participants. For the censorship issue, on which there was a wide diversity of initial attitude positions, the pro-censorship advocacy was no more effective for participants alone than in groups.

These studies are consistent with the impact perspective and do not present as much interpretational ambiguity as the correlational studies. Even so, there are a number of factors that could be responsible for the audience effects. For example, Knower (1936) suggested that the greater persuasion in the alone situation may be accounted for in one of two ways:

> The subjects in the group may have been influenced by the incipient negative responses occurring in the group

or

> The reader in the alone situation was obviously more free from distractions and thus he may have been able to absorb a greater amount of positive suggestions from the appeal presented. (p. 527)

Thus, either because participants in the groups were exposed to unfavorable reactions to the advocacy or because the others served as sources of distraction, or for both reasons the group members were less persuaded. It is important to note that the actual presence of others is required for these explanations to be viable. However, work by Latané and his colleagues suggests that, even when the actual number of people taking part is held constant or a person is actually alone, the simple *perception* that one is taking part in a task with others can influence one's behavior. For example, Latané, Williams and Harkins (1979) asked subjects to shout alone and in groups of two and six. In this study there were always six people present, but since they were blindfolded and wore earphones, they could not hear or see each other. On some trials the participants actually shouted with others, but on the crucial trials, termed pseudogroup trials, the participants were told via their headphones that they would be shouting with others but they actually shouted alone. Since each trial was accompanied by a loud masking noise delivered over the headphones, the participants were unable to tell how many other people were actually shouting. This strategem allowed Latané et al. (1979) to determine if *thinking* that one was taking part with others was sufficient to reduce individual effort, independent of any potential loss in productivity as a result of distraction or lack of coordination (Steiner, 1972) and indeed, when participants thought they were taking part with others they produced less sound than when they shouted alone. Latané et al. (1979) termed this reduction in individual effort "social loafing." Similar loafing effects have been reported in between as well as within subjects designs (Harkins, Latané, & Williams, 1980), for females as well as males (Harkins et al., 1980), and for a variety of physically effortful tasks including clapping (Harkins, et al., 1980), rope-pulling (Ingham, Levinger, Graves, & Peckham, 1974) and pumping air (Kerr & Bruun, 1981).

Division of Effort and Attitude

Of course, these findings relate to tasks involving physical effort, but evaluating persuasive messages is also an effortful activity, if conscientiously carried out. The social loafing findings suggest then that perhaps when exposed to a persuasive message in the company of others, people feel less compelled to critically evaluate the message than when they alone are to carry out the task, since there are others available to shoulder the burden. This reduced effort could lead to a reduced appreciation of the arguments and less persuasion. Of course, when actual group size manipulations are used, this loafing effect, if present, would be confounded with the effects that Knower (1936) enumerated. So, as a first step, to determine whether loafing effects could be obtained on a cognitively effortful task independent of any effects resulting from the physical presence of others, we held actual group size constant and informed the participants either that they alone were responsible for evaluating a poem and an editorial ostensibly written by another student, that they were one of four students responsible, or that they were one of sixteen evaluators (Petty, Harkins, Williams, & Latané, 1977). Consistent with the work on physically effortful tasks, subjects who were told that they were solely responsible for their evaluations reported putting greater effort into their evaluations than did subjects who shared the responsibility. In addition, the individually responsible subjects evaluated the written products more favorably than the shared responsibility subjects. This less favorable attitude towards the poem and editorial on the part of the shared responsibility (group) subjects is consistent with the notion of division of impact and replicates earlier research without the confoundings introduced by the actual presence of other people (cf. Keating & Latané, 1976; Knower, 1935, 1936). However, there are at least four different processes that could lead to this outcome. For example, a deindividuation interpretation (Zimbardo, 1970) might contend that the group evaluators experienced feelings of anonymity that made them more willing to express deviant and derogatory evaluations (see Aderman, Brehm, & Katz, 1974, for evidence consistent with this argument). Two other explanations link the more favorable evaluations by individually responsible subjects directly to the increased effort individuals perceive themselves as exerting. Jones and Gerard (1967) have suggested that

> If a person expends effort that is not readily justified by the amount of reinforcement received, he tends to create reinforcements out of the stimuli in the immediately surrounding environment. (p. 89).

This "effort justification" hypothesis would suggest that individual evaluators may have justified their increased efforts by overvaluing the communications (see also Cohen, 1959; Wicklund, Cooper, & Linder, 1967). Similarly, Brock's (1968) commodity theory predicts that the more effort one exerts attending to a communication, the higher the subjective value it will have (see also Fromkin & Brock, 1973).

A fourth explanation is suggested by the cognitive response model of attitude change (Petty et al., 1981) that we described earlier. Since both the poem and the editorial were favorably regarded (the average rating on the evaluative scales was above the midpoint for both individual and group evaluators) and the individually responsible subjects reported putting greater effort into their evaluations, the cognitive response formulation would predict that individual evaluators would be more likely to discover the merits of the communications, generate more favorable thoughts, and evaluate the products more favorably than the less-motivated group evaluators. Thus, deindividuation, dissonance, commodity enhancement, and more diligent information processing all provide potential explanations for the evaluation effect obtained by Petty et al. (1977).

Petty, Harkins, and Williams (1980) conducted two studies to distinguish among these potential explanations. Although all of these explanations make the same predictions for well-regarded materials, this is not the case if the materials are of low quality. Deindividuation, dissonance, and commodity enhancement would all still predict that individual evaluators would rate the materials more favorably, although the rationales differ. The cognitive response approach, however, would predict that the greater effort put into the evaluation of a low-quality stimulus by the individually responsible subjects should lead them to a more acute sense of the flaws of the materials and to a *less* favorable evaluation than that arrived at by the group evaluators. To test these possibilities, we had subjects evaluate a tape of a therapist interacting with a client. Subjects were led to believe either that they were the only person evaluating the therapist or that they were one of twelve. The therapist was either portrayed as highly competent and genuinely interested in the client's phobia, or as incompetent and uninterested in the client's problem. Replicating Petty et al. (1977), the individually responsible subjects reported putting more effort into their evaluations. In addition to this perceived effort measure, subjects were given three minutes to list their thoughts about the therapist's behavior (see Cacioppo, Harkins, & Petty, 1981). This thought-listing procedure provided an opportunity to look at the subjects' actual cognitive effort rather than their perceived effort. It was expected that the pattern of thoughts would be consistent with the effort the subjects reported putting into their evaluations. That is, if the individually responsible subjects were putting in greater effort, we should find that they generate more thoughts consistent with the character of the stimulus than shared responsibility subjects. Individually responsible subjects did generate more favorable thoughts in response to the good therapist than did the shared responsibility subjects. However, there were no differences for the bad therapist. Consistent with the thought-listing data, individual evaluators provided more favorable evaluations of the good therapist than group evaluators, but there were no differences for the bad therapist.

Thus, the findings for the good therapist replicated the results of the Petty et al. (1977) research and provided evidence for actual effort differences between individual and group evaluators, but the bad therapist findings were problematical. A potential explanation for the latter finding may be provided by an examination of the evaluations of the bad therapist. While these ratings were reliably worse than those of the good therapist, they were not nearly as extreme as those of the good therapist. If the bad therapist was actually more neutral than bad, the findings of no difference would not be inconsistent with the cognitive response interpretation, since greater effort put into the evaluation of a neutral stimulus would still yield a neutral evaluation, and no group/individual differences would be expected.

In a second experiment we explored this notion by having subjects evaluate one of three editorials, ostensibly written by another student. Each of the editorials was composed of eight arguments, but in one editorial the arguments were logically sound, defendable, and compelling (strong arguments message), in the second editorial the arguments were more open to refutation and skepticism (moderately weak arguments), while in the third the arguments were quite specious (very weak arguments). Crossed with this manipulation, subjects were told either that they alone were responsible for the evaluation or that they were one of ten who would be looking at a particular essay. Once again, individual evaluators reported putting greater effort into their evaluations than group evaluators. As shown in Table 7-1, analysis of the thoughts measure revealed that subjects who were individually responsible generated more favorable thoughts in response to the strong arguments and more unfavorable thoughts in response to the very weak arguments than did shared responsibility subjects. As in the previous study, there were no reliable differences in response to the moderately weak arguments. As suggested by the results of the thoughts measure, individually responsible subjects evaluated the editorial composed of strong arguments more favorably and the editorial composed of very weak arguments less favorably than did shared responsibility subjects. There were no individual/group differences in the evaluation of the editorial composed of moderately weak arguments.

These results are consistent with the cognitive response interpretation, which suggests that the greater effort put into the evaluation by the individually responsible subjects leads to a greater appreciation of the merits and flaws of the communi-

Table 7-1. Effects of Group Size and Stimulus Quality on Cognitive Effort and Evaluation[a,b]

Item	Strong Arguments		Moderately Weak Arguments		Very Weak Arguments	
	Individual	Group	Individual	Group	Individual	Group
Perceived cognitive effort	8.81_a	7.63_b	7.81_{ab}	7.04_b	8.58_a	8.10_{ab}
Negative thoughts	$.86_a$	1.40_a	1.90_{ab}	1.86_a	3.80_c	2.53_{ab}
Positive thoughts	3.76_a	2.83_b	2.00_b	2.20_b	$.96_c$	1.76_{bc}
Evaluation index	9.30_a	7.64_b	6.83_b	7.17_b	4.03_c	5.85_d

[a] From Petty, Harkins, & Williams (1980, Experiment 2).
[b] Means in the same row without a common subscript are significantly different at the .05 level by the Newman-Keuls procedure.

cations than that achieved by the shared responsibility subjects. This greater effort apparently leads to more thoughts consistent with the quality of the stimulus, and an evaluation consistent with this pattern of thoughts. The results are inconsistent with the other interpretations, each of which predicts less favorable evaluations by group evaluators for each of the editorials, regardless of their quality. These data also suggest that increasing the number of targets does not always lead to reduced persuasive impact, since when exposed to the very weak editorial, the group evaluators liked it more than the individual ones.

Factors Responsible for Division of Effort

Our series of studies suggests that divisive force fields do lead to reduced cognitive effort, but the quality of the stimulus (persuasive message) must be taken into account to predict the persuasive impact that this reduced effort will have. Moreover, while these studies do suggest the process by which effort is translated into an evaluative reaction, the process by which group evaluators come to put in less effort than individual ones is unclear. There are at least two features of the experimental paradigm that has been used in social loafing research that could contribute to reductions in effort when groups rather than individuals are assigned responsibility for a task.

External surveillance and identifiability. First, in both the studies on physical and on cognitive effort, the participants' efforts are combined in the group conditions. For example, when performing the sound production tasks, the participants think that on the group trials the sound-level meter will record the total sound output of the group. When performing the cognitively effortful tasks, the subjects are told that their reactions will be combined with those of the others to form an overall rating. Thus, on all of the tasks the subjects are led to believe that their individual outputs will not be identifiable. They can receive neither credit nor blame for their performances, and lacking this motivation for performance, the subjects loaf.

Williams, Harkins, and Latané (1981) tested this possibility by manipulating the identifiability of individual performances within the group in two experiments. In the initial phase of the first experiment, subjects shouted alone and in pseudogroups. As has been the case in previous research, when the subjects shouted alone, their ouputs were individually identifiable, but were unidentifiable when they performed in the group. In the second half of the experiment, subjects were asked to don individual microphones that supposedly permitted the monitoring of individual outputs even when the subjects performed in groups. Consistent with previous research (Latané et al., 1979), in the first half of the experiment subjects shouted more loudly when performing alone than when they thought they were shouting with the others. However, when they were told that their individual outputs could be monitored even when they performed in groups, no loafing occurred. Subjects shouted as loudly when they thought they were shouting with others as they did alone. In the second experiment, a between-subjects design was used in which subjects were told one of the following: (a) they would shout alone and in groups— identifiable when alone condition; (b) they would shout alone and in groups while wearing microphones that allowed the monitoring of their individual performances in groups as well as alone—always identifiable; or (c) they would shout alone and in groups, but since interest centered on the group's performance, their individual performances would be summed and the group totals would be examined—never identifiable. Replicating the social loafing effect, subjects shouted more loudly alone than when they thought they were shouting with others. Also, replicating the previous study, when the participants thought that their outputs could always be identified, they shouted as loudly in groups as when alone. Finally, when led to believe that the experimenters were interested in group totals, subjects put out as little effort alone as when in groups. Thus, consistent with the identifiability notion, when the experimenters could monitor the subjects' individual outputs, they worked as hard in groups as when alone, and when the experimenters monitored only the group performances, subjects worked as little alone as when in groups.

Task characteristics. These studies suggest that social loafing is, at least in part, the result of the subjects' lack of identifiability when participating in groups. When subjects can neither be praised nor blamed for their individual effort, they loaf. However, an examination of the tasks used in previous loafing research suggests at least two features of the tasks themselves that may also be required to obtain the loafing effect. First, in the loafing research, all of the subjects have shared the responsibility for working on a relatively *simple* task. Shouting, clapping, and rope-pulling are all easily accomplished. Even though the subjects are told to produce as much as they can, a maximizing task in Steiner's (1972) terminology, and each person's contribution adds to the group total, subjects undoubtedly realize that virtually anyone could perform these simple tasks. On the cognitive tasks, the subjects are asked to evaluate materials that are easily understood. After all, the subjects are told that these essays were written by their fellow students. On this optimizing task (Steiner, 1972), the subjects may feel that their efforts are redundant: The reactions they come up with are likely to be very similar to those generated by others in their group. Thus, even though their reactions will contribute to the overall rating, subjects may feel that their particular contributions are not really needed. This analysis suggests that if the tasks were made more difficult and challenging, subjects might not loaf in groups even if their individual inputs remained unidentifiable because on a challenging task, subjects would perceive that their contributions are not easily duplicated by someone else.

Secondly, in previous loafing research, in addition to the task being simple, the task was also *identical* for all group members (subjects pulled on the same rope, evaluated the same essay, etc.), and this may have contributed to social loafing by enhancing subjects' perceptions that their efforts were not needed. To remove this feature, an investigator, for example, could tell subjects that their evaluation of essays would be combined to form one overall class evaluation as in previous research (Petty et al., 1977), but that each subject would be evaluating a *different* essay from the class. Even if the task were simple and subjects remained unidentifiable in that each contributed unrecognizably to one group evaluation, loafing might not occur under these conditions because all subjects have their own unique subtask. Thus, subjects would likely perceive that their contribution was valuable and was not duplicated by another group member.

Our analysis suggests that as a result of the fact that in previous social loafing research responsibility has been shared for *one* task that is quite *simple,* the subjects may not have felt motivated to exert their maximal effort unless their work was identifiable. In other words, if the task itself does not enhance subjects' motivation to perform their best, social loafing will occur if the loafing cannot be detected. On the other hand, if the task itself provides sufficient motivation for performance, loafing may not occur even if the subjects' work remains unidentifiable. Therefore, lack of identifiability may not be a sufficient condition for social loafing. Loafing may also require that subjects feel that the group task does not afford them an opportunity to make a contribution substantial enough to warrant their best efforts.

Of course, there are undoubtedly a number of ways in which subjects could be led to believe that their efforts are needed. In the research that we describe here, we manipulated this perception in two ways. In two experiments we manipulated the difficulty of the task, testing the notion that increasing task difficulty would lead the subjects to feel that their efforts were needed since the task presented a challenge. In two other experiments, we manipulated whether subjects worked on the identical task as the others, or had their own task on which to work, testing the notion that making the participants' efforts nonredundant would make them feel needed. We expected that social loafing would occur only when the task was simple and nonchallenging or required subjects to make responses that were redundant with the contributions of other group members. When the tasks were more challenging and/or required nonredundant responses, we expected that social loafing would not occur, even if the subjects' responses were completely unidentifiable (i.e., submerged in a group score).

Task difficulty experiments. In our first experiment (Harkins & Petty, 1982), the subjects' task was to generate uses for an object. In this brainstorming task, the subjects were told either that they alone were responsible for listing as many uses for an object as they possibly could or that they shared this responsibility with nine others whose uses would be combined with their own. Crossed with this manipulation, one-half of the subjects were given an object for which pretesting had revealed that it would be difficult to generate uses, a detached doorknob, while the other half were given an object for which it was easy to generate uses, a knife. For the easy object, we predicted the typical social loafing effect: More uses would be generated by the individually responsible subjects than by those who were told the responsibility was shared. For the difficult object, however, where the task presented a challenge, we expected that shared-responsibility subjects would work as hard as those who were individually responsible.

In line with these predictions, people working alone on the easy object generated more uses than those working together, while there were no differences for the difficult object. In addition, subjects generating uses for the difficult object rated their uses as more unusual than those generating uses for the easy object.

This experiment was replicated using different objects, and once again, individual evaluators generated more uses for the easy object (a box) than did group evaluators, but there were no differences for the difficult object (a burnt-out light bulb). In addition, subjects who generated uses for the difficult object felt it less likely that the same uses would be generated by another person responding to the same object than easy-object subjects, and also felt that their uses represented more of a unique contribution unlikely to be duplicated by others. Both subjects and independent judges felt that the uses generated for the difficult object were more unusual than those generated in response to the easy object. These results are consistent with the interpretation that subjects were motivated in the difficult-object conditions by the potential for making a unique (nonredundant) contribution.[2]

---

[2] It could be argued that the equivalence in performance in the difficult object conditions was the result of a floor effect that prevented the emergence of any significant differences. Given the present data, this argument does not seem plausible. The individually responsible/difficult object subjects in both experiments generated a reasonable number of uses, an average of 7.94 in Experiment 1, and 6.28 in its replication. This level of performance left the group subjects ample opportunity to perform more poorly than individually responsible subjects. Specifically, in Experiment 1 the group subjects need only have generated five or fewer uses, and in its replication, four or fewer to have generated reliably fewer uses than the individually responsible subjects. However, in both experiments the group subjects' mean performances, if anything, exceeded that of the individual subjects' (Experiment 1: 9.25 vs. 7.94; replication: 6.64 vs. 6.28), although not significantly.

The other possibility is that the individually responsible subjects were at a ceiling and were unable to generate any more uses, no matter how hard they tried. Of course, if the individual subjects' performances were at a ceiling, the group subjects' performances were at the same ceiling since there were no reliable differences between these experimental groups. Once again, since the individual subjects' level of performance left the group subjects ample room to have generated reliably fewer uses, it seems unlikely that the performance equivalence is a ceiling artifact. In addition, in Experiment 1, there was no reliable difference in the number of uses generated under the difficult and easy conditions by the shared responsibility (unidentifiable) subjects. This finding strongly suggests that group subjects were working harder when faced with the difficult object than the easy one.

Why should the participants feel that they can make a greater contribution when the task is more difficult? Research from several sources suggests that people see themselves as above average on many dimensions. For example, Myers (1980) reports that 70% of the 829,000 high school students who recently took the Scholastic Aptitude Test felt that they were above average in leadership ability, 60% felt that they were above average in athletic ability, and 0% rated themselves as below average in ability to get along with others (60% saw themselves in the top 10%, 25% in the top 1%). Jellison and Riskind (1970), in their test of the notion that risk-taking is seen as an indicant of ability, found that on the average, subjects rated themselves as more capable, clever, competent, creative, ingenious, innovative, and insightful than average. Goethals and Zanna (1979), in their study of the role of social comparison in choice shifts, found that when asked to compare themselves to an average person on the dimensions of talent, creativity, and ability, 72% of the subjects rated themselves as above average, 17% saw themselves as average, and 1 subject (1%) felt he was moderately below average. When taking part in a simple task, subjects may not be motivated to make use of their "above average" abilities since they may feel the task could be done by anyone and others are there to do it. However, when faced with a more challenging (difficult) task, subjects may feel that their contribution is needed since they are better able than the average person to perform the task.

To test the generalizability of the finding that increasing the difficulty of the task alone is sufficient to eliminate social loafing, we replicated the basic design using a task much like those requiring physical effort (Harkins & Petty, 1982, Experiment 2). In this study the subjects simply watched a television screen, reporting seldomly occurring signals by pressing a key. As with the noise production task, identifiability was manipulated by combining the subjects' responses or collecting them separately. Thus, the subjects' responses were collected either on individual counters or on a group counter. Difficulty was manipulated by using two contrast levels, making the signals either quite easy or more difficult to detect. Consistent with other social loafing research, at high contrast levels, when the task was easy, subjects whose scores could be individually identified outperformed (i.e., fewer misses and false alarms) subjects whose scores were combined, and therefore unidentifiable. However, as with the brainstorming research, when the task was more difficult and challenging, there were no differences in performance due to identifiability.[3]

---

[3] Once again, it could be argued that this performance equivalence was the result of the task being so difficult that a floor effect prevented the emergence of any significant differences. Arguing against this interpretation is the finding that overall 77% of the 14 signals were detected. In addition, this level of performance was attained at the cost of an average of only four false alarms. To have performed reliably more poorly on the difficult task than the identifiable subjects who made 7.62 errors, the subjects who were told that their scores were not identifiable need only have made 11 or more errors (misses plus false alarms). So, although this task was more difficult than the easy one, there was still plenty of room for the unidentifiable subjects to have performed more poorly than the identifiable ones. Thus, no floor effect appears to be operating. An in Experiment 1, arguing against a ceiling artifact is

Task uniqueness experiments. Taken together, the brainstorming and vigilance studies suggest that it may not be a feeling of a lack of identifiability or accountability alone that leads to social loafing, but also a feeling that one's contribution is redundant (i.e., one's "above average" talent is not required), that one's performance does not represent a real contribution, and hence, there is no incentive for working hard. To test directly the roles of these two factors, we designed a study using the vigilance task in which the factors of interest were manipulated orthogonally. Identifiability was manipulated, once again, by keeping track of a group's responses on one counter, or on a set of four counters, one per subject. Crossed with this manipulation, in one half of the groups all of the subjects were assigned a single quadrant of the TV screen to watch (same task), while in the other half of the groups, each individual was given his or her own quadrant to watch (unique task). Fourteen signals occurred in each of the quadrants but the time of occurrence of the signals within a given quadrant was completely independent of the time of occurrence in the other quadrants. So, when watching different quadrants, subjects could make a definite contribution, since if they did not report a signal, it went unreported. When everyone watched the same quadrant, any one of the subjects could see and report a signal.

To replicate previous research on identifiability (Williams et al., 1981), we would expect better performance by subjects whose performances were individually identifiable than by those whose outputs were combined on a single counter. However, if the opportunity to make a definite contribution provides sufficient motivation to reduce social loafing, subjects whose individual scores are unidentifiable but are assigned tasks requiring nonredundant responses should perform as well as identifiable subjects. Thus, if lack of identifiability alone is sufficient to produce social loafing, we should obtain a main effect for identifiability on performance. If the lack of an opportunity to make a definite contribution to the group effort is also necessary for social loafing, as the previous experiments suggest, an identifiability $\times$ task interaction would be expected.

The results of the study supported the latter hypothesis. Despite the fact that unique-task subjects felt no more identifiable than same-task subjects when their outputs were combined, the former subjects made fewer errors than the latter. In fact, the unique task subjects performed as well as same-task participants whose outputs were identifiable. These data are presented in Table 7-2. This pattern of results for the unidentifiable (1 counter) performance cells was replicated at a higher-contrast setting. Thus, even though the subjects were performing a simple task and their responses were not identifiable, when they were responsible for monitoring a unique quadrant on the TV, no loafing occurred.

---

the fact that if the identifiable subjects were operating at a ceiling, the unidentifiable subjects were at the same ceiling since their performances were not reliably different. Yet there was ample room for poorer performance (more errors than 11). In addition, as in the previous experiment, the a posteriori tests of the interaction means revealed that the subjects whose scores were unidentifiable performed as well on the difficult task as on the easy one, suggesting that these subjects put out greater effort on the former task than on the latter one.

Table 7-2. Combined Error Index as a Function of Identifiability and Task[a,b]

Task	Identifiability	
	Identifiable (4 counters)	Unidentifiable (1 counter)
Unique (4 quadrants)	2.33_a	3.05_a
Same (1 quadrant)	2.73_a	6.08_b

[a] From Harkins & Petty (1982, Experiment 3).
[b] Means that do not share a common subscript are reliably different by the Newman-Keuls procedure, $p < .05$.

To test the generalizability of this finding, we conducted a conceptual replication, using the brainstorming task with which we began. As in the previous experiment, subjects were told either that they alone would be working on their particular task or that others would also be taking part. In this case, as in the first experiment, the task was generating uses for an object. However, rather than writing all of the uses on a sheet of paper as in the first brainstorming experiments, the subjects wrote their uses on slips of paper and put them down cardboard tubes into a common box, so that (presumably) the uses could not be associated with their authors. If brainstorming works like vigilance, then even though their outputs are unidentifiable, subjects who believe that they have their own object should generate more uses than those who believe that they have the same object for which to generate uses as everyone else.

Subjects whose outputs were unidentifiable, but who were told that they each had a different object, generated more uses than subjects whose outputs were unidentifiable but were told that they were generating uses for the same object as everyone else. Different-object subjects believed that the experimenter could tell exactly how well they performed to the same extent as same-object subjects, so that differential perceptions of identifiability do not provide a plausible interpretation for the major finding. These results are consistent with those obtained using the vigilance task. Perceptions of need are sufficient to reduce loafing even when one's contribution remains completely anonymous.[4]

Summary and conclusions. In summary, the experimental designs used in previous research on social loafing have incorporated several features that could account for the observed reductions in individual effort when groups were assigned responsibility for a task. Williams et al. (1981) have shown that one such feature is that in these studies the participants' outputs are combined. However, in addition to eliminating the potential for individual evaluation, the loafing manipulation in previous studies has also required subjects to work with others on the same simple task. The brain-

---

[4] We note that neither deindividuation (Zimbardo, 1970) nor social facilitation (Cottrell, 1972) can provide explanations for these findngs since these differences are found even when the potential for evaluation (i.e., identifiability) is held constant.

storming and vigilance studies reviewed here suggest that these task characteristics may also contribute to the loafing effect, and that loafing may be reduced by giving group members the impression that they can make a definite contribution.

Our series of studies shows that working with others on an evaluative task can lead to reduced effort, which, in turn, can affect persuasion by affecting the amount of thinking about the message content. Importantly, our research shows that these effects are above and beyond any effects attributable to the actual presence of others. Having found support for the notion that social context (i.e., the number of people evaluating a message) can influence the persuasion process, we now turn to the opposite side of the coin: the effects of multiple sources on a single target.

Multiplication of Impact

Research from several areas is consistent with the notion that increasing the number of message sources may lead to increased persuasive impact. For example, conformity pressures resulting from knowing that others support a position often lead to movement toward that attitude position simply as a result of normative influence (cf. Krech, Crutchfield, & Ballachey, 1962). Also, multiple sources may generate different arguments to support their position, and research shows that increasing the number of arguments used in a persuasive message leads to enhanced persuasion (Calder, Insko, & Yandell, 1974). Thus, multiple sources might be expected to be more persuasive as a result of conformity pressures and/or the different arguments the sources might generate. In fact, it may be that this research on conformity and number of arguments led to limited interest in the effects of multiple sources since it may have appeared that the effects of this variable were already well-documented.

However, in the previous research, *actual exposure* to persons or their arguments has been confounded with the mere knowledge that the persons or arguments existed. That is, subjects have been exposed either to the positions of one or multiple sources, or to one or multiple arguments, but subjects in the one-person or one-argument conditions have not explicitly been informed that multiple sources or multiple arguments also existed supporting the advocated position, and that they might be exposed to these sources and arguments. Thus, it was not possible to determine whether the information about the number of sources or number of arguments to which they might be exposed would have been sufficient to lead to attitude change, or if actual exposure was required for persuasion to occur.

From a social impact theory perspective (Latané, 1981), it is clear that one would predict that increasing the number of sources should increase persuasive impact, but it is less clear what the theory would predict with regard to increasing the number of different arguments or the effects of *actual* exposure versus mere knowledge of the number of sources and arguments involved. From a cognitive response theory perspective, it is clear that increasing the number of good arguments should lead to more persuasion, but increasing the number of poor arguments should lead to less persuasion. The effect on persuasion of increasing the number of sources would be determined by how increasing the number of sources affects message processing. Increasing the number of sources might plausibly increase a person's motivation to think about the arguments presented, or conversely, might distract a person from doing so.

Number of Sources and Attitudes

In an initial study designed to explore the effects of multiple sources and arguments (Harkins & Petty, 1981a), we exposed subjects to one or three arguments presented by one or three sources, but held constant background information about arguments and sources by telling all of the subjects that we had videotaped three people who advocated a particular position. Subjects were further told that each of these people had generated three arguments on the issue and that they might be exposed to these people and their arguments. This allowed a test of whether actual exposure to sources or arguments had persuasive impact beyond that achieved by the mere knowledge of the number of sources and arguments to which they might be exposed. In addition two control groups were included: an "information only" control group in which subjects were given the same background information as the other subjects but responded to the dependent measure without exposure to the sources and their messages; and an "attitude only" control group in which subjects gave their opinions on the topic without receiving any information about the existence of the sources or their arguments. As shown in Table 7-3, the "information only " manipulation was sufficient to yield more favorable attitudes than those held by the "attitude only" subjects. In fact, only when participants were exposed to multiple sources delivering multiple arguments were they more persuaded than subjects in the "information only" condition. Exposure to a single source presenting a single argument, to multiple sources who gave different versions of the same argument, or to multiple arguments given by the same source led to no more persuasion than that resulting from the background information about persons and arguments. In addition, subjects did not differ by condition in the proportion of presented arguments that they could recall, or in their estimates of the percentage of their peers they thought would support the proposal.

This pattern of results is consistent with two plausible alternative explanations. One possibility is that subjects, seeing three different sources independently generate three different, yet convincing, arguments, conclude that a large pool of good arguments in favor of the advocated position must exist, and so, it must be a position worth supporting. Subjects seeing three sources each present a variation of the same argument, or a single source (who would be motivated to avoid repeating an argument) present different arguments, would have less reason to come to this conclusion.

A second, cognitive response interpretation would suggest that subjects who are exposed to multiple sources presenting multiple arguments process the content of the message more thoroughly than subjects in the other conditions. That is, each time a source appears, the subject "gears up" to process the message. If it is a new source, and a new argument, the target thinks about the argument's implications and since the arguments are sound, favorable thoughts and persuasion result. How-

Table 7-3. Means for Attitude and Positive Thoughts Measures in Experiment 1[a,b]

Condition	Attitude	Positive Thoughts
Three-person—three-argument	1.88_a	3.75_a
Three-person—one-argument	$.30_b$	2.20_b
One-person—three-argument	$.04_b$	1.85_b
One-person—one-argument	$.03_b$	1.50_b
Information control	$.12_b$	1.95_b
Attitude control	-2.38_c	$.70_c$

[a]From Harkins & Petty (1981a, Experiment 1).
[b]Means that do not share a common subscript are significantly different at the .05 level by the Newman-Keuls procedure.

ever, if the same source appears again, even though with new arguments, the target may put less effort into thinking about the argument since this source has been heard from already. Likewise, if new sources are presented, but with the same argument, little additional processing takes place. After all, the target has heard the argument before.[5] Consistent with this interpretation, multiple-source/multiple-argument subjects generated more favorable thoughts concerning the advocated position than subjects in the other conditions (see Table 7-3).

These two possibilities were tested in a second experiment (Harkins & Petty, 1981a, Experiment 2) in which in one condition subjects were led to believe that the arguments that were presented exhausted the pool of good arguments in favor of the position. In this condition, the argument-pool explanation would predict no persuasive advantage resulting from multiple sources presenting multiple arguments, since the argument pool was limited to the number of arguments presented. Although manipulation checks revealed that the argument-pool induction was successful, limiting the argument pool did not reduce persuasion. Multiple sources presenting multiple arguments were still more persuasive than single sources presenting the same information. These results are consistent with a processing interpretation since limiting the size of the argument pool should not affect one's cognitive responses to the arguments that are actually presented. The cognitive response interpretation received further support from the results of a third experiment (Harkins & Petty, 1981a, Experiment 3) in which number of sources and argument quality were jointly manipulated. Subjects exposed to three sources presenting three con-

---

[5] This may seem inconsistent with previous research which would suggest that increasing the number of arguments (Calder, Insko, & Yandell, 1974, Insko, Lind, & LaTour, 1976) and argument repetition (Cacioppo & Petty, 1979; Harrison, 1977) should lead to enhanced persuasion. However, there are differences in methodologies that may account for these seeming inconsistencies. Our subjects, unlike those in the previous research, were all informed about the number of arguments to which they might be exposed. Also, our arguments were simple, one-sentence statements. Had we used more complex stimuli, as have previous researchers, argument repetition might have led to enhanced persuasion, as new implications of the complex arguments became apparent.

vincing arguments were more persuaded than those exposed to the same arguments presented by a single source, but, when the arguments were unconvincing, exposure to multiple sources led to *less* persuasion than that resulting from exposure to the same information from a single source. In the latter case, the enhanced thought induced by multiple sources led to greater counterargument production.

In a fourth experiment, employing only strong arguments (Harkins & Petty, 1981b), it was found that performance of a secondary, distraction task reduced the persuasion found in the multiple-source/multiple-argument condition to the levels found in the one-source/multiple-argument condition, while recall, the number of good arguments thought to exist in favor of the advocacy, and the percentage of classmates thought to support the proposal were not affected. Therefore, it appears that it was not that all processing ceased upon exposure to the distractor; rather, the additional idiosyncratic elaboration of the cogent arguments presented, which is normally elicited by exposure to multiple sources presenting multiple arguments, was not possible given the requirements of the secondary task.

Factors Responsible for Enhancement of Effort

The theory of social impact (Latané, 1981) would predict that increasing persuasion should result as the number of sources is increased. We have found that when background information is held constant, increasing the number of sources increases the amount of message processing but only when the multiple sources present different arguments in favor of the advocacy. Importantly, we are referring to the *effort* put into thinking about the message, *not* persuasion. As was the case for diffusion, we found that enhanced processing led to enhanced persuasion only when the message arguments were cogent. When unconvincing arguments were presented by multiple sources, this led to even less persuasion than when the same weak arguments were presented by a single source.

Once again, though these studies suggest the process by which effort is translated into persuasion (i.e., via cognitive responses), it is not clear what it is about multiple sources presenting multiple arguments that leads to additional thinking about the arguments presented. As was the case with the diffusion research, we conclude with some research that represents an attempt to understand the basis of this effect.

One possibility is that when multiple arguments are presented by multiple sources, the target sees the different arguments as independent bits of information. When a source appears to present his or her second argument, the target may not engage in additional thought since he or she may feel that he or she already knows what the source has to say. Only when different people present different arguments is each source-argument combination independent of the others and this independence may suggest that the sources are viewing the problem from different perspectives, drawing on different bodies of information, and so on. Given this independence, the subjects may think about each argument more thoroughly, and if the arguments are cogent, favorable thoughts and persuasion would result.

This line of reasoning suggests that, if the multiple sources presenting their different arguments were made nonindependent in some way, the persuasive advantage would disappear because subjects would no longer give enhanced scrutiny to the multiple-source arguments. We tested this notion by replicating the multiple-source/ multiple-argument and single-source/multiple-argument conditions of Harkins and Petty (1981a) and adding a multiple-source/multiple-argument condition in which the subjects were informed that the sources had formed a committee to research the issue. In the latter condition, subjects were told that the arguments generated were the result of the committee's joint efforts. As shown in Table 7-4, the data for the two replication cells duplicated previous findings: multiple-source/multiple-argument subjects generated more positive thoughts and were more persuaded than single-source/multiple-argument subjects. However, when told that the sources had colluded in the generation of their arguments, this persuasive advantage disappeared. The committee subjects were no more persuaded than single-source subjects. Thus, the persuasive advantage of having multiple sources present cogent arguments disappeared when the sources were perceived as nonindependent.

Further evidence consistent with the independence hypothesis comes from Wilder's (1977) conformity research in which he has found that the manner in which the sources of influence are grouped affects the amount of social influence that they exert. For example, when subjects perceive four people as two groups of two, these two entities exert greater social influence than when they are categorized as one group of four. That is, to the extent that the sources of influence are perceived as nonindependent, their influence is diminished.

However, while we suspect that nonindependence leads to reduced processing and less persuasion (if the arguments are cogent), this lack of independence could lead to reduced persuasion through an alternative route. It could be argued that when the target knows that the sources formed a committee to look into the issue, he or she could feel less confidence in the committee's judgment. Goethals and Nelson (1973) have shown that for matters of belief, greater confidence in the correctness of a judgment is inspired by agreement from dissimilar rather than similar others. Reckman and Goethals (1973) have shown that when emphasis is placed on accuracy of judgment, participants show a preference for partners whose interpersonal judgment styles are dissimilar from their own. As Goethals and Nelson (1973) note: "the greater the difference in perspectives converging on a judgment, the more confidently that judgment can be held" (p. 122). Of course, similarity/dissimilarity in their study referred to the degree of difference between a person him/herself and another, but the same process could operate when a target faces multiple

Table 7-4. Means for Attitudes and Positive Thoughts Measures in Committee Study I[a]

Condition	Attitude	Positive Thoughts
Three-person—Three-argument	.93$_a$	3.18$_a$
One-person—Three-argument	−.30$_b$	2.09$_b$
Committee	−.63$_b$	1.64$_b$

[a]Means that do not share a common subscript are significantly different at the .05 level by the Newman-Keuls procedure.

sources, who seem similar or dissimilar. Thus, the committee manipulation could lead to the inference that there is a commonality of perspective, resulting in reduced persuasion. Independent sources could lead to the perception of different perspectives converging on the same judgment, yielding greater confidence in their judgment.

Of course, this explanation, unlike ours, does not depend on differences in processing to account for differences in persuasion. Differences in the *inferences* made about the independence of the sources' judgments are sufficient to account for the differences in agreement. If this inferential process alone accounted for our pattern of results, the order in which the subjects were exposed to the information about whether the sources were independent or had formed a committee and the persuasive messages should not make a difference. That is, learning that the sources formed a committee after exposure to the persuasive messages should lead to the same outcome as if they had received the information prior to exposure, since the same inferences could be made in either case. If differential processing plays a role, as we suspect, the order of presentation of the source information is crucial in that only when the committee manipulation comes first could it influence the processing of the persuasive messages. If presented afterwards, it should not matter since the processing has already taken place. We tested this possibility by utilizing a pre-post design in which all of the subjects were exposed to multiple sources presenting multiple arguments, but half were told of the independence or nonindependence of the sources prior to exposure to the arguments, and half were informed subsequent to exposure to the arguments, but prior to responding to the dependent measures.

Consistent with the processing interpretation, the persuasiveness of multiple sources presenting multiple arguments was reduced only when the committee manipulation *preceded* exposure to the arguments. Learning that the sources had formed a committee after exposure to the arguments resulted in as much persuasion as that following from exposure to independent sources. Thus, it does not appear that simple inferences about the judgmental independence of the sources alone can account for the differences in persuasion. It could well be, however, that these inferences do play a role by motivating more or less processing which, in turn, depending on argument cogency, enhances or diminishes persuasive impact.

We have focused on one aspect of the committee manipulation: that is, members of a committee may be seen as sharing a perspective and this lack of independence in judgmental perspective may lead the subjects to process their messages less diligently. However, other aspects of the committee manipulation could also result in elimination of the multiple-source effect. Most simply, perhaps by labelling the multiple sources as a "committee," they are all viewed as the same source. Subjects would, therefore, respond just as they do to single sources presenting multiple arguments. Alternatively, the subjects may be influenced by their perceptions of how committees work. They may feel that certain points of view are likely to be suppressed in committees, and so, the unanimity expressed by the sources may be the result of an active campaign to bring recalcitrant committee members into line, rather than an expression of a shared perspective. If subjects believed this, they might think less about the arguments since they could not be sure that the views reflected the sources' true feelings. In addition, subjects could feel that independent sources might have been more diligent in forming their opinions than sources who are members of a committee, who share the responsibility for adopting a position on the issue. Since less thought went into it, the committee members' joint position may be less worthy of thought than the positions of the sources who arrived at their conclusions independently. Although it is not yet clear what aspect of the committee manipulation is responsible for eliminating the multiple-source/multiple-argument effect, it does appear that people are less likely to think about information that comes from committees than from independent individuals.

General Discussion

Taken together, our series of studies suggests that the social context does have important and systematic effects on the persuasion process, and in both the division and the multiplication situations, these effects appear to be mediated by the amount of cognitive effort the targets are motivated to put into processing the content of the persuasive communications received. When targets share the responsibility for evaluating persuasive messages with others, they appear to put out *less* effort than when they are solely responsible. When participants are the target of a persuasion attempt by multiple sources, each of whom contributes a different argument, they appear to put out *greater* effort than when they are exposed to a single source, even though in the latter situation, the participants have heard the same arguments and have learned about the other sources.

However, the processes that lead to the expenditure of this effort are quite different for targets and sources. In the diffusion situation (i.e., multiple targets), sharing responsibility for the same easily accomplished tasks leads the participants to feel that they cannot make a unique or worthwhile contribution, and so, they reduce their efforts. The more important, challenging, or difficult the evaluation task is, the less likely it is that group responsibility will lead to reduced effort. In the multiplication situation (i.e., multiple sources), exposure to several people who present different arguments leads to enhanced effort as long as the sources are seen as independent. The greater the perception of dependence or collusion among the sources, the less likely it is that multiple sources will lead to enhanced effort.

Despite these differences, the process that links effort and persuasion appears to be the same for multiplication and division situations: Persuasion is a function of the number and nature of cognitive responses elicited. Greater effort leads to an enhanced appreciation of the merits and/or flaws of a communication and reduced effort leads to a diminished appreciation. Thus, if the communication consists of cogent arguments, their consideration by multiple *targets* will lead to less appreciation of these merits and less persuasion than if this evaluation were conducted by a single target. The opposite occurs for messages consisting of specious arguments since the group evaluators, putting out less effort, are less aware of the message flaws than the individual evaluators and are therefore more persuaded. Similarly, the greater effort elicited by multiple independent *sources* presenting multiple, independent arguments leads to enhanced persuasion only when the arguments are cogent. If they are not, the greater cognitive effort elicited by multiple sources leads to even less persuasion than that occasioned by exposure to the same arguments presented by a single source.

In this research, we initially restricted our focus to investigating the divisive and multiplicative force fields suggested by Latané's (1981) theory of social impact. In addition to providing a conceptual framework, the theory also makes predictions concerning persuasion in these situations that we were able to test. A clear finding from our research was that under appropriate conditions, increasing the number of sources could increase the amount of cognitive effort put out by the targets, and increasing the number of targets could decrease the amount of effort they exerted. However, although these effects may be consistent with social impact theory, as noted previously, the processes that mediate effort in response to sources and targets appear to be quite different. Social impact theory is not meant to provide any insights concerning mediating processes, but its silence in this regard also means that it provides no clue as to what factors might interact with source and target manipulations to influence effort. If the mediating process were the same for both targets and sources, one could be more sanguine about the predictive utility of social impact. Importantly, social impact theory does not fare well in predicting persuasion. When the arguments making up the message were cogent, multiple sources and multiple targets did lead to enhanced and diminished persuasion, respectively. But, when the arguments were specious, exposure to multiple sources and multiple targets led to diminished and enhanced persuasion, respectively. These findings suggest that, at least when it comes to persuasion, simply knowing that the number of sources or targets has increased will not allow one to make persuasion predictions. Number manipulations, whether of sources or targets, do not seem to have simple, unitary effects on persuasion.

As a means of predicting the persuasion effects, we made use of the cognitive response model (Petty et al., 1981), which predicts that persuasion occurs primarily as a result of increases or decreases in a person's motivation and/or ability to think about the arguments that are presented. Our findings suggest that the source and target manipulations affect the participants' *motivation* to process the message arguments, and it is this motivation to think about the message arguments that mediates persuasion. The cognitive response model appears to provide a viable account of the persuasion findings that result from manipulating the number of sources and recipients of a persuasive message.

While the outcomes of these studies seem promising, a number of unresolved issues remain. For example, questions may arise as to the generalizability of these findings. For example, feeling that one can make a contribution apparently reduces the diffusion (loafing) effect, and there are probably a number of ways that this impression could be given. If participants were given a persuasive message composed of passages that appeared complex or difficult to understand, people may feel that they could make a contribution since they are likely to believe that they are better able to understand and evaluate the arguments than the average person. Similar outcomes may be obtained if participants felt that they knew more about a particular issue than other group members. Other manipulations may also reduce loafing. For example, when exposed to persuasive communications on issues that are highly personally involving, participants may not loaf, since it is important to have a veridical opinion on these issues. These possibilities suggest that the diffusion effect has low generalizability since there may be a number of factors working against it. In general, however, persuasive messages are meant to be easily understood, and, given the large number of potential issues, there is little reason to believe that most people feel very knowledgable about or personally involved in many of them.

It is also the case that in the diffusion studies, we explicitly combined the products of the participants. How often does this occur in the "real world"? First of all, there are a number of situations in which this happens. For example, juries are given joint responsibility for their decisions and the same is true of many committees. Most often, when people listen to political candidates, it is in anticipation of voting rather than filling out individual attitude questionnaires, and all votes are combined to determine the election winner. Even if there is no explicit combinatorial rule, people may still feel shared responsibility and put less effort into their evaluations when they are with others. For example, when part of a group that is listening to a persuasive communication, an individual may feel that the responsibility for evaluating the position is implicitly shared with the other members of the group, and diffusion of effort could occur.

The findings for multiplication of effort as a result of exposure to multiple sources also have implications for many persuasion settings. Our findings suggest that actual exposure to multiple sources can have persuasive effects beyond those following from simple exposure to information about the number of sources and arguments, and that this additional persuasive impact is the result of enhanced processing on the part of the targets. In addition, however, our research suggests the conditions under which exposure to multiple sources will *not* result in enhanced persuasion. For example, in the courtroom or in advertising our data suggest that any connection among the sources or their arguments will render exposure to the sources and their arguments no more efficacious than simple knowledge that they and their arguments exist. That is, if the jury perceives the defense witnesses as an entity rather than as separate sources, as is likely to be the case, the defense might be as well served to present one witness who delivers all the information and to point out the existence of the other witnesses. If potential consumers of a product see the participants in man-on-the-street interviews as truly independent, this technique would be useful. However, this perception may be unlikely given the obvious sponsorship by the responsible company. Furthermore, even if these sources were seen as independent, their advocacy would be no more effective than that of a single source, unless they generated different reasons for their use of the product.

Another problem is that cognitive effort is a central concept in our model, but we have no direct measure of it. We have used self-report measures in some of our research, and the results have been consistent with our effort interpretation. More convincing are the cognitive response data we have collected. Given the limited amount of time that participants are given to list their thoughts, we would not expect, nor have we obtained, differences in the total number of thoughts generated, but the *pattern* of thoughts generated has been consistent with the effort hypothesis. This interpretation is all the more convincing given the strong-weak argument manipulation. Just as one would expect if more effort were expended in thinking about the arguments, multiple-source/multiple-argument and single-target participants generate more favorable *thoughts* than the single-source or multiple-target participants in response to cogent arguments, but more *unfavorable* thoughts in response to specious ones. Nevertheless, a direct measure of cognitive effort would be valuable. Kahneman (1973) has suggested pupillary dilation as the single best index of mental effort, since it appears to be sensitive to both between-tasks differences in difficulty and within-task variations in effort (see also Beatty, 1982). In future research we will attempt to use a measure such as this to provide additional corroborative evidence.

As we noted in introducing our program of research on number of sources and targets of persuasive influence, we have restricted our focus in a number of ways in order to reduce the complexity inherent in many social situations. For example, in our research participants were always the targets of an influence attempt, never the sources; messages originated from outside rather than inside the group; groups were composed of unfamiliar people rather than acquaintances; and the number of people physically present in group and individual conditions was always held constant. Interestingly, the setting used in research on group polarization effects (cf., Lamm & Myers, 1978) incorporates many of the complex features that we have omitted in our research. In group polarization research, participants typically respond to some attitude item individually, and then participate in a group discussion. In this group discussion, when participants give their reasons for endorsing a given position, they are acting as the sources of a persuasive message. Additionally, in this research, the messages originate from within the group, and participants are one of multiple targets who are the recipients of multiple arguments from multiple sources. Thus, each participant acts as both a source and a target of persuasive influence. The major outcome of this kind of research is that after discussion, the average group attitude rating is more extreme than the average of the group's prediscussion ratings. That is, whatever initial tendency there was tends to be accentuated by group discussion.

One might think that this polarization tendency is opposite to what would be expected on the basis of our diffusion research. After all, in some sense the group shares responsibility for an evaluation of the attitude topic, so "why wouldn't they loaf?" Viewing this question from the perspective suggested by our research, however, makes quite clear the complexity of this setting. Participants are not only targets, they are also sources themselves and the targets of multiple sources. In addition, whatever effects actual presence might have (e.g., distraction) could also play a role.

This analysis suggests that polarization could result from the operation of multiple processes, some of which may be working in opposition to one another, but at differing strengths. We feel that a research strategy in which the various components of this setting are considered separately, as well as together, will maximize the likelihood that a thorough understanding of such phenomena will be achieved. Our research already suggests that a more fine-grained analysis of the group interaction would be fruitful. For example, our source findings would suggest that the mere number of people in the group or the mere number of different arguments expressed in the group discussion would not be as powerful a determinant of attitude polarization as *the number of different arguments that are expressed by different people.*

Additional research is required to test the generality of the effects we have obtained and to extend this work to other aspects of persuasion settings, but the research reported here suggests the utility of such an effort. Clearly, the number of sources and targets of a persuasion attempt have attitudinal effects beyond those predictable by previous research and these effects have considerable implications for persuasion attempts in naturally occurring settings.

References

Aderman, D., Brehm, S., & Katz, L. Empathic observation of an innocent victim: The just world revisited. *Journal of Personality and Social Psychology,* 1974, *29*, 342-347.

Beatty, J. Task-evoked pupillary responses, processing load, and the structure of processing resources. *Psychological Bulletin,* 1982, *91*, 276-292.

Brock, T. C. Implications of commodity theory for value change. In A. Greenwald, T. Brock, & T. Ostrom (Eds.), *Psychological foundations of attitudes.* New York: Academic Press, 1968.

Cacioppo, J. T. Harkins, S. G., & Petty, R. E. The nature of attitudes and cognitive responses and their relationships to behavior. In R. E. Petty, T. M. Ostrom, & T. C. Brock (Eds.), *Cognitive responses in persuasion.* Hillsdale, N.J.: Lawrence Erlbaum, 1981.

Cacioppo, J. T. & Petty, R. E. The effects of message repetition and position on cognitive response, recall, and persuasion. *Journal of Personality and Social Psychology,* 1979, *37*, 97-109.

Calder, B., Insko, C., & Yandell, B. The relation of cognitive and memorial processes to persuasion in a simulated jury trial. *Journal of Applied Social Psychology,* 1974, *4*, 62-93.

Cohen, A. R. Communication discrepancy and attitude change: A dissonance theory approach. *Journal of Personality,* 1959, *27*, 386-396.

Cottrell, N. Social facilitation. In C. McClintock (Ed.), *Experimental social psychology.* New York: Holt, Rinehart & Winston, 1972.

Fromkin, H. L., & Brock, T. C. Erotic materials: A commodity theory analysis of availability and desirability. *Journal of Applied Social Psychology,* 1973, *3*, 219-231.

Goethals, G., & Nelson, E. Similarity in the influence process: The belief-value distinction. *Journal of Personality and Social Psychology,* 1973, *25*, 117-122.

Goethals, G., & Zanna, M. The role of social comparison in choice shifts. *Journal of Personality and Social Psychology,* 1979, *37*, 1469-1476.

Greenwald, A. G. Cognitive learning, cognitive response to persuasion and attitude change. In A. G. Greenwald, T. C. Brock, & T. M. Ostrom (Eds.), *Psychological foundations of attitudes.* New York: Academic Press, 1968.

Harkins, S., Latané, B., & Williams, K. Social loafing: Allocating effort or taking it easy? *Journal of Experimental Social Psychology,* 1980, *16*, 457-465.

Harkins, S. G., & Petty, R. E. Effects of source magnification of cognitive effort on attitudes: An information-processing view. *Journal of Personality and Social Psychology,* 1981, *3,* 401-413. (a)

Harkins, S. G., & Petty, R. E. The multiple source effect in persuasion: The effects of distraction. *Personality and Social Psychology Bulletin,* 1981, *4,* 627-635. (b)

Harkins, S. G., & Petty, R. E. The effects of task difficulty and task uniqueness on social loafing. *Journal of Personality and Social Psychology,* 1982, *43,* 1214-1229.

Harrison, A. Mere exposure. In L. Berkowitz (Ed.), *Advances in experimental social psychology* (Vol. 10). New York: Academic Press, 1977.

Hovland, C. I. Reconciling conflicting results derived from experimental and survey studies of attitude change. *American Psychologist,* 1959, *14,* 8-17.

Ingham, A. G., Levinger, G., Graves, J., & Peckham, V. The Ringelmann effect: Studies of group size and group performance. *Journal of Experimental Social Psychology,* 1974, *10,* 371-384.

Insko, C., Lind, E., & La Tour, S. Persuasion, recall and thoughts. *Representative Research in Social Psychology,* 1976, *7,* 66-78.

Jellison, J., & Riskind, J. A social comparison of abilities interpretation of risk behavior. *Journal of Personality and Social Psychology,* 1970, *15,* 375-390.

Jones, E. E., & Gerard, H. B. *Foundations of social psychology.* New York: Wiley, 1967.

Kahneman, S. *Attention and effort.* Englewood Cliffs, N.J.: Prentice-Hall, 1973.

Keating, J., & Latané, B. Politicans on TV: The image is the message. *Journal of Social Issues,* 1976, *32,* 116-132.

Kerr, N., & Bruun, S. Ringelmann revisited: Alternative explanations for the social loafing effect. *Personality and Social Psychology Bulletin,* 1981, *7,* 224-231.

Knower, F. H. Experimental studies of changes in attitude: I. A study of the effect of oral argument on changes of attitude. *Journal of Social Psychology,* 1935, *6,* 315-347.

Knower, F. H. Experimental studies of changes in attitude: II. A study of the effects of printed arguments on changes of attitude. *Journal of Abnormal and Social Psychology,* 1936, *30,* 522-532.

Krech, D., Crutchfield, R., & Ballachey, E. *Individual in society.* New York: McGraw-Hill, 1962.

Lamm, H., & Myers, D. Group-induced polarization of attitudes and behavior. In L. Berkowitz (Ed.), *Advances in experimental social psychology.* New York: Academic Press, 1978.

Latané, B. The psychology of social impact. *American Psychologist,* 1981, *4,* 343-356.

Latané, B., Williams, K. D., & Harkins, S. G. Many hands make light the work: The causes and consequences of social loafing. *Journal of Personality and Social Psychology,* 1979, *37,* 822-832.

Myers, D. *The inflated self.* New York: Seabury Press, 1980.

Newcomb, T. M. *Personality and social change.* New York: Dryden, 1943.

Newton, J., & Mann, L. Crowd size as a factor in the persuasion process: A study of religious crusade meetings. *Journal of Personality and Social Psychology,* 1980, *39,* 874-883.

Petty, R. E., & Cacioppo, J. T. Issue involvement can increase or decrease persuasion by enhancing message-relevant cognitive responses. *Journal of Personality and Social Psychology*, 1979, *37*, 1915-1926.

Petty, R. E., & Cacioppo, J. T. *Attitudes and persuasion: Classic and contemporary approaches*. Dubuque, Iowa: Wm. C. Brown, 1981.

Petty, R. E., Harkins, S. G., Williams, K. D., & Latané, B. The effects of group size on cognitive effort and evaluation. *Personality and Social Psychology Bulletin*, 1977, *3*, 579-582.

Petty, R. E., Harkins, S. G., & Williams, K. D. The effects of group diffusion of cognitive effort on attitudes: An information-processing view. *Journal of Personality and Social Psychology*, 1980, *1*, 81-92.

Petty, R. E., Ostrom, T. M., & Brock, T. C. (Eds.). *Cognitive responses in persuasion*. Hillsdale, N.J.: Lawrence Erlbaum, 1981.

Petty, R. E., Wells, G. L., & Brock, T. C. Distraction can enhance or reduce yielding to propaganda: Thought disruption versus effort justification. *Journal of Personality and Social Psychology*, 1976, *34*, 874-884.

Reckman, R., & Goethals, G. Deviancy and group orientation as determinants of group composition preferences. *Sociometry*, 1973, *36*, 419-423.

Steiner, I. *Group process and group productivity*. New York: Academic Press, 1972.

Wicklund, R. A., Cooper, J., & Linder, D. Effects of expected effort on attitude change prior to exposure. *Journal of Experimental Social Psychology*, 1967, *2*, 416-428.

Wilder, D. Perception of groups, size of opposition, and social influence. *Journal of Experimental Social Psychology*, 1977, *13*, 253-268.

Williams, K., Harkins, S., & Latané, B. Identifiability as a deterrent to social loafing: Two cheering experiments. *Journal of Personality and Social Psychology*, 1981, *40*, 303-311.

Zimbardo, P. G. The human choice: Individuation, reason, and order, versus deindividuation, impulse and chaos, In W. Arnold & D. Levine (Eds.), *Nebraska Symposium on Motivation* (Vol. 17). Lincoln: University of Nebraska Press, 1970.

Part 3
Exchange Processes in Groups

Chapter 8

Coalition Formation: A Social Psychological Approach

S. S. Komorita and David A. Kravitz

Social interactions may be purely cooperative, as in the ideal marriage, or purely competitive, as in war. However, in most situations both tendencies are present, and an important process that occurs in such "mixed-motive" situations is the formation of coalitions. A coalition may be defined as two or more parties who agree to cooperate (pool their resources) in order to obtain some mutually desired outcome. The parties involved may be individuals, groups, or collectivities of any size. Similarly, the outcomes may be anything humans desire (money, status, power, etc.) and the resources that are pooled may be whatever is needed to obtain the desired outcome (skills, abilities, money, etc.).

Coalitions play an important role in a variety of situations. For example, a street-corner gang is a coalition of teenagers who have joined together to defend themselves against other gangs, or simply to satisfy affiliative needs. A trade union is a coalition of workers who have joined forces to obtain better working conditions and wages. The major political parties are coalitions of individuals and organizations who have joined forces to obtain greater influence over the government's policies. Finally, NATO is a coalition of nations that have pooled their economic and military resources to resist potential aggressive acts of other nations. Thus we see that coalition formation is a critical process that pervades every level of our lives, from the interpersonal to the international.

We shall begin this chapter by classifying coalition situations, and defining some necessary terms in the process. We shall then turn to a description of five theories that have been developed to predict the behavior of parties in such situations. This will be followed by a review of the empirical literature. Ten empirical generalizations will be presented and illustrated and their implications for coalition theories explicated. Finally, we shall suggest some future directions for coalition research.

Classification of Coalition Situations

Our general definition of coalition formation (defined earlier) includes a wide variety of social situations. For simplicity, and for the purpose of this chapter, we shall assume that the parties involved are individuals, and the outcomes represent some quantitative (divisible) measure, such as money or points. In addition, we shall add another constraint to this definition: The participants must not only cooperate to achieve some outcome, but they must also reach an agreement on the distribution of that outcome.

Since coalition situations vary widely, they have been categorized in a number of ways. For the purpose of describing and organizing the coalition literature, we shall classify different coalition games on the basis of the number of values (outcomes) for the different coalitions. In a *simple game* all coalitions are either "winning" or "losing." All winning coalitions are assigned (are worth) one particular value (say 100 points), and all losing coalitions are worth some smaller value (say zero). For example, consider the four-person simple game shown in Figure 8-1a. This game is called an apex game (Horowitz, 1973) and is defined as follows:

$$v(A) = v(B) = v(C) = v(D) = v(BC) = v(BD) = v(CD) = 0;$$

$$v(AB) = v(AC) = v(AD) = v(BCD) = 100;$$

$$v(ABC) = v(ABD) = v(ACD) = v(ABCD) = 100.$$

where A, B, C, and D denote the four players, and $v(\ )$ denotes the value of the coalition given within the parentheses. It can be seen that all coalitions have one of two values (100 or 0), and at least two persons are necessary to form a winning coalition. Note that among the two-person coalitions, only those that include player A are winning coalitions. Thus, player A has an advantage (bargaining strength) over the other three players in this game.

One of the main implications of this example is that there is little incentive to form large coalitions in simple games. When the value of all winning coalitions is the same, a larger number of coalition members means that the value (prize) must be divided among a large number of persons, thus reducing each person's share of the prize. For this reason only minimal-winning coalitions are likely to form in simple games. A *minimal-winning coalition* (MWC) is a winning coalition that becomes a losing coalition if any single member is deleted. The ABC coalition, for example, is not an MWC because it would still be a winning coalition if either B or C were deleted. The minimal-winning coalitions in the above game are AB, AC, AD, and BCD; the non-minimal-winning coalitions are ABC, ABD, ACD, and ABCD. Henceforth we shall ignore non-minimal-winning coalitions because they rarely form and none of the theories predicts that they will form.

The game in Figure 8-1a is called an *apex game* because there is a single "strong" (apex) player and N-1 "weak" (base) players. In apex games two types of MWCs are possible: apex coalitions of the apex player and one of the base players (AB, AC, and AD in the four-person case), and the base coalition of the N-1 base players (BCD in the four-person case). This game has been used widely in research, and we shall refer to such studies in this chapter.

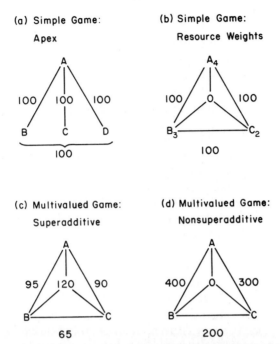

Fig. 8-1. Four types of games. Capital letters denote players and numbers denote values of coalitions; subscripts in case (b) denote the resource weights of the players and depict the game 5(4–3–2).

In contrast to simple games, in *multivalued games* the different coalitions are assigned many different values, and winning and losing coalitions are not defined. Consider the three-person multivalued game shown in Figure 8-1c. This game is defined as follows:

$$v(A) = v(B) = v(C) = 0;$$

$$v(AB) = 95; v(AC) = 90; v(BC) = 65; v(ABC) = 120.$$

It can be seen that player A again has an advantage, but for an entirely different reason than in the simple game. Player A has superior bargaining strength because the coalitions that include him or her have greater values (120, 95, 90) than the coalitions that include the other players.

In the example just given, the value of the grand coalition, the coalition of all players, is greater than the values of the smaller coalitions. Such a game is said to be superadditive. In a *superadditive game*, the value of any coalition is at least as large as the sum of the values of the disjoint (nonoverlapping) subsets of players in the coalition. The game shown in Figure 8-1d, for example, is nonsuperadditive because the value of the ABC coalition is zero, which is less than the sum of the values of the AB and C coalitions. Unlike simple games, in superadditive multivalued games there is an incentive to form larger coalitions, since larger coalitions have larger values.

Simple Games with Resource Weights

In the previous section we showed that in multivalued games the relative power of a player is based on the values of the coalitions that include the player. In a simple game, in contrast, the power of a player is based on the number and sizes of the MWCs that include the player. In many coalition experiments involving simple games, "resource weights" have been used to provide a basis (justification) for specifying which coalitions are winning or losing. In Gamson's (1961) "political convention paradigm," for example, resource weights represent votes, and a majority of the votes is necessary to form a winning coalition. Such games are called *weighted majority games*, and we shall denote such games as follows: $Q(v_1 - v_2 - \ldots - v_i - \ldots - v_N)$; where Q denotes the quota, the number of votes required to form a winning coalition; v_i denotes the number of votes controlled by player i, and N denotes the number of players. Without loss of generality we shall assume that the value of all winning coalitions is 100, and the value of all losing coalitions is zero. For convenience we shall denote the players by capital letters (A, B, C, . . ., N), in descending order of the number of votes that they control. For example, a commonly used game is 5(4-3-2), shown in Figure 8-1b. The quota is 5, and players A, B, and C control 4, 3, and 2 votes, respectively. The MWCs are therefore AB, AC, and BC. Chertkoff and Braden (1974) used this game to simulate a meeting of corporate stockholders in which the three players controlled three large blocks of stock in the company. The meeting was to determine who would control the company and thereby decide how the company's profits were to be divided. Since nobody held a majority of shares, subjects were asked to maximize their shares of the profits by forming a partnership with one of the other major stockholders. Thus, simple games can be seen as prototypes of many real-life situations in which group decisions are involved.

Another commonly used game is 9(8-3-3-3), where 9 votes are required to form a winning coalition, and the MWCs are AB, AC, AD, and BCD. If we assign a value of zero to all other coalitions, this game is identical to the simple apex game described in the previous section (shown in Figure 8-1a). Thus 9(8-3-3-3) is also a simple apex game. The only difference is that in the previous case the winning coalitions were arbitrarily determined, whereas in the present case resource weights are used as a basis for specifying the winning coalitions. When resource weights are assigned they introduce another factor that may influence the negotiations among the bargainers; one or more bargainers may appeal to justice (equity) and demand a fair or reasonable share of the reward based on the resource distribution.

Two functions of resource weights. Resource weights, hereafter denoted resources, have two distinct functions: strategic and normative. They have a *strategic function* in that they determine the number and sizes of MWCs in which the players are included. For example, in the weighted majority game 9(8-3-3-3), player A has an advantage for two strategic reasons. First, A is included in three MWCs, whereas B, C, and D are included in only two. Second, the MWCs that include A contain only two persons, whereas one of the coalitions for B, C, and D (the BCD coalition) contains three persons. This is a distinct disadvantage for B, C, and D because they must divide the prize among a larger number of players unless they join A.

The second (*normative*) function of resources is that they provide a frame of reference or basis for an equitable division of the reward. In negotiating the division of the prize some players may argue that they deserve larger shares of the prize because they are contributing more resources. In some cases such appeals to equity may be effective even when resources have no effect on the players' strategic positions in the game. The classic example of this paradox is the simple three-person game 5(4-3-2), with MWCs of AB, AC, and BC. Since all players are included in the same number and size coalitions, based on the strategic function alone, all coalitions should be equally likely for a 50-50 division of the 100 point prize. However, there is some evidence showing that the BC coalition forms more frequently than AB or AC, and that player B achieves a greater share of the prize than player C. We shall show that this relevance or irrelevance of resource weights for strategic position in the game has implications for the validity of different coalition theories.

Theories of Coalition Formation

Although a variety of coalition theories has been proposed, some of them only predict which coalitions are likely to form and others only predict the reward division among the coalition members. Since both of these dependent measures are of interest to social scientists, we shall restrict ourselves to theories that predict both variables. This restriction excludes some important normative theories (cf. Luce & Raiffa, 1957; Rapoport, 1970) because they do not predict which coalitions are likely to form. It also excludes Caplow's (1956, 1959) theory, which does not predict reward division. Accordingly, we shall describe and illustrate the following five theories that predict both dependent variables: (a) minimum resource theory (Gamson, 1961), (b) minimum power theory (Gamson, 1964); (c) weighted probability model (Komorita, 1974); (d) bargaining theory (Komorita & Chertkoff, 1973); and (e) equal excess model (Komorita, 1979).

Predictions of Theories in Simple Games

We shall initially describe and illustrate these theories with the four-person apex game (Figure 8-1a), both with and without resources. When resources are assigned, we shall use the game 9(8-3-3-3). As we showed in the previous section, the structure (pattern of MWCs) of the two games is identical, with MCWs of AB, AC, AD, and BCD.

Minimum resource theory. Gamson's (1961) minimum resource theory is based on the parity norm, which prescribes that rewards be divided in direct proportion to the resources of the coalition members. For the game 9(8-3-3-3) the theory predicts a reward division of 73 (8/11) for A and 27 (3/11) for B, C, or D in the two-person coalitions, and equal shares of 33 each in the BCD coalition. Since BCD maximizes the expectations of players B, C, and D, the theory predicts that this coalition is most likely to form.

In the BCD coalition the sum of resources of the coalition members is just large enough to meet the quota of nine votes required to form a winning coalition. For simple games this theory always predicts that the "cheapest winning" coalition will form (because each player's reward will be maximized when the joint resources are minimized), and this is the reason it is called "minimum resource" theory.

Only the normative function of resources is important in minimum resource theory (through the use of the parity norm), and the strategic function is completely ignored. This dependence on the parity norm implies that the theory is limited to games in which resources are assigned; when resources are not assigned, no predictions can be derived from the theory.

Minimum power theory. Minimum power theory was also proposed by Gamson (1964), and is based on an extension of Shapley and Shubik's (1954) index of "pivotal power." A player's *pivotal power* is based on the relative frequency with which his or her resources, when added to the resources of other players, convert a losing coalition into a winning coalition. In a four-person game there are 24 possible permutations of the players, and thus 24 possible sequences in which a winning coalition could be formed. In the apex game (Figure 8-1a), player A is pivotal in 12 cases, and players B, C, and D are each pivotal in 4 cases. Thus the pivotal power indices of players A, B, C, and D are 12/24, 4/24, 4/24, and 4/24, respectively.

Gamson proposed that the players should agree to divide the reward in direct proportion to their pivotal power indices, and thus the reward divisions should be 75–25 in AB, AC, and AD, and 33 each in BCD. Since the BCD coalition mutually maximizes expectations for players B, C, and D, the theory predicts that this coalition is most likely to form. Note that in this coalition the sum of pivotal power indices of the players is minimized. Like minimum resource theory, minimum power theory always predicts that the coalition that minimizes the sum of pivotal power indices is most likely to form in simple games.

The predictions of minimum power theory are based entirely on the pivotal power indices, which in turn depend only on the set of MWCs of the game. Thus minimum power theory is based solely on the strategic function of resources, and ignores their normative function. This means that its predictions are identical for all games that have the same pattern of MWCs. Hence, it makes identical predictions for the apex game of Figure 8-1a and for 9(8-3-3-3). This theory can be applied both to resource and nonresource games.

Weighted probability model. The basic assumption of the weighted probability model (Komorita, 1974) is that large coalitions are more difficult to form and maintain than are small coalitions. It assumes that the probability of coalition j is an inverse function of its size, given by $P_j = w_j / \Sigma w_j$; where $w_j = 1/(n_j - 1)$; n_j denotes the number of persons in coalition j; and the summation is over all MWCs. For the apex game (Figure 8-1a), the w_j values for AB, AC, AD, and BCD are 1/1, 1/1, 1/1, and 1/2, respectively, and $\Sigma w_j = 7/2$. Dividing these w_j values by Σw_j yields the probabilities of the coalitions. Thus the predicted probabilities of the AB, AC, AD, and BCD coalitions are 2/7, 2/7, 2/7, and 1/7, respectively. Note that this is the only theory that makes exact predictions of coalition frequencies.

Predictions of reward division among the coalition members are based on the probability of individual i being included in the winning coalition, denoted P_i. Given the probabilities predicted for each MWC, player A should be included in the winning coalition with $P_i = 6/7$ and for the other three players $P_i = 3/7$. Each member's share of the reward is then assumed to be directly proportional to the probability of being included in the winning coalition. Since player A's probability of inclusion is twice as large as the probability of inclusion for the other players, the model predicts reward divisions of 67-33 in the two-person coalitions. It predicts an equal share of 33 each in the BCD coalition.

Note that resources are not involved in deriving predictions. Like minimum power theory, weighted probability model is based entirely on the strategic function of resources and ignores their normative function. Hence, it can be applied both to resource and nonresource games, and it makes identical predictions for the apex game (Figure 8-1a) and for 9(8-3-3-3).

Bargaining theory. The previous theories are all static theories in that coalition frequency and reward division are predicted to be constant over all trials of a multitrial experiment. In contrast, Komorita and Chertkoff's (1973) bargaining theory predicts changes in the players' expectations and outcomes as a function of the offers, counteroffers, and outcomes of previous trials. In a one-trial game the theory assumes that players with large resources will expect and demand a share of the reward based on the parity norm, while those who have small resources will expect and demand equal shares. Thus each player will appeal to the norm of reward division that maximizes his or her share of the prize. The predicted reward division is simply the mean of these two values.

Consider the game 9(8-3-3-3) played for one trial (or the first trial of an iterated game). If player A begins negotiations with one of the others, the theory predicts that A will demand a 73-27 split (based on parity), while the other will demand a 50-50 split (based on equality). The mean of these two demands yields predicted divisions of 61-39 in AB, AC, and AD. A division of 33 each is predicted for the BCD coalition. Since the two-person coalitions maximize expectations for all players, the bargaining theory predicts that one of them is most likely to form on the first trial.

When the game is iterated over trials, the theory assumes that the bargainers will base their demands on their maximum expectations in alternative coalitions, denoted Emax. At the asymptotic level (after an indefinite number of trials), it predicts that rewards will be divided in direct proportion to these Emax values. In AB, AC, and AD, for example, player A's Emax will be 73, based on parity in the other two-person coalitions, and the other player's Emax will be 33, based on both parity and equality in the BCD coalition. Direct proportionality with respect to these Emax values of 73 and 33 yields asymptotic predictions of 69-31 in AB, AC, and AD. The predicted asymptotic division in BCD is 33-33-33.

The bargaining theory assumes that coalition frequency at the asymptote is a function of coalition instability, which in turn depends on the extent to which the coalition members are tempted to defect (to obtain higher outcomes in another coalition). It can be shown that coalition instability is minimized in the apex coalitions, and is maximized in the base coalition. Thus, bargaining theory predicts that the apex coalitions should be most (and equally) likely at the asymptote, and BCD should be least likely.

In its original form the bargaining theory could make predictions only when resources were assigned. However, Komorita and Tumonis (1980) proposed an extension of the theory to allow predictions when resources are not assigned. As in the original theory, expectations are assumed to be based on two norms of justice, where one of the norms is equality. In the apex game (Figure 8-1a), for example, where the MWCs are AB, AC, AD, and BCD, the equality norm prescribes 50-50 divisions in the two-person coalitions and 33-33-33 in BCD. The extension of the theory consists of substituting a proportionality norm based on alternatives for the parity norm based on resources. For example, if players A and B are negotiating the division of 100 points, B is expected to demand a 50-5 split (based on equality). Player A, however, is expected to demand a share that is proportional to their alternatives: 50 for A in the other two-person coalitions and 33 for B in BCD. Proportionality with respect to these alternatives yields shares of 60-40 for A and B, respectively. As in the original theory, a split-the-difference solution between equality and proportionality is assumed to be most likely on Trial 1, yielding predictions of 55-45 in AB, AC, and AD, and 33 each in BCD. Hence, one of the two-person coalitions is predicted to be most likely on Trial 1.

Expectations are assumed to converge to an asymptotic solution that is proportional to each member's maximum expectation in alternative coalitions (Emax): 60 for A in AB, AC, and AD (based on proportionality), and 33 for B, C, and D in BCD. Thus, at the asymptote a 64-36 split is predicted in AB, AC and AD, and an equal split is predicted in BCD. Thus expectations in the two-person coalitions are mutually maximized at the asymptote, and it can be shown that the instability index is minimal in the two-person coalitions and maximal in BCD. Thus, as in 9(8-3-3-3), the two-person coalitions are predicted to be most (and equally) likely at the asymptote.

In summary, the bargaining theory was originally designed for resource games, but has since been extended to games in which resources are not assigned. In resource games it is based on both the normative and strategic functions of resources. The Trial 1 predictions are based on both the normative and strategic functions of resources (through parity and equality), as are the asymptotic predictions (through proportionality with respect to maximum expectation in alternative coalitions).

Equal excess model. The equal excess model (Komorita, 1979) was proposed for games in which resource weights are not assigned. Accordingly, we shall first describe the model for the simple apex game of Figure 8-1a, in which resources are not assigned, and shall then briefly mention an extension of the model for 9(8-3-3-3) where resources are assigned.

In the prenegotiation phase of coalition formation the model assumes that each player will prefer and attempt to form the coalition that maximizes initial expectations based on equality. For the game in Figure 8-1a initial expectations of player A will be 50 in each of the two-person coalitions. The initial expectations of each of the other players will be 50 in his or her coalition with A, and 33 in BCD. Thus players B, C, and D are expected to send offers to player A, while A will be indifferent among the three two-person coalitions.

On subsequent rounds of bargaining, predictions are derived as follows. It is assumed that each player will insist on receiving at least the value of his or her best alternative. Any excess remaining after the players have all received these points will be divided equally among them. On Round 1, for example, the maximum alternatives for players A and B in the AB coalition are 50 for A (equality in AC and AD) and 33 for B (equality in BCD). The excess of 16.7 is divided equally, resulting in a predicted division of 58.3-41.7. If no agreement is reached on Round 1, to derive predictions on subsequent rounds this process is repeated with values of maximum alternatives based on the previous round. For example, if A and B negotiate on Round 2, the maximum alternative of A is 58.3 (based on Round 1 predictions in AC or AD), while for B it is 33.3 (in BCD). The excess is 8.4, and if this excess is divided equally the predicted division is 62.5-37.5. Successive iterations of this procedure will lead to stable asymptotic predictions of 67-33 in AB, AC, and AD, and 33-33-33 in BCD.

On the early rounds the two-person coalitions maximize expectations for all players, and consequently they are predicted to be most likely. At the asymptote, however, the model predicts that payoffs should converge to an equilibrium state in which the expectations of all players are equal to their respective maximum expectations in alternative coalitions, and hence none of them will be tempted to defect. This means that the likelihood of the two-person coalitions should decrease as the number of rounds required to reach agreement increases, and the likelihood of the BCD coalition should increase correspondingly.

As described above, the equal excess model is only appropriate for games in which resources are not assigned. Komorita (1979) suggested that the Trial 1 predictions of the bargaining theory might be used for initial expectations when resources are assigned. These values are then used to derive predictions for subsequent rounds. This generally results in asymptotic predictions that are identical to the asymptotic predictions when resources are not assigned.

In summary, the equal excess model was developed primarily for games in which resources are not assigned, but an extension to resource weight games was suggested. When resources are assigned, its Round 1 predictions are based on both the normative and strategic functions, while predictions on subsequent rounds are based increasingly on the strategic function of resources. Since the asymptotic predictions are the same for both resource and nonresource situations, the model implies that resource weights have effects on early rounds of bargaining but not in the late stages.

The main weakness of the model is that it does not specify the exact round on which an agreement is likely. However, it is assumed that the following situational factors encourage an agreement on the early rounds of bargaining: (a) if subjects are naive and unfamiliar with coalition bargaining; (b) if incentives to bargain competitively are negligible; and (c) if communication and information about offers and counteroffers are restricted.

Summary of predictions in simple games. The five theories vary considerably in the extent to which they focus on the normative versus strategic function of resources.

Minimum resource theory is based entirely on the normative function, and thus is at one end of this continuum. Minimum power theory and weighted probability model are at the other extreme, and are based entirely on the strategic function of resources. The predictions of both of these theories are invariant when the sets of MWCs are the same in games with and without resource assignment. Finally, bargaining theory and equal excess model are intermediate on the continuum. When resources are assigned, the Trial 1/Round 1 predictions of these two theories are based on both functions of resources. At the asymptote, the predictions of bargaining theory still are based on both functions, while the predictions of equal excess model are based entirely on the strategic function.

Table 8-1 summarizes the predictions of the five theories for the game shown in Figure 8-1a (apex game) and for the weighted majority game 9(8-3-3-3). When resources are assigned, minimum resource and minimum power theories both predict that the base (BCD) coalition should be most frequent, whereas the other theories predict that the apex coalitions should be most frequent. For the apex game without resources (Figure 8-1a), minimum resource theory is unable to make predictions. Minimum power theory predicts that the base coalition should be most frequent, but the other three theories predict that the apex coalition should be most frequent.

With regard to the predicted payoff splits, minimum resource and minimum power theories predict that the apex player's payoff should be considerably greater than do the other three theories. The other theories make remarkably similar predictions, especially at the asymptote, and it would be difficult to discriminate the comparative validities of these theories with these games. Finally, note that the asymptotic predictions of the equal excess model and of the weighted probability model coincide exactly in both games; this illustrates the fact that the asymptotic predictions of the equal excess model are based exclusively on the strategic function of resource weights. The last row of Table 8-1 shows the pooled data from several independent studies. It can be seen that the apex coalitions occurred most frequently, thus supporting the predictions of weighted probability, bargaining, and equal excess theories. Moreover, the payoff splits predicted by these theories are more accurate than those predicted by minimum resource and minimum power theories. In a subsequent section we shall show that minimum resource and minimum power theories are generally less accurate than the other three theories, and their inadequacies are not specific to these two games.

Predictions of Theories in Multivalued Games

Although the majority of coalition experiments have been restricted to simple games, in recent years experiments with multivalued games have become increasingly common. Since resources are rarely used in multivalued games, we shall restrict ourselves to the case where resources are not assigned. We shall also restrict ourselves to the predictions of two theories, bargaining theory and equal excess model. Our reasons for excluding the other three theories are that: (a) Minimum resource theory is limited to resource games, and resources are rarely used in multivalued games; (b)

Table 8-1. Predicted Coalition and Payoffs in Apex Coalition (AB, AC, and AD)[a]

Theory	Games[b]		Predicted Coalition
	9(8-3-3-3)	Apex	
Minimum resource	73-27	d	Base
Minimum power	75-25	75-25	Base
Weighted prob.	67-33	67-33	Apex
Bargaining			
E^1	61-39	55-45	Apex
E^∞	69-31	64-36	Apex
Equal excess			
E^1	64-36	58-42	Apex
E^∞	67-33	67-33	Apex
Observed results[c]	67-33 (.83)	58-42 (.87)	

[a] All theories predict an equal split (33-33-33) in the base (BCD) coalition. E^1 and E^∞ for bargaining theory and equal excess model denote Trial 1/Round 1 and asymptotic predictions, respectively.

[b] Apex refers to game in Figure 8-1a (apex game without resources).

[c] Values in parentheses denote proportion of occurrence of the apex coalition. Data are based on pooled results of studies by Chertkoff (1971), Kormorita and Tumonis (1980), Kravitz (1981), and Murnighan, Kormorita, and Szwajkowski (1977).

[d] No predictions can be derived.

minimum power theory has been shown to be very inaccurate in both simple and multivalued games (Miller, 1980a, 1980b, 1980c); and (c) an attempt to extend weighted probability model (Komorita & Tumonis, 1980) to multivalued games has proven to be unsuccessful, suggesting that the model may be limited to simple games.

Equal excess model. To illustrate the predictions of the model, we shall use the game shown in Figure 8-1d, with $v(A) = v(B) = v(C) = 0$; $v(AB) = 400$; $v(AC) = 300$; $v(BC) = 200$; and $v(ABC) = 0$. This game is a prototype of a situation in which three business people (or corporations) have the opportunity to form partnerships (or mergers), and the expected profits of the different partnerships (or mergers) differ. The predictions of the equal excess model for this game are straightforward: It was designed for this situation. The initial expectations of each player, based on equal splits, are: 200-200 for players A and B in the AB coalition: 150-150 for A and C in AC; and 100-100 for B and C in BC. According to the equal excess norm, the bargainers receive their respective alternatives and the excess is divided equally. For example, in the AB coalition player A's alternative is 150 (in AC), player B's alternative is 100 (in BC), and the excess is 150. Thus the predicted Round 1 division in AB is 225 for A and 175 for B. Similarly, it can be shown that the predicted divisions in the AC and BC coalitions on Round 1 are: AC (200-100) and BC (125-75). Since the AB coalition mutually maximizes expectations for both A and B, it is predicted to be most likely if a coalition forms on Round 1. Successive iterations of this process lead to asymptotic predictions of: AB(250-150), AC(250-

50), and BC(150-50). Note that the asymptotic expectations are in an equilibrium state in which none of the players will be tempted to defect from any coalition. This implies that the AB coalition is most likely on the early rounds but its likelihood should decrease with successive rounds of negotiations.

Bargaining theory. The bargaining theory was proposed for simple resource games. For multivalued games without resources, Komorita and Tumonis (1980) proposed an extension of the theory in which expectations based on equality and proportionality are defined in terms of the values of different coalitions instead of in terms of resources. For the game in Figure 8-1d, the equality norm prescribes AB(200-200), AC(150-150), and BC(100-100). Players A and B are predicted to initiate offers to each other because the AB coalition mutually maximizes their initial expectations. As in the original theory, each player is expected to appeal to the norm that maximizes his or her share of the reward: Player B is expected to demand an equal share (200-200), while player A is expected to demand a share that is proportional to each player's expectations in alternative coalitions. Proportionality with respect to alternatives (150 for A in AC and 100 for B in BC), yields a split of 240-160 for A and B, respectively. Thus, on Trial 1 the split-the-difference solution for AB is 220-180. Similarly, for the AC and BC coalitions, the Trial 1 predictions are 175-125 and 107-93, respectively. Since the AB coalition mutually maximizes expectations for A and B, this coalition is predicted to be most likely on Trial 1.

At the asymptote, payoffs are predicted to converge to a solution that is proportional to each member's maximum expectation in alternative coalition (Emax). Player A's Emax in AB is 200, based on proportionality in AC, while player B's Emax is 114, based on proportionality in BC. Proportionality with respect to these Emax values yields an asymptotic solution of 255-145. Similarly, the asymptotic prediction is 212-88 for AC and 114-86 for BC. It can be shown that instability is minimal in AB and maximal in BC; hence, AB is predicted to be most likely, and BC least likely.

Summary of predictions in multivalued games. Table 8-2 summarizes the predictions of the two theories for the multivalued game in Figure 8-1d. Both theories predict that AB should be most frequent and BC should be least frequent. However, equal excess also predicts that the differences in the frequencies of the three coalitions should decrease over rounds of bargaining. With regard to the predicted payoffs, the two theories make remarkably similar predictions for the AB coalition, both on the initial encounter (E^1) and at the asymptote (E^∞). Although the differences in predicted splits in the AC and BC coalitions are much larger, the frequencies of these coalitions may be too small to provide a sensitive test of the two theories. Thus, it is plausible that other types of games must be used to compare and evaluate the two theories. The last two rows of Table 8-2 show some data for this game. It can be seen that the theories do equally well in predicting reward divisions. Furthermore, as predicted by both theories, mean payoffs for player A increased with prior experience in both the AB and AC coalitions, while mean payoffs for player B in AB and for player C in AC decreased with experience.

Table 8-2. Predictions of Bargaining Theory and Equal Excess Model for Multivalued Game of Figure 8-1d[a]

Theory	Coalitions		
	AB	AC	BC
Bargaining			
E^1	220–180	175–125	107– 93
E^∞	255–145	212– 88	114– 86
Equal excess			
E^1	225–175	200–100	125– 75
E^∞	250–150	250– 50	150– 50
Observed values[b]			
E^1	209–191 (37)	204– 96 (18)	100–100 (1)
E^9	237–163 (28)	227– 73 (23)	162– 38 (5)

[a] Values of the AB, AC, and BC coalitions are 400, 300, and 200, respectively, and $v(ABC) = 0$. E^1 and E^∞ denote the Trial 1/Round 1 and asymptotic predicted values, respectively.

[b] Observed means are data from Komorita and Kravitz (1981). Values of E^1 and E^9 represent mean data for two groups of 14 triads each, who played the game for 4 trials. E^1 represent data for subjects who had no prior experience with coalition games, and E^9 represent data for subjects who had played eight trials of similar three-person games prior to playing four trials of the test game. Values in parentheses denote the frequencies of each coalition.

General Evaluation of Theories

Since recent reviews of the coalition literature are available (Miller & Crandall, 1980; Murnighan, 1978a), no attempt will be made to present an exhaustive review of this literature. Instead, we shall focus on some propositions (generalizations, hypotheses) about coalition behavior, and shall then evaluate the coalition theories in terms of these propositions. These propositions, however, should be qualified with the expression "all else being equal," since any given effect may interact with other aspects of the situation.

Simple Games

The vast majority of coalition experiments have dealt with simple resource games. In this section we shall present six propositions based on this research.

Proposition 1. In simple games the probability of a given coalition varies inversely with its size.

The last column of Table 8-1 provides some support for Proposition 1. The frequencies of the two person coalitions are .83 and .87, and by subtraction the frequencies of the three-person coalitions are .17 and .13. This inverse relation between coalition size and frequency has been obtained in virtually every study that has included MWCs of different sizes, including: Chertkoff (1971); Horowitz and Rapoport (1974); Komorita and Kravitz (1978); Komorita and Meek (1978); Kravitz (1981); Murnighan (1978b); and Murnighan, Komorita, and Szwajkowski (1977).

Minimum power theory generally predicts that larger coalitions will be more likely than smaller ones. In apex games, for example, it always predicts that the base coalition should be most frequent (cf. predictions in Table 8-1). Hence, the predictions of minimum power theory are generally inconsistent with Proposition 1 and the data supporting $P1$. In contrast, the predictions of minimum resource theory depend on the specific distribution of resources employed. Consider the two apex games: 9(8-3-3-3) and 10(6-4-4-4). In the former game, minimum resource theory predicts that the base coalition will be most frequent, whereas in the latter it predicts the apex coalitions. The predictions of the bargaining theory and equal excess model, on the other hand, are consistent with $P1$. This is largely due to their use of the equality norm, which makes small coalitions more valuable to a player than large ones. Finally, the predictions of weighted probability model are entirely consistent with $P1$, indeed $P1$ is actually one of the assumptions of the model. In summary, minimum power theory is generally inconsistent with this proposition, and minimum resource theory is only occasionally consistent. Bargaining theory, equal excess model, and weighted probability model are all consistent with Proposition 1.

Proposition 2. In simple games, a member's share of the prize in a coalition is directly related to the number of alternative MWCs that include the member, relative to the number that include other members of the coalition.

In the games shown in Figures 8-1a and 8-1b, for example, if player A negotiates with player B to form AB, player A has two alternative coalitions (AC and AD) whereas player B has only one alternative (BCD). Consistent with this difference, Table 8-1 shows that the mean share received by player A is much greater than that received by the other players.

Proposition 2 is also supported by the results of studies on veto games, a class of simple games in which one of the players, the veto player, must be included in all winning coalitions. For example, consider the veto game: 5(4-1-1-1-1). In this type of veto game the number of MWCs is N-1 and varies directly with group size. The veto player is included in all N-1 coalitions, and the other players are included in only one MWC each, the coalition with the veto player. According to Proposition 2, therefore, the payoff for the veto player should be directly related to group size. This was observed in studies by Murnighan and Roth (1980), in which group size and communication among the players were manipulated.

The predictions of minimum resource theory are based entirely on a player's resources, and do not take the number of his or her alternative MWCs into consideration. Similarly, predictions of bargaining theory and equal excess model are insensitive to the number of the player's alternatives as long as each player always *has* an alternative. Thus Proposition 2 is inconsistent with the predictions of these three theories. Minimum power theory is based on pivotal power, which is a positive function of the number of a player's alternatives. Similarly, weighted probability model bases predictions of reward divisions on the probability of being included in the winning coalition, which in turn is a positive function of the number of the player's alternatives. Thus, Proposition 2 is consistent with weighted probability model and minimum power theory, and inconsistent with minimum resource theory, bargaining theory, and equal excess model. The relative inaccuracy of the bargaining theory for veto games was also found in a study by Michener, Fleishman, and Vaske (1976).

Proposition 3. In simple games, a member's share of the reward is inversely related to the mean size of the member's MWCs, relative to the sizes of the other members' MWCs.

In the games shown in Figures 8-1a and 8-1b, for example, if player A negotiates with one of the other players, say with player B to form AB, the mean size of A's alternative coalitions is 2 (AC and AD), whereas the size of B's alternative is 3 (BCD). Since player A achieves a larger share than the others in the apex coalitions (see Table 8-1), these data support Proposition 3.

This proposition can be illustrated with a "diamond" game used by Kravitz (1981). In the four-person game 27 (16-13-11-10) the MWCs are AB, AC, and BCD. Players A, B, and C are each in two MWCs, but the mean sizes of player A's coalitions (2 players) is smaller than the mean sizes of the other players' coalitions (2.5 players). The mean reward divisions in the two-person coalitions were 59-41 and 55-45, when resources were and were not assigned, respectively. Similar effects were found in diamond games used by Michener and Sakurai (1976), and in many of the studies cited in support of Proposition 1.

Predictions of minimum resource theory are insensitive to the members' alternatives, and are therefore inconsistent with $P3$. This is also true of first trial predictions of bargaining theory and equal excess model when resources are assigned. The asymptotic predictions of these two theories depend on the players' *best* alternatives, which may be based on their smallest coalition, but do not depend on the *set* of coalitions in which they are included. Thus, these two theories may or may not be consistent with $P3$. Minimum power theory is supported because pivotal power is an inverse function of coalition size. Similarly, the weighted probability model is supported because it assumes that a player's share of the prize depends on his or her probability of being included in the winning coalition, which in turn depends on the sizes of the player's MWCs. In summary, Proposition 3 is inconsistent with minimum resource theory, is sometimes consistent with bargaining theory and equal excess model, and is perfectly consistent with minimum power theory and weighted probability model.

Proposition 4. In simple games with the same pattern of MWCs, differences in the distribution of resource weights affect the payoffs of the coalition members but have negligible effects on the frequencies of various coalitions.

Proposition 4 is supported by the results of a study by Murnighan et al. (1977) who compared three games with identical sets of MWCs but with different distributions of resources: 9(8-3-3-3), 9(8-7-1-1), and 9(8-7-7-7). In all three games the

MWCs are AB, AC, AD, and BCD. The apex coalitions occurred 83% of the time and did not differ significantly in the three games. However, the mean share for the apex player did differ significantly in the three games (means of 67, 62, and 59, respectively). Moreover, the demands of the apex player also differed significantly in the three games and were greatest in the first game and smallest in the third game.

The study by Murnighan et al. (1977) contrasted the effects of three games differing in resource weights. It is also possible to contrast the effects of games with and without resource weights but having the same pattern of MWCs. The results of such studies (Komorita & Tumonis, 1980; Kravitz, 1981) do not seem to support Proposition 4. In both studies, resource assignment had no significant effect on coalition formation and reward division. However, the results of these studies, though not statistically significant, showed a consistent effect of resource assignment. Whenever there was a strategic power difference among the players within a coalition, the stronger player received a larger share when resources were assigned than when they were not assigned. This effect of resources is illustrated in the last row of Table 8-1, which contrasts the results of the four-person apex game (Figure 8-1a) with the resource game, 9(8-3-3-3). The MWC are identical in the two games, but the apex player received a larger payoff when resources were assigned (67-33) than in the apex game where resources were not assigned (58-42).

One plausible explanation for these seemingly inconsistent results is that resources have significant effects for naive, inexperienced bargainers, and negligible effects for sophisticated bargainers who are familiar with the structure of coalition games (Chertkoff & Braden, 1974; Kelley & Arrowood, 1960; Komorita & Moore, 1976). Such changes in expectations as a function of familiarity and experience (trials/rounds) are predicted by bargaining theory and equal excess model. Both theories predict that the expectations of player A will increase over trials of bargaining because players B, C, and D will try to outbid one another to form a coalition with A. Such attractive offers from B, C, and D are assumed to increase A's level of aspiration and thus increase his or her demands on subsequent trials. The effects of resource distribution reported by Murnighan et al. (1977) are also consistent with the predictions of minimum resource theory. However, they are inconsistent with the predictions of minimum power theory and weighted probability model. Both theories assume that only the pattern of MWCs should affect coalition outcomes. It is plausible, therefore, that these two theories may be applicable only for relatively sophisticated bargainers.

In some weighted majority games the players' resources have no influence on their strategic positions (inclusion in MWCs) in the game. For example, in the game 5(4-3-2) each of the players is included in two two-person MWCs, despite having different resources. In such games resources are, by definition, strategically irrelevant.

Proposition 5. In simple games where resources are strategically irrelevant, a player's resource weight is directly related to his or her share of the reward, but is inversely related to the frequency of being included in the winning coalition.

Proposition 6. These effects of resources tend to diminish with the players' familiarity and experience with coalition games. This implies that the nor-

mative function of resources is salient for naive, inexperienced players, and the strategic function is dominant for experienced, sophisticated players.

Proposition 5 is supported by the results of game 5(4-3-2) in which the BC coalition occurs most frequently and player B receives a larger share than C (Vinacke & Arkoff, 1957). Kelley and Arrowood (1960), however, hypothesized that the BC coalition occurs most frequently because player A has not learned that power, based on resource weights, is really illusory. To test this hypothesis, they replicated game 5(4-3-2) for a large number of trials. They found that BC was most frequent in the early trials, but the frequencies of the three coalitions did not differ significantly on later trials, thus supporting Proposition 6. Many other studies also provide support for Propositions 5 and 6 (Chertkoff, 1966; Chertkoff & Braden, 1974; Chertkoff & Esser, 1977; Komorita & Brinberg, 1977; Komorita & Moore, 1976; Murnighan, 1978b; Psathas & Stryker, 1965).

Proposition 5 is consistent with the predictions of minimum resource theory and the Trial 1/Round 1 predictions of bargaining theory and equal excess model. The changes specified by $P6$ are consistent with the two dynamic theories, bargaining theory and equal excess model. Finally, if the changes given in $P6$ were to continue until all coalitions were equally likely and reward divisions were equal splits, the results would be consistent with minimum power theory and weighted probability model.

These propositions for games in which resources are strategically irrelevant suggest that: (a) minimum resource theory is limited to naive, inexperienced bargainers; (b) minimum power theory and weighted probability model are limited to sophisticated, experienced bargainers; and (c) the Trial 1/Round 1 predictions of bargaining theory and equal excess model apply to naive bargainers while the asymptotic predictions apply to sophisticated players.

Summary evaluation of theories in simple games. There is considerable empirical support for the six propositions described previously, and they have important implications for the validity of descriptive (predictive) theories of coalition formation. The six propositions, and the data supporting them, are most consistent with the assumptions and predictions of bargaining theory, equal excess model, and weighted probability model, and are generally inconsistent with the predictions of minimum resource theory and minimum power theory.

Multivalued Games

Unlike simple games in which the value of all winning coalitions is the same, in multivalued games various coalitions are assigned different values. Many experiments have been conducted on multivalued games, and the results of such studies will be used to derive some generalizations or propositions, as we did in the previous section. In this section we shall evaluate the two descriptive theories of multivalued games that were described earlier, bargaining theory and equal excess model, in terms of some propositions derived from these experiments:

Proposition 7. In nonsuperadditive multivalued games, the coalition that mutually maximizes v(S)/s *is most likely to form, where* v(S) *denotes the value of coalition* S, *and* s *denotes the number of players in* S.

To illustrate Proposition 7, consider the game shown in Figure 8-1d, with $v(A) = v(B) = v(C) = 0$; $v(AB) = 400$; $v(AC) = 300$; $v(BC) = 200$; and $v(ABC) = 0$. Proposition 7 asserts that the AB coalition should occur most frequently, and BC should occur least frequently. This game was used in a study by Komorita and Kravitz (1981), and AB, AC, and BC occurred in 66%, 32%, and 2% of the replications, respectively. The results of many other studies support *P*7 (Kahan & Rapoport, 1974; Komorita & Tumonis, 1980; Miller, 1980a, 1980b, 1980c; Riker, 1967).

The predictions of both the bargaining theory and equal excess model are consistent with Proposition 7. Both theories predict that the coalition that maximizes the payoff per member, $v(S)/s$, is most likely to form, though the equal excess model also implies that differences in the frequencies of the various coalitions should decrease over rounds of bargaining.

Very few studies have been conducted on superadditive games. In one of the few studies that systematically manipulated the value of the grand coalition, Medlin (1976) used the game shown in Figure 8-1c with the following values of the grand coalition: 95, 110, 120, 125, and 140. His results showed a systematic increase in the frequency of the ABC coalition as a direct function of its value. Thus, his results suggest that:

Proposition 8. In superadditive games, the likelihood of the grand coalition varies directly with its value: The greater its value, relative to the values of the smaller (subset) coalitions, the greater its frequency.

The predictions of the equal excess model are consistent with Proposition 8: It predicts that the likelihood of the grand coalition increases with its value. The bargaining theory, however, is ambiguous in predicting coalition outcomes in superadditive games (*P*8). Although the theory can be easily extended to such situations, additional assumptions will be required to yield specific predictions regarding the grand coalition.

Proposition 9. In multivalued games, a member's share of the prize in a coalition is directly related to the values of the member's alternative coalitions, v(S)/s, *relative to the values of other members' alternative coalitions.*

Proposition 9 applies to both superadditive and nonsuperadditive games (see Figures 8-1c and 8-1d). In the game shown in Figure 8-1d, for example, if players A and B are negotiating in the AB coalition, the value of A's alternative coalition is 300 (in AC), while the value of B's alternative coalition is 200 (in BC). Hence, *P*9 specifies that A should achieve a larger share of the prize than B. Similarly, in the game shown in Figure 8-1c (superadditive), player A's alternative coalitions (95 and 90) are greater than those of player B (95 and 65), which in turn, are greater than those of player C (90 and 65). Proposition 9 specifies that player A should receive the largest share in the ABC coalition while player C should receive the smallest share.

There is considerable evidence to support *P*9 (Funk, Rapoport, & Kahan, 1980; Kahan & Rapoport, 1974; Komorita & Kravitz, 1981; Komorita & Tumonis, 1980;

Miller, 1980b; Rapoport & Kahan, 1976), and the assumptions of both bargaining theory and equal excess model are consistent with the proposition. The two theories differ mainly in specifying the functional relation between a member's share and his or her alternatives.

Proposition 10. In multivalued games the variance of payoff shares in a coalition (deviations from equality) increases with experience with coalition games.

Proposition 10 is comparable to Proposition 6 on the diminishing effects of resources in simple games, as a function of familiarity and experience with coalition games. We shall illustrate $P10$ with the game shown in Figure 8-1d. Komorita and Kravitz (1981) directly manipulated the experience of the players prior to playing this game. In the minimal experience condition subjects had no prior experience, and in the maximal experience condition subjects were previously exposed to eight trials of similar three-person games. The mean data over four trials of the game are shown in Table 8-2, and are denoted E^1 and E^9, respectively.

It can be seen that player A's shares in both the AB and AC coalitions are larger in the maximal (E^9) than in the minimal (E^1) condition. Conversely, player C's shares in both AC and BC are smaller in the maximal than the minimal condition. The predictions of bargaining theory and equal excess model are also shown in Table 8-2. It can be seen that both theories predict an increase in player A's share and a decrease in player C's share, from E^1 to E^∞. Thus, Proposition 10 is consistent with the predictions of both theories. Moreover, these results reinforce our hypothesis (described earlier in simple games) that the Trial 1/Round 1 predictions of the theories may apply to naive, inexperienced bargainers, while the asymptotic predictions apply to sophisticated bargainers.

Summary evaluation of theories in multivalued games. There is considerable empirical support for Propositions 7-10 for multivalued games, and the predictions of both bargaining theory and equal excess model are consistent with all four propositions. The two theories make very similar predictions, and as in the case of simple games, it is difficult to differentiate their relative validities because both predict a range of outcomes.

Summary Evaluation of Theories

The five coalition theories discussed in this chapter differ in terms of their basic assumptions, their theoretical boundary conditions, and their agreement with the empirical generalizations explicated in this section. We shall now evaluate the theories with regard to these factors.

The basic assumption of minimum resource theory is that reward division will be proportional to resources. Predictions of coalition frequency follow from predicted reward divisions. Thus minimum resource theory focuses entirely on the normative function of resources, and ignores the strategic function. This exclusive attention to the normative function of resources is one of the main sources of its problems. First, minimum resource theory is limited to games in which resources are assigned, since without resources no predictions can be derived. Second, it is inconsistent with most of the empirical results for simple games. The theory is likely to be supported only when the players are inexperienced and naive.

The seminal assumption of minimum power theory is that reward division will be proportional to pivotal power. Predictions of coalition frequency follow from predicted reward divisions. Since it focuses entirely on the strategic function of resources, minimum power theory makes identical predictions for games with and without resource assignment, as long as the game structure (set of MWCs) is the same in both cases. It appears that minimum power theory is most accurate when the players are very sophisticated. The predictions of minimum power theory tend to be much too extreme, as illustrated in Table 8-1. This does not imply that the concept of pivotal power is invalid, but it does suggest that Gamson's (1964) hypothesis that rewards will be divided proportionally to pivotal power might be invalid.

Weighted probability model begins by predicting that coalition frequency will be inversely related to coalition size, due to the logistical problems of forming and maintaining large coalitions. Predictions of reward division follow from the players' probabilities of being included in the winning coalition, which depend on the predicted coalition frequencies. Like minimum power theory, weighted probability model is based entirely on the strategic function of resources and is most likely to be accurate with sophisticated players. An attempt to extend weighted probability model to multivalued games was not successful, suggesting that the theory may be limited to simple games.

The bargaining theory assumes that on the early trials players with large resource weights will argue for the parity norm, whereas those with small resources will favor equality. The actual reward division should be an equal split between these two values, and coalition frequency depends on the predicted reward splits. After this first trial players should base their demands on their best alternative coalition, and asymptotic reward divisions should be proportional to these alternatives. Coalition frequency should be an inverse function of coalition instability, which is based on the players' temptations to defect. When resources are not assigned, proportionality based on alternatives is substituted for parity on Trial 1. Thus bargaining theory attends to both the normative and strategic functions of resources, and can be applied to both games with and without resource assignment. Unlike the first three theories, bargaining theory is dynamic, predicting changes over trials. Its Trial 1 predictions tend to be most accurate with naive players, who may attend to resources more than the strategic positions in the game. Its asymptotic predictions are more appropriate for sophisticated players. The bargaining theory has been successfully extended to multivalued games, but it does have problems making predictions for superadditive games and for veto games.

Finally, equal excess model is very similar to the bargaining theory. The primary difference is the use of the equal excess norm in place of proportionality. On the early rounds the equal excess model is based on both the normative and strategic functions of resources, but at the asymptote its predictions are based entirely on the strategic function. This is consistent with observed changes over trials, and suggests that predictions for the early rounds are appropriate for naive players whereas predictions for the later rounds are appropriate for sophisticated players. The theory was developed for games without resource assignment, but incorporates the Trial 1 predictions of bargaining theory when resources are assigned. Thus it can be applied to both types of games. Finally, the equal excess model can be applied to both simple and multivalued games.

When the five theories are compared, minimum power and minimum resource theories are clearly inferior. They are static, limited in scope, and consistently inaccurate in their predictions. The other three theories are more difficult to differentiate. Weighted probability model is static and is limited to simple games. But in simple games the many comparisons between bargaining theory and weighted probability model indicate that neither is clearly superior. Equal excess model was only recently proposed, and there are few direct tests of the theory. However, the results of recent studies (Komorita & Kravitz, 1981; Komorita & Tumonis, 1980; Miller, 1980c) indicate that it is as accurate as bargaining theory and weighted probability model. Bargaining theory and equal excess model are more general than the other three theories, making predictions for games with and without resources and for both simple and multivalued games. They are both dynamic theories, predicting changes as a function of experience. This accurately describes the data, but makes it difficult to falsify the theories. These are probably the most promising general theories and it would be desirable to determine their boundary conditions, and to extend them so they yield more precise predictions.

Summary and Conclusions

Coalition formation has been studied from a variety of perspectives by many different investigators. Murnighan (1978a), in reviewing the coalition literature, divides the theoretical contributions into three major areas: (a) game theoretic models; (b) social psychological models; and (c) political coalition models. Murnighan concludes that there has been little overlap in the work of investigators in the three areas. One reason for this state of affairs is that researchers in these areas do not share a common theoretical focus. Game theorists are primarily interested in how the players will divide the prize and are not particularly concerned with which coalitions are likely to form. Social psychologists, in contrast, are concerned with both of these response measures. Moreover, game theorists focus on how a "rational" player *ought* to behave so as to maximize gain (a normative approach), while social psychologists focus on how an individual is *likely* to behave (a descriptive approach). Finally, political scientists are primarily concerned with coalitions among political parties. Hence, political coalition models are based on minimizing the ideological conflict as well as maximizing reward, whereas the complicating influence of ideology is explicitly excluded by game theorists and social psychologists.

Our review of theory and research in coalition formation has been restricted to the social-psychological approach. A review of research in the other two areas as well would have been desirable, but was clearly beyond the scope of this chapter.

The interested reader is referred to Luce and Raiffa (1957) and Rapoport (1970) for reviews of game theoretic models, and to Groennings, Kelley, and Leiserson (1970) and DeSwaan (1973) for reviews of research on political coalition formation.

Future Directions

One obvious direction for future research is to extend the generality of coalition theories. We have assumed that the participants are individuals, rather than groups or organizations; that resources of the parties represent votes, rather than the abilities and skills of individuals or economic and military resources of nations; and that the outcomes represent some quantitative measure (points, money) rather than social motives such as power, status, or control of the decision processes. These assumptions, and the monomethod approach which has accompanied them, severely limit the generality of the empirical findings, and it would be desirable to extend the boundaries of our data and theories. We have also tended to use naive subjects who are not strongly motivated, and this further limits the generality of the results.

There is also some agreement that a fruitful direction for future research is to examine the processes of coalition formation (Chertkoff, 1970; Kahan & Rapoport, 1974; Komorita & Chertkoff, 1973; Laing & Morrison, 1973; Stryker, 1972). With few exceptions, almost all theories of coalition formation focus on the outcomes of coalition bargaining and pay little attention to process variables that mediate these outcomes. One of the first attempts to examine the process of coalition formation was a study by Psathas and Stryker (1965) in which a role-playing paradigm was employed. Since then, several investigators have attempted to study the bargaining process in terms of the sequence of offers and counteroffers among the bargainers (Chertkoff & Braden, 1974; Friend, Laing, & Morrison, 1977; Kahan & Rapoport, 1974; Komorita & Moore, 1976; Rapoport & Kahan, 1976).

One of the formidable problems to be encountered in developing a process theory of coalition formation is that the bargaining processes are likely to vary with the nature of the situation (procedural rules). Investigators have used a variety of paradigms to study coalition behavior (face-to-face, convention, display, computer-controlled bargaining), and after reviewing the coalition literature, Gamson (1964) concluded that each of the theories he reviewed had some empirical support, depending on the conditions under which it was tested. Thus Gamson implied that a given theory may be quite accurate in predicting coalition outcomes in one situation but not necessarily in other situations. To the extent that this hypothesis is valid, such differential effects of situational factors should certainly apply to the processes of coalition bargaining. It can be seen that any attempt to develop a process theory of coalition bargaining is a formidable task. Nonetheless, it behooves the social scientist to make such attempts because they may lead to valuable insights regarding bargaining processes in real-life situations. Such processes invariably determine the distribution of rewards to members of society.

Acknowledgments. The preparation of this chapter was supported by a grant from the National Science Foundation (BNS 79-11103) to the first author. The authors wish to thank Charles Miller, Keith Murnighan, and Paul Paulus for many helpful comments and suggestions on earlier drafts of the manuscript.

References

Caplow, T. A theory of coalitions in the triad. *American Sociological Review*, 1956, *21*, 489-493.

Caplow, T. Further development of a theory of coalitions in the triad. *American Journal of Sociology*, 1959, *64*, 488-493.

Chertkoff, J. M. The effects of probability of future success on coalition formation. *Journal of Experimental Social Psychology*, 1966, *2*, 265-277.

Chertkoff, J. M. Sociopsychological theories and research on coalition formation. In S. Groennings, E. W. Kelley, & M. Leiserson (Eds.), *The study of coalition behavior*. New York: Holt, Rinehart and Winston, 1970.

Chertkoff, J. M. Coalition formation as a function of differences in resources. *Journal of Conflict Resolution*, 1971, *15*, 371-383.

Chertkoff, J. M., & Braden, J. L. Effects of experience and bargaining restrictions on coalition formation. *Journal of Personality and Social Psychology*, 1974, *30*, 169-177.

Chertkoff, J. M., & Esser, J. K. A test of three theories of coalition formation when agreements can be short-term or long-term. *Journal of Personality and Social Psychology*, 1977, *35*, 237-249.

DeSwaan, A. *Coalition theories and cabinet formations*. San Francisco: Jossey-Bass, 1973.

Friend, K. E., Laing, J. D., & Morrison, R. J. Game-theoretic analysis of coalition behavior. *Theory and Decision*, 1977, *8*, 127-157.

Funk, S. G., Rapoport, Am., & Kahan, J. P. Quota vs. positional power in four-person apex games. *Journal of Experimental Social Psychology*, 1980, *16*, 77-93.

Gamson, W. A. A theory of coalition formation. *American Sociological Review*, 1961, *26*, 373-382.

Gamson, W. A. Experimental studies of coalition formation. In L. Berkowitz (Ed.), *Advances in experimental social psychology* (Vol. 1). New York: Academic Press, 1964.

Groennings, S., Kelley, E. W., & Leiserson, M. (Eds.). *The study of coalition behavior*. New York: Holt, Rinehart & Winston, 1970.

Horowitz, A. D. The competitive bargaining set for cooperative *n*-person games. *Journal of Mathematical Psychology*, 1973, *10*, 265-289.

Horowitz, A. D., & Rapoport, Am. Test of the kernel and two bargaining set models in four- and five-person games. In An. Rapoport (Ed.), *Game theory as a theory of conflict resolution*. Dordrecht, Holland: Reidel, 1974.

Kahan, J. P., & Rapoport, Am. Test of the bargaining set and kernel models in three-person games. In An. Rapoport (Ed.), *Game theory as a theory of conflict resolution*. Dordrecht, Holland: Reidel, 1974.

Kelley, H. H., & Arrowood, A. J. Coalitions in the triad: Critique and experiment. *Sociometry*, 1960, *23*, 231-244.

Komorita, S. S. A weighted probability model of coalition formation. *Psychological Review*, 1974, *81*, 242-256.

Komorita, S. S. An equal excess model of coalition formation. *Behavioral Science*, 1979, *24*, 369-381.

Komorita, S. S., & Brinberg, D. The effects of equity norms in coalition formation. *Sociometry,* 1977, *40*, 351-361.

Komorita, S. S., & Chertkoff, J. M. A bargaining theory of coalition formation. *Psychological Review,* 1973, *80*, 149-162.

Komorita, S. S., & Kravitz, D. A. Some tests of four descriptive theories of coalition formation. In H. Sauermann (Ed.), *Contributions to experimental economics: Coalition forming benavior* (Vol. 8). Tubingen, West Germany: Mohr, 1978.

Kormorita, S. S., & Kravitz, D. A. The effect of prior experience on coalition behavior. *Journal of Personality and Social Psychology,* 1981, *40*, 675-686.

Komorita, S. S., & Meek, D. D. Generality and validity of some theories of coalition formation. *Journal of Personality and Social Psychology,* 1978, *36*, 392-404.

Komorita, S. S., & Moore, D. Theories and processes of coalition formation. *Journal of Personality and Social Psychology,* 1976, *33*, 371-381.

Komorita, S. S., & Tumonis, T. M. Extensions and tests of some descriptive theories of coalition formation. *Journal of Personality and Social Psychology,* 1980, *39*, 256-268.

Kravitz, D. A. Effects of resources and alternatives on coalition formation. *Journal of Personality and Social Psychology,* 1981, *41*, 87-98.

Laing, J. D., & Morrison, R. J. Coalitions and payoffs in three person sequential games: Initial tests of two formal models. *Journal of Mathematical Sociology,* 1973, *3*, 3-26.

Luce, R. D., & Raiffa, H. *Games and decisions.* New York: Wiley, 1957.

Medlin, S. M. Effects of grand coalition payoffs on coalition formation in three-person games. *Behavioral Science,* 1976, *21*, 48-61.

Michener, H. A., Fleishman, J. A., & Vaske, J. J. A test of the bargaining theory of coalition formation in four-person groups. *Journal of Personality and Social Psychology,* 1976, *34*, 1114-1126.

Michener, H. A., & Sakurai, M. M. A research note on the predictive adequacy of the Kernel. *Journal of Conflict Resolution,* 1976, *20*, 120-141.

Miller, C. E. A test of four theories of coalition formation: Effects of payoffs and resources. *Journal of Personality and Social Psychology,* 1980, *38*, 153-164. (a)

Miller, C. E. Coalition formation in characteristic function games: Competitive tests of three theories. *Journal of Experimental Social Psychology,* 1980, *16*, 61-76. (b)

Miller, C. E. Effects of payoffs and resources on coalition formation: A test of three theories. *Social Psychology Quarterly,* 1980, *43*, 154-164. (c)

Miller, C. E., & Crandall, R. Experimental research on the social psychology of bargaining and coalition formation. In P. B. Paulus (Ed.), *Psychology of group influence.* Hillsdale, N.J.: Lawrence Erlbaum, 1980.

Murnighan, J. K. Models of coalition behavior: Game theoretic, social psychological, and political perspectives. *Psychological Bulletin,* 1978, *85*, 1130-1153. (a)

Murnighan, J. K. Strength and weakness in four coalition situations. *Behavioral Science,* 1978, *23*, 195-208. (b)

Murnighan, J. K., Komorita, S. S., & Szwajkowski, E. Theories of coalition formation and the effects of reference groups. *Journal of Experimental Social Psychology,* 1977, *13*, 166-181.

Murnighan, J. K., & Roth, A. E. Effects of group size and communication availability on coalition bargaining in a veto game. *Journal of Personality and Social Psychology*, 1980, *39*, 92-103.

Psathas, G., & Stryker, S. Bargaining behavior and orientations in coalition formation. *Sociometry*, 1965, *28*, 124-144.

Rapoport, Am., & Kahan, J. P. When three is not always two against one: Coalitions in experimental three-person cooperative games. *Journal of Experimental Social Psychology*, 1976, *12*, 253-273.

Rapoport, An. *N-person game theory*. Ann Arbor: University of Michigan Press, 1970.

Riker, W. H. Bargaining in a three-person game. *American Political Science Review*, 1967, *61*, 91-102.

Shapley, L. S., & Shubik, M. Method for evaluating the distribution of power in a committee system. *American Political Science Review*, 1954, *48*, 787-792.

Stryker, S. Coalition behavior. In C. G. McClintock (Ed.), *Experimental social psychology*. New York: Holt, Rinehart & Winston, 1972.

Vinacke, W. E., & Arkoff, A. An experimental study of coalitions in the triad. *American Sociological Review*, 1957, *22*, 406-414.

Chapter 9
The Influence of Communication Upon Bargaining

Charles G. McClintock, Frank J. Stech, and Linda J. Keil

Bargaining, the mutual attempt by interdependent actors to exercise influence over each other's behaviors, occurs within a large number of animal species and across a wide range of settings. A variety of nonverbal and verbal forms of communication are employed to exercise such influence during a bargaining interaction. For example, bargaining as a nonverbal form of behavioral interaction can be observed between neighboring pairs of nest-building arctic snow buntings whose initial contacts consist of a stereotyped aerial ballet of aggressive approaches and fearful avoidances. These tacit moves and countermoves progressively produce a well-defined, mutually acceptable boundary between their nest sites thereby guaranteeing a peaceful future coexistence (Tinbergen, 1968). A verbal form of bargaining can be seen in the negotiations between the United States and the Union of Soviet Socialist Republics that have taken place repeatedly over the control of nuclear arms. These less-successful instances of human bargaining have succeeded only, after some 25 years of symbolic manuevering, in forestalling the creation of arms that neither side wanted.

In the present chapter we are principally concerned with examining how variations in the structure of communication can influence the processes and outcomes of human bargaining. In pursuing this goal, we first define bargaining as an integral part of exchange relationships, then we describe some fundamental characteristics of communication as a form of interpersonal influence, examining some of the communication dilemmas faced by bargainers. Subsequently, we outline the more basic experimental paradigms that have been employed to examine how communication influences bargaining. And finally, we review a number of empirical studies whose findings have permitted us to understand certain aspects of the relationship among structural variations in communication, the bargaining process, and its outcomes.

Bargaining

Bargaining can be defined as an exchange between two or more individuals who attempt to reach an accommodation or agreement regarding what behaviors or commodities each will or will not provide and receive subsequently from the other. In humans, it can be described as a process of decision-making because alternative future courses are suggested, considered, and then all but one are rejected.

The most fundamental requisite to bargaining is *social interaction*: the expression of behaviors by self and other that have a mutual and reciprocal effect or both one's own and other's subsequent behaviors. Hence, each individual's behavior depends, at least in part, on the motivational, perceptual, and reinforcement cues provided by the other individual (Zajonc, 1967). Put simply, each individual's behavior in an interaction is in part caused by, and is in part the cause of, each other individual's behavior. If the individuals have needs that can be satisfied only by some combination of their own and another's behaviors, the interaction implies *social interdependence*. To obtain satisfaction of various social needs, for example, love, esteem, and affiliation, the socially interdependent individual must perform behaviors (instrumental or consummatory) and obtain reinforcements which depend on another individual's behavior.

To the extent that participating actors are assumed to be rational and purposive, social interaction can be described as *strategic interaction*. Such interaction is composed of the strategic behaviors of individuals who make choices contingent upon their estimate of the actions (choices) to be made by others with whom they share interdependence. If one assumes further that individual choice is basic to strategic interaction, then one may characterize human bargaining as an instance of *interdependent decision-making*.

Interdependent decision-making has classically been the domain of mathematical game theory. And bargaining theories, particularly in economics, have been dominated by game theoretical assumptions (Young, 1975)[1] which prescribe how bargainers *should* behave rationally to achieve optimal outcomes. In social psychology, although the theory of games has had a major impact upon theories of interdependent decision-making, most conceptual and empirical work on bargaining is more descriptive than prescriptive, and more directly related to theories of social exchange than to game theory.

In bargaining, then, outcomes are jointly determined by all the affected parties or individuals. Bargained outcomes are, by definition, mutually agreeable. No bargain is ever struck until all parties agree to it. Even if the outcome of a negotiation is a break off or *deadlock,* this outcome represents a joint agreement to disagree

---

[1] There is a class of economic models of bargaining which can be described as convergence models insofar as they consider how actors move towards agreement given initially incompatible demands. These models are usually substantively tied to the economic problem of bilateral monopoly, that is an instance where a single buyer and a single seller must either reach an agreement concerning an exchange or fail to exchange their goods.

and maintain the status quo. All parties to a bargaining relationship thus, by definition, have the capability to influence the other parties, regardless of differences in
status, power, or authority, because each individual is unilaterally able to withhold
agreement, to prolong, or to end the decision-making process.

Social Exchange and Bargaining

James Coleman (1973) observes that there are two principal classes of models used
for describing social action—causal and purposive models. Causal models view human
behavior in more-or-less drive reduction and mechanistic terms as the result of prior
environmental and organismic events. Most models of human learning and socialization are causal ones. Purposive models, on the other hand, employ a somewhat
more dynamic and descriptive paradigm in which the organism is seen as monitoring
its environment, including future states, and making choices that in some manner
produce preferred outcomes. This latter orientation characterizes much of the work
in contemporary decision and game theory. Exchange theories, with the possible
exception of the work of Skinner (1981), tend to be eclectic, combining the assumptions underlying both causal-behavioristic and purposive-decision-theoretic models
of human behavior. Namely, individuals are assumed to attempt in a rational and
purposive manner simultaneously to increase the rewards to self of the behaviors or
outcomes obtained within an exchange relationship, and to reduce the costs to self
of the behaviors or outcomes produced for self or others (Thibaut & Kelley, 1959,
p. 31).

The social exchange paradigm basically assumes that social behaviors have either
positive or negative reinforcement values (or utilities) for the individual as well as
interdependent others, that they are limited in availability, that their production
implies some costs, and that their exchange through social interaction requires
allocation rules. A further major assumption is that at any given moment in an
interaction, there is a strong possibility that the needs of one or more interdependent participants are not completely satisfied by other's social behaviors, and
such participants are thus motivated to act to change other's behavior so as to
receive more rewarding outcomes. To do so participants plan to behave to achieve
such changes in a purposive manner.

A final important assumption of exchange theory is that socially interdependent
individuals will either tend to work out mutually agreeable and mutually rewarding
behavior adjustments to obtain these more rewarding outcomes for themselves, or
they will seek more rewarding alternative interactions elsewhere. The process of
"working out" these behavioral adjustments is indeed what we term *bargaining*.

Skinner's (1981) strictly behavioristic definition of exchange assumes that one
does not need to assume that parties to an exchange behave in a purposive and
rational manner. Rather, he asserts that the circumstances of social interaction create certain contingencies of reinforcement which reward some social behaviors and
punish others, leading to "selection" of particular repertoires of social behavior.
This occurs in a manner similar to Darwinian natural selection which produces species with genetic characteristics that increase the chances of their reproduction and

survival. Thus, rather than saying the individual acts to maximize rewards and minimize costs to self, Skinner seemingly suggests the social exchange relationships in fact occur in an environment that selects for adaptive social traits, and shapes and maintains socially adjusted or adaptive behaviors.

From Skinner's viewpoint, therefore, the social actor does not act, or initiate social behavior at all, and such concepts as "purpose" and "intention" have no meaning because only past consequences influence selection. What may appear to be purposive or intentional action by a social participant is, according to Skinner's selection concept, only the consequence of past selection pressures from the environments encountered in the individual's social history. Skinner acknowledges that his view is unconventional. In this chapter we will adhere to the more widespread exchange assumption that bargainers are not only motivated to reduce drive levels by responding to past contingencies of reinforcement, but they also initiate behaviors in response to the ongoing social context, as well as anticipate future events and respond to them in more-or-less rational ways.

Behavioristic Analysis of the Motivation to Bargain

The assumptions underlying the Hull-Spence drive-reduction theory of action (Spence, 1956) can be used to provide a conceptual rationale to describe the motivational dynamics of social exchange in general, and bargaining, in particular (cf. Gergen, 1969; McClintock & Keil, 1982). The theory assumes that many stimuli encountered by an individual elicit several different response tendencies. Some of these responses can be emitted simultaneously, but others are incompatible with each other. This competition between responses places a limit on the types and quantity of responses available in any situation. Competing responses can be arranged in a response hierarchy ordered on the basis of their probability of emission as an overt response. The dominant response is the most probable of emission, less probable response tendencies are subordinate.

Social interdependence implies, of course, that an individual has needs or desires for the responses that can be provided by others. Some of these social needs may be activated simultaneously producing several goal-seeking, tension-reducing behaviors that can be performed simultaneously. Other need-produced behaviors may be incompatible with one another in the sense that they cannot be produced simultaneously, for example, motivations to fight and flee. Competing needs can also be ordered in a hierarchy determined by the probability that the individual will attend that need and act to satisfy it.

Each individual, then, has a need hierarchy and a response hierarchy for any social interdependence stimulus. While we keep these two hierarchies separate for the sake of clarity, in reality, they may not be so easily differentiated. The need hierarchy governs which behaviors the individual wants from the other. The response hierarchy governs which behaviors the individual will emit for the other.

Given interdependence, only in the situation when an individual's need hierarchy and the other's response hierarchy are completely compatible (i.e., the individual's dominant need is satisfied completely by the other's dominant response, with correspondence of subordinate needs and responses) and vice versa, is bargaining unnecessary. Because of varying environmental histories among individuals, complete compatibility is generally unlikely. Any mismatch in the ordering of needs and responses is an inducement to bargaining. In effect, such asymmetries limit the frequency, type, and strength of need-satisfying responses available in a social situation, and will motivate the individual and/or the other to adjust responses and needs to enhance matching and greater reinforcement in the future.

Mixed-Motive Relations

As described above, bargaining emerges only in those ambivalent, *mixed-motive* relationships (Schelling, 1960) where need and response hierarchies have both common (coordinated) and conflicting (incompatible) ranks. If the hierarchies are completely compatible, bargaining is unnecessary. If completely incompatible (i.e., the parties' need and response hierarchies are inversely ordered), individuals would tend to break off the exchange relationship since it would be aversive and punishing for both.

In the mixed-motive relationship the need and response hierarchies of actors are sufficiently correlated that they will attempt to take advantage of the relationship, but they are also sufficiently in conflict that each actor has reason to influence the other to elicit behaviors that other is presently unwilling or unlikely to emit. This process of mutually influencing and adjusting response hierarchies is the main goal of bargaining. Namely, it is the goal of the interacting individuals to reach an agreeable coordination of responses, but at the same time it is also in the interest of each to end up receiving as many and as highly need-satisfying responses as possible.

Dynamic Influence Process

The bargaining process is even more dynamic than has been suggested thus far for not only are the valuations the other places upon outcomes only partially known (incomplete information) by each actor, but also these valuations (the need hierarchies) are assumed to be alterable as well. While actors may enter the bargaining with some firm notion of outcome preference, they cannot realistically expect an agreement that will satisfy all of their preferences. Further, in bargaining, each individual's hierarchies and the resulting preferences are altered by the receipt of information about what the other will or will not give, and will or will not accept (Ikle & Leites, 1962). It is this exchange of information that defines the *communication* aspect of the bargaining process.

When one actor nonverbally manipulates events or responses in order to change the other's evaluation of outcomes and to bring about a more favorable agreement, we term this *behavioral or tacit influence.* When the manipulation is attempted mainly through verbal communication, it may be labeled *communicated* or *negotiated influence;* when it is a by-product of the mere possession of power of one actor, it may be described as *emanated influence.* Finally, when an individual is able to volitionally produce and control these reevaluations of need by the other and hence modify the other's exchange behaviors, the first individual is said to have *power* over the other (Raven & Kruglanski, 1970).

The limit to the exercise of influence in bargaining is the value of the interaction to the participants. If one of the bargainers can afford to terminate the interaction and seek a more profitable social exchange elsewhere with other partners, the other bargainers have no further power in the exchange. They have, in fact, nothing to exchange. Thibaut and Kelley (1959) have termed this more profitable exchange the "comparison level for alternatives" and predicted the bargainer will leave the social exchange if the comparison level for alternatives is greater in value than the value of the ongoing exchange. The party then can afford to walk away and stay away, thus ends the bargaining power of the others. Of course, these latter parties may have the power to coerce the absentee to return to the social exchange. Similarly, the abandoned parties may offer some additional inducement to the absentee to return and resume bargaining. The ability to walk away from bargaining limits the power of those who wish the bargaining to continue. The vulnerability to coercion or rewards limits the power of those who would attempt to walk away from an exchange relationship.

Communication

The nature of communication in bargaining varies in the degree to which it employs verbal versus nonverbal stimuli. There are three categories of communication which are used in bargaining. Two of these are nonverbal, *tacit* and *emanation;* one is verbal, *negotiation.* Tacit communication in bargaining involves the use of signs such as gestures, moves, actions, and behaviors that make up and have functional value for an ongoing interaction, but which have little or no unique symbolic significance per se. Such tacit communication often produces what Kelley and Thibaut (1969) term *outcome influence.* At the other end of the continuum of symbolism and communication clarity is a form of communication known as negotiation, which is conducted entirely via language using symbols which facilitate the process but whose expression has little or no functional significance per se. Negotiation produces what Kelley and Thibaut call *informational influence.*

The distinction between tacit communication and negotiation is quantitative but crucial. In tacit communication, the actions the parties use to define the "rules of the game" are the same actions that constitute the interaction itself. In negotiation the symbols are distinct from the exchanges of behaviors or commodities which are being bargained over. In tacit communication there is a strong potential for confusion among the parties as to which behaviors are part of the interaction, and which are aimed at changing the course of the interaction. Even when the parties share the understanding that certain behaviors are being employed for tacit communication, if one or the other party's expectations about these behaviors are not met, or are exceeded, the mutual understanding that the parties are bargaining may falter. For example, snow buntings may actually fight if their aerial displays become too energetic. Adolescent jostling "in fun" may turn into deadly serious fights. Innocent flirtations may accelerate into love affairs. And weapon systems developed as "bargaining chips" for negotiation may become militarily attractive and be deployed for military advantage. Given such potential loss of control, one may ask why tacit bargaining is used at all by human actors. Perhaps because the moves communicated in verbal negotiation are frequently less compelling than the nonverbal ones of tacit bargaining. Talk may be cheap, and action may speak louder than words. While, for example, one might laugh at the hijacker who threatens to go to the airport and seize an airliner, the hijacker who has a gun to the head of an airplane pilot commands attention without saying anything (Baldwin, 1976).

The third form of communication in bargaining, emanation (Henrikson, 1981), has received little theoretical or empirical attention. This form of communication obtains when one individual has power over others such that they can cause others to reevaluate and modify their needs without any specific strategic attempts at outcome or informational influence. Emanation is seen as not a singular event or attempt at influence but rather a continuing form of "subtle co-optation and imitation" (Henrikson, 1981, p. 157). As a form of communication, it is neither deliberately projected toward a single target nor intended to influence a single social interaction. Instead power or influence is emanated at all potential targets, and extending across various social relationships. Influence is exercised through the apprehensions and anticipations of subjects. Bargaining by emanation thus obtains through an unarticulated rather than a strategic effort to readjust the need/response patterns of participants. That is, it occurs without the use of specific demands or sanctions of negotiation or the use of the gestures, moves, and behaviors that are instrumental in tacit forms of bargaining. In effect, communication by emanation basically involves activating response sets or expectancies that one bargainer holds for the other(s).

Although one can study and evaluate the role of signs in tacit bargaining, or the functions of emanated power in bargaining through emanation, most of the conceptual and empirical efforts in social psychology to study communication in bargaining have focused upon the effects of the presence or absence of symbolic communication upon the bargaining process and its outcomes. That is, most of the research has been devoted to that end of the bargaining continuum which focuses upon negotiations. A major assumption in these efforts is that symbolic communication is central to successful attempts to influence others and to achieve mutually profitable outcomes. Yet in some negotiation settings the ability to communicate verbally or in writing may be lacking, forbidden, interrupted, too costly, or voluntarily eschewed.

Communication Dilemmas

In the remainder of this chapter we will be concerned principally with defining and describing how variations in the availability, mode, and timing of information, whether regulated by external agents or by the parties to an exchange, influence bargaining strategies and outcomes. First, however, we examine conceptually the various communication dilemmas that confront bargainers when they are negotiating outcomes in mixed-motive settings.

Information

What is communicated in negotiation is *information* concerning the attributes of an interaction. These attributes include the actor's views of the current, past, and possible future states of the interaction; actor's needs; own and other's permissible and impermissible, possible and impossible responses; and the contingent relationship between responses and mutual outcomes of actors (Kelley & Thibaut, 1969). Interdependent actors depend on each other both for the valued social behaviors produced in the interaction (termed "outcome dependence" by Thibaut & Kelley, 1959), and for the information needed to define the nature and character of their relationship (termed "information dependence" by Jones & Gerard, 1967, and Kelley & Thibaut, 1969).

For example, the success of actor P in influencing actor O through communication depends heavily on P's ability to manipulate O's information about their relationship. P may alter his or her outcome dependency on O to his or her own advantage by exploiting O's information dependency. Information dependence, like outcome dependence, is often mutual, and each actor may attempt to improve his or her own outcomes by manipulating the information provided the other.

Information is produced and transmitted by someone or something and received by someone. The recipient decides if the information transmitted is (a) accurate (rather than distorted), that is, a faithful transmission of what was produced; (b) veridical (rather than false), that is, can be verified independently of the sender; and (c) critical (rather than trivial), that is, important to the recipient's needs and activities. Any of these three aspects may be distorted by the manipulation of information.

Complete Information

Complete information implies that actors have accurate, veridical, and critical information on the payoff matrix specifying all possible responses, the outcomes for each bargainer, for each response contingency, and knowledge of the subjective value of each outcome to all actors (Luce & Raiffa, 1957). However, such a set of conditions is purely hypothetical since in reality bargainers have at most only *incomplete information* of each other's valuations. While they may have full information on the objective extrapersonal aspects of their relationship, they have only partial subjective information on other's (and perhaps their own) valuations. Communicative influence is possible and effective because bargainers have only partial information on each other's values. If bargainers had full subjective and objective information there would be exchange but no need for communication; the situation would be totally defined for each actor and bargaining would be most efficiently conducted tacitly merely by making appropriate behavioral response adjustments.

Bargainers rarely have complete information on other's preferences and valuations because of their own unwillingness to communicate fully. This may seem illogical at first glance. Both bargainers must exchange information with each other if they hope to obtain the maximum amount of resources available in their relationship. Communication allows the bargainers to explore fully the realm of possible outcomes, identify mutually satisfying outcomes, insure full understanding of the reward contingencies, and estimate the rewards and costs to self and other of various alternative outcomes. In other words, full communication contributes to the integrative or cooperative aspects of bargaining (Walton & McKersie, 1965).

But each bargainer privately evaluates the options and responses offered by the other, and each alone knows the value to self of any given offer. Each is in sole possession of these critical pieces of information, and must rely on the other for similar information on the other's needs, preferences, values, withdrawal thresholds (also known as fallback, safety, or reserve values). In short, each bargainer's full information on the relationship depends on the other's full communication of this subjective, evaluative information.

But if increasing the "fullness" of this evaluative communication leads to an expansion of the realm of possible joint outcomes, control of this communication may lead to a greater personal share of the joint outcome for the individual bargainer, what Walton and McKersie (1965) term the distributive or competitive aspects of bargaining. Bargainers can increase their share of the joint outcome by manipulating the information about their valuations which they communicate to the other through such tactics as exaggerating their outcomes in the event of break-off, depreciating the value of offers made by the other, inflating their needs, puffing up the value of their own offers, and so forth. Such manipulated communications are far more complex than mere holding out or stony silence. They are basically *propaganda,* that is, efforts to influence the attitudes and values of the other for the ultimate purpose of influencing action (Nogee, 1963).

Communication Dilemmas: Complete Versus Incomplete Information

Kelley (1966) has analyzed the "need for information and the restraints against providing it" (p. 58) in bargaining in terms of the "dilemmas of trust" and the "dilemma of honesty and openness." Both bargainers depend on each other for information, but, as Kelley further observes, "To believe everything the other person says is to place one's fate in his hands and jeopardize full satisfaction of one's own interests. . . . to believe nothing the other says is to eliminate the possibility of accepting any arrangement with him" (p. 58).

Ideally, for distributing purposes, each party wants full information about the other's preferences and values, while disclosing minimal information about his or her own values. This is why security and espionage are sometimes aspects of negotiation. But to communicate nothing about one's own values threatens the possibility of integrative agreements, and the long-term viability of the exchange. So in order to seem to be fully communicative while in reality safeguarding information on their own valuations, bargainers manipulate the information they communicate to each other. Bargainers, in effect, have a mixed-motive relationship with respect to information dependence because they have a mixed-motive relationship with respect to outcome dependence.

Bargainers are thus forced to resolve another dilemma, that of honesty versus openness. Each must decide how much information about his or her true motives and preferences he or she can afford to reveal. The bargainer must then weigh the distributive benefits of misrepresentation or concealment against the possible damage to an integrative outcome that might result if the bargainer is too manipulative (causes the other to abandon the interaction as hopelessly unprofitable), or unsuccessfully manipulative (such that the other detects the bargainer's concealments/ misrepresentations and takes advantage of having caught out the bargainer's manipulation). Thus, the effectiveness of bargaining in facilitating outcomes for both parties depends in part on the communication between the bargainers of information being sufficiently *credible* so that both are able to perceive in the exchanged information an outcome acceptable to themselves.

In the final major section of this chapter, we will examine how bargainers resolve the communication dilemma to achieve some outcome. More specifically, we will review what is know empirically concerning how the following four factors influence bargained outcomes: (a) the availability of communication, (b) the availability of communication in interaction with the value orientations of bargainers, (c) the mode of communication, and (d) the timing of communication. We will describe first, however, the principal research paradigms that have been employed to assess the effects of the four factors upon bargaining.

Bargaining Research Paradigms

In general, empirical studies examining the role of communication in bargaining have used one of three research paradigms: (a) matrix games for two or more persons: (b) games based upon economic relations (experimental economics); and (c) role-playing analogs or simulations of real-world conflict. In reality, many of the specific tasks derived from these three paradigms have logical and mathematical forms of equivalence to one another. But despite such equivalences, subjects often respond quite differently to the particular tasks (see, for example, Pruitt, 1968, 1970), that is, mathematical task equivalence in no way ensures that the tasks have the same psychological meaning for bargainers, psychological equivalence.

Matrix Games

Matrix games are the most formalized paradigm employed in bargaining research. They reflect the mathematical game's theoretic origins of the area of experimental bargaining, and commonly use the symbols and terminology of game theory, if not always its mathematical form of analysis. The matrix game paradigm is also the most restrictive of an individual bargainer's behavior, typically offering each bargainer one of two options. In a two-person game, payoffs are defined for each of the four possible joint choices, and are generally displayed in a 2 X 2 matrix. Interdependence obtains because in most instances both bargainers' outcomes are defined by the combination of choices across *n* players, and interdependence obtains among all of those who express a preference.

In a number of studies that are reviewed subsequently, the two-person Prisoner's Dilemma Game (PDG) is employed as the experimental task; in a smaller number, the *n*-person Commons' Dilemma Game is so used (CDG). We will briefly describe these two games which, in fact, form but a subset of a variety of differently structured matrix games that can be employed to assess interpersonal choice behaviors.

Prisoner's Dilemma Game. The Prisoners' Dilemma Game (PDG) was first defined by the mathematician A. W. Tucker, subsequently popularized by Luce and Raiffa (1957), and then extensively investigated by Rapoport and Chammah (1965) among others (Gallo & McClintock, 1965). In its most common form the PDG is a two-person, binary choice game in which each player has a choice of cooperating with the other player (e.g., each of two captured culprits separated by the police keeps mum rather than rat on their partner in crime) and if both cooperate (keep mum), both are rewarded (the police can only charge the culprits with some minor offense). However, each player also has the option of defecting (confessing to the police), and each player may be tempted to choose this option by an even larger reward available to a unilateral defector (the police offer to release whichever culprit first confesses the crimes of the pair). The players realize that unilateral cooperation is heavily punished (the police will use the evidence of the defecting culprit to put the silent culprit in prison for a long time). Finally, the players realize that mutual defection is also punished but not as heavily as unilateral cooperation (if both culprits confess the police will put them both away, but will take their confessions into account and mitigate their sentences).

In summary, a sole cooperator is heavily punished, mutual defectors are punished, but less heavily (so a player who expects the other to defect is better off defecting, in terms of avoiding punishment). Mutual cooperation is rewarded, but sole defections are rewarded still more (so a player who expects the other to cooperate obtains more reward by defecting rather than also cooperating). So, regardless of whether he expects the other to defect or cooperate, the "rational, economic man" should defect, according to the classic game theory prescription. But this prescription implies the other should also defect, with the consequence that "rational" players will receive outcomes inferior to (or dominated by) the outcomes received by "irrational" players who both choose to cooperate. The mutual defection combination in the PDG is thus termed a deficient or dominated equilibrium by Luce and Raiffa (1957, p. 96) who note "there should be a law against such games!" (p. 97).

Von Neumann and Morgenstern (1964) observe that, unlike the successful game theory maximization solution in the simple situation, interdependence situations such as the PDG contain,

> some elements of an entirely different nature . . . each participant attempts to maximize a function of which he does not control all variables. This is certainly no maximization problem but a peculiar and disconcerting mixture of conflicting maximization problem . . . nowhere dealt with in classical mathematics. (pp. 11-12)

They conclude that the classic theory of games has only limited prescriptive value in such complex situations.

The Commons Dilemma Game (CDG). This game is formally an *n*-person Prisoner's Dilemma Game. Like the PDG, the payoff to each individual for defecting is higher than the payoff for cooperative behavior—regardless of what the other group members do. At the same time, all individuals in the group receive a lower payoff if all defect or compete than if all or some cooperate. Hence, as in the PDG, all players in the CDG have dominating strategies that result in a deficient equilibrium. As noted by Dawes (1980), there are important psychological differences between the two-person PDG and the *n*-person CDG. For example, in the PDG all harm visited by a player's competitive choice(s) is experienced by the one other player. In the CDG these costs are spread across a number of others. Further, in the PDG each player knows how the other has played, whereas in the CDG the choices of a particular player may be anonymous. Finally, in the repeated play of a PDG, each player, if he or she knows other's goals, has total reinforcement control over the other, that is, can facilitate or frustrate the other's obtaining a preferred outcome. The situation in the CDG is considerably more complicated since any one player's outcomes are controlled by a number of others.

Both the PDG and CDG place individuals in a setting where choices based upon protecting self-interest lead to collective ruin. For example, as regards the *n*-person Commons Dilemma Game resolving conflicts in the direction of short-term individual gain produces results analogous to those that follow from the failure to control population growth, from the unrestricted use of limited natural resources, and from the escalating pollution of the world's environment. In the Commons Dilemma, of course, individual restraint in the interest of longer-term collective interest is futile unless a substantial number of other decision-makers show similar restraint. Hence, the dilemma.

Experimental Economics

Two major economic games have been employed to study bargaining behavior: duopolies and bilateral monopolies. Here, we will describe briefly the first of the two. The latter was described earlier in Footnote 1. A duopoly is an economic relation between two sellers of a commodity each of whom controls only a part of the supply and who together control enough of the entire supply as to be the only significant source of the commodity. Further, the sellers' actions have a direct effect on the outcomes of each other, that is, they are interdependent.

The fundamental characteristic of duopoly interaction is that both actors are performing similar actions with similar consequences, producing and selling a commodity. Imagine two avocado farmers, who own all the avocado trees in town. Each faces the same problem: how much to charge per avocado and how many avocados to produce. The more they produce, the less the public will be willing to pay per avocado. If one farmer floods the market while the other restricts output, the flooder will profit more than the restrictor since both will get only a low price per piece. But both might do far better if both restricted output, and charged the consequently higher price.

Further, if both restrict output and coordinate the amount they place on the market, they could also coordinate the price they ask per avocado and, by manipulating the price and output, exact from the avocado-buying public the maximum amount the public is willing to pay ("all the market will bear"). Through coordination the farmers form a cartel, in effect a monopoly (single seller), and they are able to accrue for themselves the entire benefit available in the avocado exchange. That is, monopoly profits represent the maximum possible outcome available in any commodity exchange, thus monopoly behavior is equivalent to mutual cooperation in the PDG, which produces maximum joint outcomes.

But in duopoly, as in the PDG, each player may be "tempted" to defect. If one seller defects from the cartel and lowers price or expands production, the defector either captures the entire market (everybody buys from the lowest bidder) or reaps a greater share of the joint profits (but lowers profit per unit by flooding the market). The other seller can increase profits (but not to the monopoly level), by lowering his or her price below the other's, or expanding production. It is impossible for either to increase profits unilaterally in this situation except by lowering price or expanding output, but each such defection cycle further reduces overall profits. It is only by mutually agreeing to coordinate price and output that the sellers can regain maximum profits.

Role-Playing Simulations

The final class of paradigms considered here can be described as analogs or role-playing simulations (Crano & Brewer, 1973, p. 124) in which subjects are asked to participate in a simulation of a "real-world" mixed-motive relationship. In some sense the preceding economic games represent simplified simulations of mixed-motive relationships in the economic world. Other simulations attempt to model more complex mixed-motive interactions. One of the best known of the more complex role-playing simulations is the Deutsch and Krauss (1960) Acme-Bolt trucking game.

In this game, two players are asked to act as operators of the Acme and Bolt Trucking Companies. Each player's task is to move his or her truck of merchandise from an originating point to a destination in as little time as possible. Each player's payoffs are a direct, inverse function of the time needed to complete each trip. Each truck can move over either a main route or an alternate route. At any point along either route the player can reverse course and take the other route, with a loss of payoff because of the time consumed. The main route is the shorter path to the destination, but a secton of this route is only one lane wide and cannot be used by more than one truck at a time. On the other hand, the players can move their trucks along the lengthy and time-consuming alternate route at any time.

The times required to reach the destination along the various routes are usually such that using the alternative route yields the player little or no profit, while using the main route is profitable *if* the players coordinate their use of the one lane section. Such coordination requires a swift agreement between the players as to which will move his or her truck along the one-lane section first. Coordinating on the use of the main route leads to greater profits for both, but since the player that uses the single lane first loses the least time, both are motivated to be the first user. The trucking game combines both the problems of coordination of behaviors, and the opportunities for influence implied by the incompatibility of outcomes.

The trucking game tends to produce competitive and nonprofitable behavior by subjects, especially when subject-controlled gates are added to the paradigm. These gates, when closed, prevent the other subject from using the short, one-lane route which must be used if the player is to obtain a positive payoff. By closing the gate a given player insures the other must use the long alternative route and thus incur a loss on that trial.

As in many simulation games, the Acme-Bolt trucking game includes components of a variety of matrix and economic games. The problems of coordination in the trucking game, for example, combine features from a matrix game and an economic game which we have not described, namely, the matrix game of Chicken and the economic relationship of bilateral monopoly. Further, the opportunities for influence in the trucking game implied in its structure of outcome incompatibility are similar to those found in two matrix games, the PDG and the Maximizing Difference Game, as well as in the economic relationship of duopoly.

The preceding three paradigms permit subjects to bargain and to make interdependent decisions in interactive settings of greater or lesser complexity. We turn now to examine what has been established empirically as regards the influence of communication upon the processes and outcomes of negotiation and bargaining in such experimental settings.

Communication and Bargaining

Experimental studies of bargaining have found repeatedly that bargainers able to communicate tend to negotiate more mutually profitable and subjectively satisfying outcomes in their mixed-motive interaction than do bargainers who have only behavioral influence and no communicated influence opportunities (Hammer, 1980; Miller, Brehmer, & Hammond, 1970; Rubin & Brown, 1975; Smith, 1969; Steinfatt, Seibold, & Frye, 1974). Most of these studies compare conditions of unrestricted communication with minimal or no communication conditions. The beneficial effects of communication are not limited to one format or paradigm, but have been found (a) in the Prisoner's Dilemma Game (Deutsch, 1958; Evans, 1964; Loomis, 1959; Pilisuk & Skolnik, 1968; Radlow & Weidner, 1966; Swensson, 1967; Terhune, 1968; Voissem & Sistrunk, 1971; Wichman, 1970); (b) in experimental variations of bilateral monopoly (Daniels, 1967; Hornstein, 1965) including behavioral coordination tasks (Kelley, Condry, Dahlke, & Hill, 1965; Marwell, Schmitt, & Shotola, 1971; Mintz, 1951; Thibaut, Strickland, Mundy, & Goding, 1960) and collective bargaining tasks (Bass, 1966; Druckman, 1968); (c) in trucking game studies (Cheney, 1969; Deutsch & Krauss, 1962; Gumpert, 1967; Krauss & Deutsch, 1966; Shomer, Davis, & Kelley, 1966; and (d) in n-person Commons Dilemma Games (Bonacich, 1972, 1976; Brechner, 1977; Dawes, McTavish, and Shaklee, 1977; Edney & Harper, 1978; Harper, 1977; Jerdee & Rosen, 1974; Jorgensen & Papciak, 1981; van de Kragt, Orbell, and Dawes, 1982).

A more limited set of studies has examined whether there are structural or temporal characteristics of the communication process, or certain orientations of actors that may interact with the availability of communication to influence bargaining behaviors or outcomes. More specifically, empirical studies, using the experimental paradigms described previously, have examined three major issues: (a) whether the value orientations of bargainers interact with communication availability to influence outcomes; (b) whether the mode or the channel of communication influences outcomes; and (c) whether timing, either in terms of when the opportuinty to communicate becomes available or in terms of temporal constraints, effects bargained outcomes.

Value Orientation and Communication Availability

Value orientation refers to the attitudinal disposition that actors hold towards each other in an interaction (Rubin & Brown, 1975). Actors may evaluate the attractiveness or values of various outcome states not only in terms of the rewards and costs they afford self, but also in terms of the outcomes that they afford others with whom they are interdependent (McClintock, 1977). Three value orientations have been widely investigated in experimental bargaining: (a) *own gain,* an attempt to maximize payoffs to self (often termed "individualism" or "individualistic"); (b) *joint gain,* an attempt to maximize the sum or the payoffs to self and other ("cooperation"); and (c) *relative gain,* an attempt to maximize the positive difference between payoffs to self and other ("competition").

Experimentally, value orientations have been manipulated in two ways: first, by varying the experimenter's instructions and/or payoff schemes (e.g., rewarding competitive play), and second, by assessing motivational orientations through personality or independent interaction measures. Deutsch (1960), for example, manipulated subjects' value orientations so as to be individualistic, cooperative, or competitive, as well as the availability of communication of male subjects playing a one-trial PDG. In two of four communication conditions, subjects could pass notes before their choices in the game, or could not. Within these two levels of communication, subjects' choices in the game were announced either simultaneously, or else one player had the advantage of knowing the other's choice before having to make his choice. Subjects in a fifth condition, "reversibility," were not allowed to communicate, but were allowed to change their choice in the PDG after their mutual choices had been made and announced.

Before considering Deutsch's results, it is useful to evaluate his communication manipulations briefly in terms of the bargaining processes we have thus far outlined. Subjects in the *noncommunication reversibility* condition are able to use their changes of choice as a tacit means of behavior influence, that is, they are able to manipulate their responses in an attempt to get the other to change responses. In contrast, subjects in the *nonsimultaneous* and *simultaneous* choice condition cannot use their choice behaviors to influence the other in this one-trial game, because once their choices are made, they are fixed.

A player choosing second in the *nonsimultaneous, noncommunication* condition is confronted not with a behavioral contingency which might influence him or her, but with a behavioral fait accompli which has eliminated the mixed-motive interdependence of the game, and left the second chooser, whatever his or her motivational orientation, with a simple maximization problem. While the first chooser in the *nonsimultaneous, noncommunication* condition cannot expect to influence the other with his or her choice, the first is nevertheless caught in the communications dilemmas by the process constraint of a nonsimultaneous choice. The first chooser gives the second the advantage of information about the first's valuations, and is unable to prevent the second from exploiting this behavioral information.

On the other hand, first choosers in the *nonsimultaneous, communication* condition may be able to overcome this process constraint disadvantage by using communication to influence the other to make a choice advantageous to the first as well as to the second chooser. Any such influence would lead to higher profits for first choosers in the *nonsimultaneous, communication* condition than in the *no-communication* condition where no influence or persuasion is possible. Of course, in both conditions, second choosers should profit more than first choosers because they are in a position to exploit the commitment of first choice. For dyads in *simultaneous* conditions, the availability of communication should permit more profitable response adjustments for both players than are possible when no communication is available.

On the basis of this analysis, dyads in the *communication* conditions would be predicted to receive greater profits than dyads in *no-communication* conditions. Dyads with *nonsimultaneous choice* should receive lower profits than dyads with *simultaneous choice*. First choosers in *nonsimultaneous* conditions should suffer less exploitation if they can communicate to the second choosers than if communication is not available. Because dyads in the *reversibility* condition have a behavioral influence channel available for coordinating responses, their profits should exceed those of dyads in the *no-communication* conditions.

Deutsch (1960) found that his results supported his major predictions. First, mean dyad payoffs were significantly affected by the experimenter-induced value orientations. Cooperative dyad payoffs averaged much higher outcomes than individualistic dyads who in turn achieved higher outcomes than competitive dyads. Second, dyads in the communication conditions had higher payoffs than dyads in the no-communication conditions. Third, dyads making simultaneous choices received higher payoffs than did dyads making nonsimultaneous choices. And, in nonsimultaneous conditions, second choosers did exploit first choosers, averaging higher payoffs than first choosers. Further, this exploitation was greater in no-communication conditions than in communication conditions. And finally, higher payoffs were obtained in the reversibility than the no-communication condition.

In sum, Deutsch's subjects were better able to coordinate responses for mutually profitable outcomes when they were cooperatively oriented and when they were able to influence each other's choices, either through behavioral influence or communicated influence. As was suggested by the previous communications analysis, the nonsimultaneous process constraint reduced outcomes, but this reduction was somewhat offset if communication was available. Communication also helped disadvantaged first choosers to overcome their handicap.

What was not hypothesized by Deutsch and not suggested by the preceding communication analysis was the strong interaction between value orientation and communication opportunity that occurred. Communication opportunity and response reversibility lead to significantly greater improvements of outcomes for individualistically oriented subjects than for subjects in the competitive and cooperative orientation conditions. It appears cooperatively oriented subjects may have had no dilemma with respect to either choice or communication. Indeed, the choice in a PDG that is required to obtain outcomes consistent with cooperation and maximum joint profit is clear, and communication is unnecessary for the individual to decide upon the appropriate choice. Competitively oriented subjects also had little need to communicate to decide upon their own choice since the defection choice clearly dominates the PDG given this value orientation. Only individualistically oriented subjects needed communication to select an appropriate own gain choice since the dilemma of the PDG payoff structure is a dilemma for individualistically oriented actors—namely, if both attempt to maximize their own gain they reach a deficient equilibrium, whereas with communication or behavioral influence they can coordinate their choices to obtain a more profitable outcome.

While Deutsch (1960) manipulated value orientation by varying experimental instructions, Terhune (1968) used groups of subjects differing in their needs for achievement, affiliation, and power. Terhune assumed the affiliation motive is a desire for friendly harmonious relations while the power motive may lead to conflict, especially if attempts to control are resisted. The achievement motive was expected to produce behavior similar to that observed in Deutsch's individualistically oriented subject. Thus, Terhune hypothesized that high-need affiliation actors would be the most cooperative, those high in the need for power the most conflictive (competitive), and high-need achievers intermediate in their choice behaviors.

Subjects played 30 trials of a PDG for real money with feedback on each trial but with no communication, and then played 30 trials of the same PDG with feedback and the opportunity to communicate by means of written notes prior to making their choices. The effects of introducing communication after 30 trials without it were dramatic. The proportion of mutually cooperative choices increased from about 20% during the first 30 trials to about 70% during the last 30 trials. Unlike Deutsch's findings, there was no interaction between value orientation and communication opportunities. All three orientations showed roughly equal improvement.

Greenwood (1974) manipulated value orientation and communication opportunity to test his hypothesis that: (a) different levels of communication opportunity will have a differential effect on bargaining outcomes, and (b) motivational orientation (cooperation versus competition) will affect bargaining outcomes. The three levels of communication opportunity unrestricted, moderately restricted, and highly restricted—were used. Cooperative orientations were created by stressing that the welfare of both players were mutually important, competitive ones by emphasizing that players should outperform the other.

Subjects played a series of trials in a matrix game in which they first chose an outcome cell, and then negotiated how to redistribute points in the cell. The main effects for value orientation and communication opportunity were significant but there was no interaction between the two. Namely, both cooperation and unrestricted communication produced larger joint payoffs than the other conditions. The failure to replicate Deutsch's (1960) interaction effect can in part be attributed to changes in the task, and to Greenwood's failure to include an individualistic value condition.

In a bargaining study using a bilateral monopoly game, Kelley and Schenitski (1972) and Schenitski (1962) compared an individualistic orientation with a cooperative or group orientation, and two levels of communication availability, conversation versus written offers. They observed that actors' value orientations did not make a difference when they could converse, but when written offers were used, the cooperative orientation produced lower joint outcomes than the individualistic one. Kelley and Schenitski account for this unanticipated finding by noting that the cooperative orientation prompted actors to mention outcome options they felt might benefit others rather than following a systematic bargaining strategy that would permit them to arrive at more optimal joint outcomes. Further, the informational limitations imposed by written communication made it difficult for actors to detect that their concern for others' outcomes was producing less favorable joint outcomes.

Schulz and Pruitt (1978) partially replicated the Kelley and Schenitski studies using a somewhat different paradigm, namely a buyer and a seller who negotiated the exchange prices of three commodities. They too manipulated the value orientation of actors so as to be cooperative or individualistic and permitted two levels of communication: written offers and free verbal interaction. They observed that cooperatively oriented dyads achieved higher joint outcomes in the free verbal condition than individualistically oriented ones, a finding inconsistent with Kelley and Schenitzki's. Consistent with the latter, they observed that higher joint outcomes were not more likely to be obtained in the free verbal as compared to the more restricted written communication condition. As regards the latter, Schulz and Pruitt observe:

> having the opportunity to communicate is not itself sufficient to increase the integrative quality of bargaining solutions. For bargainers to use those communicative opportunities, they might have some form of cooperative orientation. (1978, p. 490)

Schulz and Pruitt also examined the processes that may account for the higher levels of joint outcome in the cooperative as compared to the individualistic orientation condition given communication via free verbal interaction versus written notes. They observed some important differences. Namely, in the verbal condition, cooperatively oriented dyads talked more, asked for, and gave more information than did dyads who were individualistically oriented, thereby obtaining more data about each other's needs as they were represented in their respective profit schedules. In the written notes condition, the cooperatively oriented dyads were more successful in achieving higher joint outcomes than the individualistic ones because they held more firmly to their high-priority price/profit positions, and were more likely to concede only lower-priority ones.

Given these two differing procedures for achieving high joint outcomes, Schulz and Pruitt are able to explain the difference between their own findings and those obtained by Kelley and Schenitski. First, in the latter's verbal communication condition, bargainers were not permitted to exchange information that would permit them to develop insight into what the implications of various negotiated outcomes were for other's profits, and hence what options would maximize joint outcomes. As regards the differences in achieving high joint outcomes in the written note condition, Schulz and Pruitt observe that the task employed by Kelley and Schneitski did not permit subjects an opportunity to make concessions on low-priority items and hold firm on high-priority ones, thereby permitting cooperatively oriented dyads the kind of log-rolling strategy which resulted in high joint outcomes in Schulz and Pruitt's written note conditions.

Across the studies we have reviewed which consider the interaction between the value orientation of bargainers and communication availability, there is strong evidence that the value orientation of actors may indeed interact with the nature of communication to influence bargained outcomes. In some instances this interaction produces different levels of bargained outcome; in others the interaction appears to activate different means or processes for achieving high levels of joint outcome.

Communication Modes

The modes for much of the communication which takes place among individuals are visual and auditory (Johnson, 1974). Studies manipulating the mode or channel of communication find that they are differentially related to the achievement of favorable outcomes. For example, whether subjects can see and hear each other has a measurable impact on cooperative choosing in the PDG. Wichman (1970) created four conditions in a 70-trial PDG. In one condition, Wichman's female subjects were *isolated,* in a second they could *see but not hear* each other, that is, only nonverbal communication was allowed. In a third condition they could *hear but not see* each other, that is, verbal but not visual communication. And in the fourth condition they could *both see and hear* each other. The median level of cooperative responding was 41% in isolation, 48% in see only, 72% in hear only, and 78% in see and hear. Both the ability to hear the other, and the ability to see and hear the other significantly increased cooperative choosing. It appears that subjects in the see-only condition were able to avoid communication (by not looking at each other), while subjects in the hearing conditions had no means of avoiding communication from the other. Verbal communication was thus a more effective channel of influence than nonverbal communication, but both had a positive effect on increasing joint payoffs.

Turnbull, Strickland, and Shaver (1976) examined the effects of three different modes of communication on bargaining behavior: face-to-face, audio/video, and audio. Subjects were instructed to role-play the part of chief disarmament negotiators for their assigned nations. In the face-to-face condition, subjects were seated across a table in the same room. For the other two conditions, subjects participated in separate rooms. Turnbull et al. (1976) found that face-to-face communication produced more cooperative negotiation behavior, that is, highest joint outcomes, followed by audio/video and audio-only modes of communication. The difference between the face-to-face and audio-video conditions, however, was not significant as regards cooperative behavior. Their findings suggest that visual presence plus communication is important to cooperative outcomes in negotiations. This is consistent with Weston and Kristen's (1973) assertion that cooperative outcomes are more likely to occur in the face-to-face and audio/video as opposed to audio modes because visual contact increases understanding and acceptance between participants.

Vitz and Kite (1970) examined the nature of what was actually communicated when subjects played five trials of a complex negotiation game (similar to duopoly), and were allowed either to see and hear each other, communicate by telephone, or send written messages via teletypewriters. Vitz and Kite found no observable differences in the content of communication in the face-to-face and verbal communication conditions, suggesting in this instance that the verbal content of communication was not differentially influenced by visual presence or absence. This suggests perhaps that the "increased understanding and acceptance" in Turnbull et al.'s (1976) study may have been the result of nonverbal cues. Vitz and Katz's data do not permit a comparison of bargaining effectiveness or outcomes in the three conditions.

Taking the preceding studies, together with the earlier reported results obtained by Deutsch (1960) and Terhune (1968), there appears to be relatively strong evidence that including visual channels in communication may improve bargaining outcomes. Carnevale, Pruitt, and Seilheimer (1981), however, obtained an inconsistent finding. They investigated the effects of accountability and visual versus verbal modes of communication on bargaining behavior in a bilateral monopoly game. In the visual mode, bargainers were able to see and to talk to each other. In the verbal mode, a barrier was placed between the negotiators to allow only verbal communication. Subjects engaged in a role-playing task involving a buyer and a seller who negotiated on prices for three appliances. Across all levels of accountability, being in the visual mode decreased joint benefits. When face-to-face, negotiators offered less information concerning values and used more "I's" than "We's." This finding is in contradiction to other studies which imply that visual and verbal communication are more conducive to cooperation than just verbal communication (e.g., Smith, 1969; Turnbull et al., 1976).

Thus, there exists conflicting evidence as regards the effectiveness of verbal versus verbal and visual cues in facilitating mutually profitable outcomes. Inconsistent findings can always be attributed to differences in the experimental manipulations employed in the various studies. Nevertheless, the preponderance of evidence to date is consistent with the assumption that the more communication channels available in bargaining, the more cooperative are the negotiated outcomes.

Timing of Communication

We will examine several different aspects of the timing of communication upon bargaining. First, we will evaluate the effect of whether communication occurs during the first or second half of a bargaining session. Second, we will consider the impact of permitting bargainers to communicate before a bargaining session, at regular intervals during it, or continuously. Finally, we will examine the influence of the presence or absence of time constraints upon negotiated outcomes.

Krauss and Deutsch (1966), using the trucking game paradigm, investigated the differences between communication opportunities introduced at the very beginning of the bargaining (and maintained during the initial bargaining trials), and communication opportunities introduced after subjects had experienced several bargaining trials. Further, they considered two competing hypotheses in regard to introducing the opportunity to communicate after bargaining had gone on for awhile without it. First, interacting in the bilateral gate condition of the trucking game paradigm without communication would produce deadlocks, retaliations, and heavy losses, thereby producing "barriers to communication when the opportunity to communicate was later introduced" (p. 575). Or second, the experience of early unsuccessful outcomes would lead subjects to be more receptive to innovations, and hence communication introduced later in the interaction would improve their outcomes. Krauss and Deutsch offered no specific hypotheses regarding what the effects of early communication manipulation would be relative to those of later communication.

Their first hypothesis is analogous to Newcomb's (1947) "autistic hostility" assumption, namely, as interpersonal conflict in a competitive setting intensifies and individuals see their goals or outcomes threatened by the other's behavior, communication between the actors deteriorates until they will stop communicating altogether. Their second corresponds to Kelley's (1966) strategic communication hypothesis that asserts that when an interaction becomes competitive in the absence of communication, the subsequent introduction of communication may alter the overall structure of the relationship. Introduced late in a competitive interaction, communication may alter the response-reward structure of the interaction by allowing actors to make mutually coordinated, contingent behaviors that would be impossible to arrange without communication, either by uncovering possible side payments and tradeoffs, and/or by changing the actors' valuations of own and others' outcomes.

Krauss and Deutsch tested these two competing hypotheses by having female subjects play 20 trials of a bilateral gate trucking game with verbal pretrial communication opportunities available before each of the first 7 trials (labelled "predeadlock" communication), or only before each of the 8th through the 14th trials ("postdeadlock" communication). Both groups played each of the last 15th through 20th trials without pretrial communication ("criterion" trials). Subjects were permitted to communicate during any of the 20 timed trials.

Overall they found a main effect for the predeadlock-postdeadlock manipulation with the postdeadlock dyads receiving higher payoffs in the game. That is, communication opportunities introduced early in the interaction were less effective in producing mutually profitable agreements than communication introduced later in the interaction. However, it is impossible to determine from this study whether this effect is due to the timing of the communication opportunity, or to the intervention of the experimenter in the postdeadlock dyads, and the pressure brought to bear on the bargainers when informed they could communicate "to reconsider the situation."

In an attempt to examine the same processes while employing a different task, Wandell (1968) using a 20-trial PDG game, was unable to replicate the Krauss and Deutsch (1966) results. Wandell's subjects played an "arms race" game with the ability to exchange written notes simultaneously on either the first 10 trials or on the last 10 trials. He found that communication reduced joint outcomes, and that the timing of the communication had a negligible effect on outcomes. Scodel, Ratoosh, and Minas (1959) in an earlier study also interrupted subjects playing 50 trials of the PDG after the 25th trial, and allowed them a brief interval of verbal discussion before resuming the trials with no further communication. While this brief communication produced no significant increase in cooperation compared to no-communication conditions, it did decrease the frequency of mutual defection choices relative to the first 25 trials. On the other hand, Bixenstine, Levitt, and Wilson (1966) and Bixenstine and Douglas (1967) found significant increases in cooperation when subjects were allowed a brief discussion between the 10th and 11th trials of a 20-trial PDG game.

In sum, Wandell and Scodel et al. found no improvement in outcomes with delayed communication availability relative to early availability, while Krauss and Deutsch, Bixenstine et al., and Bixenstine and Douglas found delayed communication increased joint outcomes, whereas early communication had little or no ameliorating influence. Recently, Stech and McClintock (1981), using a duopoly game, replicated the earlier Krauss and Deutsch (1966) study under conditions in which the experimenters did *not* request that subjects in the later communication condition reconsider the situation, a manipulation which Krauss and Deutsch employed because they felt it essential for breaking a previously established pattern of mutual competition. Changes in choice following such a manipulation may represent, of course, merely a response to the experimenters' demands, and tell us little about the advantage or disadvantage of later communication per se.

Stech and McClintock also employed a more complete design in which there was a baseline communication condition in which subjects were provided no opportunity to communicate either early or late. Their results indicated that dyads permitted to communicate throughout the interaction, or during the latter half, were more cooperative than those with no communication throughout, or communication during the first but not the latter half of the trials. There were no significant effects for the presence or absence of communication during the first half. Hence, as obtained in the original Krauss and Deutsch study, subjects' choice behaviors were more consistent with the strategic communication hypothesis of Kelley (1966) than with Newcomb's autistic hostility hypothesis.

The overall finding that communication introduced later in an interaction has more effect than communication introduced early suggests that bargainers may be reluctant to use communication available early in the game openly or honestly because of the mixed motive structure of their interdependent relationship. Early communication may bring the user more disadvantages than advantages. At best, bargainers may use such communication guardedly, accepting communicated information from the other with reservation. At worst, they may use early communication to trick and deceive each other, and to reject all information from the other as lies. On the other hand, communication introduced later in the interaction may refocus the bargainers' attention on the cooperative and coordinative aspects of their relation, and such aspects may emerge as a cooperative figure against the competitive ground of a previous costly interaction.

Other studies have investigated the effect of the timing of communication before and throughout the entire experimental game. Voissem and Sistruck (1971), for example, examined the effects of four different schedules of communication on cooperative game behavior: no communication, pregame communication, communication every 10 trials, and communication every trial. Subjects were randomly assigned to the experimental conditions and played a PDG with an instructed individualistic motivational orientation. Results indicate that there were significantly more individual as well as mutually cooperative responses in the communication-every-trial group than in the other groups. In addition, the results show that there was a significant increase in both individual and mutually cooperative responses in the second half of the game for the communication-every-trial group only. In the pregame communication group, there was a significant decrease in individual cooperative responses in the last half of the game as compared with the first half. Overall, there was a consistent trend of increasing individual and mutual cooperative responses with an increasing opportunity for communication.

A final timing variable that has been empirically investigated is that of time pressure of constraint. Yukl, Malone, Hayslip, and Pamin (1976) examined the effects of time pressure on bargaining behavior in a bilateral monopoly buyer-seller game using two unnamed commodities. Each commodity had different payoff values to the buyer and seller, one commodity being worth more to the buyer, the other worth more to the seller. The subject's objective was to negotiate a price which would provide a large personal payoff to self. Thus, an individualistic orientation was stressed.

Both buyers and sellers were allowed 30 minutes to negotiate. There were two levels of time pressure. In the high time pressure condition, subjects were given 30 additional payoff points, and informed that one point would be deducted for every minute of time used to make a final decision. In the low pressure condition, subjects did not receive additional points, and there were no time costs.

The findings indicated that joint outcomes were significantly greater in the low time pressure condition than in the high time pressure condition. There were also more honest disclosures of priorities in the low pressure condition than in the high time pressure condition. Further, there was more cooperative behavior in the dyads with honest communication than in the dishonest dyads. And finally, the amount of time to reach a decision was lower in the high pressure condition than in the low pressure condition. These findings imply that time pressures may inhibit mutual problem-solving by facilitating competitiveness and dishonesty in communication.

The finding that bargainers reach a decision more rapidly when time pressures exist for the resolution of conflict is consistent with a number of studies that indicate that such pressures have two effects: they result in lower demands by bargainers and more rapid concession-making (Carnevale, Sherer, & Pruitt, Note 1; Hammer & Baird, 1978; Komorita & Barnes, 1975; Pruitt & Johnson, 1970; Yukl, 1974). These processes, in turn, facilitate more rapid agreement. But as Yukl et al. (1976) found, such agreements are not necessarily ones that yield the highest levels of joint outcome.

Conclusion

One of the more consistent findings in research on bargaining is that the opportunity to communicate increases the likelihood that bargainers will obtain outcomes that maximize their joint profits or outcomes. Further, more specific research on various aspects of the communication reveals that certain intervening variables or characteristics of the communication process influence the likelihood of reaching favorable joint outcomes. In our description and review of empirical research on the relationship between communication and bargaining, we have noted a number of personal and social processes that variations in communication may influence so as to affect the quality of bargained outcomes. However, in no sense have we attempted to examine all those processes that through the manipulation of communication may influence bargained outcomes.

Messick and Brewer (1983) have recently described a number of such processes that may be the result of or co-occur with communication availability to produce more favorable collective outcomes. *First,* communication may necessitate that bargainers make public statements about their intended choices, a process that is likely to elicit norms that generate conformity pressures toward achieving some collective good. *Second,* the expression of desires and intentions may increase the level of trust that exists between players. Trust in mixed-motive settings is a basic requisite of achieving cooperative outcomes. *Third,* discussion may permit bargainers the opportunity to exercise influence, that is, to persuade the other to make choices consistent with optimizing joint outcomes. *Fourth,* the discussion of alternative choices and outcomes may create a feeling of group identity and cohesion thereby increasing the likelihood that goodness of outcomes will be defined in collective terms. And *finally,* bargainers already predisposed toward joint gain optimization may use communication as a means of problem-solving to reach preferred outcome.

Future research examining the effects of communication availability upon bargaining outcomes needs to examine in a more systematic and careful manner how the preceding processes may be elicited by communication as well as what influence they may have on the achievement of particular outcomes. Even more important to the development of the area, however, is the formulation of general theories of bargaining which take into consideration the role of communication as one of a number of processes that may influence bargaining behaviors and outcomes. Pruitt (1981) has recently set forth a careful conceptualization of what he terms integrative bargaining. In doing so he has considered formally how the exchange of concessions and various forms of problem-solving communication influence the outcomes that bargainers obtain. Obviously the future of the field will rest upon the formulation and empirical exmaination of this and similar theoretical statements.

Acknowledgment. The preparation of this chapter was partially supported by NSF Grant 80-16214. The authors would like to express their appreciation to Barry Moss for his major editorial help.

Reference Note

1. Carnevale, P. J., Sherer, P., & Pruitt, D. G. *Some determinants of concession rate and distributive tactics in negotiation.* Paper presented at the 87th annual convention of the American Psychological Association, New York, September, 1979.

References

Baldwin, D. A. Bargaining with airline hijackers. In I. W. Zartman (Ed.), *The 50% solution.* New York: Doubleday (Anchor), 1976.

Bass, B. M. Effects on the subsequent performance of negotiators of studying issues or planning strategies alone or in groups. *Psychological Monographs,* 1966, *80* (whole No. 614).

Bixenstine, V. E., & Douglas, J. Effect of psychopathology on group consensus and cooperation choice in a six-person game. *Journal of Personality and Social Psychology,* 1967, *5,* 32-37.

Bixenstine, V. E., Levitt, C. A., & Wilson, K. V. Collaboration among six persons in a prisoner's dilemma game. *Journal of Conflict Resolution,* 1966, *10,* 488-496.

Bonacich, P. Norms and cohesion as adaptive responses to political conflict: An experimental study. *Sociometry,* 1972, *35,* 357-375.

Bonacich, P. Secrecy and solidarity. *Sociometry,* 1976, *39,* 200-208.

Brechner, K. C. An experimental analysis of social traps. *Journal of Experimental Social Psychology,* 1977, *13,* 552-564.

Carnevale, P. J. D., Pruitt, D. G., & Seilheimer, S. O. Looking and competing: Accountability and visual access in integrative bargaining. *Journal of Personality and Social Psychology,* 1981, *40,* 111-120.

Cheney, J. H. The effects upon the bargaining process of positive and negative communication options in equal and unequal power relationships. *Dissertation Abstracts,* 1969, *30,* 2146-2147-A.

Coleman, J. *The mathematics of collective action.* Chicago; Aldine, 1973.

Crano, W. D., & Brewer, M. B. *Principles of research in social psychology,* New York: McGraw-Hill, 1973.

Daniels, V. Communication, incentive, and structural variables in interpersonal exchange and negotiation. *Journal of Experimental Social Psychology,* 1967, *3,* 47-74.

Dawes, R. M. Social dilemmas. *Annual Review of Psychology,* 1980, *31,* 169-193.

Dawes, R. M., McTavish, J. & Shaklee, H. Behavior, communication, and assumptions about other people's behavior in a commons dilemma situation. *Journal of Personality and Social Psychology,* 1977, *35,* 1-11.

Deutsch, M. Trust and suspicion. *Journal of Conflict Resolution,* 1958, *2,* 265-279.

Deutsch, M. The effect of motivational orientation upon trust and suspicion. *Human Relations,* 1960, *13,* 123-139.

Deutsch, M., & Krauss, R. M. The effect of threat upon interpersonal bargaining. *Journal of Abnormal and Social Psychology,* 1960, *61,* 181-189.

Deutsch, M., & Krauss, R. M. Studies in interpersonal bargaining. *Journal of Conflict Resolution,* 1962, *6,* 52-76.

Druckman, D. Dogmatism, prenogotiation experience, and simulated group representation as determinants of dyad behavior in a bargaining situation. *Journal of Personality and Social Psychology,* 1967, *6,* 279-290.

Druckman, D. Prenegotiation experience and dyadic conflict resolution in a bargaining situation. *Journal of Experimental Social Psychology,* 1968, *4,* 367-383.

Edney, J. J., & Harper, C. S. The effects of information in a resource management problem: A social trap analog. *Human Ecology,* 1978, *6,* 387-395.

Evans, G. Effect of unilateral promise and value of rewards upon cooperation and trust. *Journal of Abnormal and Social Psychology,* 1964, *69,* 587-590.

Gallo, P. S., Jr., & McClintock, C. G. Cooperative and competitive behavior in mixed-motive games. *Journal of Conflict Resolution,* 1965, *9,* 68-78.

Gergen, K. J. *The psychology of behavior exchange.* Reading, Mass.: Addison-Wesley, 1969.

Greenwood, J. G. Opportunity to communicate and social orientation in imaginary reward bargaining. *Speech Monographs,* 1974, *41,* 79-81.

Gumpert, P. *Some antecedents and consequences of the use of punitive power by bargainers.* Unpublished doctoral dissertation, Teacher's College, Columbia University, New York, 1967.

Hammer, W. C. The influence of structural, individuals and strategic differences on bargaining outcomes: A review. In D. L. Harnett & L. L. Cummings (Eds.), *Bargaining behavior: An international study.* Houston: Dame, 1980.

Hammer, W. C., & Baird, L. S. The effect of strategy, pressure to reach agreement and relative power on bargaining behavior. In H. Sauerman (Ed.), *Contribution to experimental economics* (Vol. 7). Mohr: Tubingen, 1978.

Harper, C. S. Competition and cooperation in a resource management task: A social trap analogue. In S. Weidman & J. R. Anderson (Eds.), *Priorities for environmental design research.* Washington, D. C.: Environmental Research Association, 1977.

Henrikson, A. K. The emanation of power. *International Security,* 1981, *6*(1), 152-164.

Hornstein, H. A. The effects of different magnitudes of threat upon interpersonal bargaining. *Journal of Experimental Social Psychology,* 1965, *1,* 282-293.

Ikle, F. C., & Leites, N. Political negotiation as a process of modifying utilities. *Journal of Conflict Resolution,* 1962, *6,* 19-28.

Jerdee, T. H., & Rosen, B. Effects of opportunity to communicate and visibility of individual decisions on behavior in the common interest. *Journal of Applied Psychology,* 1974, *59,* 712-716.

Johnson, D. W. Communication and the inducement of cooperative behavior in conflicts: A critical review. *Speech Monographs,* 1974, *41,* 64-78.

Jones, E. E., & Gerard, H. B. *Foundations of social psychology.* New York: Wiley, 1967.

Jorgenson, D. O., & Papciak, A. S. The effects of communication, resource feedback, and indentifiability on behavior in a simulated commons. *Journal of Experimental Social Psychology,* 1981, *17,* 373-385.

Kelley, H. H. A classroom study of the dilemmas in interpersonal negotiations. In K. Archibald (Ed.), *Strategic interaction and conflict: Original papers and discussion.* Berkeley, California: Institute of Interational Studies, 1966.

Kelley, H. H., Condry, J. C., Jr., Dahlke, A. E., & Hill, A. H. Collective behavior in a simulated panic situation. *Journal of Experimental Social Psychology,* 1965, *1,* 20-54.

Kelley, H. H., & Schenitzki, D. P. Bargaining. In C. McClintock (Ed.), *Experimental social psychology.* New York: Holt, Rinehart and Winston, 1972.

Kelley, H. H. & Thibaut, J. W. Group problem solving. In G. Lindzey & E. Aronson (Eds.), *Handbook of social psychology* (Vol. IV., 2nd ed.). Reading, Mass.: Addison-Wesley, 1969.

Komorita, S. S., & Barnes, M. Effects of pressures to reach agreement in bargaining. *Journal of Personality and Social Psychology,* 1975, *32,* 699-705.

Krauss, R. M., & Deutsch, M. Communication in interpersonal bargaining. *Journal of Personality and Social Psychology,* 1966, *4,* 572-577.

Loomis, J. L. Communication, the development of trust, and cooperative behavior. *Human Relations,* 1959, *12,* 305-315.

Luce, R. D., & Raiffa, H. *Games and decisions: Introduction and critical survey.* New York: Wiley, 1957.

Marwell, G., Schmitt, D. R., & Shotola, R. Cooperation and interpersonal risk. *Journal of Personality and Social Psychology,* 1971, *18,* 9-32.

McClintock, C. G., & Keil, L. J. Equity and social exchange. In R. Cohen & J. Greenberg (Eds.), *Equity and justice in social behavior.* New York: Academic Press, 1982.

McClintock, C. G. Social motivation in settings of outcome interdependence. In D. Druckman (Ed.), *Negotiations: Social psychological perspectives.* Beverly Hills: Sage, 1977.

Messick, D. M., & Brewer, M. B. Solving social dilemmas: A review. In L. Wheeler (Ed.), *Review of personality and social psychology.* Beverly Hills: Sage, 1983.

Miller, M. J., Brehmer, B., & Hammond, K. R. Communication and conflict reduction. A cross cultural study. *International Journal of Psychology,* 1970, *5,* 75-87.

Mintz, A. Non-adaptive group behavior. *Journal of Abnormal and Social Psychology,* 1951, *46,* 150-159.

Newcomb, T. M. Autistic hostility and social reality. *Human Relations,* 1947, *1,* 69-86.

Nogee, J. L. Propaganda and negotiation: The ten-nation disarmament committee. *Journal of Conflict Resolution,* 1963, *7,* 510-521.

Pilisuk, M., & Skolnick, P. Inducing trust: A test of the Osgood proposal. *Journal of Personality and Social Psychology,* 1968, *8,* 121-133.

Pruitt, D. G. Reciprocity and credit building in dyads. *Journal of Personality and Social Psychology,* 1968, *8,* 143-147.

Pruitt, D. G. Motivational processes in the decomposed prisoner's dilemma game. *Journal of Personality and Social Psychology,* 1970, *14,* 227-238.

Pruitt, D. G. *Negotiation behavior.* New York: Academic Press. 1981.

Pruitt, D. G., & Johnson, D. G. Mediation as an aid to saving face in negotiation. *Journal of Personality and Social Psychology,* 1970, *14,* 239-246.

Radlow, R., & Weidner, M. F. Unenforced commitments in "cooperative" and "non-cooperative" non-constant-sum games. *Journal of Conflict Resolution*, 1966, *10*, 497-505.

Rapoport, An., & Chammah, A. M. *Prisoner's dilemma: A study in conflict and cooperation*. Ann Arbor, Mich.: University of Michigan Press, 1965.

Raven, B. H., & Kruglanski, A. W. Conflict and power. In P. Swingle (Ed.), *The structure of conflict*. New York: Academic Press, 1970.

Rubin, J. Z., & Brown, B. R. *The social psychology of bargaining and negotiation*. New York: Academic Press, 1975.

Schelling, T. C. *The strategy of conflict*. Cambridge, Mass.: Harvard University Press, 1960.

Schenitzki, D. P. *Bargaining, group decision-making, and the attainment of maximum joint outcome*. Unpublished doctoral dissertation, University of Minnesota, 1962.

Schulz, J. W. & Pruitt, D. G. The effects of mutual concern on joint welfare. *Journal of Experimental Social Psychology*, 1978, *14*, 480-492.

Scodel, A., Ratoosh, P., & Minas, J. Some personality correlates at decision making under conditions of risk. *Behavioral Science*, 1959, *4*, 19-28.

Shomer, R. W., Davis, A. H., & Kelley, H. H. Threats and the development of coordination: further studies of the Deutsch and Krauss trucking game. *Journal of Personality and Social Psychology*, 1966, *4*, 119-126.

Skinner, B. F. Selecting consequences. *Science*, 1981, *213*, 501-504.

Smith, D. H. Communication and negotiation outcome. *Journal of Communication*, 1969, *19*, 248-256.

Spence, K. W. *Behavior theory and conditioning*. New Haven: Yale University Press, 1956.

Stech, F. J., & McClintock, C. G. Effects of communicating timing on duopoly bargaining outcomes. *Journal of Personality and Social Psychology*, 1981, *40*, 664-674.

Steinfatt, T. M., Seibold, D. R., & Frye, J. K. Communication in game theoretic models of conflicts: Two experiments. *Speech Monographs*, 1974, *41*, 23-35.

Swensson, R. G. Cooperation in the prisoner's dilemma game I: The effects of asymmetric payoff information and explicit communication. *Behavioral Science*, 1967, *12*, 314-322.

Terhune, K. W. Motives, situation, and interpersonal conflict within prisoner's dilemma. *Journal of Personality and Social Psychology Monograph Supplement*, 1968, *8*, 1-24.

Thibaut, J. W., & Kelley, H. H. *The social psychology of groups*. New York: Wiley, 1959.

Thibaut, J. W., Strickland, L. H., Mundy, D., & Goding, E. F. Communication, task demands, and group effectiveness. *Journal of Personality*, 1960, *28*, 156-166.

Tinbergen, N. *Curious naturalists*. New York: Doubleday (Anchor), 1968.

Turnbull, A. A., Strickland, L., & Shaver, K. G. Medium of communication, differential power, and phrasing of concessions: Negotiating success and attributions to the opponent. *Human Communication Research*, 1976, *2*, 262-270.

van de Kragt, A., Orbell, J. M., & Dawes, R. M. *The minimal contributing set as a solution to public goods problems.* Paper presented at the annual meeting of The American Psychological Association, Washington, D. C., 1982.

Vitz, P. C., & Kite, W. R. Factors affecting conflict and negotiation within an alliance. *Journal of Experimental Social Psychology,* 1970, *6,* 233-247.

Voissem, N. H., & Sistrunk, F. Communication schedule and cooperative game behavior. *Journal of Personality and Social Psychology,* 1971, *19,* 160-167.

Von Neumann, J., & Morgenstern, O. *Theory of games and economic behavior.* New York: Wiley, 1964.

Walton, R. E., & McKersie, R. B. *A behavioral theory of labor negotiations: an analysis of social interaction system.* New York: McGraw-Hill, 1965.

Wandell, W. A. Group membership and communication in a prisoner's dilemma setting. *Dissertation Abstracts,* 1968, *28,* 4767-4768-B.

Weston, J. R., & Kristen, C. *Teleconferencing: A comparison of attitudes, uncertainty and interpersonal atmosphers in mediated and face-to-face group interaction.* Prepared for the Department of Communications, Ottawa, Canada, 1973.

Wichman, H. Effects of isolation and communication on cooperation in a two-person game. *Journal of Personality and Social Psychology,* 1970, *16,* 114-120.

Young, O. R. (Ed.) *Bargaining: Formal theories of negotiation.* Urbana: University of Illinois Press, 1975.

Yukl, G. A. The effects of situational variables and opponent concessions on a bargainer's perception, aspirations and concessions. *Journal of Personality and Social Psychology,* 1974, *29,* 227-236.

Yukl, G. A. Effects of information, payoff magnitude, and favorability of alternative settlements on bargaining outcomes. *Journal of Social Psychology,* 1976, *98,* 269-282.

Yukl, G. A., Malone, M. P., Hayslip, B., & Pamin, T. A. The effects of time pressure and issue settlement order on integrative bargaining. *Sociometry,* 1976, *39,* 277-281.

Zajonc, R. B. *Social psychology: An experimental approach.* Belmont, California: Brooks/Cole, 1967.

Zartman, I. W. Negotiation as a joint decision-making process. *Journal of Conflict Resolution,* 1977, *21,* 619-638. [Reprinted in I. W. Zartman (Ed.), *The negotiation process.* Beverly Hills, California: Sage, 1978]

Chapter 10
Procedural Justice, Participation, and the Fair Process Effect in Groups and Organizations

Jerald Greenberg and Robert Folger

The vast body of theory and research on justice in groups and organizations has focused primarily on issues of *distributive justice* (Homans, 1961), that is, the manner in which resources are distributed, and on responses to these distributions (for recent reviews, see Freedman & Montanari, 1980; Greenberg, 1982). Another fundamental type of justice manifest in groups and organizations, but one that has received considerably less attention, concerns the rules and processes through which resources are allocated, that is, *procedural justice* (Leventhal, 1976; Thibaut & Walker, 1975; Tyler & Caine, 1981). For example, in considering the fairness of pay raises, workers may not only take into account how much pay they receive relative to others, but also such procedural factors as who made the decision, and what criteria were taken into account (see Lawler, 1971). Concerns of this type, focusing on the *process* of allocation, rather than on the outcome of allocation per se, fall into the domain of procedural justice.

This chapter will focus on procedural justice in group and organizational settings. Indeed, it is within such contexts that the procedures by which allocation decisions are made take on particular significance. Consider, for example, the trend toward democratization of the workplace during the 20th century (Blumberg, 1968). While not adopted universally, practices that allow employees some direct control over various aspects of their working conditions, or allow them some degree of influence in decisions made regarding those working conditions, are becoming increasingly common. This growing popularity appears to be spread by the belief that participation is an effective way of fostering productivity, in conjunction with the attitude that it offers a morally attractive alternative to many of the oppressive facets of organizational life (Locke & Schweiger, 1979; Strauss, 1977).

Psychological folklore suggests that this participatory trend will have positive benefits. An illustration of the alleged benefits of participation is provided by an example taken from the literature on interpersonal justice. In reviewing various forms of perceived injustice. Deutsch (1975) observed that "much social psychological research" (not cited in Deutsch's article) identifies unfair decision-making practices as the "most fundamental" form of injustice. He then went on to say that "people are more apt to accept decisions and their consequences if they have participated in making them" (p. 139). Another way of stating this idea is that if the *process* is perceived as being fair (e.g., because it allows for participation), then there is a greater likelihood that the *outcomes* resulting from that process will be considered fair. The tendency for perceptions of procedural justice to influence perceptions of distributive justice in this particular way, and hence to contribute to the acceptance of decisions, has been called the *fair process effect* (Folger, Rosenfield, Grove, & Corkran, 1979). This chapter will examine the fair process effect, and possible explanations of this effect. Particular attention will be paid to its limiting conditions.

We will begin by briefly reviewing the organizational contexts in which democratically oriented procedures and participatory practices have emerged. One purpose of this brief overview will be to demonstrate that theorists have used terms such as "participatory" to group together, rather loosely, a very wide variety of operations. Our position is that these operations are multifaceted—indeed, they may be too complex and diverse to be assimilated by any single psychological mechanism (i.e., fair process effects may occur for different reasons in different settings). This review will be followed by an examination of several social-psychological constructs that are applicable in this context. The concluding point to be made is that just as there are a variety of relevant concepts, there are also differences in the effects of democratic and participatory arrangements in different circumstances, that is, enhanced satisfaction and acceptance of decisions cannot be expected to occur in every instance. In fact, it is only by taking into account the diversity of operations and relevant psychological mechanisms that some less well-known tendencies—tendencies that run counter to the fair process effect and thus to the conventional wisdom of psychological folklore—can be explained.

Participation in Organizational Contexts

There are several common organizational practices that are participatory in nature. Our presentation will highlight four such practices: participatory management programs, nonauthoritarian leadership styles, flexible work schedules, and cafeteria-style pay plans. These represent examples of programs or operations that give employees the freedom to control either their work inputs (such as the type of work performed), their outcomes (such as the type of benefits derived from their labor), or both.

Participatory Management Programs

Perhaps the most obvious example can be seen in participative management programs (for reviews, see Dachler & Wilpert, 1978; Locke & Schweiger, 1979). Although the exact specifications of such programs vary from organization to organization, they generally involve the introduction of procedures that increase the role of workers in the running of their companies (i.e., the opportunity to exert some influence) (see Strauss, 1977; Tannenbaum & Schmidt, 1958). Policies in which management considers workers' recommendations in making decisions is a typical example. Such policies may take various forms ranging from simple consultation with workers through making joint decisions with them, to giving them total control over decisions (Heller & Yukl, 1969). The effectiveness of such programs in improving productivity and satisfaction has long been noted (e.g., Coch & French, 1948; Lawrence & Smith, 1955; Ritchie & Miles, 1970), although it is by no means unequivocal (Locke & Schwieger, 1979).

Special programs such as the well-known Scanlon Plan involve especially active cooperation between workers and managers, who get to share the labor-cost savings resulting from their participation in organizational activities. Such plans have been recognized as effective in raising company productivity and lowering employee grievances (Lesieur & Puckett, 1969). Accordingly, this form of worker participation in management procedures regarding work inputs and outcomes has been seen as beneficial to both workers and management.

Nonauthoritarian Leadership Styles

The literature on leadership styles reveals some analogous effects. For example, the classic research by Lewin, Lippitt, and White (1939) showed that democratic leadership fostered greater group cohesiveness than either autocratic or laissez-faire leadership styles. Analogously, nonauthoritarian leadership led to greater member satisfaction in a study by Shaw (1955). Thus, leadership styles that allowed members some say in determining their outcomes and inputs were preferred to other styles. Related research has shown the leaders tend to be more persuasive when group members have a say in selecting them and elected leaders were more influential than appointed leaders (Hollander & Julian, 1970). Similar positive effects of nonauthoritarian leadership styles have been well documented (Bass, 1981). However, the results have not been unequivocal: Several theoretical perspectives on leadership recognize that participatory leadership styles may only be effective under certain situations (e.g., see Chemers, Chapter 2, this volume; Fiedler, 1978; Vroom & Yetton, 1973).

Flexible Work Schedules

Other organizational programs give workers a voice in determining their inputs only. What comes to mind here is flexitime, the practice according to which employees are given some freedom in determining their working hours (Cohen & Gadon, 1978). Recent research has shown that compared to typical conditions in which workers have no say in determining their working hours, employees working under self-determined, flexible schedules tend to be more satisfied with their jobs (Golembiewski, Yeager, & Hilles, 1975; Orpen, 1981), are absent less frequently (Kim & Campagna, 1981), are sometimes more productive (Schein, Maurer, & Novak, 1977), and enjoy greater ease in commuting to and from their jobs (Hicks & Klimoski, 1981).

Cafeteria-Style Pay Plans

On the output side, there are cafeteria-style approaches to compensation that allow employees to select the combination of fringe benefits they desire. Such programs have been described as beneficial in reducing turnover (Lawler, 1981), and evidence suggests that they are often well received (Nash & Carroll, 1975). To summarize, organizational practices that give individuals some influence in determining their work inputs and/or their outcomes tend to be accepted, and sometimes result in improved productivity.

Summary Evaluation of Participatory Effects in Organizations

The preceding overview of organizational practices represents what might be termed the "promise" of participation—namely, that there are a variety of ways of implementing participatory programs in organizations. It should be noted, however, that not all reviews of these applications have been optimistic about this promise (e.g., see Dachler & Wilpert, 1978; Yukl, 1981). Indeed, a review by Locke and Schweiger (1979) has a decidedly negative tone. Specifically, in reviewing 46 studies of participative decision-making (PDM) containing productivity measures, 22% of the investigations found PDM to be superior to other decision-making practices, and an identical number found it to be inferior, with 56% yielding equivocal results. The results were clearer, although not totally unambiguous, in the case of the 43 studies including satisfaction measures. PDM was associated with higher satisfaction than other practices in 60% of the studies, and lower satisfaction in only 9%, with the remaining 31% of the cases yielding equivocal findings.

Given that there has not been complete consistency in the impact of participatory programs in organizations, it is useful to consider the psychological mechanisms that might affect such results. We will consider several psychological mechanisms that could account for the fair process effect, and we will pay particularly close attention to those that can explain instances of both the presence of the effect and its absence, or even reversal. In addition, the diversity of practices already outlined can be made more theoretically manageable if we reduce the variations into their underlying basic forms. We have identified two forms of participation that are conceptually fundamental—"choice" and "voice." The former represents a more direct form of influence over outcomes, and the latter, a more indirect form. Each of these basic forms is discussed in a separate section in the following, and within each section, some mechanisms that can account for the results of that particular form of participation are presented. As an interpretation of the effects of voice turns out to call for the consideration of more mechanisms than is the case with choice, our discussion of voice will be lengthier and more detailed. In neither case, however, have we tried to be exhaustive in our consideration of the possible mechanisms, and some of the mechanisms that are mentioned receive only sketchy treatment. Our purpose has been to deal with some of the mechanisms in detail rather than to attempt to indicate the entire range of conceivably relevant mechanisms.

Participation in the Form of Choice

If and when participatory practices do yield greater satisfaction and acceptance of decisions, a simple explanation that comes immediately to mind can be invoked—namely, these practices may increase the extent to which people get what they want (cf. Folger, 1977; Locke & Schweiger, 1979; Mitchell, 1973). Certainly it should be no great surprise that people who get what they want are happier than people who do not, and it should likewise be clear that participatory procedures might tend to accomplish this goal more than nonparticipatory procedures. There are some considerations, however, that lie below this superficial simplicity.

To begin with, it is important to note that if this explanation were the whole story, there would be no psychological significance in participation per se. Giving people what they want could be accomplished, after all, in a totally autocratic and nonparticipatory manner, although it might be argued that participation provides a more efficient means of determining just what it is that people desire to have (where "participation" means asking them).

Asking people what they want and then letting them have the desired outcomes is closely related to having people choose their own outcomes. When participation comes in the form of choice, the key question—as the earlier remarks have suggested —is whether the act of providing a choice produces any *incremental* satisfaction over and above that produced by obtaining the desired outcome itself. Obviously, demonstrations of an added process contribution to satisfaction must involve a choice versus no-choice comparison across a constant level of outcomes. Interpreting the results from such a comparison is a problem in that ceiling effects might well obscure any evidence of participation-produced satisfaction (i.e., even people who have no choice but who get what they want might be so happy as to be near the endpoint of a satisfaction scale).

There is another complication of choice as well. The act of choosing involves making a commitment to an outcome and assuming responsibility for it. Both from an attributional standpoint and from the perspective of theories such as cognitive dissonance (e.g., Insko, Worchel, Folger, & Kutkus, 1975), the act of making a commitment to, and thereby assuming responsibility for, one's decision has an effect on one's attitudes toward outcomes. However, the specific nature of those attitudes (whether they become accepting or rejecting of the outcomes) depends on the magnitude of the outcome. Studies by Folger and his colleagues (Folger, Rosenfield, & Hays, 1978; Folger, Rosenfield, Hays, & Grove, 1978) illustrate this point.

The theoretical basis for these studies was a clarification of the relationship between equity and dissonance suggested by Deci and Landy (in Deci, 1975). According to this perspective, opposite reactions to either low (inequitably disadvantageous) or high (inequitably advantageous) outcomes are mediated by choice. The results of two experiments confirmed this hypothesis. Specifically, subjects who chose to work for low compensation showed greater enthusiasm and satisfaction than those who had no choice about working for low compensation. On the other hand, subjects who had a choice about whether or not to work for an overly generous rate of compensation were *less* satisfied than those who had no choice about receiving this rate of compensation. (Performance findings that paralleled the results of satisfaction measures were also obtained.)

These findings suggest that there are circumstances under which choice of a desirable outcome does *not* produce greater satisfaction than procedures involving the absence of choice. Basically, the problem is the possibility of an "overjustification effect" (see Lepper & Greene, 1978): People can lose enthusiasm for what was an intrinsically interesting activity by virtue of choosing to be rewarded in a generous fashion for having performed that activity (presumably due to the self-attribution "I'm doing it for the reward"). It is beyond the scope of this chapter to review the various qualifications necessary to specify the precise conditions under which this effect can occur (e.g., Rosenfield, Folger, & Adelman, 1980), but reference to the effect is sufficient to indicate one reason why the relationship between participation and satisfaction is not straightforward even when people choose desirable outcomes. As we shall see, the relationship is even more complex when it comes to the other underlying form that participation can take—voice.

Before turning from choice to a consideration of voice, it is necessary to comment briefly on the underlying basis for our distinction between the two. This distinction is closely akin to the one made by Thibaut and his colleagues (Houlden, LaTour, Walker, & Thibaut, 1978; Thibaut & Walker, 1978) regarding differences between "decision control" and "process control" in structures for dispute resolution (especially those structures adopted within formal legal systems). *Decision control* has been defined as "the degree to which any of the participants may unilaterally determine the outcome of the dispute," and *process* control as "control over the development and selection of information that will constitute the basis for resolving the dispute" (Thibaut & Walker, 1978, p. 546).

In the case of legal disputes, the outcome is "unilaterally determined" by a judge or jury. There are, however, important differences between decision control in the legal context and choice as an element of participatory procedures in organizational contexts. For example, it is sometimes true that the decision a judge is allowed to make must be selected from among a discrete set of alternatives prescribed by law (e.g., guilty vs. innocent; and if guilty, death vs. life imprisonment). In such cases, the available options are often determined by legal precedent and are backed by centuries of moral reasoning about the welfare of citizens and the state. The point is that there is a degree of social consensus about these being the *only* "reasonable" options.

Within an organizational context, on the other hand, there may be considerable debate about the *content* of the options that should be made available to workers. For example, management may offer workers a choice regarding the *time* of day at which coffee breaks occur. From the workers' point of view, this choice may be less meaningful than a choice about the *length* of breaks (e.g., an option of one 30-minute break or two 15-minute breaks).

This matter of the content of options is important because it implies that there are *levels* of unilateral control. At the highest level is the selection of the specific content of options to be made available. This type of control is typically reserved exclusively by management (although this statement is not meant to deny the societal and organizational-climate constraints that managers and owners may feel when they establish company policies)—in fact, the exercise of this type of control is probably responsible for the contention by Tannenbaum and Cooke (1979) that a degree of hierarchical control remains within *all* organizational systems, even the most allegedly "democratic" (for which reason Tannenbaum & Cooke argue that all such organizations actually represent points on a continuum of oligarchy). Workers' control by the act of choice exists at a lower level. It is "unilateral" or direct control because workers are not literally *forced* into settling for any particular option (although it is important to note that they may feel considerably *constrained* if none of the choices is desirable), but it is not complete control because the available options have been predetermined.

Another way of putting the matter is to emphasize that choice may engender only a partial and limited sense of control. *Choice* and *control* are not synonymous. In fact, we have used the term "choice" at this point rather than the term "control" because we wish to emphasize that the psychological mechanisms(s) underlying the effects of choice may or may not involve a sense of control. The sense of personal control may well be a highly important psychological mechanism (see further discussion of this issue in the following sections) and it may well be at least partly responsible for the effects of choice. Even where a sense of control is partially involved, however, it is possible that several other psychological mechanisms also contribute to the observed effects (e.g., satisfaction or dissatisfaction with the outcomes received).

For example, an act of choice—selecting among options, thereby rejecting others —often involves making a *commitment* as well as exercising some unilateral control. The effects of commitment, in turn, have been adumbrated in terms of a variety of psychological mechanisms, including (cf. Cialdini, Cacioppo, Bassett, & Miller, 1978): self-perception (Bem, 1967); dissonance (Festinger, 1957); and behavioral "freezing" (Lewin, 1947) or increased resistance to change (Kiesler, 1971). The theoretical differentiation among these various constructs, although important to an understanding of the effects of choice, is a task beyond the scope of the present chapter. Similarly, we will not explore the various possible interrelationships between choice and control, although there is a considerable literature on this subject (e.g., Deci, 1980; Perlmuter & Monty, 1979; Steiner, 1970).

Participation in the Form of Voice

Participation as choice, because it represents a somewhat direct control over out-comes, is probably not as common as more indirect forms of participation. We have chosen to group the remainder of these participatory forms under the heading of *voice* to emphasize the common element they share in allowing for the expression of opinion in decision-making. The term "voice" has been borrowed in a slightly modified version from Hirschman (1970), who distinguished it from *exit* in referring to two basic classes of political and economic activity: interest articulation within a system (voice) versus the decision to remove oneself from the system (exit). Hirschman's analysis was focused primarily on such situations as those faced by consumers/voters whose favorite product/political party begins to decline in its capacity to provide satisfaction. To exercise voice by articulating one's interests to those in charge (of the company manufacturing the product or of the political party) is to attempt reform; to "exit" by switching brands or parties to give up on reform. Without intending to imply the various connotations reflected in Hirschman's usage, we have adopted the term "voice" as a shorthand for the variety of ways that subordinates in an organization communicate their interests to their superiors in an attempt to exert influence over the decisions their superiors will make. (These terms have been similarly applied to organizational contexts by Farrell, Note 1, and by Spencer, Note 2.)

A line of investigation that is important to understanding the role of voice, especially as it relates to procedural justice, is the pioneering research of Thibaut and Walker (1975) and their associates. This research, which uses a laboratory analog of judicial decision-making, consistently reveals stronger preference for the adversary system (a legal system, such as that used in the United States, that imbues control over the process to the disputants themselves) than for the inquisitorial system (a legal system, such as that used in many European countries, in which the process of dispute resolution is relegated to a third party). Specifically, research (e.g., LaTour, 1978; Lind, Kurtz, Musante, Walker, & Thibaut, 1980; Walker, LaTour, Lind, & Thibaut, 1974) suggests that satisfaction with verdicts is greater among defendants who have some voice in their own defense than among those who have no voice. This line of research has established that defendants' satisfaction with verdicts, and the perceived fairness of these verdicts, was greater when procedures allowed them to present evidence in support of their case. So pervasive was this effect, in fact, that it extended even to the outcome that would otherwise have been the most intolerable of all—namely, the situation in which subjects perceived themselves to be innocent but were found guilty. Subjects found guilty after they had exercised voice were more accepting of the verdict than were subjects who had no voice and were found guilty (LaTour, 1978; Walker et al., 1974).[1]

An important frame of reference is established by the previously cited research. In particular, it is useful to consider the situation in which people think they are innocent and are found guilty—the otherwise intolerable outcome found to be more acceptable under adversary as opposed to inquisitorial arrangements—as a test for assessing the impact of participatory procedures. The significance of this situation is that by pertaining to low-quality outcomes, it thereby avoids the possible ceiling effects mentioned in connection with our discussion of choice.

---

[1] It is ironic that reactions to the adversary system are so positive since it has also been shown (Lind, Thibaut, & Walker, 1973) that "the evidence presented and assembled for decisionmaking by autocratic processes represents the discovered evidence more accurately than does that presented by adversary processes" (Thibaut & Walker, 1978, p. 547).

Effectance and Reactance Explanations

Thibaut and Walker's (1975) analysis of the adversarial system postulates that its distinguishing feature is a balance of control: Control over the final determination of outcomes to be awarded is vested in a neutral third party, and control over evidence bearing on that determination is vested equally in the parties disputing the outcome distribution issue. The framing of participatory procedures in terms of control has been an influential perspective contributed by this work, and so it is with respect to the issue of control that we will begin our examination of the psychological mechanisms germane to voice.

The desire for control has been termed the *effectance* motive (White, 1959). According to the effectance perspective, people have a general orientation (i.e., cutting across specific types of outcomes) to increase the degree of freedom they possess to manipulate the environment and to control outcomes. Any increment in control over outcomes should produce an increment in satisfaction. Adversary procedures are better received than inquisitorial procedures, according to an effectance explanation, because the former offer greater control over evidence presentation than the latter. Presumably, this greater satisfaction with the adversary *procedure* simply "spills over" generalized positive affect to the *outcomes* derived from that procedure as well.

An alternative perspective on control is offered by *reactance* theory (Brehm, 1966), and the most recent exposition of that theory (Brehm & Brehm, 1981) strongly contrasts reactance and effectance. Whereas effectance is seen as a desire for control *in general* (i.e., for the process itself rather than for the particular outcomes it entails), reactance is described as a motivation regarding *specific* freedoms. One implication of this distinction is that according to effectance, a loss of control in one area of one's life can be offset by gaining control in another area, whereas reactance maintains that the threat to a freedom is motivationally arousing until that specific freedom is restored.

A second distinction between reactance and effectance is that while effectance suggests an ever-vigilant search for new opportunities to *gain* control, reactance is quiescent until the *loss* of control occurs or is threatened. Brehm and Brehm's (1981) review of the evidence for a motive to gain control argues that the conclusive study demonstrating the existence of this motive has yet to be performed (and suggests that it is unlikely to be forthcoming, given the methodological problems they point out). Given that the reactance motive can accommodate the evidence as well, it would appear to offer a more parsimonious explanation than the construct of effectance.

A reactance interpretation of the fair process effect implies that the effect is something of a misnomer. What is responsible for the effect, from a reactance perspective, is *not* an increment of satisfaction because of voice, but a decrement in satisfaction in the conditions used for comparison—those in which the freedom to exercise voice has been denied, which can therefore aptly be named *mute* procedures. Under the test case of low outcomes, "voice" procedures show greater acceptance of other intolerable decisions than do "mute" procedures because the latter add the insult of reactance to the injury of inequity (Folger, 1977).

Social Influence Explanation

Both the effectance and reactance constructs are limited in their ability to explain the effects of variations in procedures. The effectance construct is relevant only to positive effects of control. Reactance is restricted to negative effects of the deprivation of control. These limitations become apparent in light of evidence, which we will consider in the following, that voice can produce either positive reactions (the fair process effect) or negative reactions (those that Folger et al., 1979, have termed the *frustration effect*). For that reason, we will examine yet a third psychological mechanism—social influence processes. We believe that social influence processes are capable of accounting for both fair process and frustration effects. Before considering the social influence explanation, however, we should note that it is not incompatible with reactance. Reactance predicts negative responses to mute procedures but does *not* address what occurs with voice (i.e., where control is gained, not lost). Therefore, the reactance explanation is not necessarily disconfirmed by evidence that certain independent processes (e.g., forms of social influence) can make responses to voice just as negative as responses to mute procedures (or even more so).

Our social influence explanation considers allocation situations from the perspective of the psychology of groups. All allocation situations entail at least that most minimal of groups, the dyad, because the necessity of distributing outcomes implies that more than one person will receive some portion of the available benefits. A standard primitive situation (typical of laboratory experiments) actually involves a three-person group consisting of a decision-maker, or allocator, and two recipients, or co-workers.

Considered from the perspective of psychological processes relevant to groups, one of the most fundamental elements of the decision-making that leads to an allocation is that people in the group can differ in their opinions about what will constitute a fair distribution of benefits. For example, while all might agree that productive contributions to the group should be rewarded relative to the size of the contribution (a generalized equity notion), they might very well disagree about what *kinds* of contributions are to count the most. Thus, although equity may be "in the eye of the beholder" (Walster, Berscheid, & Walster, 1973); people differ in their perceptions of what is fair and equitable (Greenberg, 1983).

Furthermore, judgments of outcome fairness cannot be evaluated by the kinds of objective criteria that constitute checks on "physical reality" (cf. Festinger, 1954). What we are emphasizing is that perceptions of outcome fairness involve not only the social comparison of one's own outcome/input ratio to that of others, as proposed originally in Adams's (1965) equity formula, but also the comparison of one's own *opinions* (about such things as the proper application of that formula) with others' opinions. Many situations involve an inherent ambiguity about what is fair. Indeed, if that were not the case, it would be difficult for an experimentally manipulated unfair outcome allocation to be viewed by subjects as something another person might plausibly do, and therefore equity experiments would be impossible to conduct because of subject suspicion. Given a degree of ambiguity and uncertainty regarding the correctness of one's own opinion, the door is opened to being influenced by other people's opinions. (It should be noted that the fairness of outcomes in organizational contexts can be every bit as ambiguous as the fairness of outcomes in laboratory contexts, especially when the former situations involve such things as subjective performance appraisals.)

Our position is that the fair process effect can be explained in terms of this susceptibility to influence via social comparison. Participation in decision-making is, after all, a matter of expressing opinions about what the decision should be. For example, participation may take the form of workers' opinions about their salaries being expressed to a supervisor in charge of salary decisions. When the decision is made, it then represents the final opinion of the supervisor—an opinion against which workers can compare their own.

The nature of social influence in the situation just described can be explicated in attributional terms, just as Ross, Bierbrauer, and Hoffman (1976) analyzed the Asch conformity paradigm in terms of the attributional dilemmas it posed. Consider what happens when a worker's voiced salary request is denied (thus establishing the appropriate test condition, to which we referred earlier, of a poor outcome). Clearly there is a difference of opinion between the worker and the supervisor. Because participation has occurred, however, this difference of opinion is likely to be evaluated in a way that it would not be if participation had not occurred. The act of participation makes the supervisor's decision a *reply* to a voiced request, and hence the supervisor's opinion is one that he or she expresses *despite opposition*. An opinion expressed despite opposition has attributional implications that differ from those that exist when there is no opposition (i.e., when the same opinion/decision of a supervisor occurs in a situation in which the worker has no voice).

What is the attributional implication of opinions expressed despite opposition? In Kelley's (1972) terms, this situation creates the tendency for *augmentation* to occur. "Augmentation" refers to the enhanced perception of a cause's being responsible for an effect when the causal factor produces the effect despite conditions that should inhibit it. For example, when a time of 10 seconds in a 100-yard dash is accomplished despite a 25-mile-per-hour wind blowing in the runner's face, greater athletic ability is attributed to the person who achieved that feat than to a person in another heat whose identical time was recorded when the wind was calm. According to the logic of augmentation, people should be more inclined to believe that a speaker's true attitude is responsible for his or her public pronouncements, rather than perceiving that these pronouncements are extrinsically motivated by such considerations as the desire to win popularity, to the extent that those pronouncements are made in the face of opposition.

In a study that supports this line of reasoning, Mills and Jellison (1967) showed that a speech representing a position said to be unpopular with the audience was perceived by subjects as being more sincere than when the same position was adopted in a speech to an audience for whom it represented a popular stand (subjects in the former condition were also more persuaded). Similar effects have been found by Eisenger and Mills (1968), in a study in which the extremity of an argument (connoting its unpopularity) enhanced the perception of its sincerity. (In both studies, factors such as communicator credibility were held constant.)

The worker-supervisor situation is analogous. To recapitulate our argument, we began by presuming that opinions regarding fairness involve a degree of ambiguity. Given uncertainty and the accompanying susceptibility to social influence via social comparison, the worker has some tendency to look toward the supervisor's opinion as a source of information to begin with (Festinger, 1954), and the role of supervisor may bestow a certain degree of authority to any occupant of that position. It is our contention that in addition to these tendencies, an augmentation effect can provide a further impetus toward the worker's acceptance of the supervisor's opinion. Just as the unpopularity or extremity of a speaker's position has been shown to increase the persuasiveness and perceived sincerity of the speaker in laboratory contexts (Eisinger & Mills, 1968; Mills & Jellison, 1967), so the unpopularity of a supervisor's opinion (i.e., when it opposes the worker's own expressed viewpoint) might increase the perceived reliability of the supervisor as a source of information. In this fashion, the provision of voice can lead to greater acceptance of outcomes, and it is this connection between a procedure and the perception of outcomes generated by the procedure that we have referred to as the fair process effect. The absence of a participatory process makes it easier to perceive an allocator's decision as having been made without much thought, whereas participation can contribute to the perception that it was a considered judgment.

The preceding analysis has suggested that the motive to increase one's sphere of control is not the only psychological mechanism that can explain why people given voice respond more positively than those receiving outcomes via a mute procedure. In fact, we have identified not one but two alternative mechanisms—reactance and social influence processes. It is our opinion that it would be a mistake to propose an *experimentum crucis* that would test the relative explanatory power of these mechanisms. The diversity of procedures (and the multifaceted complexity of any given procedure) make it unlikely that any one mechanism can provide a complete explanation. The implementation of a participatory process involves enough variables in a real-world setting to make it likely that elements of all three mechanisms—effectance, reactance, and social influence—might simultaneously play a role.

Despite this plea for theoretical eclecticism, we will focus attention in the remainder of our discussion of those social influence processes that we identified from the standpoint of a group perspective. Our reason for emphasizing this particular perspective is not based on our conviction that it will ultimately prove to be superior to the others, but rather that it alone appears capable of taking into account certain curious effects that sometimes arise from voice procedures. Given the less-than-perfect consistency of results from participatory studies, however, it is useful to consider carefully those mechanisms that can explain instances in which voice procedures do *not* produce greater outcome satisfaction than mute procedures.

Limiting Conditions of the Fair Process Effect

Voice and Opinion Diversity

In introducing the social influence perspective, we developed the idea that fairness judgments affecting feelings of satisfaction are subjective impressions susceptible to social comparison. Within that context, the influence of an authority's opinion (as reflected in the allocation decision) was said to be greater when that opinion is expressed despite opposition (the worker's voiced objection) than when the same opinion is expressed under circumstances where no objection was allowed. This description, however, focuses exclusively upon only two opinions: the opinion of the decision-maker and the opinion of the subordinate participating by means of a voice in the decision-making process. The situation may be more complicated, however, when more than two parties are involved, as an experiment by Thibaut, Friedland, and Walker (1974) suggests.

The Thibaut et al. experiment actually involved five persons, each of whom was involved in a laboratory experiment using an industrial simulation. Four subjects played the role of separate corporations. The fifth person was a confederate assigned the role of "government" in a bogus random drawing. The corporations had to pay taxes to the government, and the instructions identified two different taxation policies that could be adopted. One policy was markedly more disadvantageous to the corporations than the other and thus provides the appropriate test case for our analysis.

The determination of which tax policy would be implemented was made by means of either a participatory or a nonparticipatory decision-making procedure. In the nonparticipatory conditions, the government was allowed to make a decision unilaterally, whereas all five parties voted under the participatory arrangement. Experimental control of the decision was maintained in the participatory case by bogus feedback that the vote had been split among the four corporations and the government had broken the tie.

A key measure reflecting satisfaction with tax policy was the amount of taxes paid relative to taxes owed. Payment of taxes was subject to the corporations' discretion because opportunities to cheat on tax payment had been designed into the structure of the games (the government was allowed to monitor compliance with the tax regulations only on certain trials of the game). The results from this measure showed that when a policy disadvantageous to the corporations was in effect, the participatory conditions yielded more cheating than the nonparticipatory conditions.

Clearly these results seem directly contrary to the tendency for participatory procedures to produce greater acceptance of a decision than nonparticipatory procedures. From a group perspective, however, they can be explained in terms of the same social influence processes previously outlined. Just as our earlier discussion of social influence drew a parallel with the basic Asch conformity paradigm, it is helpful in this case again to refer to a finding from one of Asch's variations.

The variation to which we refer (see Asch, 1951) involves a break in the uniformity of group pressure that is placed upon someone whose opinion deviates from the group. Our earlier analysis referred to a subordinate whose opinion differed from the decision-maker's, and hence this subordinate faced a "unanimous" opinion of only one person. The situation in the participatory conditions of the Thibaut et al. experiment, however, involved a diversity of opinion and hence a break in unanimity. It is in light of the results of Asch variation (namely, that a break in unanimity by a single confederate "ally" yields a much greater tendency for a subject to stick to his or her own opinion than when there is no such ally) that the Thibaut et al. findings can be explained in social influence terms.

From this standpoint, a critical difference between the participatory and nonparticipatory conditions is the presence or absence of feedback about the opinions of the other corporations. In the absence of a participatory vote, each corporation knew only the judgment of that person in the authority-figure role of government. By contrast, each subject in the participatory conditions knew that one other corporation had also voted for the favorable tax policy. Apparently the validation of one's own opinion by an ally enables a person to maintain a more resolute posture in opposition to an authority figure, thereby increasing the tendency for expressions of dissatisfaction to occur.

In summary, two aspects of the Thibaut et al. findings stand out. First, in contrast to the typical fair process effect, the results indicated *less* acceptance of the decision when subjects had voice than when they did not. Second, this effect can be explained in terms of social influence processes.

This discussion of the Thibaut et al. experiment represents a reinterpretation of a study not originally designed to test a social influence analysis. A weakness in addition to the post hoc nature of the interpretation is that the voice versus mute (participatory/nonparticipatory) procedural manipulation is confounded with the presence versus absence of awareness of an opinion that validates the subject's own. A more informative experimental design is one that manipulates feedback about other subjects' opinions independently of the procedural opportunity for participation in decision-making. Two such experiments have been reported by Folger et al. (1979).

The aim of the studies by Folger et al. was to use a participatory procedure that *did* enhance acceptance of the decision when subjects received no feedback that validated their own opinions, and to compare this procedure with one that combined voice and information about a concurring opinion. Each experiment involved a decision-maker's allocation of the rewards going to two workers. A salient norm of equitable distribution, which corresponded to what workers indicated privately was their perception of how much they should receive, was violated by the decision-maker's allocation.

The rules governing the process by which the allocation decision would be made were announced prior to the decision. In the *mute* conditions, this announcement stated that the allocation was solely the decision-maker's prerogative. Each subject in the voice conditions, on the other hand, believed that he or she alone had been randomly chosen to transmit his or her own opinion regarding a fair allocation to the decision-maker. Independently of this procedural manipulation, subjects were given one of two types of information regarding what the "other subject" had privately indicated the allocation should be. Half of the subjects in each experiment learned that the other subject's opinion allegedly coincided with their own (and hence it disagreed with the decision-maker's opinion). The information given to the remaining subjects differed by experiment. In Experiment 1, the subjects were given false information about the other's opinion that made it appear to coincide with the decision-maker's judgment. The corresponding subjects in Experiment 2 were simply given no feedback at all about the other subject's opinion.

The results of these two experiments were similar. When there was nothing to confirm the subject's perception of an allocation inequity (i.e., when the other subject's opinion "supported" the decision-maker or when no information about the other subject's opinion was provided), "voice" subjects expressed greater satisfaction than "mute" subjects and showed additional evidence of having accepted the decision (e.g., they gave more money to the decision-maker when it was their turn to allocate). When the feedback regarding the other subject's opinion *did* confirm the subject's own perception of fairness, however, the fair process effect was *not* evident: In both experiments comparisons of the mute and voice conditions yielded no significant differences. Moreover, there were some tendencies for the voice procedure to produce *less* satisfaction than the mute procedure.

This hint of a tendency for participation to "backfire" obviously needs further exploration. The evidence for it in the context of the paradigm we have been discussing is minimal and merely suggestive. It is, however, consistent with a general hypothesis that expressions of dissatisfaction tend to be strengthened the more a person has reason to be convinced (via interpersonal validation) of an inequity. The final situation to be described, although somewhat specific, represents perhaps the most dramatic evidence—at least in terms of statistical significance—of the possibility that the normal acceptance-enhancing properties of voice sometimes may be reversed.

Voice and the Partial Improvement of Outcomes

The unique circumstances under which voice has been most clearly shown to have deleterious effects on outcome satisfaction involve what might be called "incomplete restoration of equity." The following sequence of events describes this situation in the abstract: first, a recipient has (perceives) an inequitably low level of outcomes; next, a request is made for outcomes to be raised to an equitable level; and finally, the outcomes are raised, but not to such an extent that the inequity is entirely redressed. A real-life example might involve someone's feeling underpaid, asking for a raise that would put his or her salary at what is perceived as the deserved level, and then getting only half of what was requested.

A study by Thibaut (1950) provides an experimental analog of such a situation. The subjects in Thibaut's experiment were a group of children divided into two teams. During three rounds of game-playing prior to the experimental manipulation, the experimenter had always favored the same team (e.g., allowing them to throw beanbags at a target while the other team had to pick up the beanbags). The experimenter left the room for a few minutes after these three rounds, and one of his assistants, who had been watching and taking notes as an observer, persuaded the disadvantaged team to ask the experimenter to reverse the roles of the teams and replay the last game. The manipulation, administered by the experimenter upon his return, involved granting this request or turning it down.

Measures of hostility showed that the subjects whose request had been granted expressed more anger than those whose request was denied. This finding is unusual for two reasons. First, it is an instance of a participatory procedure (voice) being followed by dissatisfaction rather than satisfaction. Second, the greater dissatisfaction came from those who received the outcome they *wanted*, rather than from those who remained deprived! Nevertheless, the pattern of results is entirely consistent with our earlier social influence analysis. The subjects who did not receive what they wanted represent the familiar test case to which we have made reference several times. The effect is the same augmentation-derived tendency to accept the judgment of an authority figure whose unfavorable allocation is made despite voiced opposition. The group whose outcomes improved as a result of voice, on the other hand, parallel those subjects in the Thibaut et al. (1974) and Folger et al. (1979) experiments who had their opinions confirmed by social comparison—the difference being that the latter received self-validating information regarding the opinions of other subjects, whereas the voice-improvement group in the Thibaut study had their perception of the existence of a previous inequity verified by the compensatory action of the experimenter. The compensation was only partial, however, in that only one game of three was replayed. Thus, a cumulative inequity remained in effect, and the previous injustice of the two earlier games was, if anything, made more salient by the experimenter's tacit admission of guilt.

Once again we have indulged in a post hoc explanation. Another possible weakness in interpretation is that the Thibaut study had no "mute" nonparticipatory group with which comparisons could be made. An experiment by Folger (1977), however, addresses these problems.

The subjects in Folger's study were given small amounts of money during each of ten different pay periods that occurred in the course of the experiment. In each case, the amount a "worker" subject received was the result of an allocation by his manager in which the manager decided how to divide some money (the same amount each pay period) between the two of them. Prior to the first pay period all workers had recorded the division they perceived as being fair, and these perceptions were challenged by substantially inequitable pay decisions favoring the manager/allocator on the first two pay periods. At this point, the subjects in the voice condition were allowed to send a note to the manager revealing their recorded statement of what they perceived as being the fair way to divide the money, whereas subjects assigned to the mute condition were given no such opportunity. Thereafter, on pay periods 3-10, the size of the allocation to the worker gradually increased (to the same extent in both groups) while the amount to the manager declined. On the tenth pay period, the division was an even split for the first time. All pay decisions were actually controlled by the experimenter so that the net result was a cumulative inequity involving total pay for the manager that was twice the size of the total received by the worker/subject.

Under these conditions, workers in the voice condition displayed significantly greater dissatisfaction than mute workers. This is one more example of a situation in which a participatory procedure has produced *less* acceptance of a decision than a nonparticipatory procedure. Again, the results fit the prediction from a social influence analysis. The voice-improvement workers received a begrudging endorsement of their position in the form of the manager's gradual "conversion" to a 50-50 allocation. Given this reluctant acceptance of the validity of sharing evenly, the overall unevenness of the total amounts stood out as an unacceptable situation.

Interestingly, the identical sequence of payments apparently took on a different meaning when the absence of voice (mute condition) precluded subjects' being able to feel responsible for having caused a change in the manager's allocation behavior (i.e., these subjects were not as dissatisfied as those in the voice condition). These results thus take on special significance in suggesting that the very possibilities for increased worker influence characteristic of participatory arrangements may actually engender greater worker resentment under some circumstances.

Summary

A variety of results involving voice procedures thus seem capable of being explained in terms of social influence. When voice produces the fair process effect, the explanation focuses upon augmentation associated with a decision-maker's opinion being expressed despite opposition. As we have seen, however, other effects of social influence may override or short circuit augmentation, such that voice does not result in a fair process effect. The form of social influence taking place in these latter cases seems to involve inferences from what is known about others' opinions (peers or the decision-maker) that serve to validate one's own perception of an inequity.

These negative (nonacceptance) reactions to voice, which have been the focus of this section on the *limitations* of the fair process effect, have been categorized by Folger et al. (1979) as instances of a *frustration effect*. The point in using such a term is to call attention to the possibility that voice can raise expectations; such expectations, in turn, may subsequently be dashed. In other words, voice procedures can represent one way in which *relative deprivation* is experienced as the result of "if only" thoughts (e.g., "If only the supervisor had seen things my way") that create an alternative frame of reference against which to compare existing reality (cf. Folger, Rosenfield, Rheaume, & Martin, 1983; Folger, Rosenfield, & Robinson, 1983). As was the case in our discussion of choice, however, we have not attempted an exhaustive treatment of possible underlying mechanisms. *Public commitment,* for example, might account for some instances of dissatisfaction resulting from voice procedures. That is, the voiced expression of one's opinions tends to bolster them, thus leading to intransigence rather than acceptance. Further social influence analyses should also be extended to include the effects of such factors as the credibility and status of the source, as well as the degree to which individuals believe that the opinions they express are actively considered by those making a decision.

Conclusion

Our discussion of the psychological mechanisms surrounding the use of participation has been intended to raise questions rather than to provide definitive answers. Certainly there is sufficient evidence to warrant the conclusion that increased participation will not always enhance satisfaction. We have suggested some theoretical reasons why this conclusion should not be surprising, but the process of exploring concepts that can account for the different effects of participation has revealed a diversity of psychological mechanisms to match the variety of procedures encompassed under the heading of democratized arrangements. Given this state of affairs, we can only hope that others will treat this topic area as one much in need of further investigation, rather than continuing the historical trend of allegiance to the conventional wisdom about the allegedly beneficial effects of participatory decision-making.

Acknowledgment. The authors gratefully acknowledge the helpful comments of Chuck Behling, Paul Paulus, Harry Reis, and John Slocum on earlier drafts of this chapter. The second author would also like to acknowledge encouragement from J. Stacy Adams that was responsible for several of the investigations herein reported.

Reference Notes

1. Farrell, D. *Exit, voice, loyalty, and neglect as responses to job dissatisfaction.* Paper presented at the meeting of the Academy of Management, New York, August 1982.
2. Spencer, D. G. *Employee voice and employee retention.* Paper presented at the meeting of the Academy of Management, New York, August 1982.

References

Adams, J. S. Inequity in social exchange. In L. Berkowitz (Ed.), *Advances in experimental social psychology* (Vol. 2). New York: Academic Press, 1965.

Asch, S. E. Effects of group pressure upon the modification and distortion of judgements. In H. Guetzkow (Ed.), *Groups, leadership and men*. Pittsburgh: Carnegie Press, 1951.

Austin, W. Justice, freedom, and self-interest in intergroup conflict. In W. G. Austin & S. Worchel (Eds.), *The social psychology of intergroup relations*. Monterey, Calif.: Brooks/Cole, 1979.

Bass, B. M. *Stogdill's handbook of leadership*. New York: Free Press, 1981.

Bem, D. J. Self-perception: An alternative interpretation of cognitive dissonance phenomena. *Psychological Review,* 1967, *74*, 183-200.

Blumberg, P. *Industrial democracy: The sociology of participation*. New York: Schocken, 1968.

Brehm, J. W. *A theory of psychological reactance*. New York: Academic Press, 1966.

Brehm, S. S., & Brehm, J. W. *Psychological reactance: A theory of freedom and control*. New York: Academic Press, 1981.

Cialdini, R. B., Cacioppo, J. T., Bassett, R., & Miller, J. A. Low-ball procedure for producing compliance: Commitment then cost. *Journal of Personality and Social Psychology,* 1978, *36*, 463-476.

Coch, L., & French, J. R. P. Overcoming resistance to change. *Human Relations,* 1948, *1*, 512-533.

Cohen, A. R., & Gadon, H. *Alternative work schedules*. Reading, Mass.: Addison-Wesley, 1978.

Dachler, H. P., & Wilpert, B. Conceptual dimensions and boundaries of participation in organizations: A critical evaluation. *Administrative Science Quarterly,* 1978, *23,* 1-39.

Deci, E. L. *Intrinsic motivation.* New York: Plenum, 1975.

Deci, E. L. *The psychology of self-determination.* Lexington, Mass.: D. C. Heath, 1980.

Deutsch, M. Equity, equality, and need: What determines which value will be used as the basis of distributive justice? *Journal of Social Issues,* 1975, *31,* 137-150.

Eisenger, R., & Mills, J. Perception of the sincerity and competence of a communicator as a function of the extremity of his position. *Journal of Experimental Social Psychology,* 1968, *4,* 224-232.

Festinger, L. A theory of social comparison processes. *Human Relations,* 1954, *7,* 117-140.

Festinger, L. *A theory of cognitive dissonance.* Evanston, Ill.: Row, Peterson, 1957.

Fiedler, F. E. Contingency model and the leadership process. In L. Berkowitz (Ed.), *Advances in experimental social psychology* (Vol. 11). New York: Academic Press, 1978.

Folger, R. Distributive and procedural justice: Combined impact of "voice" and improvement on experienced inequity. *Journal of Personality and Social Psychology,* 1977, *35,* 108-119.

Folger, R., Rosenfield, D., Grove, J., & Corkran, L. Effects of "voice" and peer opinions on responses to inequity. *Journal of Personality and Social Psychology,* 1979, *37,* 2253-2261.

Folger, R., Rosenfield, D., & Hays, R. P. Equity and intrinsic motivation: The role of choice. *Journal of Personality and Social Psychology,* 1978, *36,* 557-564.

Folger, R., Rosenfield, D., Hays, R., & Grove, J. Justice vs. justification effects on productivity: Reconciling equity and dissonance findings. *Organization Behavior and Human Performance,* 1978, *22,* 465-473.

Folger, R., Rosenfield, D., Rheaume, K., & Martin, C. Relative deprivation and referent cognitions. *Journal of Experimental Social Psychology,* 1983, *19,* 172-184.

Folger, R., Rosenfield, D., & Robinson, T. Relative deprivation and procedural justifications. *Journal Personality and Social Psychology,* 1983.

Freedman, S. M., & Montanari, J. R. An integrative model of managerial reward allocation. *Academy of Management Review,* 1980, *5,* 381-390.

Golembiewski, R. T., Yeager, S., & Hilles, R. Factor analysis of some flexitime effects: Attitudinal and behavioral consequences of a structural intervention. *Academy of Management Journal,* 1975, *18,* 500-509.

Greenberg, J. Approaching equity and avoiding inequity in groups and organizations. In J. Greenberg & R. L. Cohen (Eds.), *Equity and justice in social behavior.* New York: Academic Press, 1982.

Greenberg, J. Overcoming egocentric bias in perceived fairness through self-awareness. *Social Psychology Quarterly,* 1983, *46,* 152-156.

Hicks, W. D., & Klimoski, R. J. The impact of flexitime on employee attitudes. *Academy of Management Journal,* 1981, *24,* 333-341.

Hirschman, A. O. *Exit, voice and loyalty: Responses to declines in firms, organizations, and states.* Cambridge, Mass.: Harvard University Press, 1970.

Hollander, E. P., & Julian, J. W. Studies in leader legitimacy, influence, and innovation. In L. Berkowitz (Ed.), *Advances in experimental social psychology* (Vol. 5). New York: Academic Press, 1970.

Homans, G. C. *Social behavior: Its elementary forms.* New York: Harcourt, Brace, & World, 1961.

Houlden, P., LaTour, S., Walker, L., & Thibaut, J. Preference for modes of dispute resolution as a function of process and decision control. *Journal of Experimental Social Psychology,* 1978, *14*, 13-30.

Insko, C. A., Worchel, S., Folger, R., & Kutkus, A. A balance theory interpretation of dissonance. *Psychological Review,* 1975, *82*, 169-183.

Kelley, H. H. Causal schemata and the attribution process. In E. E. Jones, D. E. Kanouse, H. H. Kelley, R. E. Nisbett, S. Valins, & B. Weiner (Eds.), *Attribution: Perceiving the causes of behavior.* Morristown, N.J.: General Learning Press, 1972.

Kiesler, C. A. *The psychology of commitment: Experiments linking behavior to belief.* New York: Academic Press, 1971.

Kim, J. S., & Campagna, A. F. Effects of flexitime on employee attendance and performance: A field experiment. *Academy of Management Journal,* 1981, *24*, 729-741.

LaTour, S. Determinants of participant and observer satisfaction with adversary and inquisitorial modes and adjudication. *Journal of Personality and Social Psychology,* 1978, *36*, 1531-1545.

Lawler, E. E., III. *Pay and organizational effectiveness.* New York: McGraw-Hill, 1971.

Lawler, E. E., III. *Pay and organization development.* Reading, Mass.: Addison-Wesley, 1981.

Lawrence, L. C., & Smith, P. C. Group decision and employee participation. *Journal of Applied Psychology,* 1955, *39*, 334-337.

Lepper, M. R., & Greene, D. *The hidden costs of reward.* Hillsdale, N. J.: Lawrence Erlbaum, 1978.

Lesieur, F. G., & Puckett, E. S. The Scanlon plan has proved itself. *Harvard Business Review,* 1969, *47*(5), 109-118.

Leventhal, G. S. Fairness in social relationships. In J. W. Thibaut, J. T. Spence, & R. C. Carson (Eds.), *Contemporary topics in social psychology.* Morristown, N.J.: General Learning Press, 1976.

Lewin, K. Group decision and social change. In T. M. Newcomb & E. L. Hartley. *Readings in social psychology.* New York: Holt, 1947.

Lewin, K., Lippitt, R., & White, R. Patterns of aggressive behavior in experimentally created "social climates." *Journal of Psychology,* 1939, *10*, 271-299.

Lind, E. A., Kurtz, S., Musante, L., Walker, L., & Thibaut, J. W. Procedure and outcome effects on reactions to adjudicated resolution of conflicts of interest. *Journal of Personality and Social Psychology,* 1980, *39*, 643-653.

Lind, E. A., Thibaut, J., & Walker, L. Discovery and presentation of evidence in adversary and nonadversary proceedings. *Michigan Law Review,* 1973, *71,* 1129-1144.

Locke, E. A., & Schweiger, D. M. Participation in decision-making: One more look. In B. M. Staw (Ed.), *Research in organizational behavior* (Vol. 1). Greenwich, Conn.: JAI Press, 1979.

Mills, J., & Jellison, J. M. Effect on opinion change of how desirable the communication is to the audience the communicator addressed. *Journal of Personality and Social Psychology,* 1967, *6,* 98-101.

Mitchell, T. R. Motivation and participation: An integration. *Academy of Management Journal,* 1973, *16,* 670-679.

Nash, A. N., & Carroll, S. J., Jr. *The management of compensation.* Monterey, Calif.: Brooks/Cole, 1975.

Orpen, C. Effect of flexible working hours on employee satisfaction and performance: A field experiment. *Journal of Applied Psychology,* 1981, *66,* 113-115.

Perlmuter, L. C., & Monty, R. A. *Choice and perceived control.* Hillsdale, N.J.: Lawrence Erlbaum, 1979.

Ritchie, J. B., & Miles, R. E. An analysis of quantity and quality of participation as mediating variables in the participative decision making process. *Personnel Psychology,* 1970, *23,* 347-359.

Rosenfield, D., Folger, R., & Adelman, H. F. When rewards reflect competence: A qualification of the overjustification effect. *Journal of Personality and Social Psychology,* 1980, *39,* 368-376.

Ross, L., Bierbrauer, G., & Hoffman, S. The role of attribution processes in conformity and dissent: Revisiting the Asch situation. *American Psychologist,* 1976, *31,* 148-157.

Schein, V. E., Maurer, E. H., & Novak, J. F. Impact of flexible working hours on productivity. *Journal of Applied Psychology,* 1977, *62,* 463-465.

Shaw, M. E. A comparison of two types of leadership in various communicants. *Journal of Abnormal and Social Psychology,* 1955, *50,* 127-134.

Spencer, D. G. *Employee voice and employee retention.* Paper presented at the meeting of the Academy of Management, New York, August 1982.

Steiner, I. D. Perceived freedom. In L. Berkowitz (Ed.), *Advances in experimental social psychology* (Vol. 5). New York: Academic Press, 1970.

Strauss, G. Managerial practices. In J. R. Hackman & J. L. Suttle (Eds.), *Improving life at work.* Santa Monica, Calif.: Goodyear, 1977.

Tannenbaum, A. S., & Cooke, R. A. Organizational control: A review of research employing the control graph method. In C. J. Lammers & D. Hickson (Eds.), *Organizations: Alike and unlike.* London: Routeledge and Kegan Paul, 1979.

Tannenbaum, R., & Schmidt, W. H. How to choose a leadership pattern. *Harvard Business Review,* 1958, *36,* 95-101.

Thibaut, J. An experimental study of the cohesiveness of underprivileged groups. *Human Relations,* 1950, *3,* 251-278.

Thibaut, J., Friedland, N., & Walker, L. Compliance with rules: Some social determinants. *Journal of Personality and Social Psychology*, 1974, *30*, 782-801.

Thibaut, J., & Walker, L. *Procedural justice: A psychological analysis.* Hillsdale, N.J.: Lawrence Erlbaum, 1975.

Thibaut, J., & Walker, L. A theory of procedure. *California Law Review*, 1978, *66*, 541-566.

Tyler, T. R., & Caine, A. The role of distributional and procedural fairness in the endorsement of formal leaders. *Journal of Personality and Social Psychology*, 1981, *41*, 642-655.

Vroom, V. H., & Yetton, P. W. *Leadership and decision making.* Pittsburgh: University of Pittsburgh Press, 1973.

Walker, L., LaTour, S., Lind, E. A., & Thibaut, J. Reactions of participants and observers to modes of adjudication. *Journal of Applied Social Psychology*, 1974, *4*, 295-310.

Walster, E., Berscheid, E., & Walster, G. W. New directions in equity research. *Journal of Personality and Social Psychology*, 1973, *25*, 151-176.

White, R. W. Motivation reconsidered: The concept of competence. *Psychological Review*, 1959, *66*, 297-333.

Yukl, G. A. *Leadership in organizations.* Englewood Cliffs, N.J.: Prentice-Hall, 1981.

Part 4
Interaction in Groups

Chapter 11
Loneliness, Sex-Role Orientation and Group Life: A Social Needs Perspective

Phillip Shaver and Duane Buhrmester

Most group dynamics researchers, understandably enough, have been more concerned with group-level processes than with the needs and feelings of individual group members. Thus, while many important structural and dynamic group phenomena have been identified—social facilitation, rejection of deviants, coalition formation, creation of leadership and status hierarchies—relatively little is known about the needs that cause individuals to join groups in the first place and that give groups so much power over their members. Presumably, individuals join groups and yield to group demands because group life offers certain rewards which cannot be obtained easily or at all in nongroup settings. We know intuitively that being rejected by attractive groups or consigned to low-status positions within them is psychologically painful, but most group researchers have taken this for granted rather than attempting to explain it. In the present chapter we consider how loneliness, an emotional state that arises when certain social needs go unmet, may be related to group life.

Just as important as group researchers' neglect of loneliness has been loneliness researchers' failure to say how membership in groups may reduce or augment loneliness. The most complete and up-to-date anthology of research on loneliness (Peplau & Perlman, 1982) hardly mentions groups (the word "group" does not even appear in the index). Because of the dearth of research directly linking loneliness with group life, we will have to indulge in some speculative leaps if we want to integrate the two research areas conceptually. Fortunately, many indirectly relevant theoretical and empirical stepping stones are available, so we need not leap too far at any single juncture.

Our exposition will be divided into four sections: (a) a review of current conceptions of loneliness, focusing on the idea that loneliness results when an individual fails to satisfy important social needs; (b) an exploration of the social needs and "provisions" (Weiss, 1974) associated with group life; (c) an examination of social orientations and skills related to individuals' attainment of social provisions from groups, with special attention being paid to so-called "masculine" and "feminine" relational styles; and (d) a reconsideration of several well-known group phenomena

—cohesiveness, conformity, leadership styles, and group-entry behavior—from a social needs perspective. If we fulfill our mission, the desirability of referring to individuals' social needs in explanations of group processes will be evident, and several important questions for future research will be raised.

Current Conceptions of Loneliness

Loneliness is an emotional state, like anger or fear. Unlike many other emotions, however, loneliness is not easy to detect with behavioral measures. At present, it can best be operationalized simply by asking people whether or not they feel lonely (Rubenstein & Shaver, 1980, 1982a), or by asking whether they lack companionship, feel left out, feel out of tune with the people around them, and so on (that is, without explicitly using the word "loneliness"; see Russell, 1982; Russell, Peplau, & Ferguson, 1978). Fortunately, the most popular measures of loneliness correlate highly with each other and meet standard reliability and validity criteria (Russell, 1982).

Representative national surveys indicate that around one-quarter of American adults feel lonely at any given time (Bradburn, 1969; for adolescents the proportion is even higher: Brennan, 1982; Rubenstein & Shaver, 1982b), and interviews suggest that almost everyone experiences loneliness occasionally (Peplau & Perlman, 1982; Rubenstein & Shaver, 1982b). The reasons people give for feeling lonely include: having no spouse or lover, feeling "different," being misunderstood, having no close friends, coming home to an empty house, being socially or geographically isolated, moving, and changing jobs or schools (Buhrmester, Shaver, Furman, & Willems, Note 1; Cutrona, 1982; Rubenstein & Shaver, 1980, 1982a). These can all be characterized as *situational causes* of loneliness, several of which are clearly related to group life. We also know that certain *personality characteristics* predispose some people to loneliness: shyness, poor social skills, self-defeating attribution patterns, self-destructive coping styles, and a history of significant social losses (Jones, 1982; Shaver & Rubenstein, 1980). No doubt, many episodes of loneliness are due to an interaction of situational and dispositional factors (for example, see Shaver et al., Note 2).

To date, there is no universally accepted or even dominant conceptualization of the causes of loneliness. Perlman and Peplau (1981) "view loneliness as a discrepancy between one's desired and achieved levels of social relations" (p. 32). The precise nature of "desire" is left unaddressed. According to Weiss (1973), "Loneliness appears always to be a response to the absence of some particular type of relationship or, more accurately, a response to the absence of some particular relational *provision*" (p. 17, italics added). As discussed in the following, Weiss has gone further than other loneliness theorists in his efforts to tie the notion of social provisions to a conception of social needs. For present purposes, it is worth noting that both the Perlman-Peplau discrepancy notion and Weiss's hypothesis about relational provisions point to the existence of social desires or needs; in other words, the concept of loneliness seems naturally to call for a larger social-motivational theory or conceptual framework. Therefore, if we are to connect loneliness with group life, it will prove useful to explore the motives and incentives for joining and participating in social relationships and groups.

Loneliness as Emotional and Social Isolation

Weiss (1973) has been able to distinguish two forms of loneliness, which he calls "emotional isolation" and "social isolation." In a study of Parents Without Partners, an organization for single, divorced, and widowed parents, Weiss found that despite the organization's success in providing friendship, support, and advice, members still tended to feel the absence of a stable attachment relationship; they still longed for a missing form of intimacy. A subsequent study of recently relocated married couples yielded a very different pattern of results. Couple members were not likely to be emotionally isolated, since they had an intimate relationship with a spouse; instead they suffered from social isolation. They longed for involvement with friends and community. This was especially true for nonworking wives, many of whom intensely missed their old social network. In contrast, most of the husbands immediately became involved with a work group of some kind, and this protected them to some extent from social isolation (Weiss, 1973).

Factor analytic studies (Rubenstein & Shaver, 1980, 1982a) have produced further evidence for Weiss's distinction. When people are asked how loneliness *feels*, two distinct factors emerge which seem to correspond to emotional and social isolation. The first includes the following adjectives: desperate, panicked, helpless, afraid, without hope, abandoned, and vulnerable. The second includes: impatient, bored, desiring to be elsewhere, uneasy, angry, and unable to concentrate.[1] Moreover, people's self-reported *reasons* for loneliness produce two corresponding factors: (a) having no spouse or sexual partner, breaking up with a spouse or lover (emotional isolation); and (b) feeling different, being misunderstood, not being needed, having no close friends (social isolation).

Weiss (1974) has elaborated his hypothesis that people seek specific "relational provisions" from each of the several kinds of relationships they maintain by proposing a list of six basic provisions and speculating about the emotional consequences of deprivation or fulfillment of each. For example, being deprived of intimacy or emotional attachment causes a person to feel emotionally isolated. Being deprived of participation in a group or community involving companionship, shared interests, organized activities, and meaningful roles causes a person to feel alienated, bored, uneasy, aimless—in a phrase, socially isolated. Because Weiss (1973) has studied intimacy in connection with marriage or marriage-like relationships, he tends to associate social but not emotional isolation with group life. However, *if we entertain the*

---

[1] Actually, there are four "feelings" factors. Besides the two described in the text, there are "Self-Deprecation" and "Depression." Rubenstein and Shaver (1982a) view the first two, emotional and social isolation, as primary and the latter two as *consequences* of them. If emotional or social isolation persists too long and seems uncontrollable, the lonely person tends to become overly self-critical and depressed.

possibility that groups can provide or promote psychological intimacy in addition to offering social engagement or involvement, it becomes possible to ask how participation in groups might alleviate both emotional and social isolation. This is the step we wish to take next.

Social Provisions of Group Life

If loneliness comes in two forms, emotional isolation and social isolation, and each is due to an absence or deficiency of certain social provisions, then it seems likely that there are two basic categories or kinds of provisions. We know from previous work (Weiss, 1973) that one can be labelled "intimacy" and the other, "social integration" (which for reasons to be discussed later we prefer to call "integrated involvement"). In this section we want to explore the possibility that participation in groups can supply a person with provisions from *both* categories and thereby prevent or substantially alleviate loneliness. Rather than begin with an abstract analytic discussion of the provisions themselves, we would like to consider first how groups might differ in their capacity for satisfying intimacy and integration needs. Casual observation suggests that some kinds of groups are better than others at providing intimacy and emotional support, just as some are more likely than others to meet members' needs for social activity and meaningful, identity-enhancing projects. This suggests that we ought to be able to characterize naturally occurring groups in terms of the provisions they offer to typical members. Once this characterization is attempted, it will be easier to say in detail what the provisions themselves are like.

Figure 11-1 displays a two-dimensional conceptual scheme which can be used to characterize groups. As a first approximation to reality, the two dimensions are portrayed as orthogonal because Weiss's writings and existing loneliness research suggest that it is possible to be both socially and emotionally isolated at the same time, or to be in one state without being in the other. (This assumed orthogonality will be discussed in more detail later.) The vertical dimension, representing the cluster of provisions that prevent emotional isolation, is labelled "Psychological Intimacy"; the horizontal dimension, representing the cluster of provisions that alleviate social isolation, is labelled "Integrated Involvement." Each point identified in the space corresponds to a familiar kind of group. At present, the locations of the points are only approximate and based more on intuition than research; but in principle the properties of groups could be assessed empirically in terms of our two-dimensional framework and each group located precisely.

At the lower left of the figure, where both psychological intimacy and integrated involvement are low, we have "an audience of unrelated individuals." Presumably, this kind of collectivity meets very few of a person's needs for intimacy and social integration. A person in the middle of a crowd, as the phrase "lonely in a crowd" suggests, can be both emotionally and socially isolated despite social stimulation. In the upper right-hand corner, where both psychological intimacy and integrated involvement are high, we have the "ideal commune," a utopian community which meets its members' needs for both intimacy and involvement. In the United States,

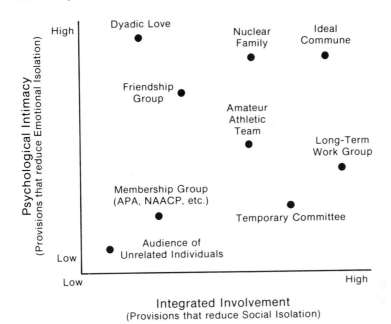

Fig. 11-1.

the prototypes most often used to depict ideal community are the close extended family and the friendly small town (Rubenstein & Shaver, 1982b), two naturally occurring group forms which have probably become somewhat romanticized as they have become less common. There have also been some deliberate attempts to build special kinds of communities. Interestingly, studies of 19th- and 20th-century communes (e.g., Kanter, 1972) indicate that for some reason the attainment of tightly knit community among nonfamily members almost always occurs at the expense of dyadic intimacy, a price few people have been willing to pay.

> Since [dyadic] relationships can interfere with group cohesion, couples [were] often seen as threats to communal groups. Sexual attachments, it was thought, would drain members of their emotional energy and divide their loyalty; even strong nuclear families were seen as harmful to the group as a whole. Many successful communities solved this problem by calling for either free love and group marriage or celibacy. Thus, all group members had similar sexual ties: all or nothing . . . . half of the successful groups separated parents from children at an early age . . . . The sense of community, a great antidote for loneliness, is central to utopian philosophy. Members of successful communes were called upon to renounce their own attachments and replace them with "collective unity." (Rubenstein & Shaver, 1982b, p. 147)

Perhaps a better example of ideal community is the extended farm family, portrayed in television fantasies like "The Waltons." What we are calling integrated involvement—participation in an organized, goal-directed group which assigns activities, roles, and identities to individuals—was supposedly guaranteed in such families, since members had to work together effectively in order to survive. Unlike other business enterprises, however, the farm family—at least as depicted in "The Waltons" —was concerned not just with members' economic productivity but also with their emotional needs. Dinner table conversation focused on family members' feelings, problems, and personal concerns, and smaller group (often dyadic) conversations centered even more on self-disclosure and emotional support. Whether or not "The Waltons" accurately represents small-town and family farm life, it reflects very well Americans' wish that a single group could provide intimacy as well as inte-grated involvement. (Later in this chapter we will take up the questions of why it is sometimes difficult to obtain both intimacy and integrated involvement from the same group and why intimacy is often attained in dyadic relationships rather than in groups.)

The contemporary nuclear family, at least in its middle- and upper-middle-class forms, provides less in the way of role involvement and work assignments and rela-tively more in the way of intimacy than more traditional, hierarchical families did (Veroff, Douvan, & Kulka, 1981), which is why we have placed the "nuclear family" a little higher and to the left of the "ideal commune" in Figure 11-1.

At the upper left of the figure we have placed "dyadic [romantic] love." This is not a group form at all, except in a very special sense, but it represents the extreme of intimacy, with equal role status, no business-like tasks (at least until love becomes institutionalized in marriage), and a maximum of mutual self-disclosure and affec-tion. It usually involves sex as well—which, in addition to providing its own rewards, meets needs for psychological intimacy, touch, and affection in a powerful way. This kind of love is, theoretically at least, what kept the mobile couples in Weiss's (1973) study from feeling emotionally isolated.

In the lower right-hand corner of Figure 11-1, various kinds of teams and work groups appear. These can be highly involving, giving individuals meaningful goals (even if only for a few hours), and typically include hierarchies and specific role assignments (outfielder, legal advisor, etc.). There is usually little focus on intimacy, although as group or team members come to know each other personally (if they do) some intimacy may develop, which is why we have placed "long-term work group" and "amateur athletic team" above "temporary committee."

Other groups fall at different points in the space, depending on our estimate of the psychological intimacy and integrated involvement they provide to typical group members. Most members of the American Psychological Association, for example, gain very little in the way of involvement from membership, and experi-ence even less intimacy (although APA conventions may provide opportunities for both). Friendship groups no doubt vary in intimacy and involvement as well. To the best of our knowledge, little attempt has been made to measure the provisions ob-tained by individuals from the groups they belong to, or the provisions they lack because of failing to participate in appropriate groups. In principle, however, there is no reason why these variables cannot be assessed systematically. Doing so would establish some important empirical links between loneliness and group life.

Elaborating the Two Dimensions: Psychological
Intimacy and Integrated Involvement

With these examples in mind, it is possible to state more clearly what we mean by psychological intimacy and integrated involvement, and to relate these constructs to earlier writings (see Table 11-1). Psychological intimacy, as Weiss (1973, 1982) has noted, is akin in certain respects to "attachment" as discussed by Harlow (see Harlow & Mears, 1979) and Bowlby (1969). Attachment between infants and their adult caretakers (usually mothers) involves feelings of trust, familiarity, safety, and warmth. The infant is presumably without defenses, and the mother is more open and giving than in most other relationships. Intimacy between adults involves many of the same features (Rubenstein & Shaver, 1982b, Chapter 2; Weiss, 1982). Another component of intimacy is what Carl Rogers (1959) called "unconditional positive regard," a willingness to accept and support another person emotionally regardless of that person's current behavior or contribution to the relationship. A third component is mutual self-disclosure (Archer & Earle, Chapter 12, this volume; Derlega & Chaikin, 1975; Jourard, 1971), a more adult form of openness and dropping of defenses. Self-disclosure goes along with an atmosphere of security, acceptance, and emotional support, because most people are unwilling to express their deepest thoughts and feelings without an assurance of sympathy and continued involvement. This is especially true for emotional catharsis (Scheff, 1979), the process by which a person discharges pent-up feelings. Most people cannot express such feelings except within the context of an intimate, secure relationship. Another aspect of intimacy involves care, nurturance, and giving of oneself without keeping accounts. The rules of fairness in an intimate relationship center around individuals' needs and the desirability of equality rather than around equity (Deutsch, 1975; Mills & Clark, 1982).

When a person suffers from insufficient intimacy, he or she not only feels lonely, but also fails to express or discharge pent-up feelings (a risk to health, according to Scheff); experiences low self-esteem (reporting, for example, that "no one really cares about me," according to Rubenstein and Shaver); is vulnerable to clinical depression (Weeks, Michela, Peplau, & Bragg, 1980); feels anxious and insecure; and

Table 11-1. Two Categories of Social Provisions

Psychological Intimacy	Integrated Involvement
Affection and warmth	Enjoyable and involving activities and projects (alleviation of boredom)
Unconditional positive regard	
Opportunity for self-disclosure and emotional expression	Social identity and self definition
	Being needed for one's skills
Lack of defensiveness, lack of concern for social presentation	Social comparison information
	Opportunity for power and influence
Giving and receiving nurturance	Conditional positive regard (approval for contributions to group goals)
Security and emotional support	
	Support for one's beliefs and values

reports a wide range of mental and physical symptoms (Lynch, 1977; Rubenstein & Shaver, 1982b). Therefore, absence of intimacy is not a trivial matter.

Intimacy, as cozy as it may sound, does not necessarily mean the absence of conflict. In a study we conducted recently in collaboration with Wyndol Furman, affection and conflict were measured separately in college students' descriptions of their family relationships. The two dimensions proved to be essentially uncorrelated. In new relationships with first-year college friends and dates, however, the two dimensions proved to be highly (negatively) correlated; and a pattern of low affection or high conflict marked a budding relationship as likely to fail. Evidently, part of family or friendship-group intimacy is a feeling of security strong enough to allow for conflict.

While intimacy seems most common in dyadic relationships—mother and infant, two people in love, a Rogerian therapist and his or her client—it can also arise in certain kinds of groups. We have already mentioned the family, which in our society is the model of a group that accepts its members unconditionally and permanently, and attempts to meet each member's needs regardless of his or her current contributions. (When a child is seriously ill, it's a rare parent who asks, "What have you done for me lately?") Groups of close friends—especially female friends, as we will explain later—also provide group members with many aspects of intimacy. Members of such groups may discuss hurt feelings, doubts, and secrets without fear of rejection, and support each other without immediate regard for equity. Encounter groups and therapy groups are deliberately designed to produce a similar atmosphere (Lakin, 1972). The goal is equalitarian interaction aimed at the expression of private feelings, mutual support, self-insight, and (at least in the case of therapy groups) self-improvement. While critics have questioned the value of the "instant intimacy" provided by encounter groups (see, e.g., Archer & Earle, Chapter 12, this volume) and have described socially oriented therapy as "the purchase of friendship," these creations of modern society can be sympathetically viewed as attempts to overcome the loneliness of emotional isolation.

Integrated involvement, our second category of social provisions, is less characteristic of dyadic interactions and more obviously connected with group life. We use the adjective "integrated" to suggest the importance of group *structure*. Many task-oriented groups assign members to interlocking roles, so that work or organized play can benefit from a division of labor. Moreover, many groups array roles hierarchically, so that some people—the leaders—are more central and influential. These features of group structure are associated with certain social provisions—public recognition of one's contributions, promotions, power—which are less common in groups whose main purpose is to provide intimacy. The term "involvement" is meant to suggest two additional features of task-oriented groups. One is goal-directed *activity*. Socially isolated individuals commonly say, "I'm bored" or "I have no one to *do* things with" (Rubenstein & Shaver, 1982a, 1982b). Task-oriented groups provide goals and incentives for individual members and automatically confer meaning on their activities, at least for a while. Hitting a volleyball back and forth across a net may seem meaningless in itself, but in the context of two organized teams seeking to win, each player can be totally engaged—no less than if the goal were to erect a building or manufacture goods of some kind. Another aspect of involvement is a set of feelings including acknowledged importance to the group, *being needed*—not "needed" as a nurturer or unique personality, but as a competent, talented occupant of certain group roles.

The right-hand column of Table 11-1 displays some of the specific provisions offered by groups that supply integrated involvement. Just as psychologically intimate groups provide what Rogers calls unconditional positive regard, integrated-involving groups are a source of *conditional* positive regard. Approval is given not because a group member needs it or because all members deserve it equally, but because a member has contributed something of special value to the group. While psychologically intimate groups tend to distribute rewards according to a norm of need or equality (Deutsch, 1975; Mills & Clark, 1982), integrated-involving groups tend to follow the norm of equity: Each member gets rewarded according to his or her contributions.

Most of the existing laboratory research on group processes (as summarized, for example, by Cartwright & Zander, 1968) focuses on groups that are integrated and involving in our terms: teams, work groups, problem-solving groups, and so on. Not surprisingly, most well-known group phenomena—social facilitation (Zajonc, 1965, 1980), social comparison processes (Festinger, 1954; Suls & Miller, 1977), conformity (Asch, 1951, 1956), normative and informational influences of reference groups (Kelley, 1952)—are typical of integrated-involving groups, not necessarily of groups whose main provisions are intimate in nature.

There is an implicit tone of threat or anxiety in many write-ups of group studies. Groups are portrayed as promoters of evaluation apprehension (Cottrell, 1968, 1972), rejection of deviants (Levine, 1980; Schachter, 1951), and rigid conformity (Asch, 1956; Cartwright & Zander, 1968, Chapter 11). Group leaders are depicted as strict allocators of rewards and punishments. At the extreme, this picture of groups seems compatible with philosopher Jean-Paul Sartre's (1963) startling claim that "scarcity" and "terror" are the forces holding most groups together (see also Cumming, 1965).

In our view, this negative portrayal of groups is misleading. Certain rewards of integrated involvement—pride of accomplishment, admiration and respect from others, participation in meaningful activities (where meaning is conferred by group consensus), support for shared beliefs and values, exercise of authority and influence, public recognition of group members' identities—cannot be obtained in the same form in intimacy-oriented, equalitarian groups. Conditional and unconditional positive regard are quite different, yet both are highly desirable. The norms of equality and equity are incompatible in most situations; and while many people prefer equality in general, few would choose never to be rewarded in proportion to their actual contributions. The "terror" of group life, then, to the extent that it exists at all, is the price paid for the performance-related rewards offered by integrated-involving groups. The field of group research could use new ways to measure and conceptualize the rewards provided by particular groups to each of their members. Within an appropriate conceptual framework, the rewards of group life would stand out as clearly as the threat of losing them does now.

Both our two-dimensional group classification scheme (Figure 11-1) and the question of whether task-oriented groups are inhumane (i.e., nonintimate) are reminiscent of earlier writings. The grandfather of all such distinctions among group types is Toennies (1887/1961), whose work *Gemeinschaft und Gesellschaft* contrasted traditional, communal society with the then emerging modern industrial society. The two forms of society were presented as opposites or alternatives, and Toennies, like many other late-19th-century social thinkers, was clearly worried that human beings were about to suffer terribly from the demise of Gemeinschaft. More recently, Parsons and Bales (Parsons & Bales, 1955; Parsons, Bales, & Shils, 1953), influenced to some extent by Toennies, distinguished between two major forms of social behavior, "instrumental" and "expressive." As summarized by Glennon (1979):

> For Parsons, instrumental behavior includes an emphasis on task fulfill-ment, productivity, and efficiency. A person who is acting instrumentally in a social relationship would typically inhibit emotions, act from self-interested motives, rely on standardized or "objective" codes for judgment, evaluate others in terms of performance or achievement, and display involv-ment with the other that is limited to specific aims. Any instrumental rela-tionship is construed as a means to an end. Expressive behavior, on the other hand, emphasizes such integrative goals as emotional fulfillment, group cohesiveness, and stability. A person who is acting expressively would typically show emotion, be oriented toward collective interest, rely on personal relational criteria for the evaluation of others, judge others in terms of their personal qualities, and show a wide interest in the other. Here the relationship is an end in itself, to be enjoyed for its own sake and not because of a specific interest. (pp. 27-28)

It is clear that Parsons, like Toennies, thought of instrumental and expressive behaviors as antithetical and mutually exclusive: "the variables we have stated are dichotomies and not continua . . . each concept sets up a polarity, a true dilemma" (Parsons & Shils, 1964, p. 91). For this reason, a group, in order to function smoothly, was thought to require *two* leaders, one (the "task leader") to focus attention on goal attainment and the other (the "socioemotional leader") to relieve tension and promote solidarity (see Bales & Slater, 1955).

Parsons and Bales derived many of their ideas not just from Toennies's analysis of societal types but also from informal familiarity with sex roles in the American family, where the male was supposed to be primarily instrumental in orientation and the female primarily expressive. (Their 1955 book was titled *Family, Sociali-zation, and Interaction Process*.) In fact, so-called "instrumental" and "expressive" behaviors, as portrayed in Glennon's distillation of Parsons' writings, immediately make more sense if one thinks of them in terms of masculinity and femininity. Not surprisingly, even Toennies (1887/1963) had noticed a connection between femi-ninity and Gemeinschaft:

> All activity which expresses itself in a direct manner, either originally or from habit or memory, as a consequence and expression of life itself, be-longs to the realm of women. Thus, all expressions and outbursts of emo-tions and sentiments, conscience, and inspired thoughts are the specific truthfulness, naivete, directness, and passionateness of the woman, who is in every respect the more natural being (pp. 151-153).

One need not agree with this somewhat quaint and sexist outburst in order to see that the distinction between Gemeinschaft and Gesellschaft, like the later distinction between expressiveness and instrumentality, was heavily influenced by social theorists' conceptions of the psychological differences between males and females.

Thinking about this persistent influence on social theory has led us to wonder how our two social provision dimensions are related to sex-role orientations. Anyone familiar with the recent literature on sex roles cannot help noticing that our portrayal of psychological intimacy and integrated involvement as orthogonal dimensions is similar to the current view that masculinity and femininity are independent rather than mutually exclusive constructs. In the following section we will examine the possibility that so-called "masculine" and "feminine" social styles are each especially well suited to the attainment of one of our two types of social provisions. A brief review of recent studies on sex differences in social behavior will help to illuminate the two provision dimensions and the ways in which they are related to group members' conduct. It is important to keep in mind, however, that in the present chapter we are more interested in the social styles per se than in the fact that they happen to be traditionally associated with gender.

Parallels Between the Provision Dimensions and Masculine and Feminine Social Styles

Not long ago—before 1970 or 1975, say—it would have been difficult to relate our group classification scheme to masculinity and femininity, because masculinity and femininity were conceptualized as opposite ends of a single continuum, not as two orthogonal dimensions. For centuries it was easy to believe that masculinity and femininity were antithetical, since "male versus female" is clearly a biological *dichotomy*, and to be like a male or like a female (that is, to be masculine or feminine) was to be like one or the other mutually exclusive alternative. In recent years, however, psychological masculinity and femininity have been reconceptualized as independent dimensions (see, for example, Bem, 1974; Spence & Helmreich, 1978). The two trait clusters shown in Table 11-2, taken from Spence and Helmreich's Personal Attributes Questionnaire (PAQ), correspond fairly well with our intuitive

Table 11-2. Characteristics of Psychological Masculinity and Femininity[a]

Femininity	Masculinity
Able to devote self to others	Independent
Emotional	Active
Gentle	Competitive
Helpful to others	Can make decisions easily
Kind	Never gives up easily
Aware of others' feelings	Self-confident
Understanding	Feels superior
Warm	Stands up well under pressure

[a]Based on Spence and Helmreich's Personal Attributes Questionnaire.

conceptions of masculinity and femininity (and, incidentally, probably would not have surprised someone of Toennies's generation); but instead of being opposites, they are empirically uncorrelated. In other words, it is possible for an individual to be *both* masculine and feminine (i.e., psychologically androgynous) in terms of the PAQ. (An important qualification to this statement will be considered later.)

There is an obvious parallel between femininity, as defined by Spence and Helmreich, and our intimacy dimension (compare the left-hand columns of Tables 11-1 and 11-2). The feminine behaviors are precisely the ones that would facilitate psychological intimacy in dyads and groups. Moreover, masculinity as operationalized by the PAQ suits a person well for membership in task-oriented groups, groups that provide what we have been calling integrated involvement (compare the right-hand columns of the two tables).

In terms of the orthogonal-dimensions approach to masculinity and femininity, gender differences in achievement behavior and social style are due to mean gender differences in masculinity and femininity (males being more "masculine" on the average, females more "feminine"). When masculinity and femininity are controlled for, gender differences in social psychological variables usually disappear (e.g., Olds & Shaver, 1980; Spence & Helmreich, 1978). Therefore, in the following brief review of studies relevant to the present chapter we will include some that focus on gender differences as well as some that measure masculinity and femininity directly.

There is increasing evidence that males and females exhibit different social styles and establish different kinds of relationships and groups, even in childhood. Lever (1976), for example, observed elementary school children and found that boys played outdoors more often than girls; boys also played more often in large age-heterogeneous groups, and played games that were competitive and lasted longer than girls' games. Lever attributed the time difference to two factors: the boys' games typically required more skill and were therefore less likely to become boring, and the boys were better able to resolve inevitable disputes.

> During the course of this study, boys were seen quarreling all the time, but not once was a game terminated because of a quarrel and no game was interrupted for more than seven minutes. (Lever, 1976, p. 482)

In contrast, disputes among girls tended to end the game, as if harmony were more valuable than any activity that threatened to disrupt it. Commenting on this and related studies, Gilligan (1982) says:

> From the games they play, boys learn both the independence and the organizational skills necessary for coordinating the activities of large and diverse groups of people. By participating in controlled and socially approved competitive situations, they learn to deal with competition in a relatively forthright manner—to play with their enemies and compete with their friends—all in accordance with the rules of the game. In contrast, girls' play tends to occur in smaller, more intimate groups, often the best-friend dyad, and in private places. (pp. 9-11)

In a recent study by Furman and Willems (Note 3), fourth-grade children were brought into a playroom/laboratory where they encountered a same-sex, same-age stranger. There were strong sex differences in the way the children related to each other: Boys tended to plunge right into organized play without spending much time getting to know each other; girls tended to interweave play with a mutal exchange of self-revealing information. At the end of the play session, boys' feelings that they liked each other seemed to be based on the fun they'd had playing together, not on what they had learned about each other through mutual self-disclosure. This study, in combination with Lever's (1976), indicates that feminine and masculine social styles, each well-adapted for either intimacy or integrated involvement, are already well established in childhood.

Buhrmester and Furman (Note 4) asked college-student males and females about their participation in group life. No sex differences were reported in the total number of groups belonged to (formal plus informal), but there was a tendency for males to belong to more formally organized groups and a powerful difference in the frequency of becoming a leader of a formal group. Moreover, satisfaction with participation in organized groups was unrelated to loneliness or self-esteem among females, but was negatively related to loneliness and positively related to self-esteem for males. (For both sexes, satisfaction with informal friendship groups was negatively correlated with loneliness.) Finally, being a leader of a formally organized group correlated with loneliness in opposite directions for males and females (-.11 vs. +.24, a significant difference), and the same pattern was evident for measures of emotional isolation (-.22 vs. +.35) and self-esteem (+.34 vs. -.10). In other words, for males being a leader of a formally organized group was associated with less loneliness, less emotional isolation, and higher self-esteem; for females, being a leader was actually a negative experience in terms of these social adjustment variables. Evidently, the differences in childhood behavior documented by Lever and Furman equip males and females for easy adjustment to different kinds of groups and group roles later in life.

In the same study, Buhrmester and Furman examined correlations between Spence and Helmreich's masculinity and femininity scales, on the one hand, and measures of loneliness, social isolation, intimacy, and self-esteem, on the other. With male and female subjects combined, masculinity correlated most highly with self-esteem and the absence of social isolation, while femininity correlated most highly with intimacy. Because of this pattern, androgynous subjects (those who scored above the median on both masculinity and femininity) were favorably situated on all four dimensions: They were low in loneliness and social isolation and high on intimacy and self-esteem. In a related study, Ickes and Barnes (1978) compared the quality of male-female interactions when dyads containing partners with various combinations of masculine and feminine qualities were observed. The most favorable interactions occurred between pairs of androgynous persons, the least favorable between masculine-feminine pairs.[2] In other words, the smoothest and most reward-

---

[2] It may seem odd that the traditional marriage combination—masculine male, feminine female—is a poor match psychologically. But this striking finding was confirmed in a large survey study of marital satisfaction (Shaver, Pullis, & Olds, Note 5). It suggests to us that traditional sex roles were "designed" by cultural evolution to meet economic rather than psychological needs (see also Harris, 1979).

ing interactions occurred when both partners were able to contribute "masculine" (instrumental) *and* "feminine" (expressive) behaviors to the relationship.

Wheeler, Reis, and Nezlek (1983) asked male and female college students to keep detailed records of all their social interactions for two weeks. Each interaction was described in terms of sex composition, number of people present, intimacy, self-disclosure, satisfaction, and several other dimensions. At the end of the two-week period, subjects filled out various questionnaires, including the UCLA loneliness scale and the PAQ. The best predictor of *not* being lonely, for both males and females, was a composite *intimacy* score. The next best predictor was time spent with females, which the authors took as evidence that females know how to foster intimacy. (Time spent with males was unrelated to loneliness.) Finally, PAQ femininity was negatively associated with loneliness for both males and females, suggesting that femininity (as measured by the PAQ) is a social orientation or set of social skills that encourage intimacy.

For college students, at least, loneliness seems to be more highly related to the intimacy of interactions than to their frequency or duration. Several investigators (e.g., Cutrona, 1982; Shaver et al., 1981; Solano, Note 6; Wheeler et al., 1983) have found that interaction *quality*—which usually has something to do with intimacy— is more important than *quantity* (number of friends, number of organizations belonged to, number of dates, and so on). This may mean either that intimacy is more important than what we have been calling integrated involvement, or that most college students can easily meet their needs for involvement but have a harder time attaining intimacy. (This would fit with Erikson's, 1982, notion that the major developmental "crisis" of early adulthood concerns "intimacy vs. isolation.") It may also be due to an imbalance in the UCLA loneliness scale and in existing measures of interaction quality, which seem to stress intimacy more than integrated involvement (Reis, Note 7).

We have mentioned that intimacy in groups is associated with adherence to norms of distributive justice based on need and equality, while integrated-involving groups tend to follow the norm of equity (payment proportional to task-oriented contributions). In a recent review of gender differences in reward allocation behavior, Major and Deaux (1982) concluded that females more often than males distribute rewards on the basis of need and equality rather than equity—especially when the allocators themselves are among the reward recipients. This is still another way in which a "feminine" social orientation seems conducive to intimacy in group settings.

To summarize, the burgeoning literature on gender differences in social behavior suggests that females are socialized for intimacy, while males are socialized in ways that suit them for participation in integrated-involving groups and organizations. This is not because males can comfortably do without intimacy, we believe, but rather because they learn to count on females to provide it for them (Rubenstein & Shaver, 1982b). Most male-male interactions (among college students at least) are not very intimate and, at least according to current measures, not very satisfying (Wheeler et al., 1983). On the other hand, males derive much of their self-esteem, feelings of belonging, and sense of meaning and engagement from participation in organized groups. Females seem less comfortable than males with competition, leadership, performance evaluations, task-related assignment of rewards, and so on

—the sources of satisfaction offered by integrated-involving groups. In our view, these average gender differences are due, not to inherent biological proclivities (although we cannot totally rule out that possibility), but to socialization of males and females for different roles in society—in particular, for different roles in family and work groups.

Traditionally, males have exchanged purchasing power and social status (provisions gained in integrated-involving work groups) for nurturance and sexual and psychological intimacy (provisions gained in a marital or family setting). Recent changes in American society have called this arrangement into question. Women have entered the workforce and professional schools in increasing numbers, forcing them (it would seem) to participate in groups that operate by "male" standards. At the same time, an increasing number of men have become more concerned with marital and family intimacy and have been frustrated by their inability to contribute fully to it (Veroff et al., 1981). The idea that masculinity and femininity are compatible (because they are orthogonal) has gained prominence, and the ideal of androgyny—of maximal behavioral flexibility—has been widely disseminated. If the parallels we have drawn between the dimensions of sex-role identity and the categories of social provisions are valid, today's androgynous men and women should find it easier than their parents did to attain both kinds of provisions directly, without having to barter one for the other; and it should be more feasible than ever before to create work groups that provide both intimacy and involvement.

Group Phenomena Viewed from a Social Needs Perspective

If the general approach we have been developing is correct—that is, if group members' behavior is motivated by a desire to obtain one or both of the two kinds of social provisions, psychological intimacy and integrated involvement—then these two dimensions (or something parallel to them) should show up repeatedly in studies of well-known group phenomena such as cohesiveness, conformity, and leadership. The purpose of the next few sections is to explore this possibility.

Two Kinds of Cohesiveness

Some groups are more closely knit than others, a fact which group researchers have attempted to capture in the concept of "cohesiveness." Cartwright (1968), in an influential review, accepted (as do we) Festinger's (1950) definition of cohesiveness: "the resultant of all forces acting on members to remain in the group." Since we have been talking throughout this chapter about the social provisions of groups and the negative emotional consequences of rejection and isolation, the chapter is, in the established language of group dynamics, an essay on cohesiveness.

Cohesiveness has been measured in a variety of ways: in terms of group members' attractiveness to each other, ratings of the group's overall attractiveness to members, closeness or identification with the group, expressed desire to remain in the group, or some combination of these. From our perspective, attractiveness is due to the receipt by members of certain social provisions. Therefore, another reasonable index of cohesiveness would be the extent to which a particular group meets members' needs for intimacy and/or integrated involvement. If this is a productive line of thinking, we would expect cohesiveness to appear in two major forms, one corresponding to intimacy and the other to integrated involvement.

In fact, different measures of cohesiveness have not all correlated highly with each other, which suggests that the construct is multidimensional. And when Hagstrom and Selvin (1965) factor-analyzed their 19-item cohesiveness scale, two factors emerged.

> Hagstrom and Selvin believe that the first factor measures the instrumental attractiveness of groups. . . . The second, they feel, measures intrinsic attractiveness—the degree to which members are attracted to close personal association with others in the group." (Cartwright, 1968, p. 95)

These two factors seem to correspond well with our integrated involvement and intimacy dimensions.

It seems reasonable to speculate, then, that cohesiveness is an indication, at the group level of analysis, that members are receiving important social provisions from participation and are thus unlikely to feel lonely. If a particular group is cohesive in both of Hagstrom and Selvin's senses ("instrumental" and "intrinsic"), members are especially unlikely to be lonely. If the group is cohesive in only one of the two senses, members will feel the absence of certain provisions unless they are obtaining them in sufficient quantity from other groups or dyadic relationships (which may in fact be the norm, in a society where most adults seem to want both a marriage and membership in work or leisure-time activity groups). These speculations are empirically testable.

Cohesiveness and Conformity

Cartwright (1968) has carefully analyzed the *determinants* and *consequences* of group cohesiveness. His list of determinants fits well with our social needs perspective:

> (a) [the member's] *motive base for attraction*, consisting of his needs for affiliation, recognition, security, . . .; (b) the *incentive properties of the group*, consisting of its goals, programs, characteristics of its members, style of operation, prestige, or the properties of significance for [the member's] motive base; (c) his *expectancy*, the subjective probability, that membership will actually have beneficial or detrimental consequences for him; and (d) his *comparison level*—his conception of the level of outcomes that group membership should provide. (p. 96)

In our terms, cohesiveness depends on the degree to which group members' social needs are satisfied. Members whose needs (for affiliation, recognition, security, prestige, etc.) are not met by the group can be expected to be relatively uninvolved and disloyal—in addition to feeling emotionally and socially isolated. They are likely to be on the lookout for more attractive, more fulfilling groups.

Research on the *consequences* of cohesiveness also fits comfortably within a social needs framework. Cohesive groups, by definition, retain members longer.

Research shows, more specifically, that cohesive groups reduce members' anxiety levels and increase their feelings of security and self-esteem (Cartwright, 1968). Because cohesiveness is associated with individual members' need-fulfillment, it fosters member conformity and rejection of deviants. If the group is rewarding, especially compared with imaginable alternatives (Thibaut & Kelley, 1959), members will be reluctant to risk censure or rejection.

Conformity as the Avoidance of Isolation

Festinger (1950) proposed that "pressure toward uniformity" in groups is based partly on the group's need to foster behavior leading to goal attainment. In terms of our two-dimensional classification of group provisions (Table 11-1), this particular pressure toward uniformity is related to integrated involvement. In theory, the group should exercise this kind of pressure by threatening to withhold one or more of the provisions of integrated involvement (e.g., role assignment, conditional positive regard, participation in enjoyable projects). Cartwright and Zander (1968, p. 142) talk about another kind of pressure toward uniformity, based on the need to maintain the group itself:

> "Pressures against behavior that may bring disgrace to the group or divide
> the group and threaten its existence or make members uncomfortable and
> ready to resign also seem to ensure that the group survives."

We would add to this list several pressures based more directly on threats to intimacy—for example, withdrawing emotional support, refusing to listen to a group member's desires and feelings, withholding affection. In short, there may be two general kinds of pressures toward uniformity which are rarely distinguished in the literature because their dynamics (involving threat) and results (conformity or rejection) are so similar.

These pressures may have different consequences for different individuals. It seems likely that a person whose needs of a certain type are being satisfied by other relationships could resist group pressures related to those needs better than a person who has no outside support and no known alternative sources of provisions. This hypothesis gains informal support from all the newspaper stories about beleaguered public officials whose spouses and family members stand faithfully behind them in times of crisis and challenge. It may also be related to the relatively unstudied strength of religious individuals who believe God loves them or wants them to act in certain ways, regardless of mundane social pressures.

We know quite a bit about the ways in which groups try to control deviant and recalcitrant members' behavior (Cartwright & Zander, 1968; Levine, 1980). At first, persuasive communications are actively directed toward the deviant; if these do not quickly result in comformity, the communications become increasingly hostile. Eventually, if the deviant still insists on being contrary (or creative and autonomous, depending on one's point of view), he or she is likely to be punished, isolated, ignored, or rejected (Levine, 1980; Schachter, 1951).

A group has potent punishment for a member who persists in deviating
despite pressure on him to shift: it may redefine its boundaries so as to

> exclude the deviant, thereby protecting uniformity among members. Rejec-
> tion of a deviant can be accomplished in various ways. He may be set apart
> so that no one talks or listens to him, he may be dropped from activities of
> the group, or he may be expelled. Obviously, the more attractive the group
> is to a member, the more he wishes to avoid such extreme sanction. Para-
> doxically, the greater the cohesiveness of a group, the more likely the mem-
> bers are to reject the persistently deviant member. (Cartwright & Zander,
> 1968, p. 145)

Most of the available studies of rejection of deviants from groups do not include
measures of the deviants' feelings. In fact, in most studies the focus of research
attention has been on the behavior of the majority, and the deviant has been a confederate of the experimenter. In one experiment, however, Pepitone and Wilipizeski
(1960) found that rejected deviants were both self-depreciating and angry. These are
two of the most commonly reported characteristics of lonely individuals, according
to recent studies (Jones, 1982). Moreover, loneliness research with children (Hymel,
Asher, Renshaw, & Geraci, Note 8) has established an empirical connection between
sociometric isolation (or noncentrality) in the classroom and self-reported loneliness.
Brennan (1982), in a review of research on adolescent loneliness, found a sizable
negative correlation between group membership and loneliness. Similar findings
have been obtained in studies of adults (e.g., Fischer & Phillips, 1982; Rubenstein &
Shaver, 1980). Finally, several researchers have correlated measures of loneliness
with more group-oriented measures of alienation, anomie, normlessness, and power-
lessness, and all have obtained strong relationships (Johnson, 1981; Jones, 1982). It
seems safe to conclude that rejection from groups or reluctance to attempt group
entry is a cause of loneliness. (See section on group entry, which follows.) It would
be interesting to know whether the different ways groups have of dealing with nonconformity—for example, withdrawal of affection versus exclusion from certain
group roles and activities—relate to the deviant's subjective feelings of social or
emotional isolation. It would also be interesting to know how deviants weigh the
rewards and costs of their positions. For some, presumably, the rewards of individ-
uality and of loyalty to private convictions (or to other individuals and groups) outweigh the temporary pain of isolation and loneliness.

Two Facets of Group Leadership

A huge body of research has been devoted to the topic of group leadership (Cartwright & Zander, 1968, Chapter 24; Chemers, Chapter 2, this volume; Stogdill,
1974). Of special interest to us are studies relating to the following questions:
What are the functions of group leadership? What styles of group leadership have
been identified? What are the consequences of different leadership styles? By now
it should come as no surprise that the two dimensions we have been highlighting
show up frequently in studies addressing each of these questions.

Cartwright and Zander (1968), in their discussion of the function of group leadership, decided that leadership has to do with *influence*, and in particular with influence that promotes one or more group objectives. According to Cartwright and
Zander, group objectives fall into two categories:

(a) the achievement of some specific group goal and (b) the maintenance or strengthening of the group itself. Examples of member behaviors that serve functions of *goal achievement* are "initiates action," "keeps members' attention on the goal," "clarifies the issue," "develops a procedural plan," "evaluates the quality of work done," and "makes expert information available." Examples of behaviors that serve the functions of *group maintenance* are "keeps interpersonal relations pleasant," "arbitrates disputes," "provides encouragement," "gives the minority a chance to be heard," "stimulates self-direction," and "increases the interdependence among members." (p. 306)

Similarly, when characteristics of group leaders are examined, two factors emerge which correspond to these group functions (Fleishmann, Harris, & Burtt, 1955; Halpin & Winer, 1952). The first cluster has been termed "initiating structure" and involves defining roles for task completion, establishing channels of communication, and creating organizational structure to get a job done. The second group of leader characteristics has been called "consideration" and includes friendship, mutual trust, respect, and warmth between group members and leader. Leaders high on the first dimension are often referred to as "task-oriented," "production-oriented," or "work-centered," while those high on "consideration" are said to be "human-relations oriented," "employee-oriented" or "group-centered" (Chemers, Chapter 2, this volume; Katz & Kahn, 1978; Stogdill, 1974). It should be obvious that these two dimensions of leadership closely parallel our dimensions of integrated involvement and psychological intimacy. Leaders who are good at initiating structure are likely to provide members with a meaningful sense of role involvement, for example, while leaders high in interpersonal consideration are likely to create an atmosphere conducive to emotional expression and intimacy.

A large number of studies have been designed to determine the effects of different leadership styles on group productivity and satisfaction (see Fiedler & Chemers, 1974, Katz & Kahn, 1978, and Stogdill for reviews). Generally, a task-oriented style is associated with greater productivity, while human-relations-oriented leaders seem to engender greater feelings of satisfaction in group members and hence promote group maintenance. In his review of early studies, Shartle (1956) concluded that the optimum group leader has both task-oriented and human-relations skills, thus promoting both cohesiveness and productivity. A subsequent study of Japanese coal mine supervisors (Misumi & Tasaki, 1965) reached the same conclusion. Groups with leaders who emphasized both task achievement and group cohesion fostered higher morale and higher production levels than groups in which either production or group maintenance was the sole focus of the leader's efforts.

As mentioned earlier, Parsons and Bales (for points discussed here, see also Bales & Slater, 1955, and Heinicke & Bales, 1953) conceived of the two functions of leadership as antithetical and thus as unlikely to coexist within a single person's behavior. In fact, they thought it likely that *two* leaders rather than one would usually be necessary to keep group members both happy and productive. This bipolar picture of leadership functions was based primarily on laboratory studies of initially leaderless small groups. Cartwright and Zander (1968) summarized arguments suggesting that leaders who emerge in such situations may be perceived as unduly aggressive or unequalitarian. In more natural and long-lasting groups, however, leadership may arouse less hostility. Certainly, the framework we have outlined here suggests that leaders who simultaneously facilitate both intimacy and integrated involvement will be especially well liked. And in fact, Stogdill (1974), in his review of leadership studies, found little correlation (i.e., no negative correlation) between leader behaviors that foster cohesiveness and satisfaction, on the one hand, and those that increase productivity on the other. In his terms,

> the results surveyed suggest that group cohesiveness and productivity respond to two different patterns of leader behavior. A leader needs to exhibit some degree of both forms of behavior in order to have a group that is productive and cohesive. (pp. 406-407)

Stogdill obviously implies that the two different behavior patterns do not require two separate leaders.

In terms of Spence and Helmreich's (1978) masculinity and femininity dimensions, the ideal leadership profile could be characterized as "androgynous"—that is, as including both masculine instrumentality and feminine sensitivity to others' feelings and needs. To date there has been little research on the leadership styles or effectiveness of people with different PAQ scores, so we can only speculate about the possibility that the optimal leader is androgynous.

Of course, it is likely that particular leadership styles are effective only in certain situations or for certain kinds of groups. According to Stogdill (1974, p. 406):

> person-oriented leadership tends to increase member satisfaction in small interaction-oriented groups. Work-oriented leadership is associated with member satisfaction in large, task-oriented groups.

Research inspired by Fiedler's (1978) "contingency model of leadership effectiveness" (reviewed extensively in this volume by Chemers, Chapter 2, and elsewhere by Strube & Garcia, 1981) indicates that task-oriented leaders are most effective under conditions of very high or very low task structure and control, whereas interpersonally oriented leaders are most effective under conditions of intermediate structure and control. In our opinion, controversies in the research literature concerning these and other recent theories of group leadership are likely to be resolved only if investigators consider the social and nonsocial needs and objectives of leaders and group members in particular situations. (For similar views see Graen & Schiemann, 1978, Hollander, 1978, and House & Dressler, 1974.)

Thinking specifically about loneliness, it is interesting to speculate that when it arises in the context of group life, it does so in part because the leader's style fails to engender the kinds of interactions necessary to meet members' social needs. Leaders who facilitate too little intimacy, as compared with group members' needs or expectations, for example, foster emotional isolation; those who fail to provide involvement and direction breed boredom, restlessness, and feelings of social isolation.

Group Entry Behavior, Rejection, and Withdrawal

If belonging to a group is rewarding, it should be of considerable concern to people, from early childhood on, to be able to enter desirable groups at will. In recent years, developmental psychologists have studied the sociometric structure of classroom groups and have systematically observed the ways in which children succeed or fail in their attempts to enter attractive groups. Since we do not yet have similar data on adult group-entry behavior, it may be useful to draw tentative conclusions from studies of children.

Elementary-school classrooms are clearly divided along popularity lines as early as fourth grade (Asher & Gottman, 1981). Some children are popular, and they tend to form an interlocking clique at the top of the social pyramid. Other, less popular children are not as well integrated into a group, and they spend much of their free time alone. Sometimes the unpopular children try to form friendships with each other, but these attempts frequently fail. Being unpopular has been explicitly linked with loneliness by Hymel et al. (Note 8); unpopular children tend to report feeling lonely.

What distinguishes socially successful from socially unsuccessful children? Dodge and Coie (Note 9) collected sociometric ratings from fourth-grade boys and identified four social types: popular, average, rejected (actively disliked), and neglected (ignored). When the subjects were experimentally placed in new groups of strangers, popular boys again rapidly became leaders. They asserted rules in a positive way, avoided giving offense, and did not appear to be possessive. They seemed to be norm-setters in every situation. Rejected boys got into fights, made more aversive comments, and were more possessive. When not talking inappropriately, they left the group to play by themselves. The other boys viewed them as disruptive, said they talked too much, and actively avoided them. Neglected children made fewer comments and seemed reluctant to lead or stand out. This study clearly indicates that children exhibit fairly stable social styles which are related to their ability to obtain valued social provisions from groups.

When attempting to join a play group, unpopular children tend to ask questions, make irrelevant comments about themselves, or state their feelings (Putallaz & Gottman, 1981). All of these strategies

> attempt to call the group's attention to the user. That is, unpopular children seem to try to exert control and divert the group's attention to themselves rather than attempt to integrate themselves into the ongoing conversation of the group. . . . When used by children, these strategies have a high probability of resulting in the group's ignoring or rejecting them. (p. 140)

There are remarkable similarities between unpopular children's self-focus and lack of tact and the social ineptitude of lonely college students. Jones, Freeman, and Goswick (1981) videotaped conversations between lonely and nonlonely college students, and then compared the conversations with those between nonlonely students. The lonely students proved to be more self-preoccupied; they seemed to focus on their own thoughts and feelings and missed conversational leads offered by their partners. In the end, the lonely subjects felt awkward and were convinced that their partners disliked them. In a subsequent study, Jones, Hobbs, and Hockenbury (1982) successfully attempted to change these dysfunctional social and attentional patterns through social skill retraining. Two weeks after the intervention, subjects from the experimental group showed much more normal behavior and reported feeling less lonely, self-conscious, and shy. This study is reminiscent of one conducted by Furman, Rahe, and Hartup (1979) in which withdrawn preschoolers participated in "therapeutic" play sessions with slightly younger peers. Weeks later, the subjects were unobtrusively observed in the preschool setting and found to be much less withdrawn. The observations indicated that the formerly withdrawn youngsters were now more adept at exercising leadership and expressing kindness, two forms of behavior they had rarely shown before.

Taken together, these recent studies of children and college students indicate that loneliness is due in part to being rejected or ignored by desirable groups, and that rejection is in turn due to identifiable failures in the group entry process or inadequate social skills. These deficiencies can be greatly reduced by one or another form of social skill training.

Summary, Conclusions, and Future Directions

There is ample evidence that people who belong to fewer groups, or have smaller social networks, or are unpopular are also lonelier than their more socially accepted and connected peers. But loneliness is not simply a matter of quantity of social interactions or number of groups to which one belongs. The two most influential conceptions of loneliness speak of a discrepancy between desired and actual social contact or of an absence of desired (or needed) relational provisions. Research indicates that there are two major types of loneliness: emotional isolation and social isolation; and this suggests that there are two major categories or clusters of provisions—psychological intimacy and integrated involvement. Each cluster can be obtained by individuals, at least to some extent, by membership in groups. Our two provision dimensions are reminiscent of Parsons and Bales's distinction between instrumental and expressive behavior, a distinction that in turn is related to the traditional distinction between masculinity and femininity. Recent research indicates that masculinity and femininity, for a long time thought to be opposites, can be meaningfully operationalized as independent dimensions. This is compatible with our own representation of the two social provision dimensions as orthogonal rather than antithetical. In fact, "masculinity" and "femininity" may be viewed as clusters of social orientations and behaviors that equip a person for membership in integrated-involving and psychologically intimate groups. When we look directly at research on cohesiveness, conformity, rejection of deviants, and leadership, we repeatedly find evidence for the existence of two major provision dimensions. Cohesiveness takes two forms, "instrumental" and "intrinsic"; cohesiveness increases conformity, most likely because deviant members of cohesive groups feel they have a lot to lose;

leadership, like cohesiveness, comes in two major forms, "task-oriented" and "interpersonally oriented." If a person cannot obtain desired or needed social provisions, for whatever reason—inadequate social skills, poor group leadership, holding unpopular opinions, failing to contribute instrumentally to a task-oriented group and being ostracized or rejected as a result—he or she feels lonely and either seeks more satisfying relationships or becomes increasingly isolated and depressed.

In the process of attempting to integrate the diverse literatures concerned with loneliness and group life, we have touched upon several ambiguities, gaps in the record, and testable questions for future research. In this final section we would like to return briefly to a few of these.

1. What exactly are the social provisions of group life? We have done everything we can to specify these in terms of relevant research and theory, but further research is needed to explore the validity of our speculations. We have reasoned backwards, in a sense—from types of loneliness to the missing provisions that presumably cause them. It would now be useful to attack the problem head on, so to speak, by discovering the full set of motives for joining and remaining loyal to certain groups.

2. Are we correct in proposing two major clusters of provisions, and in representing these clusters as more-or-less orthogonal? The orthogonality hypothesis is based on evidence that a person can be lonely in one of two major ways without being lonely in the other, or can be lonely in both ways at the same time. Representing the provisions as orthogonal has the advantage of making them parallel to masculinity and femininity; and, as we have shown, there are good reasons for expecting this parallelism.

At points in our argument, however, we came across unmistakable evidence that there is some tension or incompatibility between task and interpersonal orientations. How is it possible, for example, for a group to support or reward its members both conditionally and unconditionally at the same time? How is it possible to operate simultaneously according to need and equity principles? Interestingly, a similar problem has arisen in research on sex-role orientations. Spence and Helmreich (1978), while trying to measure masculinity and femininity as two separate and independent dimensions, found that certain scale items (e.g., "not at all aggressive . . . very aggressive," "very submissive . . . very dominant," "feelings easily hurt . . . feelings not easily hurt") refused to conform to this scheme. Instead, these items formed a distinct *bipolar* factor which Spence and Helmreich labelled "masculinity-femininity." Along the same lines, there is at least *some* evidence for Parsons and Bales's notion that people have a hard time acting simultaneously as task and socio-emotional leaders.

More work needs to be done to discover whether specific masculine and feminine behaviors are simultaneously compatible, which we doubt, or can be productively alternated or selected in appropriate (but different) situations by an androgynous person, which seems more likely. Similarly, it is important to delineate the precise ways in which an optimal leader balances, say, "initiating structure" with socio-emotional "consideration." Stogdill (1974) clearly implies that this is a matter of *behavior alternation*, not of specific behaviors being simultaneously task- and interpersonally oriented.

3. We have placed familiar types of groups into a two-dimensional space (Figure 11-1) based on the provisions which they seem to provide to typical members. It is obviously important to try to measure these provisions directly by questioning members of various kinds of groups and then (a) to factor analyzing the provision variables to see whether in fact they form two major dimensions, and (b) examining the correlation between factors to see whether it is in fact near zero, as the orthogonality hypothesis implies.

4. To what extent can groups fully satisfy people's needs for intimacy and integrated involvement? In order to maintain the present chapter's focus on group life, we have said little about the fact that most adults seem to want at least one intimate dyadic relationship and are rarely satisfied solely by group membership. Moreover, we have talked as if groups *as a whole* can be intimate; but informal observation suggests that intimacy occurs more easily and more frequently in dyads than in groups. We cannot tell yet whether groups are inherently nonintimate (perhaps intimacy interferes with the attainment of other group goals) or tend to fragment into dyads or small pieces when intimacy is allowed (as the ideologies of utopian communities suggest), or whether researchers have simply devoted relatively little attention to intimacy in naturally occurring groups.

As more efforts are made to map peoples' full "social networks" or "social support systems," it should be possible to determine the role groups play in the average person's social life.

5. Are there differences of the kinds we would predict between predominantly male and predominantly female (or "masculine" and "feminine") groups? Surprisingly little research has been directed at this issue. Do masculinity and femininity influence leadership style? Are they related to performance and satisfaction in different kinds of group settings?

While working on this chapter we found that much of the sex-role literature presents masculinity as incompatible with social life. Masculinity is linked with independence and individual achievement, or (in the Gilligan book, 1982, referred to earlier) as related to fear of social connectedness. The image is that of the Marlboro man, hiking mountain trails or sitting in the woods *alone* (except for his favorite cigarette). Our analysis of the parallels between sex-role and social provision dimensions suggests an alternative way to think about masculinity. Perhaps it is a collection of attitudes and social skills which suits a person, whether male or female, to obtain rewards from task-oriented groups, groups which emphasize productivity, division of labor, hierarchy, and equity. Masculinity, in this case, would be viewed not in terms of isolation or independence, but in terms of enhanced participation in certain kinds of groups.

Besides the several specific research questions raised here, there has been implicit in our remarks a call for a more general social-motivational perspective. In attempting to integrate the two fairly separate bodies of research on loneliness and group process, we have found it necessary to rely heavily on several interlocking notions: that people have basic social needs, analogous to physical needs such as hunger; that when these social needs go unsatisfied, people feel lonely and are motivated to behave in ways that will increase their chances of obtaining the social provisions they lack; and that this process underlies such familiar group phenomena as cohesiveness and conformity. The concept of social need has not been very popular during the successive reigns in psychology of behaviorism and cognitivism, but we see no way of avoiding it in the long run. As psychology moves toward a reconsideration of emotions and close personal relationships, which seems to be the emerging trend, the time is ripe for a reconsideration of social needs. In an era when loneliness ranks high among people's personal complaints—when Americans are, perhaps almost literally, "hungry" for intimacy and community—this scientific turn of events is very welcome indeed.

Acknowledgments. The authors are grateful to Wyndol Furman, Cindy Hazan, Howard Markman, Paul Paulus, Anne Peplau, Dan Perlman, Harry Reis, Gwen Sorrell, and Robert S. Weiss for helpful comments on an earlier draft of this chapter.

Reference Notes

1. Buhrmester, D., Shaver, P., Furman, W., & Willems, T. *Social skills and relationship development during a life transition.* Paper presented at the American Psychological Association Convention, Washington, D.C., August, 1982.

2. Shaver, P., Furman, W., Buhrmester, D., & Willems, T. *State and trait loneliness during the transition to college.* Paper presented at the American Psychological Association Convention, Los Angeles, 1981.

3. Furman, W., & Willems, T. *The acquaintanceship process in middle childhood.* Paper presented at the International Conference on Personal Relationships, Madison, Wisconsin, 1982.

4. Buhrmester, D., & Furman, W. *Sex-role differences in socioemotional adjustment to college.* Unpublished manuscript, University of Denver, 1983.

5. Shaver, P., Pullis, C., & Olds, D. *An analysis of contemporary marriage: A report on the LHJ "Intimacy Today" survey.* Unpublished technical report. New York: Societal Data Corporation, 1980.

6. Solano, C. *The social reality of feeling lonely: Friendship and reciprocation.* Unpublished manuscript, 1982.

7. Reis, H. Personal communication, 1982.

8. Hymel, S., Asher, S., Renshaw, P., & Geraci, R. *Loneliness in children: Development of a self-report measure.* Paper presented at the Annual Convention of the American Educational Research Association, 1981.

9. Dodge, K. A., & Coie, J. D. *Behavioral patterns among socially rejected, average, and popular fifth graders.* Paper presented at the Fifth Biennial Southeastern Conference on Human Development, Atlanta, 1978.

References

Asch, S. E. Effects of group pressure upon the modification and distortion of judgments. In H. Guetzkow (Ed.), *Groups, leaders, and men.* Pittsburgh: Carnegie Press, 1951.

Asch, S. E. Studies of independence and conformity: I. A minority of one against a unanimous majority. *Psychological Monographs,* 1956, *70* (9, Whole No. 416).

Asher, S. R., & Gottman, J. M. *The development of children's friendships*. London: Cambridge University Press, 1981.

Bales, R. F., & Slater, P. Role differentiation in small decision-making groups. In T. Parsons & R. F. Bales (Eds.), *Family, socialization and interaction process*. Glencoe, Illinois: Free Press, 1955.

Bem, S. L. The measurement of psychological androgyny. *Journal of Consulting and Clinical Psychology*, 1974, *42*, 155-162.

Bowlby, J. *Attachment and loss, Vol. 1: Attachment*. New York: Basic Books, 1969.

Bradburn, N. *The structure of psychological well-being*. Chicago: Aldine, 1969.

Brennan, T. Loneliness at adolescence. In L. A. Peplau & D. Perlman (Eds.), *Loneliness: A sourcebook of current theory, research and therapy*. New York: Wiley-Interscience, 1982.

Cartwright, D. The nature of group cohesiveness. In D. Cartwright & A. Zander (Eds.), *Group dynamics: Research and theory*. New York: Harper and Row, 1968.

Cartwright, D., & Zander, A. *Group dynamics: Research and theory*. New York: Harper & Row, 1968.

Cottrell, N. B. Performance in the presence of other human beings: Mere presence, audience, and affiliation effects. In E. C. Simmel, R. A. Hoppe, & G. A. Milton (Eds.), *Social faciliation and imitative behavior*. Boston: Allyn & Bacon, 1968.

Cottrell, N. B. Social facilitation. In C. G. McClintock (Ed.), *Experimental social psychology*. New York: Holt, 1972.

Cumming, R. D. *The philosophy of Jean-Paul Sartre*. New York: Random House, 1965.

Cutrona, C. E. Transition to college: Loneliness and the process of social adjustment. In L. A. Peplau & D. Perlman (Eds.), *Loneliness: A sourcebook of current theory, research and therapy*. New York: Wiley-Interscience, 1982.

Derlega, V., & Chaikin, A. *Sharing intimacy*. Englewood Cliffs, N.J.: Prentice-Hall, 1975.

Deutsch, M. Equity, equality and need: What determines which values will be used as the basis of distributive justice? *Journal of Social Issues*, 1975, *31*, 137-149.

Erikson, E. H. *The life cycle completed: A review*. New York: W. W. Norton, 1982.

Festinger, L. Informal social communication. *Psychological Review*, 1950, *57*, 271-282.

Festinger, L. A theory of social comparison processes. *Human Relations*, 1954, *7*, 117-140.

Fiedler, F. E. The contingency model and the dynamics of the leadership process. In L. Berkowitz (Ed.), *Advances in experimental social psychology* (Vol. 11). New York: Academic Press, 1978.

Fiedler, F. E., & Chemers, M. M. *Leadership and effective management*. New York: Scott-Foresman, 1974.

Fischer, C. S., & Phillips, S. L. Who is alone? Social characteristics of people with small social networks. In L. A. Peplau & D. Perlman (Eds.), *Loneliness: A source-*

book of current theory, research and therapy. New York: Wiley-Interscience, 1982.

Fleishmann, E., Harris, E., & Burtt, H. *Leadership and supervision in industry: An evaluation of supervisory training programs*. Columbus: Ohio State Bureau of Educational Research, 1955.

Furman, W., Rahe, D., & Hartup, W. Rehabilitation of socially-withdrawn preschool children through mixed-age and same-age socialization. *Child Development*, 1979, *50*, 915-922.

Gilligan, C. *In a different voice*. Cambridge, Mass.: Harvard University Press, 1982.

Glennon, L. M. *Women and dualism: A sociology of knowledge analysis*. New York: Longman, 1979.

Graen, G., & Scheimann, W. Leader-member agreement: A vertical dyad linkage approach. *Journal of Applied Psychology*, 1978, *63*, 206-212.

Hagstrom, W. D., & Selvin, H. C. The dimensions of cohesiveness in small groups. *Sociometry*, 1965, *28*, 30-43.

Halpin, A., & Winer, B. *The leadership behavior of the airplane commander*. Columbus: Ohio State University Research Foundation, 1952.

Harlow, H. F., & Mears, C. *The human model: Primate perspectives*. New York: Halstead Press, 1979.

Harris, M. *Cultural materialism: The struggle for a science of culture*. New York: Random House, 1979.

Heinicke, C., & Bales, R. F. Developmental trends in the structure of small groups. *Sociometry*, 1953, *16*, 7-38.

Hollander, E. P. *Leadership dynamics*. New York: Free Press, 1978.

House, R. J., & Dressler, G. The path-goal theory of leadership: Some post hoc and a priori tests. In J. G. Hunt & L. L. Larsen (Eds.), *Contingency approaches to leadership*. Carbondale, Ill.: Southern Illinois University Press, 1974.

Ickes, W., & Barnes, R. D. Boys and girls together—and alienated: On enacting stereotyped sex roles in mixed-sex dyads. *Journal of Personality and Social Psychology*, 1978, *36*, 669-683.

Johnson, J. *An attribution model of loneliness*. Unpublished doctoral dissertation, New York University, 1981.

Jones, W. H. Loneliness and social behavior. In L. A. Peplau & D. Perlman (Eds.), *Loneliness: A sourcebook of current theory, research and therapy*. New York: Wiley-Interscience, 1982.

Jones, W., Freeman, J. E., & Goswick, R. The persistence of loneliness: Self and other determinants. *Journal of Personality*, 1981, *49*, 27-48.

Jones, W. H., Hobbs, S. A., & Hockenbury, D. Loneliness and social skill deficits. *Journal of Personality and Social Psychology*, 1982, *42*, 682-689.

Jourard, S. M. *The transparent self* (2nd ed.). New York: Van Nostrand Reinhold, 1971.

Kanter, R. M. *Commitment and community*. Cambridge, Mass.: Harvard University Press, 1972.

Katz, D., & Kahn, R. L. *The social psychology of organizations* (2nd ed.). New York: Wiley, 1978.

Kelley, H. H. Two functions of reference groups. In G. E. Swanson, T. M. New-comb, & E. L. Hartley (Eds.), *Readings in social psychology*. New York: Holt, Rinehart and Winston, 1952.

Lakin, M. *Interpersonal encounter: Theory and practice in sensitivity training*. New York: McGraw-Hill, 1972.

Lever, J. Sex differences in the games children play. *Social Problems,* 1976, *23*, 478-487.

Levine, J. M. Reaction to opinion deviance in small groups. In P. B. Paulus (Ed.), *Psychology of group influence*. Hillsdale, N.J.: Lawrence Erlbaum, 1980.

Lynch, J. *The broken heart: The medical consequences of loneliness*. New York: Basic Books, 1977.

Major, B., & Deaux, K. Individual differences in justice behavior. In J. Greenberg & R. L. Cohen (Eds.), *Equity and justice in social behavior*. New York: Academic Press, 1982.

Mills, J., & Clark, M. C. Communal and exchange relationships. In L. Wheeler (Ed.), *Review of personality and social psychology* (Vol. 3). Beverly Hills, Calif.: Sage, 1982.

Misumi, J., & Tasaki, T. A study on the effectiveness of supervisory patterns in a Japanese hierarchical organization. *Japanese Psychological Review,* 1965, *7*, 151-162.

Olds, D. E., & Shaver, P. Masculinity, femininity, academic performance, and health: Further evidence concerning the androgyny controversy. *Journal of Personality,* 1980, *48*, 223-341.

Parsons, T., & Bales, R. F. (Eds.), *Family, socialization and interaction process*. Glencoe, Ill.: Free Press, 1955.

Parsons, T., Bales, R. F., & Shils, E. H. *Working papers in the theory of action*. Glencoe, Ill.: Free Press, 1953.

Parsons, T., & Shils, E. H. (Eds.), *Toward a general theory of action*. New York: Harper Torchbooks, 1964.

Pepitone, A., & Wilipizeski, C. Some consequences of experimental rejection. *Journal of Abnormal and Social Psychology,* 1960, *60*, 359-364.

Peplau, L. A., & Perlman, D. (Eds.), *Loneliness: A sourcebook of current theory, research and therapy*. New York: Wiley-Interscience, 1982.

Perlman, D., & Peplau, L. A. Toward a social psychology of loneliness. In S. Duck & R. Gilmour (Eds.), *Personal relationships 3: Personal relationships in disorder*. London: Academic Press, 1981.

Putallaz, M., & Gottman, J. M. An interactional model of children's entry into peer groups. *Child Development,* 1981, *52*, 986-994.

Rogers, C. R. A theory of therapy, personality, and interpersonal relationships, as developed in the client-centered framework. In S. Koch (Ed.), *Psychology: A study of a science* (Vol. 3). New York: McGraw-Hill, 1959.

Rubenstein, C., & Shaver, P. Loneliness in two northeastern cities. In J. Hartog, J. Audy & Y. Cohen (Eds.), *The anatomy of loneliness*. New York: International Universities Press, 1980.

Rubenstein, C., & Shaver, P. The experience of loneliness. In L. A. Peplau & D. Perlman (Eds.), *Loneliness: A sourcebook of current theory, research and therapy*. New York: Wiley-Interscience, 1982. (a)

Rubenstein, C., & Shaver, P. *In search of intimacy*. New York: Delacorte, 1982. (b)

Russell, D. The measurement of loneliness. In L. A. Peplau & D. Perlman (Eds.), *Loneliness: A sourcebook of current theory, research and therapy*. New York: Wiley-Interscience, 1982.

Russell, D., Peplau, L. A., & Ferguson, M. Developing a measure of loneliness. *Journal of Personality Assessment*, 1978, *42*, 290-294.

Sartre, J.-P. [*In search of a method.*] In Hazel Barnes (Trans.), *Critique de la raison dialectique*. New York: Knopf, 1963.

Schachter, S. Deviation, rejection, and communication. *Journal of Abnormal and Social Psychology*, 1951, *46*, 190-207.

Scheff, T. J. *Catharsis and healing, ritual and drama*. Berkeley: University of California Press, 1979.

Shartle, C. *Executive performance and leadership*. Englewood Cliffs, N.J.: Prentice-Hall, 1956.

Shaver, P., & Rubenstein, C. Childhood antecedents of adult loneliness. In L. Wheeler (Ed.), *Review of personality and social psychology* (Vol. 1). Beverly Hills, Calif.: Sage, 1980.

Spence, J., & Helmreich, R. *Masculinity and femininity: Their psychological dimensions, correlates, and antecedents*. Austin, Texas: University of Texas Press, 1978.

Stogdill, R. M. *Handbook of leadership: A survey of theory and research*. New York: Free Press, 1974.

Strube, M. J., & Garcia, J. E. A meta-analytical investigation of Fiedler's contingency model of leadership effectiveness. *Psychological Bulletin*, 1981, *90*, 307-321.

Suls, J., & Miller, R. L. (Eds.), *Social comparison processes: Theoretical and empirical perspectives*. Washington, D.C.: Hemisphere, 1977.

Thibaut, J. W., & Kelley, H. H. *The social psychology of groups*. New York: Wiley, 1959.

Toennies, F. Gemeinschaft and Gesellschaft. In T. Parsons, E. Shils, K. D. Naegele, & J. R. Pitts (Eds.), *Theories of society*. New York: Free Press, 1961. (Originally published, 1887.)

Toennies, F. *Community and society*. New York: Harper Torchbooks, 1963.

Veroff, J., Douvan, E., & Kulka, R. *The inner American: A self-portrait from 1957 to 1976*. New York: Basic Books, 1981.

Weeks, D. G., Michela, J. L., Peplau, L. A., & Bragg, M. E. The relation between loneliness and depression: A structural equation analysis. *Journal of Personality and Social Psychology*, 1980, *39*, 1238-1244.

Weiss, R. S. *Loneliness: The experience of emotional and social isolation*. Cambridge, Mass.: MIT Press, 1973.

Weiss, R. S. The provisions of social relationships. In Z. Rubin (Ed.), *Doing unto others*. Englewood Cliffs, N.J.: Prentice-Hall, 1974.

Weiss, R. S. Issues in the study of loneliness. In L. A. Peplau & D. Perlman (Eds.), *Loneliness: A sourcebook of current theory, research and therapy*. New York: Wiley-Interscience, 1982.

Wheeler, L., Reis, H., & Nezlek, J. Loneliness, social interaction, and sex roles. *Journal of Personality and Social Psychology*, 1983, *42*, in press.

Zajonc, R. B. Social facilitation. *Science,* 1965, *149*, 269-274.

Zajonc, R. B. Compresence. In P. B. Paulus (Ed.), *Psychology of group influence*. Hillsdale, N.J.: Lawrence Erlbaum, 1980.

Chapter 12
The Interpersonal Orientations
of Disclosure

Richard L. Archer and Walter B. Earle

Why a piece on *self*-disclosure in a book devoted to group processes? For those who accept the current liberal definition of the term self-disclosure no explanation is necessary. By this definition it is the act of revealing personal information *to others*, so self-disclosure is inherently social in nature and a part of the traffic among group members. But for those who are purists or simply less familiar with the thrust of the literature the question is a real one. Self-disclosure would obviously appear to refer to the act of reporting one's self-conception. Viewed from this perspective it is primarily a phenomenon for personality theory, not group dynamics.

The truth is that, historically, both perspectives have been represented in the research literature on self-disclosure. We will briefly trace the undeniably *intra*personal origins of the self-disclosure concept as a key to personality. Then we will explain how a "midlife crisis" in research findings spurred social psychologists to transform self-disclosure into an *inter*personal mechanism for developing relationships. This review will set the stage for a radical yet sensible proposal: that the current focus on the social aspects of disclosure favors a marriage between self-disclosure and group process.

If we may pursue the courtship metaphor, it would appear that, like the suitor kept perpetually waiting in the parlor, the young field of personal communication has been pining for a chance to join theoretical forces with the fine old family of group processes. Why have these advances been spurned? We can point to possible causes for the noticeably low profile of communication, especially intimate communication, in the group processes literature. Perhaps this state of affairs has to do with overly restrictive assumptions about who constitutes a group and what the business of groups is. On the other hand, a close look at the assumptions disclosure researchers hold about relationships makes this reluctance to embrace more understandable: The transformation of self-disclosure into an interpersonal concept has been far from complete because the perspective of the individual persists.

Our task of bringing self-disclosure and group processes together, then, is much more constructive and conceptual than it is reconstructive and historical. Since disclosure's intrapersonal roots have tended to blind theorists and especially researchers to the full range of roles personal communications play in social interaction, we will try to organize and identify them anew. An expanded typology of the uses of disclosure will be presented. It will include the more group-oriented uses such as describing a relationship as well as the more individually oriented ones such as describing the self. A relative feast of research illustrating some of these orientations is available, but apparently at the cost of producing famine where investigation of the others is concerned. But merely pointing out this neglect will probably not motivate researchers to end it. We intend to convince personality and social psychologists that a broader notion of disclosure provides a bridge that could unify self and group processes with theoretical advantages for both.

We are getting a bit ahead of ourselves, however. First, let us examine the two traditional approaches to personal communication, one based on the self, the other on the group, and the more recent interest in the role of self-disclosure in developing relationships.

Self-Disclosure Tradition

Obviously, self-disclosure, whether taken at face value or interpreted in some fashion, provides a unique and valuable source of information about what a person is like. Consequently, it comes as no surprise that reviewers have been able to relate the concept broadly to the writings of theologians, social philosophers, and psychotherapists (see Altman & Taylor, 1973; Doster & Nesbitt, 1979; Goodstein & Reinecker, 1974). The more proximate roots of the self-disclosure notion in psychology, however, are to be found in the work of Lewin (1935, 1936), Rickers-Ovsiankina (1956), and Jourard (1964). Among them they gave self-disclosure a name, proposed its relationships to personality, and devised research paradigms to study it (see Archer, 1979; Cozby, 1973).

Lewin was first, and perhaps foremost, a personality theorist. His dynamic theory of personality depicts the self as a series of concentric circles (boundaries) sectioned into wedges (regions). The self, then, is seen as a circular library in which information is shelved according to its centrality and type. The boundaries must be permeated to access the self-information that lies within, so the more central aspects of the self are by definition more difficult to obtain, and hence private. By scrutinizing an individual's self-disclosure, or the lack of it, others may trace the depth and breadth of that individual's personality. (For a more complete account see Altman and Taylor, 1973).

It remained for one of Lewin's students, Rickers-Ovsiankina (1956), to operationalize this concept of self-disclosure (which Lewin termed "social accessibility"). Rickers-Ovsiankina drew up a self-report measure composed of a number of potential topics for self-disclosure. Students were asked to indicate the ones they were prepared to reveal to each of three prospective targets varying in the closeness of their relationship to the respondent (stranger, acquaintance, best friend). Rickers-Ovsiankina used this type of instrument to investigate regularities in social accessibility across topics and targets, as well as some individual differences (e.g., Rickers-

Ovsiankina, 1956; Rickers-Ovsiankina & Kusmin, 1958). Both the consistencies and the variations were duly interpreted in terms of Lewin's theory of personality structure. Thus, self-disclosure came to be regarded as a *mirror* of the self without any direct attempt to test the proposition empirically.

At this point the torch was passed from the Lewinian theorists to the practitioners of psychotherapy. Concurrently, but independently of Rickers-Ovsiankina, a clinical psychologist named Jourard crafted a similar individual difference measure and dubbed the dimension self-disclosure (Jourard & Lasakow, 1958). Jourard most certainly regarded self-disclosure as a mirror of the self, or in his terms, a symptom of personality. Unfortunately, the proposed structure of *The Transparent Self* (Jourard, 1971b) was never made as explicit as Lewin's concept of personality. Suffice it to say that he accepted the humanistic notions of personal growth put forth by Maslow (1954) in self-actualization theory and Rogers (1958) in client-centered therapy. This growth orientation led Jourard to take a step further and portray self-disclosure as an actual *maker* of the self.

Jourard's views are paraded in a pair of quotations from his aforementioned book (Jourard, 1971b). He claimed that "every maladjusted person is a person who has not made himself known. . . and in consequence does not know himself" (p. 32). A need to reveal the self to at least one significant other is posited. One may, of course, suppress the need, but "in the effort to avoid [disclosure], a person provides for himself a cancerous kind of stress" (p. 33). For Jourard, disclosure is a mirror of self into which the revealer as well as the listener may gaze. Failing to engage in this kind of simultaneous self-discovery and self-representation is said to result in an ambiguous self-concept, unfulfilling relationships with others, and psychophysiological symptoms of stress.

Informal observations of clients undergoing psychotherapy and a clinician's intuition were the real sources for Jourard's ideas about self-disclosure. On the other hand, his scientific curiosity enticed him to initiate a surprisingly broad program of controlled investigations that provided the first significant body of findings in the area (Jourard, 1971a). Like Rickers-Ovsiankina, his early studies focused on descriptive and demographic issues and personality correlates of disclosure. Later efforts broke with tradition and examined it as a medium of interaction. Except in the case of introversion and possibly neuroticism, the flurry of attempts by Jourard and his fellow practitioners to link the absence of self-disclosure with personality and psychopathology were generally a failure (Archer, 1980; see Archer, 1979, and Goodstein & Reinecker, 1974, for reviews). Instead, it was the social interaction studies that bore fruit, beginning with the demonstrations of a listener's increased liking for a revealer (Jourard, 1959) and reciprocity of disclosure exchange (Jourard, 1959; Jourard & Landsman, 1960) within preexisting groups of men and women.

While a battery of self-report measures furnished both Jourard and Rickers-Ovsiankina with a justifiable expedient for exploring relationships between self-disclosure and personality, it was clearly an indefensible research strategy for answering questions about social interaction. Consequently, the later studies of Jourard and his students were increasingly based upon an experimental laboratory paradigm in which subjects met each other for the first time and exchanged disclosure face-to-face (Jourard, 1971a). Often the other was the experimenter who manipulated the independent variables through his or her own self-disclosures to or physical and eye contact with the subject (e.g., Jourard & Friedman, 1970).

The paradigm used in these studies piqued the interest of social psychologists. Even more intriguing was the implication that self-disclosure was a chief instigator and lubricant for relationships (see Cozby, 1973). However, these social interaction findings were somewhat tangential to the original accounts of disclosure as a mirror and maker of personality. Faced with a lack of evidence, reviewers of the disclosure-personality literature challenged the validity of the self-report measures of disclosure (Cozby, 1973; Goodstein & Reinecker, 1974) and the adequacy of the simple correlational, trait-based research designs (Altman & Taylor, 1973; Chaikin & Derlega, 1974). As remedies they urged the adoption of multidimensional measures (Chelune, 1979) and person-situation interactional research designs (Archer, 1979). However the new designs and measures were all aimed at differences in social behavior. In the name of rehabilitating the disclosure-personality research, the critics were, for all intents and purposes, bidding investigators to turn their attentions toward the role of disclosure in social interaction.

Traditional Role of Communication in Groups

Whatever the relationship between self-disclosure and the self, few would disagree with the claim that disclosures constitute much of the communication within groups. Nevertheless, communications have rarely occupied the limelight in studies of group process. While investigators of self-disclosure were finding their bearings in personality and then losing them, in the field of group dynamics communication had quietly settled into the supporting role Festinger (1950) had assigned it. Not until the comparatively recent interest in encounter groups did communications receive a title role in the groups literature (see Cartwright & Zander, 1968, and Shaw, 1981, for reviews), and these were unusual groups indeed.

In his review of "informal social communication," Festinger (1950) identified three sources of pressure to communicate within (and among) groups. The first and best supported was pressures toward uniformity. These pressures within a group were said to arise from the members' needs to validate their beliefs, to find social reality for them in consensus. In addition, a desire for group locomotion or movement toward a shared goal could be a source of such pressures if consensus was perceived as instrumental to its attainment. These effects of group locomotion on communication were convincingly demonstrated in a discussion-group context by Schachter (1951). According to Festinger, both validation and locomotion needs give rise to communication among group members in the form of influence attempts designed to reduce the discrepancies among their views. This should be especially true if the group is a cohesive one in which membership is highly valued and the issues involved are central to the group's existence.

The second set of pressures to communicate described by Festinger (1950) was forces to change position in the group. Members of the group desiring more status and power within it should address more communications to the high and the mighty in an effort to gain entry. Both early experimental laboratory (Thibaut, 1950) and correlational field studies (Hurwitz, Zander, & Hymovitch, 1953) have found this hypothesized directional flow of communication up the organizational ladder. Conversely, the studies on communication networks (see Shaw, 1964, for a review) show that channeling communications through an individual will increase the likelihood that he or she will become a group leader.

While communications arising both from pressures toward uniformity and to change position in the group are viewed as instrumental, the last source of communications named by Festinger (1950) is not. The existence of an emotional state in group members is expected to produce communications which are consummatory. In other words, someone feeling joyful or angry will want to express it to others, whether it influences them or not. Festinger was anticipating the outcome of the research on fear and affiliation by Schachter (1959). The results of those studies and others (e.g., Gerard & Rabbie, 1961; Zimbardo & Formica, 1963) have usually been interpreted to mean that attempts to communicate in emotional situations stem more from social comparison needs than from a desire for social support or an urge to express feelings. However, Shaver and Klinnert (1982) have recently marshalled considerable evidence from primate and infant studies to support an anxiety-reduction interpretation.

Festinger's (1950) description of pressures to communicate is general enough to apply to persons engaged in intimate, personal communications as well as those participating in impersonal ones. For example, close relationships may simply be viewed as highly cohesive groups. Individuals trying to develop a sense of self through disclosure could also reasonably be seen as searching for social reality. On the other hand, there is no special consideration given to describing intimacy in this account of informal social communication, nor does it address itself to the motives for developing close relationships. A look at the methodological trends in group dynamics helps to explain why not.

Festinger and his fellow pioneers in group dynamics drew many of their hypotheses about communication from their field study of social pressures within and between the residents of Westgate and Westgate West, a pair of housing projects for families of M.I.T. students (Festinger, Schachter, & Back, 1950). Obviously, theirs was a very rich and complex data set centered on a population with many forms of ongoing social contact and overlapping close relationships among pairs and larger groupings. Understandably, they turned to experimental designs for less equivocal tests of their hypotheses (e.g., Schachter, 1951). Randomly selected groups of three or more strangers replaced friends and acquaintances. Specific and narrowly defined tasks replaced the coffee klatch and the bridge party. Unfortunately, in eliminating the ambiguities concerning the causal links between social pressures and communication, they also sacrificed much of this interactional diversity and most of the context of lasting relationships in which it was embedded.

In the 1960s, just as the interest in laboratory research on social comparison and affiliation came to an end, encounter groups became a cultural phenomenon (see Back, 1973; Lakin, 1972). Variously termed encounter, experiential, sensitivity-training, or simply training groups (T-groups), these groups also showed considerable variety of form and purpose. However, Lakin (1972; see Shaw, 1981) has identified some constants: (a) facilitating emotional expressiveness; (b) generating feelings of belongingness; (c) fostering a norm of self-disclosure as a condition of group membership; (d) sampling personal behaviors; (e) making sanctioned interpersonal comparison; (f) sharing responsibility for leadership and direction with the appointed leader. Encounter groups differ from typical problem-solving or task-oriented groups in that members place primary importance on the group experience itself (Lakin, 1972) and that the broadly defined goal is valid communication (Bennis & Shepard, 1956).

Encounter groups were certainly not devised for research purposes. The reasons why they reached fad-like proportions, like Jourard's interests in self-disclosure, are usually traced to the general disenchantment with the overorganized, impersonal, and rootless nature of today's culture and to the influence of the humanistic growth psychologies. But when investigators began to use them as a vehicle to study group dyanmics, encounter groups could be seen as an attempt to replace the intimate communication and close relationships that experimental laboratory studies ruled out.

Encounter groups were an odd sort of group, not because they reinstated intimate communication, but because of the way in which they did so. Rather than to follow the obvious approach of returning group dynamics to the study of ongoing relationships in natural settings, encounter group researchers strove to inject intimacy into a short-term task group composed of strangers! Admittedly, encounter groups are less structured and their goals are initially more ambiguous than the typical task group, but as they develop, members define norms and state purposes in far more concrete terms than in everyday relationships. (See Bennis & Sheppard, 1956, and Winter, 1976, for analyses of encounter group development.) Friendships are seldom so limited and definite in their duration or activities either.

The effectiveness of encounter groups in promoting self-knowledge and developing openness is uncertain (Shaw, 1981). In any case, researchers would be unwise to consider them analogs of normal close relationships for the purpose of investigating group processes. Interestingly enough, Schein and Bennis (1965) have included isolating the group, insuring that the members will not meet again, and encouraging an attitude that the group is temporary and game-like among their conditions for creating a "psychologically safe" environment in encounter groups. It seems that if *participants* confuse the artificial encounter group with a naturally occurring friendship, they are in for an unpleasant and perhaps even a traumatic experience.

Relationships: Where the Self Joins the Group

As those social psychologists interested in attraction began to explore self-disclosure as a basis for relationship formation between pairs of individuals, those steeped in group dynamics could have been and should have been their natural allies. However, group processes research was focused firmly on task groups and, as we have seen, the notion of relationships as groups constituted to perform the task of intimate communication was not a particularly convincing one. Moreover, that kind of thinking had produced encounter groups and the subsequent public furor over their benefits and dangers.

There was also the issue of size. A relationship, like the tango, typically takes two. Even though dyadic interchanges seem to be the most frequent type of social interaction (Wheeler & Nezlek, 1977), traditionalists may have wondered whether a dyad was big enough to be a representative group. Given the controversies involved in deciding what kind of group a relationship is, it is not so surprising that group processes research largely ignored relationships and self-disclosure as well.

Left to themselves, attraction researchers first conducted a campaign to exorcise from self-disclosure the humanistic values that Jourard had invested in it (Cozby, 1973). Early experiments destroyed the illusion that intimate disclosure inevitably produced attraction (Derlega, Harris, & Chaikin, 1973; Ehrlich & Graeven, 1971). Pragmatically, investigators attempted to describe the kind of disclosure and the circumstances under which liking would be the result. These studies pointed up the operation of situational norms of disclosure intimacy (e.g., Chaiken & Derlega, 1974) and the attributional concept of personalistic disclosure in first encounters (e.g., Jones & Archer, 1976; Rubin, 1975).

Among the disclosure researchers, only Altman and Taylor (1973) attempted to go beyond first encounters to construct a thorough-going theory of relationship development with self-disclosure as the cornerstone and prime mover. For this reason, along with its familiarity, their social penetration theory (Altman & Taylor, 1973) will be our instrument for exploring the assumptions made by disclosure theorists and investigators about relationships. Keep in mind, however, that these assumptions are also implicit in most of the other work on self-disclosure.

Altman and Taylor (1973) opt for the new term *social penetration* over the traditional term *self-disclosure* to reflect their interest in a broad range of nonverbal as well as verbal exchanges of intimacy involved in forming relationships (Taylor, 1979). They borrow their conception of the self as a series of concentric circles from Lewin's (1935) personality theory (discussed earlier). A growing relationship between two individuals is seen as a mutual process of inquiry and disclosure in which they share selves. Since the process is said to proceed inward from superficial to adjacent intimate levels and to expand across levels of intimacy as they are reached, social penetration may by represented as an ever-widening and deepening wedge in the circular self. Altman and Taylor (1973) attribute this characteristic wedge relationship between the depth and breadth of disclosure to the influence of rewards and costs.

The picture of participants in a relationship as dependent upon one another for rewards is drawn by Altman and Taylor (1973) from Thibaut and Kelley's (1959) theory of interdependence. Like Thibaut and Kelley (1959), they see each participant conducting an ongoing evaluation of past and present rewards and costs in order to predict the future. The ratio of rewards to costs and the magnitude of each are taken into account. The actual returns are measured against prior expectations for the relationship (comparison level, CL) and potential alternatives for other relationships (comparison level for alternatives, CL_{alt}). These calculations enable each participant to determine rationally whether to pursue or terminate the union and what the next move will be if the decision is to forge ahead.

Returning to the notion of the social penetration wedge. Altman and Taylor (1973) predict this pattern of exchange because it should tend to maximize rewards and minimize costs. They claim we pursue intimate exchanges because those exchanges are by nature more rewarding than superficial ones. The move to adjacent levels of intimacy and expansion across levels is grounded on our expectation that rewarding interactions are more likely where similar behaviors and topics are involved (see Byrne, 1971).

Although intimacy can be more rewarding, it can also be correspondingly more costly if more central feelings, desires, and values conflict. This observation leads Altman and Taylor (1973) to predict a differential, slowing rate of social penetration in the later as opposed to earlier and middle stages of developing relationships. Thus, the give-and-take of rewards in the form of self-disclosure drives the machinery of social penetration to manufacture close relationships in a slow and systematic fashion, unless and until prohibitive costs are encountered. In that event, the participants are said to pull out of the relationship by gradually reducing the depth and breadth of exchange. In other words, the social penetration process reverses itself.

As may be seen from the foregoing summary, Altman and Taylor's (1973) complex, multivariate account of social penetration processes is not so much a new theory as it is a clever integration of a pair of previous ones. Self-disclosure is the linchpin through which this is achieved, and although the theory suffers in terms of specificity by bringing nonverbal as well as verbal intimacy within its domain, it is certainly a credible attempt to *explain* the role of disclosure in relationships. Much of the existing evidence on disclosure exchange in lab and field settings can be fitted into its framework. Furthermore, with its differential-rates-of-exchange notion, the theory manages to *predict* an increase in immediate disclosure reciprocity during acquaintanceship followed by a decrease in such reciprocity when the relationship becomes a close one. This effect has been demonstrated with friends and married partners here and abroad, (Derlega, Wilson, & Chaikin, 1976; Morton, 1978; Won-Doornink, 1979) and is among the most important findings in the literature to date. It is only after looking beyond these obvious strengths of the theory to its assumptions about the nature of relationships that we find cause to question it.

Altman and Taylor's choice of the penetration metaphor is very revealing. Rooted in the boundary concepts of Lewin and the reward/cost concepts of Thibaut and Kelley, the social penetration process pictures relationship development as a matter of overcoming one's own and one's partner's resistance to get the goods. The stakes involved are high. Those who give in to self-disclosure may gain the joys of being close, but they simultaneously risk embarrassment and rejection. In addition to these more palpable social risks, there may also be a sense of loss. Self-disclosure makes the private self public (see Runge & Archer, 1981), opening it up for inspection and reinterpretation by an other. Thus, an overlooked cost of building a relationship may be a feeling that some personal uniqueness and integrity have been forfeited.

Despite the costs of sacrificing privacy and even some "self-hood," the rewards of exchange are considered strong enough by Altman and Taylor to propel us toward one another. But notwithstanding the inspiration taken from Thibaut and Kelley's ideas of *inter*dependence, the social penetration process is always viewed from the standpoint of its rewards for the *individual*. While the relationship may be advantageous for both participants, it seems more like mutual exploitation than symbiosis. In sum, we are left with the vivid picture of two individuals chipping away at their own and each other's selves, each for his or her own ends.

Perhaps in trying to characterize the individualistic rewards orientation of social penetration we have gone too far and presented a caricature. If our criticism seems extreme, we hasten to add that both Altman and Taylor have been forthright critics of their own theory. Taylor (1979) shares our concern over the largely molar approach to intimate exchange taken by social penetration theory. He has urged that a molecular approach to the phenomenon based upon the attributional concept of personalism (e.g., Jones & Archer, 1976; Taylor, Gould & Brounstein, 1981) be pursued at this point. Altman and his colleagues (Altman, Vinsel, & Brown, 1981) agree with our contention that social penetration theory really focuses on individuals, not relationships. They advocate a dialectic approach to relationships examining cycles of openness-closedness and stability-change. Something of this missing dyadic perspective is incorporated into the new dialectic approach by considering the degree of synchrony among the cycles of the participants. However, neither Taylor's (1979) nor Altman et al.'s (1981) suggestions are able or intended to move social penetration theory away from its firm foundations in individual rewards.

Social penetration theory provides an account of individuals at the point of embarkation that is similar to Levinger's (Levinger, 1974; Levinger & Snoek, 1972) contemporaneous but less-often cited levels of pair relatedness. Levinger's model of relationships also charts the course of two unrelated persons from zero contact (level 0) through awareness (level 1) and surface contact (level 2). But eventually Levinger's couple reaches mutuality (level 3), an intersection of originally separate selves evidenced by joint goals and activities and a "we-feeling." Altman and Taylor (1973, pp. 129-142) only hint at the origins of this creative aspect of relationships. Just as Tolman's cognitive theory of learning was accused of leaving the rat "buried in thought" (Guthrie, 1952) the social penetration theory of relationships can be charged with abandoning the participants before they become a couple. They describe the journey, but not its end.

There are several possible reasons why Altman and Taylor (1973) and most other disclosure theorists and researchers paint such an individualistic and incomplete picture of relationships. First of all, there is a pervasive if implicit theme in much of contemporary social-psychological research that humans would do better without groups (Buys, 1978). If relationships, like other groups, are viewed from this one-sided perspective as sources of deindividuation, groupthink, contagion, and the like, they are certainly not something to be rushed into.

In addition, the research traditions of disclosure investigators themselves take a cautious view of intimacy. Altman's background in nonverbal research where intimacy was conceptualized as an invasion of personal space (Felipe & Sommer, 1966), a producer of affiliative conflict (Argyle & Dean, 1965), and an intruder on privacy (Altman, 1975) probably influenced social penetration theory. In fact, Altman et al. (1981) feel that the chief weakness of the theory is that it still overemphasizes openness! Other self-disclosure investigators were interested in intimacy from the standpoint of impressions management. Should persons reveal or conceal deviant acts (Derlega et al., 1973) and socially stigmatizing events (Jones & Archer, 1976;

Jones & Gordon, 1972) to ingratiate themselves with others? These investigators allowed a particular issue in which intimacy was linked with negativity to become the foundation for broader speculation about the role of norms and personalism in acquaintance.

Last and not least is that insidious term, *self*-disclosure. Interest in disclosure and personality is fading while interest in relationships is blossoming. But, like the legendary Lorelei of the Rhine who enticed sailors to their doom on the rocks, the word itself calls investigators back to the perspectives and goals of the individual. Who, then, can fault researchers from the group processes perspective for failing to heed the call?

The Uses of Disclosure

Disappointment with the limitations of traditional views of intimate communication has led us to take a new look at the issue of function. The idea that self-disclosure may fulfill a number of different functions has been reintroduced to the literature by Derlega and Grzelak (1979). Archer (1980) has focused primarily upon disclosure's uses in developing a self-conception. In the present context, we will confront the functional issue, "what is self-disclosure used for?", in terms of the aforementioned broadly social definition of disclosure as *the act of revealing personal information to others.* From the discloser's point of view, its functions can then be seen as corresponding to several *interpersonal orientations.* These orientations differ in the amount of *listener uniqueness* and *listener contribution* called for.

Listener uniqueness refers to the degree to which disclosure is aimed at a particular listener. Listener contribution is the degree to which the listener must respond to the disclosure with something of him- or herself. Since these two listener dimensions tend to covary in social interaction, they may be collapsed into a single dimension of intra-to-interpersonal communication along which our interpersonal orientations can be ordered.

Our plan is to present a comprehensive classification of the self-disclosure functions that are associated with each orientation (see Figure 12-1).[1] Supportive evidence from the current research will be offered when it is available. By taking this tack we wish to call attention to the way in which researchers have tended to focus on a few of the orientations and their corresponding functions to the detriment of the whole. This approach should also underline the special need for a more adequate conceptualization of disclosure's role in relationships.

---

[1] At first blush some readers may feel that such a wide-ranging approach comes perilously close to equating disclosure with communication itself and thus, robbing the word of any special meaning. We recognize some merit in the notion that, in the broadest sense, all communications disclose something about the communicator. But rest assured that we view disclosure as a subset of communication. It is a form of communication that has intimacy (see Archer, 1980) and self-reference as its hallmarks.

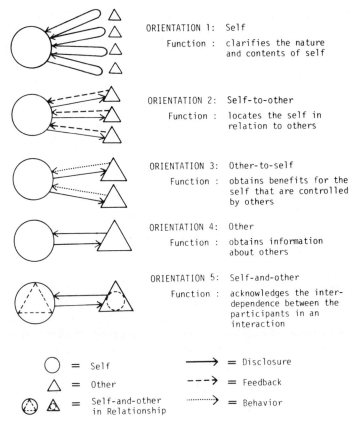

ORIENTATION 1: Self
    Function : clarifies the nature
               and contents of self

ORIENTATION 2: Self-to-other
    Function : locates the self in
               relation to others

ORIENTATION 3: Other-to-self
    Function : obtains benefits for the
               self that are controlled
               by others

ORIENTATION 4: Other
    Function : obtains information
               about others

ORIENTATION 5: Self-and-other
    Function : acknowledges the inter-
               dependence between the
               participants in an
               interaction

○ = Self   ⟶ = Disclosure
△ = Other   ---> = Feedback
⬡ ⧌ = Self-and-other   ·········> = Behavior
        in Relationship

Fig. 12-1.

Orientation 1: Self

The primary function of *self*-oriented disclosure is to *clarify the nature and contents of the self*. This kind of disclosure is at least marginally social because: (a) the presence of others provides a legitimate opportunity to disclose and (b) revealing the information gives it an existence outside the mind of the discloser, a social reality. Both listener uniqueness and listener contribution are low, however, because when we make a *self*-oriented disclosure to others, we are mainly talking to ourselves.

According to Bem (1972), individuals gain self-knowledge through inferences based on observations of their own behavior. This notion is consistent with the finding of Fishbein and Laird (1979) that voluntary disclosure or concealment of self-information in a conversation will correspondingly affect the revealer's subsequent judgment of its positivity or negativity, respectively. This implies that everyday self-disclosures will be a potent source of self-insight—even if the discloser did not initially intend them to be. Let us suppose that like Julie Andrews we find ourselves repeatedly revealing that bright copper kettles and warm woolen mittens are our favorites. Presumably then, such things will sooner or later show up in our self-concept.

Perhaps it is not so surprising then, that some clinical psychologists regard talking to oneself as a result of, rather than a reason for, therapy. From a behavior-modification perspective, Meichenbaum (1977) describes the role of "self-talk" in mediating behavior change. In the form of questions and answers about the task at hand it provides a means of self-instruction, thereby increasing attention and memory. The written form of self-talk advocated by the depth psychologist Progoff (1975) is aimed at altering perceptions of self in the broadest sense. In his journal workshops he claims that by learning to record events in an intensive personal journal,

> the actions and inner experiences that accompany them in a person's life, can be brought into a form definite enough so that they can be reflected and perceived. (Progoff, 1975; p. 21)

In addition to helping us define ourselves for ourselves, *self*-oriented disclosure also aids us in defining ourselves for others. At minimum, it may simply be a statement that "I exist." It is a means of calling attention to oneself as is a cough, a facial gesture, or a particular movement of the body.

Statements to others frequently go beyond a mere "I exist" to "I stand for. . . ." We may have something that we urgently need to convey about our selves, regardless of the response (or lack of response) it evokes in others. For example, a women may consider herself to be a rugged enthusiast of the out-of-doors, a conquerer of the wilderness. However, she may have little actual experience with which to substantiate this self-conception (e.g., an afternoon of cross-country skiing at a nearby state park). According to Wicklund and Gollwitzer (1981), this state of affairs will arouse a motive to gain completeness, leading her to develop *alternative* ways of affirming outdoor skills (self-symbolizing). For example, she might make frequent trips to the local wilderness outfitter's to purchase the latest in top-of-the-line equipment. Alternatively, she might, in conversations with others, disclose about her "backwoods exploits."

Self-oriented disclosures may also serve a need for reaffirming aspects of one's self-conception that have been threatened outright, for example, by discrepant feedback from others. Swann (in press) argues that when people receive self-discrepant feedback, they will actively strive to verify their original self-conceptions. In a recent experiment by Swann and Hill (1982), subjects who had been given self-discrepant feedback on the dimension of dominant-submissive subsequently attempted to undermine this feedback. They behaved in a relatively more/less dominant fashion (i.e., more like their "true selves") toward the person providing the feedback than did subjects who had received self-consistent feedback. Presumably *self*-oriented disclosure offers an alternative way of refuting a challenge to the self-concept by allowing the discloser to emphasize to others what he or she is "really like." The prevalence of this form of disclosure on TV talk shows, where celebrities' public images are often discrepant from their private self-conceptions, is legendary.

Given that the research area in question is ostensibly concerned with *self*-disclosure, the lack of studies addressed to *self*-oriented disclosure is somewhat ironic. While retaining the individual as the unit of analysis, disclosure researchers have largely ignored Jourard's (1971b) claim that disclosure makes the self more concrete and tangible. One reason for this may lie in the popularity of social exchange theory (e.g., equity, Adams, 1965; Walster, Berscheid, & Walster, 1973) as an explanation for disclosure motivation (see Archer, 1979). Viewing disclosure as an offer implies that it is the target's response—whether he or she honors it—that really matters.

Orientation 2: Self-to-Other

We now turn from a discussion of disclosure that proceeds independently of audience involvement to a consideration of disclosure that *does* require a response from the target. The primary function of *self-to-other* disclosure is to *locate the self in relation to others* on some dimension of interest. It is thus designed to answer the single question, "Where do I stand.?" Particularly in situations that are new or ambiguous, there are often no objective reference points for evaluating important abilities and opinions (Festinger, 1950, 1954). Furthermore, *self*-oriented disclosure is inadequate for evaluation purposes. For example, a man may want to know whether the folk wisdom about "fighters" and "lovers" (i.e., that one cannot be good at both) applies to him. If he wants to know where he stands on either of these dimensions, it will not be sufficient for him to simply observe his own behavior. Likewise, the mere assertion that "I am the world's greatest fighter/lover" will not be satisfactory either. The information he seeks can only be obtained by comparing himself directly (observation) or indirectly (verbal mediation) to others on the dimensions of lovemaking and fighting ability. Disclosure that permits such comparison represents a social extension of the self that was absent in Orientation 1. It requires a response from the target of disclosure. In addition, it is an implicit acknowledgment of a common bond between discloser and target, since the discloser's level of ability on the dimsnsion in question exists only in relation to the target's (this is equally true in the domain of opinion, where "rightness" is the judgment criterion).

Self-to-other disclosure thus reflects a different interpersonal orientation than its predecessor as just discussed. The exercise of the former requires an interaction between discloser and target, so listener contribution is higher. However, the intended goal of the interaction is still quite limited. It is a simple request for information, with no necessary implications for future involvement between the partners. It follows, despite the fact the listener uniqueness is higher, that the basis for choosing a comparison person will be fairly nonspecific. Anyone who might have some knowledge or experience bearing on the relevant judgment dimension will be fair game for an inquiry. Given a choice, we will most likely choose a comparison person who is somewhat similar, since the information obtained from this informant will often be more diagnostic (see Latané, 1966). However, this qualification still leaves a rather large potential field of disclosure targets. .

Because *self-to-other* disclosure does not require any degree of prior contact between the parties, it is subject to socially determined norms of appropriateness, so as to protect individuals from overly intimate intrusions by others. In general, these oft-demonstrated proscriptions for disclosure (e.g., Chaikin & Derlega, 1974) operate so as to prevent unpleasant surprises. If, in his search for comparison information on lovemaking, a man presents a candid self-assessment to a female stranger on a subway train, he will almost certainly be rebuffed. The awareness of this possibility is likely to restrict information-gathering activities to more appropriate targets (e.g., acquaintances, friends, or roommates, Rubin & Shenker, 1978) in more suitable social settings (e.g., over a drink, Rohrberg & Sousa-Poza, 1976) in the comforts of one's living room, Brundage, Derlega, & Cash, 1977.

It also means that the target's response to the substantive content of one's disclosure, as well as to its intimacy level, can be highly informative (e.g., in determining whether or not the target is a good comparison person for me). For example, if one of us notices that a listener owns an Alfa-Romeo, we may reveal our most private sports car fantasies (off limits even to our wives) in an instant. Daher and Banikiotes' (1976) experiment confirmed the notion that people feel an affinity for others whose disclosure promises to be similar in content and intimacy.

By now it should be apparent that a considerable part of the disclosure literature is pertinent to the *self-to-other* orientation. Social comparison needs, from the group literature discussed earlier, are typically cited as a motivational basis for this kind of interpersonal communication. Schachter's (1951) classic study found that communications addressed to the deviant were longer and more personal in content. More recently, Latané, Ekman, and Joy (1966) observed that subjects in the "same boat," who worked in pairs under conditions of shared stress (moderately painful electric shocks), made more personal statements to each other during a free interaction period than did subjects in conditions where stress was not shared, or no one was stressed. The need to compare may explain why complete strangers quickly develop such surprising levels of intimacy when thrown together in the midst of a crisis or disaster only to go their separate ways when it is over.

Orientation 3: Other-to-Self

Frequently we are not so much interested in the answer to the *self-to-other* question, "Where do I stand?", as we are in the one for the question, "Where do I stand with you?" (i.e., "How are you going to behave toward me?"). The primary function of *other-to-self* disclosure is to *obtain benefits for the self that are controlled by others*. In interpersonal terms, the stakes here are much higher than in Orientations 1 and 2; and so, correspondingly, are listener uniqueness and listener contribution. The goal is to create a favorable impression of ourselves in the eyes of the target so that he or she will do certain things for us. For this reason, the criteria for choosing a target for disclosure must be more particularistic and the techniques more subtle.

For example, let us say that Bob is visiting the office of a particular accounting firm where he would like to be employed at a future time. There is one person in particular, the owner of the firm, whose views will prevail in any decision to hire. Bob wants to cultivate this person and to make himself attractive. Positive, intimate disclosure provides an obvious and tempting route to ingratiation (Jones & Wortman, 1973; Schneider & Eustis, 1972). Disclosure (whether positive or negative) can also directly influence the target's behavior toward the revealer in the desired direction. For example, Langer and Abelson (1972) found that prefacing a legitimate request for help with disclosure of one's personal state ("I'm really upset and distressed") resulted in more helping than when the request itself came first. The trick here, though, since Bob is trying to make a good impression, is for him to disclose personal information without revealing anything that is *inappropriately* intimate. He will probably want to match the intimacy and positivity of his self-statements to those of his target (Schneider & Eustis, 1972) to keep himself eligible for membership in and comparison with the new reference group. Bob would also be wise to (a) time his revelations to occur after a decent interval so as to appear modest (Jones & Gordon, 1972), and (b) temper his claims so they will not be at variance with the sort of information the target may *already* have obtained through more dispassionate sources (Baumeister & Jones, 1978).

Taking the perspective of the would-be employer, Ebenezer, would yield a different set of strategies. Low disclosure (relative to the job applicant) would seem most prudent. It would maintain the proper social distance between self and applicant, and would avoid personal involvement that might jeopardize the existing power differential. The use of nondisclosure as a strategy of high-power persons is consistent with the results of a study of communication patterns is a large business organization conducted by Slobin, Miller, and Porter (1968). They found greater willingness to self-disclose *up* the status hierarchy (from subordinate to boss) than vice versa. Slobin et al. have attributed this asymmetrical disclosure pattern primarily to low-power ingratiation motives. However, data from a recent experiment by Earle, Giuliano, and Archer (Note 1) imply that the asymmetrical pattern may result not only from the low-power partner's attempt to redefine the terms of the relationship (in the direction of greater equality), but also from the corresponding reluctance of the high-power partner to reopen negotiations on this issue.

In our example, then, it is likely that an asymmetrical pattern of disclosure between Bob and Ebenezer would result, with the job applicant doing the "chasing" and the boss doing the "running." However, another possible scenario would involve multiple "suitors," all wooing each other for the same or different reasons. In any case, the chief purpose of disclosure here is to establish unilateral control over the course of the interaction.

Other-to-self disclosure need not always be employed indirectly in crafting self-presentational strategies. There are probably circumstances under which the information revealed is itself of direct value and may be traded for attraction, favors, and other considerations. Petty and Mirels (1981) have argued along these lines that Brock's (1968) commodity theory pertains to disclosure. The theory states that resources have value to the extent that they are perceived to be scarce or unavailable to others. Consistent with this notion, Petty and Mirels' experiment indicated that people perceive intimate information as scarce. Furthermore, when (female) subjects' perceptions of its scarcity were eliminated, intimate disclosure did not lead to attraction.

Orientation 4: Other

The basic function of *other*-oriented disclosure is to *obtain information about others*. This is essentially different from the *self-to-other* orientation, in that the information sought here includes (a) non-self-relevant information, and hence (b) information about the potentially unique (nonnormative) characteristics of the target. It is likewise distinguishable from *other-to-self* disclosure because control (learning about the target so as to be able to manipulate him or her) is only one of the possibilities here. For example, seeking information about the other may simply be a gesture of recognition for that individual, in the same way that recognition of self is implicated in *self*-oriented disclosure. It's a way of saying, "Here's what I'm feeling, I wonder what *you're* feeling" and implies that "you count," "you're important," and so on. Alternatively, information acquisition may serve to assess the possible outcome of future interaction with this person (Altman & Taylor, 1973). *Other*-oriented disclosure is thus defined by the polar extremes of polite interest and relationship formation. Whichever is the case, this kind of disclosure requires greater listener contribution and implies greater listener uniqueness. It "works" as a way to obtain information because of the reciprocity phenomenon.

Since the disclosure reciprocity effect has been "cussed and discussed" at length by so many reviewers (e.g., Altman & Taylor, 1973; Archer, 1979; Chaikin & Derlega, 1974; Cozby, 1973), we do not intend to devote much space to retelling a well-plowed field. Suffice it to say that it is an often replicated finding that in a brief conversation or in the course of a relationship people tend to match one another in the intimacy and amount of self-information they reveal. Admittedly, in both types of social interaction there are limits, alternatives, and exceptions to the rule of reciprocity (e.g., Archer & Berg, 1978; Berg & Archer, 1980; Berg & Archer, 1982; Morton, 1978). However, it seems clear that reciprocal disclosure is a phenomenon of social life. Consequently, disclosure of one's own is a useful tool for collecting intelligence about others.

Orientation 5: Self-and-Other

Although Orientations 2-4 are social in the sense that they are aimed at evoking a response from the target, they are not necessarily social in any larger group sense. They require a response to "me" (the discloser) but not consideration of "us" (the discloser-recipient unit). In contrast, *self-and-other* disclosure functions to *acknowledge the interdependence between the participants in an interaction. Self-and-other* disclosure reflects the maximal degree of listener uniqueness and listener contribution because it explicitly or at least implicitly denotes the existence of a particular *relationship.* We certainly do not claim that this is the only (or even the most frequent) type of disclosure that occurs within the context of relationships. However, we do intend to indentify some of the distinctive elements of disclosure that only the awareness of or desire for a relationship can produce.

Initially, *self-and-other* disclosure can serve as a *symbol* of the bond that exists or is desired between the participants. Several experiments in first-encounter situations indicate that personalistic disclosure, the sort that sets the recipient apart from others as far as the revealer is concerned, is the surest path from intimacy to attraction (Archer & Burleson, 1980; Petty & Mirels, 1981; Taylor et al., 1981). At an even more basic level, participants in an interaction seem to be seeking signs of responsiveness in their partner's disclosure. They like corresponding patterns of content and intimacy that convey understanding, concern, and a willingness to continue and develop the interaction (Berg & Archer, 1980; Berg & Archer, 1982; Davis & Perkowitz, 1979).

Beyond its value as a symbol of the relationship's existence, *self-and-other* disclosure eventually enables the participants to arrive at a *definition* of that relationship (see Morton, Alexander, & Altman, 1976). If Dick reveals to Jane that he enjoys calling the shots, then they have defined mutually satisfactory ground rules for future interaction. Crises will arise to the extent that these definitions come into conflict. If Jane defines the relationship as an arena for sexual experimentation, and Dick conceives of it as a platonic encounter between two intellectuals, then the relationship is heading for trouble. The origin of a "crisis" can be either an acute disagreement on this issue, or the cumulative residue of chronic misunderstanding, resulting from the failure of one or both parties to disclose their own (implicit) definitions of the form of the relationship. In either case, the continued survival of the relationship may well depend upon whether mutual disclosure is now forthcoming. The few investigations of disclosure within marriages based upon case studies (Kamorovsky, 1962) and self-report measures (Hendrick, 1981; Levinger & Senn, 1967) all find that disclosure is related to marital satisfaction.

Unfortunately, the processes involved in defining relationships through *self-and-other* disclosure have so far received little in the way of attention from investigators. Thanks to a number of theorists, however, the future for such research may be bright. That the patterns of disclosure appear to change as relationships deepen and mature provides one point of departure. Altman and Taylor (1973) have reasonably interpreted the decline in reciprocity as evidence for greater flexibility in exchange brought about through the availability of additional channels of communication. Clark and Mills' (1979) distinction between exchange and communal relationships and Wegner and Giuliano's (in Wegner, 1982) demonstration of "group awareness" lead to a more daring interpretation. The definition of the relationship itself may have changed. Participants may no longer view themselves as incurring and discharging debts to one another, but rather as permanently obliged to meet each other's needs.

Another way to address the relationship-defining aspects of *self-and-other* disclosure is provided by the latest version of the theory of interdependence (Kelley & Thibaut, 1978). In applying this general model of interpersonal relations to close relationships, Kelley (1979) maintains that participants (a) are interdependent in terms of the consequences of their specific behaviors, with both commonality and conflict of interest, (b) are responsive to the other's as well as their own outcomes, and (c) attribute the outcomes of their interaction to the other's dispositions, both positive and negative.

Viewed in the terms of the theory, *self-and-other* disclosure provides a medium for couples to inform one another directly about their conceptions of and wishes for individual and joint outcomes rather than being forced to rely solely upon inferences based on behavior. In this way mutual disclosure may serve as a "hot line" to explain motives and so prevent unnecessary escalation of conflict. Even when the dispositions partners attribute to one another are uncomplimentary and in dispute, these perceptions should come as less of a surprise.

The issue of attributional conflict, disagreement between partners about the causes of one another's behavior (Kelley, 1979), brings to mind a third source of insight into *self-and-other* disclosure: the systems theory of communication (Watzlawick, Beavin, & Jackson, 1967; see Penman, 1980, for a review). Watzlawick et al. note that when communication is viewed as a system, a circular feedback loop instead of a linear chain, it makes little sense to single out one message as cause and another as effect. The mutual influence the participants have on one another leads to an uninterrupted sequence of interchanges. Nevertheless, partners tend to see such interchanges as causal chains and "punctuate" the sequence of events in different ways. To take an example from Watzlawick et al., a couple may have a marital problem involving the husband's passive withdrawal and the wife's nagging criticism. The husband may view the origins of the problem as, "She nags, so I withdraw." The wife, on the other hand, will probably view it in the opposite manner, "He withdraws, so I nag." An outside observer, the marriage counselor perhaps, sees only a mutually determined sequence of nagging and withdrawing.

Self-and-other disclosure, termed meta-communication by Watzlawick et al. because it is communication about communication, offers the participants an avenue through which to share perspectives on problematic interchanges. They may both learn that the punctuation each imposes upon the sequence is the key to breaking a vicious circle.

Orienting Disclosure to Group Processes

It is time to look more closely at the point at which we have arrived. The reader may have noticed that the ordering of the interpersonal orientations in the previous section could be considered hierarchical. If the act of disclosure is viewed as storytelling, then *self*-oriented disclosure is concerned with establishing the subjective truth value of that story ("This is me, isn't it?"). *Self-to-other* disclosure attempts to verify the story's correspondence with others of a similar nature ("Where do I stand?"), while *other-to-self* disclosure conspires to pleasingly package it for consumption ("how will it play in Peoria?"). Soliciting stories that are relevant or simply of interest from others is the goal of *other*-oriented disclosure ("How's it going for *you*?"), while for *self-and-other* disclosure it is the weaving of two or more such stories together like a novel or soap opera ("Will we live happily ever after?").

By now it should be clear why we are so uncomfortable with the term *self*-disclosure: Although all of these orientations involve disclosure only the first is completely "self-ish." They steadily become more interpersonal. We tend to accept the implication of the hierarchical configuration that the more self-oriented are also the more fundamental. Yet a single sequence of disclosures may find the revealer(s) taking any and all of these orientations, intra- and interpersonal, at one point or another.

The advantages of conceptualizing disclosure in terms of several interpersonal orientations and the functions they serve are twofold, and deal with perspective. This scheme brings into focus where investigators have been and where they ought to be going both in self-disclosure and in group processes.

Whenever self-disclosure investigators congregate they complain and wonder about why their research has had such a limited impact on mainstream social psychology. Categorizing their efforts in terms of our scheme suggests an answer. Most self-disclosure studies fall into the *other-to-self* and *other* orientations. Investigators have been obsessed with finding simple relationships between disclosure and attraction and simple explanations for disclosure reciprocity. The result of these single-minded, laboratory-bound, and generally unsuccessful quests (see Archer, 1979; Lynn, 1978) has been a tendency to forget their oft-repeated claim that their real interests lie in the relationships questions of the *self-and-other* orientation. Ironically enough, it was the failure of the same sort of single-minded approach that led disclosure researchers to abandon their original interest in the role of disclosure in personality. Now the field finds itself unwittingly marooned in social exchange and self-presentation and neither fish (the study of developing self-conceptions through communication) nor fowl (the study of developing relationships through communication).

The way off these shoals seems clear enough in terms of the orientations. Instead of just paying lip service to relationships, most disclosure researchers should actually focus their investigations on the *self-and-other* questions central to relationships. It would also be a good idea if a few of them with a personality bent would finally explore the part disclosure plays in developing and structuring the self (the *self* orientation) instead of simply assuming that it does and how it does.

While self-disclosure aficionados have recently begun to whisper their concerns in private, followers of group process have long since made public their fears that it, too, has become a backwater of social psychology (Pepitone, 1981; Steiner, 1974). We would add to their list of contributing causes an overly narrow definition of communication and of the group itself. Most of what investigators of group dynamics have had to say about disclosure lies within our *self-to-other* and *other-to-self* orientations. These undoubtedly reflect major uses of disclosure in laboratory task groups of the business analog or experiential variety consisting or three or more persons. Unfortunately, they leave untouched the intimate dyadic exchanges that constitute such a large and significant proportion of our lives.

Our remedy for making waves with group processes again also turns on the analysis of the interpersonal orientations of disclosure. More investigators of groups should concentrate on how people develop and change their notions of what their ad hoc social groups, especially close relationships, are through *self-and-other* disclosure. In addition to exploring this fundamental issue, it would also be wise if even some of those interested in more traditional questions of group process took the role of disclosure into account. The payoffs might be surprising.

Is there any reason why the *self* and *other* in our scheme should not be groups and their spokespersons rather than individuals? This kind of substitution would unlock the implications of disclosure for intergroup relations (see Austin & Worchel, 1979, for a review), and vice versa. Does some form of leadership emerge in disclosing dyads as it does in other groups? Davis' (1976) acquaintanceship work suggests that it does in the person of the higher disclosing member and Miller, Berg, and Archer's (1983) findings imply that responsive people make more effective leaders in interactions involving intimacy. Does disclosure within the group fall victim to the social loafing phenomenon that saps group productivity in other spheres (Latané, Williams, & Harkins, 1979)? The results of a study of disclosure in dyads and triads by Taylor, DeSoto, & Lieb (1979) suggest it might. Does disclosure provide a lever to exert minority influence in situations involving the exercise of power (Moscovici & Faucheaux, 1972)? Perhaps so, because even a disliked deviant can coax reciprocal disclosure out of her partner (Derlega et al., 1973).

We could go on with these examples, but we think the point has been made: The group processes family would do well to reconsider the suitor in the parlor. Disclosure in its present form may not look like much of a catch, but like all prospective husbands, marriage may change it for the better. Furthermore, it is well to remember that the fine old family, for all of its respectability, is sorely in need of a little youthful vigor. They really need each other.

Of course it will not be easy at first. Traditions die hard. We will have to consider process variables rather than just depth and breadth, and to employ the group rather than the individual as our unit of analysis. Moreover, we will be forced to step outside the laboratory to learn new methods of sampling interpersonal behavior when and where it occurs (e.g., Wheeler & Nezlek, 1977) and new techniques for analyzing sequences of communication (e.g., Penman, 1980). Studying relationships is a complex proposition that gives us all pause. But it is about time we heeded those lonely voices crying in the wilderness (e.g., Huston & Levinger, 1978; Pepitone, 1981; Steiner, 1974) for a truly *social* social psychology instead of just feeling guilty about it.

Our ambivalence about embarking upon the study of anything so enigmatic as relationships brings to mind the final scene from the movie, *Annie Hall,* in which Woody Allen ponders the reason he continues to cultivate relationships despite his frequent and disillusioning break-ups. He likens it to the dilemma of the man whose brother thought he was a chicken. When asked by the psychiatrist why he did not turn his brother over to an institution, he answered, "I would, but I need the eggs." Thinking we can ever understand the role of personal communication in relationships may be just as preposterous, but social psychology needs the eggs.

Acknowledgment. The authors wish to thank Irwin Altman, Toni Giuliano, George Levinger, Bill Swann, John Thibaut, Robin Vallacher, and Dan Wegner for their invaluable comments on the initial drafts of this chapter. Preparation of the chapter was supported by NIMH Grant 33199 to the first author.

Reference Note

1. Earle, W. B., Giuliano, A., & Archer, R. L. *Lonely at the top: The effect of power and information flow in the dyad.* Unpublished manuscript, University of Texas at Austin, 1983.

References

Adams, J. S. Inequity in social exchange. In L. Berkowitz (Ed.), *Advances in experimental social psychology* (Vol. 2). New York: Academic Press, 1965.

Altman, I. *The environment and social behavior.* Monterey, Calif.: Brooks/Cole, 1975.

Altman, I., & Taylor, D. A. *Social penetration: The developments of interpersonal relationships.* New York: Holt, Rinehart and Winston, 1973.

Altman, I., Vinsel, A., & Brown, B. B. Dialectic conceptions in social psychology: An application to social penetration and privacy regulation. In L. Berkowitz (Ed.), *Advances in experimental social psychology* (Vol. 14). New York: Academic Press, 1981.

Archer, R. L. The role of personality and the social situation. In G. J. Chelune (Ed.), *Self-disclosure.* San Francisco: Jossey-Bass, 1979.

Archer, R. L. Self-disclosure. In D. M. Wegner & R. Vallacher (Eds.), *The self in social psychology.* New York: Oxford University Press, 1980.

Archer, R. L., & Berg, J. H. Disclosure reciprocity and its limits: A reactance analysis. *Journal of Experimental Social Psychology,* 1978, *14,* 527-540.

Archer, R. L., & Burleson, J. A. The effects of timing of self-disclosure on attraction and reciprocity. *Journal of Personality and Social Psychology,* 1980, *38,* 120-130.

Argyle, M., & Dean, J. Eye-contact, distance and affiliation. *Sociometry,* 1965, *28,* 289-304.

Austin, W. G., & Worchel, S. (Eds). *The psychology of intergroup relations.* Monterey, Calif.: Brooks/Cole, 1979.

Back, K. W. *Beyond words: The story of sensitivity training and the encounter movement.* Baltimore: Penguin Books, 1973.

Baumeister, R. F., & Jones, E. E. When self-presentation is constrained by the target's knowldege: Consistency and compensation. *Journal of Personality and Social Psychology,* 1978, *36,* 608-618.

Bem, D. Self-perception theory. In L. Berkowtiz (Ed.), *Advances in experimental social psychology* (Vol. 6). New York: Academic Press, 1972.

Bennis, W. G., & Shepard, H. A. A theory of group development. *Human Relations,* 1956, *9,* 415-437.

Berg, J. H., & Archer, R. L. Disclosure or concern: A second look at liking for the norm breaker. *Journal of Personality,* 1980, *48,* 245-257.

Berg, J. H., & Archer, R. L. Responses to the self-disclosure and interaction goals. *Journal of Personality,* 1980, *48,* 245-257.

Berg, J. H., & Archer, R. L. Responses to self-disclosure and interaction goals. *Journal of Experimental Social Psychology,* 1982, *18,* 501-512.

Brock, T. C. Implications of commodity theory for value change. In A. G. Greenwald, T. C. Brock, & T. M. Ostrom (Eds.), *Psychological foundations of attitudes.* New York: Academic Press, 1968.

Brundage, L. E., Derlega, V. J., & Cash, T. F. The effects of physical attractiveness and need for approval on self-disclosure. *Personality and Social Psychology Bulletin,* 1977, *3,* 63-66.

Buys, C. J. Humans would do better without groups. *Personality and Social Psychology Bulletin,* 1978, *4,* 123-125.

Byrne, D. *The attraction paradigm.* New York: Academic Press, 1971.

Cartwright, D., & Zander, A. (Eds.). *Group dynamics: Research and theory* (3rd ed.). New York: Harper & Row, 1968.

Chaikin, A. L., & Derlega, V. J. *Self-disclosure*. Morristown, N. J.: General Learning Press, 1974.

Chelune, G. J. Measuring openness in interpersonal communication. In G. J. Chelune (Ed.), *Self-disclosure*. San Francisco: Jossey-Bass, 1979.

Clark, M. S., & Mills, J. Interpersonal attraction in exchange and communal relationships. *Journal of Personality and Social Psychology*, 1979, *37*, 12-24.

Cozby, P. C. Self-disclosure: A literature review. *Psychological Bulletin*, 1973, *79*, 73-91.

Daher, D. M., & Banikiotes, P. G. Interpersonal attraction and rewarding aspects of disclosure content and level. *Journal of Personality and Social Psychology*, 1976, *33*, 492-496.

Davis, D., & Perkowitz, W. T. Consequences of responsiveness in dyadic interactions: Effects of probability of response and proportion of content-related responses. *Journal of Personality and Social Psychology*, 1979, *37*, 534-550.

Davis, J. D. Self-disclosure as an acquaintance exercise: Responsibility for level of intimacy. *Journal of Personality and Social Psychology*, 1976, *33*, 787-792.

Derlega, V. J., & Grzelak, J. Appropriateness of self-disclosure. In G. J. Chelune (Ed.), *Self-disclosure*. San Francisco: Jossey-Bass, 1979.

Derlega, V. J., Harris, M. S., & Chaikin, A. L. Self-disclosure reciprocity, liking, and the deviant. *Journal of Experimental Social Psychology*, 1973, *9*, 277-284.

Derlega, V. J., Wilson, M., & Chaikin, A. L. Friendship and disclosure reciprocity. *Journal of Personality and Social Psychology*, 1976, *34*, 578-582.

Doster, J. A., & Nesbitt, J. G. Psychotherapy and self-disclosure. In G. J. Chelune (Ed.), *Self-disclosure*. San Francisco: Jossey-Bass, 1979.

Ehrlich, H. J., & Graeven, D. B. Reciprocal self-disclosure in a dyad. *Journal of Experimental Social Psychology*, 1971, *7*, 389-400.

Felipe, N., & Sommer, R. Invasions of personal space. *Social Problems*, 1966, *14*, 206-214.

Festinger, L. Informal social communication. *Psychological Review*, 1950, *57*, 271-282.

Festinger, L. A theory of social comparison processes. *Human Relations*, 1954, *7*, 117-140.

Festinger, L., Schachter, S. S., & Back, K. *Social pressures in informal groups: A study of human factors in housing*. New York: Harper & Row, 1950.

Fishbein, M. J., & Laird, J. D. Concealment and disclosure: Some effects of information control on the person who controls. *Journal of Experimental Social Psychology*, 1979, *15*, 114-121.

Gerard, H. B., & Rabbie, J. M. Fear and social comparison. *Journal of Abnormal and Social Psychology*, 1961, *62*, 586-592.

Goodstein, L. D. & Reinecker, V. M. Factors affecting self-disclosure: A review of the literature. In B. Maher (Ed.), *Progress in experimental personality research* (Vol. 7). New York: Academic Press, 1974.

Guthrie, E. R. *The psychology of learning*. (Rev. Ed.). New York: Harper & Row, 1952.

Hendrick, S. S. Self-disclosure and marital satisfaction. *Journal of Personality and Social Psychology*, 1981, *40*, 1150-1158.

Hurwitz, J. I., Zander, A. F., & Hymovitch, B. Some effects of power on the relations among group members. In D. Cartwright & A. Zander (Eds.), *Group dynamics: Research and theory.* Evanston, Ill.: Row, Peterson, 1953.

Huston, T., & Levinger, G. Interpersonal attraction and relationships. In M. R. Rosenzweig & L. Porter (Eds.), *Annual Review of Psychology* (Vol. 29). Palo Alto, Calif.: Annual Reviews, 1978.

Jones, E. E., & Archer, R. L. Are there special effects of personalistic self-disclosure? *Journal of Experimental Social Psychology,* 1976, *12,* 180-193.

Jones, E. E., & Gordon, E. M. Timing of self-disclosure and its effects on personal attraction. *Journal of Personality and Social Psychology,* 1972, *24,* 358-365.

Jones, E. E., & Wortman, C. *Ingratiation: An attributional approach.* Morristown, N. J.: General Learning Press, 1973.

Jourard, S. M. Self-disclosure and other-cathexis. *Journal of Abnormal and Social Psychology,* 1959, *59,* 428-431.

Jourard, S. M. *Self-disclosure: An experimental analysis of the transparent self.* New York: Wiley, 1971.(a)

Jourard, S. M. *The transparent self.* New York: Van Nostrand, 1964.

Jourard, S. M. *The transparent self* (rev. ed.). New York: Van Nostrand Reinhold, 1971.(b)

Jourard, S. M., & Friedman, R. Experimenter-subject "distance" and self-disclosure. *Journal of Personality and Social Psychology,* 1970, *15,* 278-282.

Jourard, S. M., & Landsman, M. J. Cognition, cathexis, and the "dyadic effect" in men's self-disclosing behavior. *Merrill Palmer Quarterly,* 1960, *6,* 178-186.

Jourard, S. M., & Lasakow, P. Some factors in self-disclosure. *Journal of Abnormal and Social Psychology,* 1958, *56,* 91-98.

Kelley, H. H. *Personal relationships.* New York: Lawrence Erlbaum, 1979.

Kelley, H. H., & Thibaut, J. W. *Interpersonal relations: A theory of interdependence.* New York: Wiley, 1978.

Kamorovsky, M. *Blue-collar marriage.* New York: Random House, 1962.

Lakin, M. *Interpersonal encounter: Theory and practice in sensitivity training.* New York: McGraw-Hill, 1972.

Langer, E. J., & Abelson, R. P. The semantics of asking a favor: How to succeed in getting help without really dying. *Journal of Personality and Social Psychology,* 1972, *24,* 26-32.

Latané, B. Studies in social comparison-introduction and overview. *Journal of Experimental Social Psychology,* 1966, Supplement 1, 80-94.

Latané, B., Ekman, J., & Joy, V. Shared stress and interpersonal attraction. *Journal of Experimental Social Psychology,* 1966, Supplement 1, 80-94.

Latané, B., Williams, K., & Harkins, S. Many hands make light the work: The causes and consequences of social loafing. *Journal of Personality and Social Psychology,* 1979, *37,* 822-832.

Levinger, G. A three-level approach to attraction. Toward an understanding of pair relatedness. In T. L. Huston (Ed.), *Foundations of interpersonal attraction.* New York: Academic Press, 1974.

Levinger, G., & Senn, D. J. Disclosure of feelings in marriage. *Merrill Palmer Quarterly,* 1967, *13,* 237-249.

Levinger, G., & Snoek, J. D. *Attraction in relationship: A new look at interpersonal attraction*. Morristown, N.J.: General Learning Press, 1972.

Lewin, K. *A dynamic theory of personality*. New York: McGraw-Hill, 1935.

Lewin, K. *Principles of topological psychology*. New York: McGraw-Hill, 1936.

Lynn, S. J. Three theories of self-disclosure exchange. *Journal of Experimental Social Psychology*, 1978, *5*, 466-479.

Maslow, A. H. *Motivation and personality*. New York: Harper, 1954.

Meichenbaum, D. *Cognitive behavior modification: An integrative approach*. New York: Plenum Press, 1977.

Miller, L. C., Berg, J. H., & Archer, R. L. Openers: Individuals who elicit intimate self-disclosure. *Journal of Personality and Social Psychology*, 1983, *44*, 1234-1244.

Morton, T. L. Intimacy and reciprocity of exchange: A comparison of spouses and strangers. *Journal of Personality and Social Psychology*, 1978, *36*, 72-81.

Morton, T. L., Alexander, J. F., & Altman, I. Communication and relationship definition. In G. R. Miller (Ed.), *Explorations in interpersonal communication research*. (Sage Annual Reviews of communication research, Vol. 5). Beverly Hills, Calif.: Sage, 1976.

Moscovici, S., & Faucheaux, C. Social influence, conformity bias, and the study of active minorities. In L. Berkowtiz (Ed.), *Advances in experimental social psychology* (Vol. 6). New York: Academic Press, 1972.

Penman, R. *Communication processes and relationships*. London: Academic Press, 1980.

Pepitone, A. Lessons from the history of social psychology. *American Psychologist*, 1981, *36*, 972-985.

Petty, R. E., & Mirels, H. L. Intimacy and scarcity: Effects on interpersonal attraction for males and females. *Personality and Social Psychology Bulletin*, 1981, *7*, 493-503.

Progoff, I. *At a journal workshop*. New York: Dialogue House Library, 1975.

Rickers-Ovisiankina, M. A. Social accessibility in three age groups. *Psychological Reports*, 1956, *2*, 283-294.

Rickers-Ovsiankina, M. A., & Kusmin, A. A. Individual differences in social accessibility. *Psychological Reports*, 1958, *4*, 391-406.

Rogers, C. *Client-centered therapy*. Boston: Houghton Mifflin, 1951.

Rohrberg, R. B., & Sousa-Poza, J. F. Alcohol, field-dependence, and dyadic self-disclosure. *Psychological Reports*, 1976, *39*, 1151-1161.

Rubin, Z. Disclosing oneself to a stranger: Reciprocity and its limits. *Journal of Experimental Social Psychology*, 1975, *11*, 233-260.

Rubin, Z. & Shenker, S. Friendship, proximity and self-disclosure. *Journal of Personality*, 1978, *46*, 1-22.

Runge, T. E., & Archer, R. L. Reactions to the disclosure of public and private self-information. *Social Psychology Quarterly*, 1981, *44*, 357-362.

Schachter, S. Deviation, rejection, and communication. *Journal of Abnormal and Social Psychology*, 1951, *46*, 190-207.

Schachter, S. *The psychology of affiliation*. Stanford, Calif.: Stanford University Press, 1959.

Schein, E. H., & Bennis, W. G. *Personal and organizational change through group methods: A laboratory approach.* New York: Wiley, 1965.

Schneider, D. J., & Eustis, A. C. Effects of ingratiation motivation, target positiveness, and revealingness on self-presentation. *Journal of Personality and Social Psychology,* 1972, *22,* 149-155.

Shaver, P., & Klinnert, M. Implications of developmental research for Schachter's theories of affiliation and emotion. In L. Wheeler (Ed.), *Review of personality and social psychology* (Vol. 3). Beverly Hills, Calif.: Sage, 1982.

Shaw, M. E. Communication networks. In L. Berkowitz (Ed.), *Advances in experimental social psychology* (Vol. 1). New York: Academic Press, 1964.

Shaw, M. E. *Group dynamics: The psychology of small group behavior* (3rd ed.). New York: McGraw-Hill, 1981.

Slobin, D. I., Miller, S. H., & Porter, L. W. Forms of address and social relations in a business organization. *Journal of Personality and Social Psychology,* 1968, *8,* 289-293.

Steiner, I. Whatever happened to the group in social psychology? *Journal of Experimental Social Psychology,* 1974, *10,* 94-108.

Swann, W. B. Self-verification: Bringing social reality into harmony with the self. In J. Suls and A. G. Greenwald (Ed.), *Psychological perspectives on the self* (Vol. 2). Hillsdale, N.J.: Lawrence Erlbaum, in press.

Swann, W. B., & Hill, C. A. The temporal stability of laboratory-induced changes in self-ratings. *Journal of Personality and Social Psychology,* 1982, *43,* 59-66.

Taylor, D. A. Motivational bases. In G. J. Chelune (Ed.), *Self-disclosure.* San Francisco: Jossey-Bass, 1979.

Taylor, D. A., Gould, R. J., & Brounstein, P. J. Effects of personalistic self-disclosure. *Personality and Social Psychology Bulletin,* 1981, *7,* 487-492.

Taylor, R. B., DeSoto, C. B., & Lieb, R. Sharing secrets: Disclosure and discretion in dyads and triads. *Journal of Personality and Social Psychology,* 1979, *37,* 1196-1203.

Thibaut, J. An experimental study of the cohesiveness of underpriveleged groups. *Human Relations,* 1950, *3,* 251-278.

Thibaut, J. W., & Kelley, H. H. *The social psychology of groups.* New York: Wiley, 1959.

Walster, E., Berscheid, E., & Walster, G. W. New directions in equity research. *Journal of Personality and Social Psychology,* 1973, *25,* 151-76.

Watzlawick, P., Beavin, J. H., & Jackson, D. D. *Pragmatics of human communication.* London: Faber & Faber, 1967.

Wegner, D. M. Justice and the awareness of social entities. In J. Greenberg & R. L. Cohen (Eds.), *Equity and justice in social behavior.* New York: Academic Press, 1982.

Wheeler, L., & Nezlek, J. Sex differences in social participation. *Journal of Personality and Social Psychology,* 1977, *35,* 742-754.

Wicklund, R. A., & Gollwitzer, P. M. Symbolic self-completion, attempted influence, and self-deprecation. *Basic and Applied Social Psychology,* 1981, *2,* 89-114.

Winter, S. K. Developmental stages in the roles and concerns of group co-leaders. *Small Group Behavior,* 1976, *7,* 349-362.

Won-Doornink, M. J. On getting to know you: The association between the stage of a relationship and reciprocity of self-disclosure. *Journal of Experimental Social Psychology,* 1979, *15,* 229-241.

Zimbardo, P. G., & Formica, R. Emotional comparison and self-esteem as determinants of affiliation. *Journal of Personality,* 1963, *31,* 141-162.

Chapter 13
Influences of Past Relationships on Subsequent Ones

William Ickes

How do past relationships influence subsequent ones? This question is an important one for social psychology in general and for the study of group processes in particular. Since it is almost axiomatic that past relationships *do* influence relationships formed later, our attempt to study the nature of this influence may reward us with an increased capacity to understand and even predict the interaction that occurs in dyads and larger groups.

Assuming that past relationships influence subsequent ones, what forms does this influence take? Do past relationships serve as "templates" for future relationships, such that individuals tend to gravitate toward new interaction partners with whom they can replicate important features of previous relationships with earlier partners? Or, do past relationships have less influence on one's choice of specific partners for future interactions than on one's more general style of relating to new interaction partners? If the influences exerted by past relationships can be identified, what are their limiting conditions and what are their implications for our understanding of interpersonal behavior and group processes?

Like most interesting questions in the social sciences, the questions posed above are considerably easier to ask than to answer. Entire volumes on the socialization process and its effects on personality and social development have been written to provide frameworks for simply addressing such questions, let alone answering them. Given the scope and complexity of the task, the goal of this brief chapter is, by constraint, fairly modest. Instead of exploring all of the possible ways past relationships might influence subsequent ones, I will focus on only one specific and necessarily limited attempt to answer questions such as those posed above: that provided by Walter Toman's (1961, 1969, 1976) "family constellation" theory.

In defense of this limitation in scope, there are a number of reasons why Toman's theory offers a useful focus for the chapter. First, Toman's theory is perhaps the best known and theoretically most explicit attempt to use aspects of past relationships to predict aspects of later ones. Second, the particular "past relationships" used as the basis for such prediction—individual's long-term interactions with their siblings—are intuitively compelling as predictors. Because sibling relationships are assumed to exert a pervasive impact on the individual's social development over a period that typically extends from early childhood through late adolescence, they should permit a strong test of the proposition that past relationships influence subsequent ones. Third, the particular "subsequent relationships" that the theory attempts to predict—heterosexual friendship, dating, and marriage relationships—have traditionally been of special interest and importance to clinical, personality, and social psychologists (cf. Berscheid, in press; Gottman, 1979). Fourth, a considerable body of empirical research has been conducted which bears either directly or indirectly on Toman's theory and therefore permits a reasonably clear evaluation of its predictive validity. For all of these reasons, Toman's "family constellation" theory may provide a useful starting point for our inquiry.

The chapter begins with a brief description of Toman's theory and continues with a review of studies explicitly designed to test it. The results of other relevant studies are then examined—studies that were not designed as tests of Toman's hypotheses but that raise important questions about the adequacy of his theoretical model. Following this review, a study is described that permitted a test of the competing predictions derived from Toman's theory and from the set of research findings in conflict with it. The results of this study are discussed and their broader theoretical implications are explored. In the final section, some speculations are offered regarding the development of a more adequate theoretical model of the influences that past relationships exert on subsequent interactions in dyads and small groups.

Toman's "Family Constellation" Theory

Toman (1961, 1969, 1976) has stated the essential thesis of his "family constellation" theory in the following way:

> whatever people a person chooses for spouses, friends, partners, assistants, superiors, and the like, will be co-determined by the kind of people a person has been living with the longest, most intimately, and most regularly, and by all incidental losses of such people. In short: new interpersonal relationships will be co-determined by old ones. More precisely and elaborately: *new (extra-familial...) interpersonal relationships will duplicate the earliest (intra-familial...) interpersonal relationships in degrees varying from complete duplication to none at all. What is more: the closer the new relationships come in kind to the old ones, ... other things being equal, the better will the person be prepared for the new ones, and the greater their likelihood to last and to be happy and successful.* (Toman, 1969, p. 6, italics in original)

According to Toman, the earliest interpersonal relationships that individuals experience and use as templates for their subsequent relationships are those with parents and siblings. Although the influence of relationships with parents is expected to have the greatest impact on only children, it is assumed that in families of two, three, four, or more children the influence of sibling relationships will predominate. It is further assumed that two characteristics of the individuals involved in these early relationships—their sexes and their age ranks—are of major importance in determining the influence that their intrafamilial relationship will exert on their future, extrafamilial ones.

> The implication is that people learn predominantly from their siblings a kind of senior or junior attitude to others and a capacity to relate well to members of the opposite sex. Toman believes that people who have had no siblings of senior rank experience what he calls "rank conflict" with those who are of senior rank, and that those who have had no opposite sex siblings experience "sex conflict" with members of the opposite sex. (Birtchnell & Mayhew, 1977, p. 18)

In other words, to the extent that two individuals complement each other by providing each other with the same configuration of sex and age-rank relations that each experienced in an early, intrafamilial relationship, their own relationship is expected to be mutually rewarding and successful. Conversely, to the extent that two individuals fail to complement each other in one or both of these respects, their relationship is expected to be unrewarding and unsuccessful.

The theory's predictions regarding sex and age-rank complementarity are assumed to generalize across both same-sex (male-male, female-female) and mixed-sex (male-female) dyads. However, the mixed-sex cases (heterosexual dyadic relationships) have received the greatest theoretical and empirical attention because of their implications for mate selection and marital satisfaction. For prototypic cases involving dyad members from two-sibling families, the theory predicts that heterosexual dyadic relationships will be most successful and satisfactory when (a) the older brother of a younger sister is paired with the younger sister of an older brother, or (b) the younger brother of an older sister is paired with the older sister of a younger brother. Because the age ranks of the partners in each of these relationships are complementary, the partners are expected to have minimal conflict over seniority rights. Also, because each of the partners is used to relating with someone of the opposite sex, potential sex conflicts are expected to be minimal as well.

On the other hand, heterosexual dyadic relationships should be least successful and satisfactory when neither sex nor age-rank complementarity occur, that is, when (a) the older brother of a younger brother is paired with the older sister of a younger sister, or (b) the youngest brother of an older brother is paired with the younger sister of an older sister. In these cases, the potential for both sex conflict and age-rank conflict is expected to be maximal, and the resulting interactions are expected to be the least rewarding of any of the 16 combinations involving male and female dyad members who are each from two-sibling families. Other combinations—those in which only one of the two types of complementarity occur—are expected to reveal intermediate levels of interactional satisfaction and success.

Research Designed to Test Toman's Theory

A number of studies have been designed to test the major predictions of Toman's theory. Toman's own research (Toman, 1959, 1962, 1964; Toman & Gray, 1961) was the first to appear, and although Toman claimed that the bulk of his findings were supportive (e.g., Toman, 1964), an evaluation of these studies by Birtchnell and Mayhew (1977) led them to draw a very different conclusion. They argued that:

> [none] of these studies are methodologically adequate to test this theory. In the paper introducing his theory, Toman was concerned with sibling matches of patients' parents and referred to a series of 40 cases among whose parents there was not a single fully optimal match. In 31 of the cases there were either sex or rank conflicts or both, and in seven he found examples of the worst possible types of matches. He did not have a control group with which to compare these cases. In one small study of 40 marriages he showed a just significant tendency for complementarity in mate selection but did not consider marital success (Toman, 1964). Toman and Gray (1961) studied parents of disturbed children compared with parents of college students and other married couples. They considered rank and sex of partners' siblings separately, i.e., not in combination, and the results were significant in the anticipated direction. His only study of divorced and nondivorced married couples (Toman, 1962) involved 16 couples in each group. Again he calculated what he called "total conflict disposition" which involved summating the results of the first two comparisons and dividing by two. This is not the same, of course, as examining rank by sex for each couple. His results were once more significant in the anticipated direction. (pp. 18-19)

Given that Toman's own findings were not only somewhat mixed but also open to criticism on methodological grounds, independent attempts to test the theory should be of particular interest and importance. The first of these independent studies, conducted by Levinger and Sonnheim (1965), tested the hypotheses that the partners in normal marriages will "(a) show greater birth-order complementarity, (b) show greater sibling sex complementarity, [and] (c) show greater combined birth rank and sex complementarity" than the partners in distressed marriages (p. 138). Levinger and Sonnheim found no support for any of these hypotheses in their comparisons of 24 "disturbed" and 36 "normal" married couples.

Other independent tests of the theory that also have focused on its predictions regarding mate selection and marital satisfaction have similarly failed to find any support for them. In survey studies conducted in the United States by Kemper (1966) and Touhey (1971), and in England by Birtchnell and Mayhew (1977, Study 1), no evidence was found for the hypothesized relationships between the subjects' birth orders and those of their spouses, despite the fact that the sample sizes in all three studies were large (246, 200 and 2000, respectively). A significant relationship between the birth orders of husbands and wives was found in a survey of 146 faculty members at a large state university (Ward, Castro, & Wilcox, 1974); however, this relationship was in a direction *opposite* that predicted by Toman's theory.

A study by Mendelsohn, Linden, Gruen, and Curran (1974) found support for Toman's predictions regarding both sex complementarity and rank complementarity in 64 heterosexual, college-age couples who had been paired in what was ostensibly a "computer dating program." On the other hand, no such support was found by Birtchnell and Mayhew (1977, Study 2) in a survey study of friendship formation involving a much larger sample of university undergraduates (145 males and 184 females).

Taken collectively, the studies most directly relevant to Toman's theory fail to provide much support for it. As Birtchnell and Mayhew (1977, p. 32) have noted, it is probably unfortunate that most of the support has come from Toman's own research.

Other Relevant Research

The predictive validity of Toman's theory is called into question not only by the results of studies explicitly designed to test it, but by the results of other relevant studies as well. Specifically, there are a number of studies in the birth-order literature that are also relevant to Toman's predictions, even though the studies were not designed to test these predictions.

The birth-order literature suggests that differences in the early social experience of first- and later-born individuals underlie a range of behavioral differences observed later in the life span. Because first-borns interact more, and more exclusively, with adults than do later-borns during their early years, first-borns tend to become adult-oriented whereas later-borns tend to become peer-oriented (Markus, 1981; McArthur, 1956; Sells & Roff, 1963). This difference in orientation appears to be related to findings indicating that first-borns actually receive more parental attention, direction, and control than do later-borns (Jacobs & Moss, 1976; Schaller, 1978; see also Conners, 1963).

Among the best-established consequences of this differential socialization are: (a) the greater propensity of first-borns to conform to authority (e.g., Adams, 1972) and to identify with and adopt task-oriented leadership roles (e.g., Chemers, 1970; Hardy, 1972; Hardy, Hunt, & Lehr, 1978); (b) the greater educational attainment of first-borns, including college attainment (see reviews by Adams, 1972, and Warren, 1966, but also see Smelser & Stewart, 1968); and (c) the greater achievement and intelligence of first-borns (e.g., Belmont & Marolla, 1973; Breland, 1973; Zajonc & Markus, 1975; Zajonc, Markus, & Markus, 1979).[1] As if these apparent advantages of first-borns over later-borns were not enough, first-borns also (d) have more pride in themselves (Howarth, 1980) and higher self-esteem (Schwab & Lundgren, 1978);

---

[1] Although the "confluence model" of Zajonc and his colleagues acknowledges that the average intellectual performance of first-borns invariably exceeds that of last-borns in studies of older adolescents and adults (Zajonc et al., 1979, p. 1333), the pattern of differences is demonstrated to be much more complicated in studies conducted during subjects' childhood and early adolescent years. The "confluence model" (e.g., Zajonc & Markus, 1975; Zajonc et al., 1979) offers a compelling account of the entire pattern of age-related differences based on the assumption that "effects previously thought to be associated with birth order [per se] are . . . mediated substantially by family size and the spacing of births" (Zajonc et al., 1979, p. 1328).

(e) are accorded more status than their later-born siblings as a function of age (Eisenstadt, 1956; Moore, 1969); (f) are perceived as dominant in sibling interactions (Sutton-Smith & Rosenberg, 1968, 1970); and (g) are more likely to administer punishment to a same-sex peer in a Buss-type shock paradigm (Ickes, Note 1).

The picture is not entirely one-sided, however, as Markus (1981) and others have noted. By becoming adult-oriented and internalizing adult standards for intellectual performance and achievement, first-borns also tend to become more stressed, anxious, and neurotic than later-borns (Howarth, 1980; Sutton & McIntire, 1977). Moreover, first-borns apparently fail to develop their social skills to the degree that later-borns do. Because first-borns typically have only adult roles to model early in life whereas later-borns have both adult and peer (i.e., sibling) roles to model, later-borns seem to develop a wider repertoire of role-playing skills. These social skill differences are suggested by (a) the greater self-reported participation of later-borns in drama, and (b) peer ratings indicating that later-borns are better than first-borns at the type of role-playing that acting requires (Sutton-Smith & Rosenberg, 1966). Such differences also are evidenced by studies indicating that, relative to first-borns, later-borns (c) are rated by themselves (McArthur, 1956) and by their teachers (Miller & Maruyama, 1976) as more socially skilled, (d) are rated by their peers as more popular (a finding that generalizes across the variables of age, race, sex, and socioeconomic status) (Miller & Maruyama, 1976; Schachter, 1964), and (e) are more accepting of their peers in return (Sells & Roff, 1963).

Although the wider range of role models available to later-borns than to first-borns may account in part for these social skill differences, Miller and Maruyama (1976) have identified another, possibly more important factor in the relative status and power of first- versus later-born siblings:

> Because age grading—the hierarchical awarding of status as a function of age—apparently occurs universally in childhood and adolescence (e.g., Eisenstadt, 1956; Moore, 1969), younger children must typically grow up possessing less power than their older siblings. Indeed, first-borns are perceived as dominant in sibling interactions (Sutton-Smith & Rosenberg, 1968). Therefore, if later-born children are to obtain even a modicum, if not a fair share of positive outcomes, they must develop their interpersonal skills—powers of negotiation, accommodation, tolerance, and a capacity to accept less favorable outcomes—to a degree not typically found in first-born children. On the other hand, first-born children, by virtue of the higher status implicit in age grading, possess greater power and may simply take or achieve what they want quite arbitrarily. (p. 123)

Taken collectively, the findings just reviewed suggest a simple, straightforward prediction regarding birth order and social behavior: Later-borns will evidence greater social skills and be more successful in peer interactions than will first-borns.

Clearly, however, this simple, empirically based prediction is somewhat at odds with predictions deriving from Toman's family constellation theory. Toman proposes that "the role a person has had in early intra-familial relationships will carry over into adult relationships" (Levinger & Sonnheim, 1965, p. 137) such that people will prefer to affiliate with, date, and marry partners "who enable them to replicate an early relationship with a sibling of the opposite sex" (Birtchnell & Mayhew, 1977, p. 19). Accordingly, heterosexual dyadic relationships should be most successful and satisfactory when both rank and sex complementarity occur, i.e., when (a) the older brother of a younger sister is paired with the younger sister of an older brother or (b) the younger brother of an older sister is paired with the older sister of a younger brother.

In contrast, the prediction deriving from the birth-order studies just reviewed is that heterosexual dyadic relationships should be most successful and satisfactory when both the male and the female are later-borns. Unlike Toman's theory, this contrasting prediction requires no assumptions about rank complementarity or the desirability of replicating an early relationship with an opposite-sex sibling.

A Test of Competing Predictions

Given these competing predictions and the fact that the available research did not provide unequivocal support for one prediction at the expense of the other, additional research was warranted. For this reason, Ickes and Turner (1982) conducted a study which sought to clarify the influences of birth order in mixed-sex dyads composed of a male and a female who each had a sibling of the opposite sex. The design of the study—a between-dyads factorial in which the first- versus last-born status of the male and female dyad members were varied orthogonally—permitted a test of the competing predictions described above.

The study employed an unstructured interaction paradigm that has proven particularly useful for revealing the influence of dispositional factors on behavior occurring in the initial interaction of two strangers (Ickes & Barnes, 1977, 1978; Ickes, Patterson, Rajecki, & Tanford, 1982; Ickes, Schermer, & Steeno, 1979; Rajecki, Ickes, & Tanford, 1981). The major advantages of the paradigm are: (a) it tends to minimize the influence of situational factors while maximizing the influence of dispositional ones; (b) it permits the unobtrusive measurement of spontaneous, unstructured interaction behavior that is relatively uncontaminated by task demands or other traditional sources of bias; and (c) it yields a wide range of behavioral and self-report measures that can be analyzed at both the between-dyads and within-dyads levels of analysis. For detailed reviews and discussions of the paradigm, see Ickes (1982; in press).

The subjects in the study were 40 male and 40 female undergraduates who—according to pretest data—each had a sibling of the opposite sex and were either the first-born or the last-born in their families. Within the constraints imposed by their gender and birth order, the subjects were randomly (and without their knowledge) assigned to membership in a mixed-sex dyad of one of four types: (a) a first-born male paired with a first-born female, (b) a first-born male with a last-born female, (c) a last-born male with a first-born female, and (d) a last-born male with a last-born female.

After being contacted by telephone and scheduled to participate at the same time, the subjects in each dyad reported to separate waiting areas—a procedure designed to ensure that they would not meet or interact before the experimental session began. The experimenter met them, established that they did not know each other, and escorted them into a "waiting room." There, they were invited to be seated on a large couch. The experimenter then left them alone together, ostensibly to retrieve some questionnaires to be used in the study, and timed a 5-minute interval in which the subjects' behavior was covertly audio- and videotaped. Upon returning to the room, the experimenter explained the need for deception and obtained the subjects' written permission releasing the tapes for use as data. The subjects were then asked to complete posttest questionnaires concerning their perceptions of self and other during the 5-minute interaction period. Following the collection of these self-report data, the subjects were thanked for their participation and released.

Several behavioral measures were subsequently coded from the videotapes by raters who were kept blind to the subjects' birth orders. Specifically, there were measures of such "static" behaviors as who sat first, who talked first, interpersonal distance, body orientation, and body posture; and of such "dynamic" behaviors as the total frequency and duration of verbalizations, directed gazes, mutual gazes, expressive gestures, and positive affect expressed as smiles and laughter. Data analyses were performed for these various behavioral measures as well as for the self-report data taken from the subjects' postinteraction questionnaires.

The results of the study did not support Toman's complementarity hypotheses. Instead, the data supported the empirically derived hypotheses predicting greater interactional involvement when the male and female dyad members were last-born rather than first-born. These findings emerged in two sets of effects: those involving the males' birth order and those involving the females' birth order.

Effects for the Males' Birth Order

The behavioral data for the males' birth order indicated that dyad members talked to each other longer, asked each other more questions, and looked at each other more in the last-born male (LB♂) dyads than in the first-born male (FB♂) dyads. There were also some intriguing differences in the behavior of the male and female members within the LB♂ and FB♂ dyad types (Table 13-1). As the data in the first row of Table 13-1 indicate, the last-born males talked to their female partners almost twice as long as the first-born males talked to theirs. Although the females' talking did not vary as a function of the males' birth order, the greater amount of time the female partners of last-born males spent in the "listener role" (Duncan, 1969, 1972; Duncan & Fiske, 1977) helps account for the fact that they looked at their male partners nearly twice as long as did the female partners of first-born males (Table 13-1, second row).

Additional findings indicated that the females in the LB♂ dyads enjoyed their interactions with the relatively talkative last-born males. Specifically, these females tended to smile more frequently, provided their partners with over twice as many verbal reinforcers or "back-channel" responses ("Right," "Uh-huh," "I see," etc.), and expressed substantially more liking for their partners on a postinteraction liking measure than did the females in the FB♂ dyads.

The reasons why the last-born males evoked more responsiveness and liking from

Table 13-1. Effects of Males' Birth Order by Sex of Dyad Members

Dependent Measures	First-Born Male Dyads		Last-Born Male Dyads		Interaction $F(1, 36)$
	Males	Females	Males	Females	
Verbalizations (duration[2])	56.0	79.3	102.0	87.1	4.35[b]
Directed gazes (duration)	65.0	54.5	81.0	102.9	3.38[c]
Positive affect (frequency)	5.4	6.4	5.4	9.6	4.32[b]
Positive affect (duration)	6.9	7.3	4.2	9.7	5.68[d]
Verbal reinforcers (frequency)	5.6	4.3	5.0	9.0	4.91[b]
Number of questions asked	4.2	4.3	6.9	5.8	3.43[c]
Number of conversation sequences initiated	0.6	1.2	0.8	0.6	3.83[c]
Liking for partner	42.4	29.4	41.6	47.3	5.13[b]

[a]Measures of duration are in seconds.
[b]$p < .05$.
[c]$p \leqslant .075$.
[d]$p < .025$.

their partners than did the first-born males are hinted at in a number of apparently converging results. First, the last-born males directly signalled their interest in and involvement with their partners by asking them more questions than the first-born males asked theirs. Second, the data from one of the posttest questionnaire items revealed that the last-born males rated themselves as having tried more than the first-born males "to compensate for their partners' failure to initiate conversation, act friendly, etc." Third, an examination of individual liking dimensions revealed that the last-born males were perceived to be significantly more "self-assertive," "exciting," and "friendly" than were the first-born males.

All of these data converge to suggest that, compared to the males with older sisters, the males with younger sisters did not interact well with strange females. The first-born males did not talk much, asked relatively few questions, let their female partners initiate most of the conversation sequences, and were perceived by their partners as relatively unassertive, unexciting, and unfriendly. This pattern of behavior and impressions contrasted sharply with that characteristic of the last-born males who talked nearly twice as long, asked more questions, and evoked more gazes, verbal reinforcers, and self-reported liking from their female partners.

Effects for the Females' Birth Order

The effects involving the females' birth order were similar to those for the males' birth order in suggesting that the last-born females may have been better interaction partners than the first-born females. The data revealed that the last-born females were twice as likely as the first-born females to initiate the conversation in their dyads. They were also rated as significantly more "likeable" by their male partners, and were found to smile significantly more frequently and longer than their partners, whereas the first-born females did not differ from their partners in the frequency and duration of smiling.

Taken in sum, these findings indicate that there are facilitative social effects associated with the last-born status of females as well as that of males. The overall pattern of data suggests, however, that the effects due to the females' birth order may be more subtle and indirect than those due to the males' birth order, perhaps because gender-relevant stereotypes prescribe that males should take a more active role than females in providing the content and structure for initial, mixed-sex interactions (Ickes, 1981; Ickes & Barnes, 1978).

Checks on Possible Mediating Variables

Because previous studies in the author's program of research have revealed substantial influences on interaction behavior of the dyad members' sex-role orientations (Ickes, 1981; Ickes & Barnes, 1978; Ickes et al., 1979; LaFrance & Ickes, 1981), it was reasonable for us to wonder if sex-role differences may have mediated the present results. Such mediation would be highly plausible if, for example, males and females, with older opposite-sex siblings are more likely to become androgynous than are males and females with younger, opposite-sex siblings. (For a review of work demonstrating that—in initial, unstructured encounters—androgynous individuals typically have more involving and personally satisfying interactions than nonandrogynous individuals, see Ickes, 1981).

To determine if the subjects with older, opposite-sex siblings indeed had acquired a more androgynous orientation than those with younger, opposite-sex siblings, we analyzed the subjects' pretested scores on the Bem Sex Role Inventory (Bem, 1974). The results of this analysis revealed that birth order (whether the males' or the females') was *not* significantly related to the subjects' sex-role orientations, neither as main effects nor in interaction with the other variables. A similar analysis based on the subjects' ages also failed to yield any significant results. It appears, then, that the reported influences of the subjects' birth order on their interaction behavior were *not* mediated by corresponding differences in their ages or sex-role orientations.

Theoretical Implications

The results of the Ickes and Turner study clarify the influence of birth order in mixed-sex dyads by revealing, for both males and females, the facilitative social effects of having an older, opposite-sex sibling. These findings are consistent with predictions derived from most of the previous empirical research, but they are inconsistent with the predictions derived from Toman's (1961, 1969, 1976) theory. By supporting the first set of predictions at the expense of the second, the data can be used to argue for a theory of birth-order influences in heterosexual dyads that does not require any assumption about rank complementarity. In other words, lastborn status per se may account for the acquisition of certain social skills that promote success in heterosexual relationships; Toman's stipulation that the success of such relationships will depend upon the participants' rank complementarity appears to be both unnecessary and unwarranted.

Obviously, the study described above did not test all of the important aspects of Toman's theory. In particular, it did not permit an evaluation of Toman's assumption that sex-complementarity is important in promoting the success of heterosexual relationships. Because all of the subjects in the study had opposite-sex siblings, it could not be determined whether their dyadic interactions were, on the average, qualitatively or quantitatively better than those of males and females with same-sex siblings. For this reason, the applicability of Toman's sex-complementarity hypothesis to mixed-sex dyads must remain somewhat open to question.

By the same token, the data just presented do not address the related questions of whether sex complementarity and rank complementarity are important to the success of same-sex relationships. Although the data discredit the hypothesized influence of rank complementarity in mixed-sex dyads, they do not preclude the possibility that either or both types of complementarity may affect the interaction of same-sex dyads. Definitive tests of these possibilities must also await future research.

The Ickes and Turner data do more, however, than simply discredit the assumed importance of rank complementarity in heterosexual relationships. In addition, they reconfirm and further specify the effect of last-born status on the acquisition of certain social skills. In the case of males with older sisters, these social skills appear to include such elements as the ability to carry the weight of initial conversation with someone of the opposite sex, to generate questions for one's female partner, to compensate for the partner's failure to initiate interaction, act friendly, and so on, and to elicit a relatively high level of gazes, smiles, verbal reinforcers, and self-reported liking from the partner. In the case of females with older brothers, last-born status appears to foster the ability to initiate interaction with a strange male and to provide a warm and responsive context for the interaction by doing most of the smiling that occurs.

If we may speculate a bit in an attempt to characterize more abstractly the nature of these sex-differentiated social skills, it appears that the social skills of the last-born males are used to provide much of the actual content and structure of the interaction, whereas the social skills of the last-born females are used to create a favorable (i.e., responsive and supportive) context or "climate" for the interaction. Again, however, the generality of such differences must be questioned. It is possible that the greater social skills of last-born males and females are routinely displayed in patterns reflective of the "content/context" distinction, but it is also possible that these sex-differentiated patterns of behavior occur only in those initial, mixed-sex interactions in which the male is expected to take the lead.

What socialization process(es) could account for the specific social skill advantages of these last-born males and females? Two possibilities are suggested. The first possibility is that, in the course of attempting to engage their older, opposite-sex siblings in conversation or in other forms of social interaction, individuals try out a variety of "social engagement" behaviors, only some of which are reinforced. As time passes, the reinforced behaviors become well-established as part of a repertoire of social engagement and social competence skills, whereas the nonreinforced behaviors become extinguished. The development of such skills in individuals with younger, opposite-sex siblings is less likely, however, because the greater power of these individuals (based on their relative size, intellectual development, etc.) permits them to demand their younger siblings' attention and social engagement directly, without having resort to the trial-and-error use of more subtle and indirect social skills (cf. Miller & Maruyama, 1976). Obviously, this type of explanation relies on a "social conditioning" view of the socialization process in which the feedback provided by an older, opposite-sex sibling (in the form of acceptance or rebuff of the younger sibling's attempt at social engagement) constitutes the reinforcement for the younger child's acquisition and refinement of specific social skills.

A second possible explanation for the differential socialization of children with older versus younger opposite-sex siblings puts less emphasis on the children's interaction with their opposite-sex siblings than on the amount of contact the children are likely to have with their siblings' same-sex friends (who also are of the opposite sex with respect to the children themselves). According to this account, individuals with older, opposite-sex siblings are likely to have relatively many opportunities to encounter and interact with their siblings' same-sex friends, thereby acquiring a repertoire of social engagement and social competence skills in the same manner previously described. In contrast, individuals with younger, opposite-sex siblings are typically less likely (and often less willing) to have contact with their siblings' same-sex friends, and thus fail to acquire and refine such skills to the same degree.

These two alternative socialization processes are obviously *not* mutually exclusive (i.e., both could contribute to the resulting social skill differences, either additively or in interaction). These interrelated processes could also help to explain the differential patterns of social skills displayed by the male and female last-borns in the Ickes and Turner study. Specifically, these socialization processes may reinforce males for providing the structure and content of a mixed-sex interaction but reinforce females for providing a supportive context for such interaction. The motive for these differential patterns of reinforcement may derive from the socializing agents' conceptions of appropriate gender-specific behavior in mixed dyads. If so, the resulting reinforcements can apparently influence the specific patterns of social skills acquired by male and female last-borns without necessarily influencing their psychological sex-role orientations.

Speculations and Directions for Future Research

To the various implications already discussed, I would like to add some further speculations. These speculations focus on a complementary way to conceptualize the influence of past relationships on subsequent relationships—one that employs the language and metaphor of *role theory* in sociology (e.g., Goffman, 1959; Linton, 1936; Merton, 1957; Parsons, 1951; Turner, 1962, 1978; for reviews see Biddle, 1979; McCall & Simmons, 1978; Stryker & Statham, in press). In the discussion to follow, the questions we have been considering may be recast in the language of role theory to read: Do past role relationships constrain and codetermine subsequent ones? How are these constraints affected by the range and content of the role repertoires that social actors have acquired? What are the more general implications of such differences for the interactions that occur in dyads and in larger groups?

Dramaturgical Metaphor and the "Range" Continuum

The utility of theatrical performance as a metaphor for everyday social life has been apparent for centuries, appearing at least as early as Shakespeare's speech explaining why "all the world's a stage." During the last half-century, role theorists have gotten considerable mileage out of this dramaturgical metaphor, with Goffman's (1959) essay on the presentation of self being perhaps the prime example. For our present purposes, the most important aspect of the analogy between theatrical performance and everyday social performance is that concerning the process(es) by which professional social actors acquire and develop the repertoire of roles they are able to play. As an analytic tool for supplementing earlier discussions by others of the processes involved in role acquisition and role taking (e.g., Baldwin, 1897; McCall & Simmons, 1978; Stryker & Statham, in press; Turner, 1978), I would like to propose the following conception of the "range" continuum.

The "range" continuum: Professional actors. Professional actors frequently are compared and contrasted in terms of the "range" of roles they are able to play (see Figure 13-1). At one extreme of the range continuum is the "one-role" actor or actress. Specific examples of this theoretical extreme are necessarily hard to find, for if an actor were in fact able to play one and only one role (Hamlet, for example), it is doubtful that he would survive long in the acting profession. We may, however, identify a position close to the "one-role" extreme as belonging to the "one-character" actor or actress. Whereas the "one-role" actor or actress is limited to the portrayal of a single role in which the setting, the plot, and the roles of the other cast members are all fixed and relatively invariant across productions, the "one-character" actor or actress is limited only insofar as his or her character is relatively fixed; the other elements (setting, plot, etc.) may all vary considerably.

To illustrate the "one-character" actor or actress, we might use John Wayne and Lucille Ball as specific examples. Both of these performers are noted for having

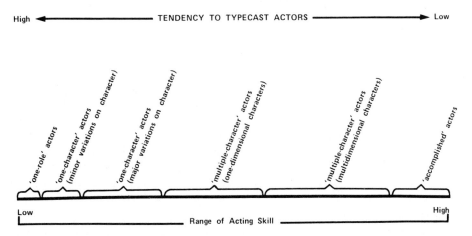

Fig. 13-1. The "range" continuum.

created essentially *one* memorable character with whom they are strongly identified. In nearly all of Mr. Wayne's films, he portrayed the same gruff-but-likeable trouble-shooter who had a lumbering walk, a talent for effective leadership, and the courage and savvy needed for effective action. Of course, in different films, this character was given different names and asked to confront different kinds of trouble in different locales and time periods, but it was still basically the same "John Wayne character" who outwitted and outgunned the Apaches in Arizona and the Japanese at Iwo Jima. Similarly, Ms. Ball's "Lucy character" was essentially the only constant in the different television series in which she appeared—series which varied considerably in their settings, supporting cast members, and the circumstances in which the "Lucy character" found herself. As with the "John Wayne character," much of the enduring appeal of the "Lucy character" derived from its relatively stable, predictable, trans-situational nature. Just as the audience could look forward to John Wayne "saving the day" in even the most difficult situations, viewers could count on Lucy to be the same scheming, scatterbrained, ineptly manipulative person in whatever context she was viewed, and could therefore anticipate the fun that would result when one of her schemes backfired.

The "one-character" actor or actress may represent only one subcategory of the more generic category of "character" actors. With regard to the other subcategories, some character actors are able to portray significant variations on the same character (e.g., a funny, obese Southern law-enforcement officer versus a cruel and sadistic one), whereas other character actors have the acting range necessary to portray many different characters. The different characterizations offered by these "multiple-character" actors may often be rather superficial, stereotyped, and one-dimensional, but as one moves toward the other extreme of the range continuum, these multiple characterizations become increasing more complex, differentiated, and multidimensional. At this extreme of the continuum, the "multiple-character" actor shades into and becomes the compleat or "accomplished" actor.

In contrast to the "one-character" actor described above, the "accomplished" actor not only can create a character just as unique, vivid, and memorable as the "Lucy character" or the "John Wayne character," but can then go on to create a *different* (but similarly unique, vivid, and memorable) character in his next dramatic appearance, and in the one after that, and so on. Indeed, each characterization may be so strikingly different from the one(s) that preceded it that viewers may find it difficult to accept the fact that they are watching the same person performing each of these roles. The contrasts between the characters portrayed by Dustin Hoffman in such films as *The Graduate, Midnight Cowboy, Little Big Man,* and *Tootsie* can be used to illustrate this conception of the accomplished actor, as can the contrasts between the characters portrayed by Meryl Streep in *The Deerhunter, The French Lieutenant's Woman,* and *Sophie's Choice.* When viewing such actors and actresses, one must be prepared to be surprised, since consistency in certain elements of their performance from one role to the next may be the exception rather than the rule.

The most obvious advantage to professional actors and actresses of increasing their range of role-playing skill is that they are better able to avoid being typecast. As the upper portion of Figure 13-1 indicates, the range of an actor's skills is assumed to be inversely related to the strength of the tendency to typecast the actor.

The nontypecast actor tends to have more opportunities than the typecast actor to play a variety of different roles in different dramaturgical contexts and genres.

Assuming that actors and actresses can be compared and contrasted on a continuum reflecting the range of their abilities, we should note a few additional qualifying assumptions. First, in case it is not already obvious, when the terms "one-dimensional" and "multidimensional" are used to describe an actor's characterizations, they should be interpreted in the looser sense intended by films and drama critics instead of in the stricter sense typically intended by scientists. Second, it should be acknowledged that nearly all self-respecting actors attempt to increase their range throughout their professional careers, and that most, if not all, of them succeed to some degree in this attempt. For example, Peter Sellers, a good multiple-character actor whose different characterizations were perhaps a bit too stylized and one-dimensional throughout most of his career (in, for example, *Dr. Strangelove* and *The Many Faces of Fu Manchu*), apparently created in the role Chance the gardener (in *Being There*) a characterization of such richness and sublety that many critics marked the performance as evidence that Sellers had attained the range of a fully accomplished actor (Schickel, 1980). Third, some actors who have transcended their earlier, more limited range may, for one reason or another, still get typecast into roles that do not permit them to display the added range they have acquired. Thus, it was not until John Wayne was given the somewhat off-beat role of Rooster Cogburn in *True Grit,* and was therefore able to display a greater range than his previous roles had allowed, that he was voted an Academy Award by his peers.

The "range" continuum: Nonprofessional social actors. Like the professional actors described previously, nonprofessional social actors can be compared and contrasted in terms of the "range" of roles and characterizations they are able to enact. Some social actors seem to be limited to the "one-role" or "one-character" extreme, whereas others have the acting range and role repertoire necessary to portray multiple characters of varying complexity and dimensionality. Actors at the first extreme appear to be essentially the same "character" regardless of changes in the situation, the other participants, or the operative "script" (Abelson, 1976; Schank & Abelson, 1977). On the other hand, actors at the second extreme seem to become very different "characters" in different situations, with different coactors, or when different social "scripts" are operative.

In current social-psychological theory, Snyder's (1974, 1979) conception of *self-monitoring* coincides most closely with the notion of the "range" continuum developed here. In his research, Snyder has sought to identify individuals who, like professional actors, are able to monitor and manage the verbal and nonverbal aspects of their self-presentation effectively in order "to create the most favorable situated identities for themselves in their social encounters" (Snyder, 1979, p. 88). These *high self-monitoring individuals,* like professional actors, are assumed to have the abilities and motivations required for effective impression management. These abilities and motivations include

a knowledge of the interpretations that others place upon our acts, a desire to maintain situationally appropriate identities, a wide range of self-presentational skills, and the willingness to use this repertoire of impression management strategies. (Snyder, 1979, p. 88)

Snyder's (1974) Self-Monitoring Scale has been used to identify not only high self-monitoring individuals but a contrasting population of *low self-monitoring individuals*—individuals who are relatively lacking in the abilities and motivations necessary to modify their self-presentations from one situation to the next. The results of several studies have supported the construct validity of the Self-Monitoring Scale, showing, for example, that professional actors score higher on the scale than nonactors (Snyder, 1974). Other findings have indicated that, relative to low self-monitoring individuals, high self-monitoring individuals can (a) better express intentionally displayed emotions (Snyder, 1974), (b) portray different assigned "roles" more effectively and convincingly (Lippa, 1976), (c) deceive others more successfully (Krauss, Geller, & Olson, 1976), (d) infer others' emotional states more accurately (Geizer, Rarick, & Soldow, 1977; Krauss, Geller, & Olson, Note 2), and (e) construct "richer, better articulated, and more informative" cognitive representations of prototypic character types (Snyder & Cantor, 1980).

It is tempting to try to equate Snyder's self-monitoring dimension with the "range" continuum in Figure 13-1, with low self-monitoring individuals corresponding to "one-role" or "one-character" actors and high self-monitoring individuals corresponding to "accomplished" actors. Although such a strict theoretical equivalency is probably not warranted, there appears to be at least a strong analogical relationship between the two conceptions. Drawing on this analogy, let us consider how the notion of the "range" continuum may be useful in developing a more adequate model of the influences that past relationships have on subsequent ones.

Consider first the fact that Toman's theory tends to characterize all human beings as "one-role" actors. In his view, individuals are compelled to go through life trying to replicate—again and again—the same type of role relationship they experienced during their earliest formative years. In this sense, they resemble the "one-role" actors represented in Figure 13-1, seeking to play the same role again and again, and repeatedly gravitating toward partners who can perform the complementary roles. As Figure 13-1 suggests, however, such "one-role" actors may be statistically rare and not at all characteristic of the population as a whole. Instead, most actors, whether professional or nonprofessional, manage to acquire a set of role-taking and self-presentation skills that increase their range as actors and thereby increase the range of "roles" and "role relationships" in which they can perform successfully.

This line of thinking suggests some interesting implications. First, it suggests that Toman's model may not be universally applicable, as he assumes, but may apply instead to only a small segment of the general population. Specifically, the model may apply only to those individuals whose socialization was so limited, so lacking in opportunities for them to acquire role-taking and self-presentation skills, that they are habitually compelled to reenact the only "roles" and "role relationships" they know and understand. These unfortunate and socially stunted individuals are *typecast* in the almost-literal sense of being molded into a fixed, unyielding form. Second, this line of reasoning suggests that a more adequate model of the influence that past relationships have on subsequent ones would incorporate the full continuum of actor categories represented in Figure 13-1. Indeed, at least as much attention should be devoted to the categories in the middle and at the extreme right of the continuum as to those at the extreme left. Third, this reasoning suggests that the central concern of a more adequate model should be the task of accounting for aspects of present and future relationships in terms of the range and content of the role-taking and self-presentation skills acquired in past relationships.

Directions for Future Research

If we push the third of these implications to its logical conclusion, it is clear that what is ultimately needed is a coherent theoretical specification of how one's past participation in certain types of relationships leads to the acquisition of certain types of role-playing and self-presentation skills. Providing such specification will be an extraordinarily long and difficult task, and much of the necessary empirical work will have to be done by researchers in the area of social development. Ideally, such research should be based on the direct observation and classification of the various role relationships in which individuals engage on a day-to-day basis. It should focus on such variables as the sheer number of role relationships in which the individual is able to participate, the individual's relative power and status within these relationships, the specific role-playing and self-presentation skills most likely to be modeled, imitated, and reinforced, and the opportunities individuals have to practice and refine such skills. Such research should take the form of both cross-sectional and longitudinal studies, and should encompass the entire developmental span of childhood, adolescence, and young adulthood.

Obviously, we would have to wait a very long time before the accumulation of research of the type proposed above would be sufficient to allow us to see the outlines of a general, comprehensive theory of the processes by which participation in past relationships influences behavior in subsequent ones. In the meantime, it is probably not necessary to leave all of the empirical and conceptual work to the developmental social psychologists. There is, for example, important work that personality psychologists can do as well. Personality psychologists can add to our knowledge through their study of the various individual difference factors that appear to be implicated in the processes of interest. By exploring both the antecedent conditions that give rise to the observed individual differences and the behavioral consequences or correlates of these differences, personality psychologists may act as catalysts in speeding up the process of theoretical integration.

Consider, for example, how the personality researcher might employ the existing information about the individual difference variables of birth order and self-monitoring to further our understanding of the processes by which past relationships influence subsequent ones. Now that existing research has implicated each of these variables in the types of processes our potential theory seeks to account for, the personality researcher could extend this line of inquiry in a number of ways.

First, the researcher could attempt to catalog both the antecedent conditions and the behavioral consequences of these individual difference variables. There are, for example, certain obvious "antecedents" to the variable of birth order that are essentially inherent in the meaning of this variable. Thus, important antecedent conditions of being last-born are: (a) the fact of having one or more siblings whose birth occurred before that of the subject, and (b) the resultant experience, in the vast majority of cases, of interacting over an extensive period of time with siblings who were larger, stronger, and cognitively more advanced than the subject during his or her formative years. Somewhat in contrast to the birth-order variable, the antecedent conditions that give rise to individual differences in the self-monitoring variable are not obviously inherent in the meaning of this construct. Moreover, attempts to find clearcut antecedents of the trait of self-monitoring have to date been largely unsuccessful (Snyder, Note 3). We do, however, have a great deal of information about the behavioral consequences and correlates of self-monitoring (see Snyder, 1979, for a review), and, as the first part of this chapter has attempted to document, we have also begun to develop a fairly clear picture of the behavioral consequences and correlates of birth order.

Once the personality researcher has determined the antecedents and consequences of the process-relevant individual difference variables, a second and related line of inquiry would be to assess both the analogical and the empirical relationships between these predictor variables. The analogical strategy would be to look for overlap or at least similarity in the antecedent conditions and/or behavioral consequences of the individual difference variables. If an apparent overlap or similarity exists (e.g., last-borns and high self-monitors both seem to be more adept at acting and role-taking), the analogical strategy may suggest an appropriate empirical strategy (e.g., simply correlating the two variables) to determine whether or not the relationship suggested by the analogy has any basis in fact.

If the expected empirical relationship does not emerge (e.g., to date, no significant correlation between birth order and self-monitoring has been reported, to my knowledge), the researcher may then conclude either (a) that the relationship suggested by the analogy does not hold in reality (i.e., the analogy was false and misleading), or (b) that the relationship does hold, but in a more qualified way than that suggested by the original interpretation of the analogy. For example, the analogical relationship between birth order and self-monitoring may point toward a true relationship between these two variables that could be demonstrated *within* families (e.g., last-borns will have higher self-monitoring scores at age 18 than their first-born siblings did when tested at the same age) but could not be demonstrated *between* families (e.g., last-borns compared to first-borns from different families may not have reliably different self-monitoring scores because of family socialization differences that mask or override the influence of the birth-order variable).

Alternatively, it may be that the form of the relationship is not linear, as originally assumed, but curvilinear instead. Such an alternative explanation could simultaneously account both for the failure to find a significant linear relationship between birth order and self-monitoring, and for Ickes and Barnes' (1977) observation that individuals with *moderate* self-monitoring scores may be able to get along with a greater range of people than individuals with either high or low self-monitoring scores. If first-borns tend to become either high or low self-monitors, whereas last-borns tend to become moderates, both of the findings reported previously would make sense. Moreover, an interesting new question would be raised about the factor(s) that might cause first-borns to be pushed to one extreme or the other.

As this example illustrates, the process of searching for the presence or absence of analogical relationships between relevant individual difference variables will typically lead the researcher to formulate specific hypotheses that are amenable to empirical test. Subsequent attempts to test these hypotheses will either tend to support the validity of the analogy (in which case additional aspects of the analogy may be tested, to determine how far it may be extended), or will tend to question its validity (in which case more qualified tests of the analogy may be attempted). Regardless of the outcome, the researcher can profit conceptually from the information acquired. If the apparent analogy breaks down empirically at every point, the researcher is likely to conclude that the individual difference variables are implicated in genotypically different processes that only appear to be similar at a superficial, phenotypic level. This will lead the researcher to search for differences in the processes rather than similarities, and to test additional hypotheses relevant to these differences. On the other hand, if the apparent analogy is supported, in either a qualified or an unqualified way, the researcher is likely to know more about the nature of the process than he or she did originally. By exploring other aspects of the analogy (and thus determining to what extent it holds, and at what point, if any, it breaks down), the researcher can bring information pertinent to each of the individual difference variables to bear in understanding the common process in which both variables are implicated.

Conclusions

We are a long way from having a general, comprehensive theory of the processes by which participation in past relationships influences behavior in subsequent ones. We are, however, beginning to make some progress toward this goal. For example, we can conclude from the research reviewed in this chapter that a theory such as Toman's, which views individuals' adult relationship as severely constrained by simple features of the intrafamilial relationships they experienced during their earliest formative years, does not do justice to the range of role-taking and self-presentation skills acquired by most individuals. We can also conclude that a more adequate theory of the socialization process should focus on the means by which such role-taking and self-presentation skills are acquired, and on those features of the individual's social world that determine the particular forms these skills will take. Although developmental social psychologists are probably in the best position to observe and record the relevant processes as they unfold, personality psychologists— through the study of process-relevant variables such as birth order and self-monitoring—may also have important insights to offer about the means by which past relationships influence subsequent ones.

Reference Notes

1. Ickes, W. Unpublished material, 1971.
2. Krauss, R. M., Geller, V., & Olson, C. *Modalities and cues in perceiving deception.* Paper presented at the meeting of the American Psychological Association, Washington, D. C., 1976.
3. Snyder, M. Personal communication, 1982.

References

Abelson, R. P. Script processing in attitude formation and decision-making. In J. Carroll & T. Payne (Eds.), *Cognition and social behavior.* Hillsdale, N.J.: Lawrence Erlbaum, 1976.

Adams, B. N. Birth order: A critical review. *Sociometry,* 1972, *35*(3), 411-439.

Baldwin, J. M. *Social and ethical interpretations in mental development.* New York: Macmillan, 1897.

Belmont, L., & Marolla, F. A. Birth order, family size, and intelligence. *Science,* 1973, *182,* 1096-1101.

Bem, S. L. The measurement of psychological androgyny. *Journal of Consulting and Clinical Psychology,* 1974, *42,* 155-162.

Berscheid, E. Interpersonal attraction. In G. Lindzey & E. Aronson (Eds.), *Handbook of social psychology* (3rd ed.). Reading, Mass.: Addison-Wesley, in press.

Biddle, B. J. *Role theory: Expectations, identities and behavior.* New York: Academic Press, 1979.

Birtchnell, J., & Mayhew, J. Toman's theory: Tested for mate selection and friendship formation. *Journal of Individual Psychology,* 1977, *33,* 18-36.

Breland, H. M. Birth order effects: A reply to Schooler. *Psychological Bulletin,* 1973, *80,* 810-212.

Chemers, M. The relationship between birth order and leadership style. *Journal of Social Psychology,* 1970, *80,* 243-244.

Conners, C. K. Birth order and needs for affiliation. *Journal of Personality,* 1963, *31*(3), 409-416.

Duncan, S. D., Jr. Nonverbal communication. *Psychological Bulletin,* 1969, *72,* 118-137.

Duncan, S. D., Jr. Some signals and rules for taking speaking turns in conversations. *Journal of Personality and Social Psychology,* 1972, *23,* 283-292.

Duncan, S. D., Jr., & Fiske, D. W. *Face-to-face interaction: Research, methods, and theory.* Hillsdale, N. J.: Lawrence Erlbaum, 1977.

Eisenstadt, S. N. *From generation to generation.* Glencoe, Ill.: Free Press, 1956.

Geizer, R. S., Rarick, D. L., & Soldow, G. F. Deception and judgment accuracy: A study in person perception. *Personality and Social Psychology Bulletin,* 1977, *3,* 446-449.

Goffman, E. The presentation of self in everyday life. New York: Doubleday, 1959.

Gottman, J. *Marital interaction: Experimental investigations.* New York: Academic Press, 1979.

Hardy, R. C. A developmental study of the relationships between birth order and leadership style for two distinctly different American groups. *Journal of Social Psychology*, 1972, *87*, 147-148.

Hardy, R. C., Hunt, J., & Lehr, E. Relationship between birth order and leadership style for nursery school children. *Perceptual and Motor Skills*, 1978, *46*, 184-186.

Howarth, E. Birth order, family structure and personality variables. *Journal of Personality Assessment*, 1980, *44*, 299-301.

Ickes, W. Sex-role influences in dyadic interaction: A theoretical model. In C. Mayo & N. Henley (Eds.), *Gender and nonverbal behavior*. New York: Springer-Verlag, 1981.

Ickes, W. A basic paradigm for the study of personality, roles, and social behavior. In W. Ickes & E. S. Knowles (Eds.), *Personality, roles, and social behavior*. New York: Springer-Verlag, 1982.

Ickes, W. A basic paradigm for the study of unstructured dyadic interaction. In H. Reis (Issue ed.), *New directions for methodology of behavioral science: Naturalistic approaches to studying social interaction*. San Francisco: Jossey-Bass, 1983.

Ickes, W., & Barnes, R. D. The role of sex and self-monitoring in unstructured dyadic interactions. *Journal of Personality and Social Psychology*, 1977, *35*, 315-330.

Ickes, W., & Barnes, R. D. Boys and girls together—and alienated: On enacting stereotyped sex roles in mixed-sex dyads. *Journal of Personality and Social Psychology*, 1978, *36*, 669-683.

Ickes, W., Patterson, M. L., Rajecki, D. W., & Tanford, S. Behavioral and cognitive consequences of reciprocal versus compensatory responses to pre-interaction expectancies. *Social Cognition*, 1982, *1*, 160-190.

Ickes, W., Schermer, B., & Steeno, J. Sex and sex-role influences in same-sex dyads. *Social Psychology Quarterly*, 1979, *42*, 373-385.

Ickes, W., & Turner, M. On the social advantages of having an older, opposite-sex sibling: Birth order influences in mixed-sex dyads. *Journal of Personality and Social Psychology*, 1983, in press.

Jacobs, B. S., & Moss, H. A. Birth order and sex of sibling as determinants of mother-infant interaction. *Child Development*, 1976, *47*, 315-322.

Kemper, T. D. Mate selection and marital satisfaction according to sibling type of husband and wife. *Journal of Marriage and the Family*, 1966, *28*, 346-349.

LaFrance, M., & Ickes, W. Posture mirroring and interactional involvement: Sex and sex-typing effects. *Journal of Nonverbal Behavior*, 1981, *5*(3), 139-154.

Levinger, G., & Sonnheim, M. Complementarity in marital adjustment: Reconsidering Toman's family constellation hypothesis. *Journal of Individual Psychology*, 1965, *21*, 137-145.

Linton, R. *The study of man*. New York: Appleton-Century, 1936.

Lippa, R. Expressive control and the leakage of dispositional introversion-extraversion during role-played teaching. *Journal of Personality*, 1976, *44*, 541-559.

Markus, H. Sibling personalities: The luck of the draw. *Psychology Today*, June 1981, 35-37.

McArthur, C. Personalities of first and second children. *Psychiatry*, 1956, *19*, 47-54.

McCall, G. J., & Simmons, J. L. *Identities and interactions* (Rev. ed.), New York: Free Press, 1978.

Mendelsohn, M. B., Linden, J., Gruen, G., & Curran, J. Heterosexual pairing and sibling configuration. *Journal of Individual Psychology*, 1974, *30*, 202-210.

Merton, R. K. *Social theory and social structure* (Rev. ed.). Glencoe, Ill.: Free Press, 1957.

Miller, N., & Maruyama, G. Ordinal position and peer popularity. *Journal of Personality and Social Psychology*, 1976, *33*, 123-131.

Moore, W. E. Social structure and behavior. In G. Lindzey & E. Aronson (Eds.), *The handbook of social psychology* (2nd ed.). Reading, Mass.: Addison-Wesley, 1969.

Parsons, T. *The social system*. Glencoe, Ill.: Free Press, 1951.

Rajecki, D. W., Ickes, W., & Tanford, S. Locus of control and reactions to a stranger. *Personality and Social Psychology Bulletin*, 1981, *7*, 282-289.

Schachter, S. Birth order and sociometric choice. *Journal of Abnormal and Social Psychology*, 1964, *68*, 453-456.

Schaller, J. A critical note on the conventional use of the birth order variable. *Journal of Genetic Psychology*, 1978, *133*, 91-95.

Schank, R., & Abelson, R. P. *Scripts, plans, goals, and understanding: An inquiry into human knowledge structures*. Hillsdale, N.J.: Lawrence Erlbaum, 1977.

Schickel, R. Sellers strikes again. *Time*, March 3, 1980, 64-68.

Schwab, M. R., & Lundgren, D. C. Birth order, perceived appraisals by significant others, and self-esteem. *Psychological Reports*, 1978, *43*, 443-454.

Sells, S., & Roff, M. Peer acceptance-rejection and birth order. *American Psychologist*, 1963, *18*, 355.

Smelser, W. T., & Stewart, L. H. Where are the siblings? A re-evaluation of the relationship between birth order and college attendance. *Sociometry*, 1968, *31*, 294-303.

Snyder, M. The self-monitoring of expressive behavior. *Journal of Personality and Social Psychology*, 1974, *30*, 526-537.

Snyder, M. Self-monitoring processes. In L. Berkowitz (Ed.), *Advances in experimental social psychology* (Vol. 12). New York: Academic Press, 1979.

Snyder, M., & Cantor, N. Thinking about ourselves and others: Self-monitoring and social knowledge. *Journal of Personality and Social Psychology*, 1980, *39*, 222-234.

Stryker, S., & Statham, A. Symbolic interaction and role theory. In G. Lindzey & E. Aronson (Eds.), *Handbook of Social Psychology* (3rd ed.). Reading, Mass.: Addison-Wesley, in press.

Sutton, J. M., & McIntire, W. G. Relationship of ordinal position and sex to neuroticism in adults. *Psychological Reports*, 1977, *41*, 843-846.

Sutton-Smith, B., & Rosenberg, B. G. The dramatic sibling. *Perceptual and Motor Skills*, 1966, *22*, 993-994.

Sutton-Smith. B., & Rosenberg, B. G. Sibling consensus on power tactics. *Journal of Genetic Psychology*, 1968, *112*, 63-72.

Sutton-Smith, B., & Rosenberg, B. G. *The sibling*. New York: Holt, Rinehart & Winston, 1970.

Toman, W. Family constellation as a character and marriage determinant. *International Journal of Psycho-Analysis*, 1959, *40*, 316-319.

Toman, W. *Family constellation: Its effect on personality and social behavior* (1st ed.). New York: Springer, 1961.

Toman, W. Family constellation of the partners in divorced and married couples. *Journal of Individual Psychology*, 1962, *18*, 48-51.

Toman, W. Choices of marriage partners by men coming from monosexual sibling configurations. *British Journal of Medical Psychology*, 1964, *37*, 43-46.

Toman, W. *Family constellation: Its effect on personality and social behavior* (2nd ed.). New York: Springer, 1969.

Toman, W. *Family constellation: Its effect on personality and social behavior* (3rd ed.). New York: Springer, 1976.

Toman, W., & Gray, B. Family contellation of "normal" and "disturbed" marriages: An empirical study. *Journal of Individual Psychology*, 1961, *17*, 93-95.

Touhey, J. C. Birth order and mate selection. *Psychological Reports*, 1971, *29*, 618.

Turner, R. H. Role-taking: Process versus conformity. In A. Rose (Ed.)., *Human behavior and social process*. Boston: Houghton Mifflin, 1962.

Turner, R. H. The role and the person. *American Journal of Sociology*, 1978, *84*, 1-23.

Ward, C. C., Castro, M. A., & Wilcox, A. H. Birth-order effects in a survey of mate selection and parenthood. *Journal of Social Psychology*, 1974, *94*, 57-64.

Warren, J. R. Birth order and social behavior. *Psychological Bulletin*, 1966, *65*, 38-49.

Whalen, C. K., Flowers, J. V., Fuller, M. J., & Jernigan, T. Behavioral studies of personal space during early adolescence. *Man-Environment Systems*, 1975, *5*(5), 289-297.

Zajonc, R. B., & Markus, G. B. Birth order and intellectual development. *Psychological Review*, 1975, *82*, 74-88.

Zajonc, R. B., Markus, H., & Markus, G. B. The birth order puzzle, *Journal of Personality and Social Psychology*, 1979, *37*, 1325-1341.

Author Index

Subject Index